INTERNATIONAL MONEY AND THE REAL WORLD

INTERNATIONAL MONEY AND THE REAL WORLD

Paul Davidson

A HALSTED PRESS BOOK

John Wiley & Sons
New York

First published 1982 by
THE MACMILLAN PRESS LTD
London and Basingstoke
First Published in the U.S.A.
by Halsted Press, a Division
of John Wiley & Sons, Inc.,
New York.

ISBN 0–470–27256–2

Printed and bound in Great Britain
at The Pitman Press, Bath

Library of Congress Cataloging in Publication Data

Davidson, Paul.
    International money and the real world.
    "Sequel to [author's] Money and the real world" –
Pref.
    "A Halsted Press book."
    Includes bibliographical references.
    1. International finance.   2. Money.   I. Title.
HG3881.D329 1982   332'.042   81–6777
ISBN 0–470–27256–2   AACR2

To Louise, Greg, Diane, Robert, and Cindy

'In recent years most people have become dissatisfied with the way the world manages its monetary affairs. Yet they distrust the remedies which are suggested. We do badly; but we do not know how to do better.'

J. M. Keynes, *A Treatise on Money*, 1930

Contents

Preface

In a 1978 review of the second edition of my *Money and the Real World*, the reviewer in the *Economic Journal* stated

> Since the book was published, Davidson's contention that Keynesian monetary theory has to be seen in the context of economic uncertainty has become a conventional wisdom . . . . [Now] it would be interesting to have . . . Davidson's views on how his models could be extended to deal with an open economy; despite its emphasis on 'reality', Davidson's world is definitely the closed economy of Keynes' *General Theory*.

This volume does provide the theoretical extension called for in this *E. J.* review. Although the analysis presented here swims against the existing mainstream approach to international monetary theory, hopefully it will also become a 'conventional wisdom' within a few years.

Why didn't I provide these theoretical additions in my earlier work? The manuscript for *Money and the Real World* was completed in the spring of 1971. It attempted to provide an analysis of the real world by utilizing a simple but 'realistic' monetary model – one describing the operation of a 'closed' entrepreneurial economy employing time-oriented monetary contracts to organize production *and* exchange activities. All the contractual obligations in this system were denominated in terms of a single uniform currency. At that time I believed that in order to get our monetary theory 'right' and to gain insight into the workings of the real economic world in which we lived, it was essential to logically demonstrate why an unfettered market system could suffer high levels of unemployment, stagnation and price instability if (1) liquidity pressures were not promptly offset by an alert monetary authority able to exert discretionary powers and (2) if governments did not prevent effective demand failures and incomes inflation pressures. If a free market system could display, even in such a rarefied, simple, closed economy model, such poor economic performance, then it seemed reasonable to believe that the more complicated open economy systems were even less likely to achieve socially desirable economic results. Moreover, in the spring of 1971 the Bretton Woods system was still in force and therefore the major trading partners were linked via a quasi-unionized monetary system for settling contracts. Thus, the real world complications due to international trade could be laid aside for the time being while the basic concepts of monetary analysis were clarified.

During the ensuing decade of the seventies, the national and international economic system has been racked by destabilizing events – the collapse of Bretton Woods and the move to variable exchange rates, the energy price explosion and the ensuing struggle over the distribution of world income and wealth, etc. The discussion of international aspects of Post Keynesian Theory can no longer be postponed.

This volume is a logical sequel to *Money and the Real World*, and as such is a response to the 1978 suggestion of the *Economic Journal* reviewer's request for theoretical extension. It is, however, not sufficient to focus on the closed *v.* open economy dichotomy. It is also essential to analyse the bifurcation of economies into Unionized Monetary Systems (UMS) and Non Unionized Monetary Systems (NUMS), where the latter use different monetary units (in the absence of the institution of fixed exchange rates) in specifying contractual obligations among trading partners at home and abroad.[1] These contractual agreements affect and control the production and purchasing flows among and within nations. The existence of NUMS introduce complications which, in appropriate circumstances, make economic growth and purchasing power stickiness over time even more difficult to achieve than in the simple closed UMS model of Keynes' *General Theory* or my *Money and the Real World*. Having already placed the theory of employment, money and prices on the proper track via the closed UMS model, it is now essential to expand our theoretical analysis to a NUMS world which is more descriptive of the real world in which developed economies have chosen to live since the collapse of the Bretton Woods agreement.

This volume attempts to deal head on with the complex and difficult questions of international liquidity, money, contracts and financial institutions. The analysis will not provide the unique optimal equilibrium solutions which, though so dear to the hearts of neoclassicists, are irrelevant to the problems of real world economic processes incessantly moving through time towards an uncertain and unpredictable future. Instead, it adopts a taxonomic approach which analyses the directional effects of various factors on first one and then another set of circumstances. This volume presents a catalogue, so to speak, which does not claim to resolve the issues with the delusive exactness of a solution to an algebraic model. This classificatory approach (which is the system of Marshall, Keynes and Shackle) permits economists to be roughly right rather than precisely wrong.

It is my firm belief that we must get theory correct before we can develop proper policy suggestions; therefore, the emphasis of this volume is on theory. Nevertheless, suggestions for policy solutions to our pressing economic problems are not ignored. Guiding principles and necessary requirements are suggested for developing institutional arrangements to internationally coordinate monetary, fiscal *and* incomes policies among trading nations. Once the theoretical relationships are uncovered and the path for further development indicated, the details of the day-to-day operations of such institutional structures are easily left to others to flesh out.

In conclusion, I would like to thank Rutgers University for providing me with a Faculty Academic Study Program (FASP) leave between January and June of 1980 which gave me time to concentrate my attention on these matters. I also must thank the Institute of Advanced Studies in Vienna, Confindustria in Rome and my colleagues in Italy (Sergio Parrinello, Alessandro Roncaglia, Paolo Sylos-Labini and especially my former student, Jan Kregel) for providing me with various forums to present my ideas and try out drafts of various chapters as they were being developed. I also wish to thank Victoria Chick- and Ed Williams for their help and extensive comments on the Multinational and Eurocurrency discussions.

Finally, I wish to thank my wife Louise, for her generous support and encouragement not only during the writing of this volume but over the years. If it were not for her, many petty (from hindsight) problems as well as the major traumatic event our family experienced would have so diverted my concentration and energies that it would have been impossible to complete this volume.

Princeton, New Jersey
April 1981

1 Solving the Crisis in Economic Theory

Except for a few brief years in the 1930s, the development of monetary theory and international trade theory has been dominated by a pre-Keynesian, i.e. neoclassical, logic. Although this analytical approach may have been useful as a rough approximation a century or more ago when economic affairs were organized on a significantly different basis than currently and our previous knowledge of the economic system was negligible, this neoclassical view has hampered the development of an economic theory which is relevant for the fundamental problems which plague twentieth century developed, market-oriented, production economies organized on a forward money contracting basis. Unfortunately, until we get our theory right, the ability of economists to provide sound guidelines to policy makers facing hard, important, and urgent economic problems will be severely restricted. Thus it is incumbent upon those of us who believe that the study of economics is for 'practical purposes', that we take the critical leap forward and bring monetary theory and international trade theory into effective contact with the real world. To do so we must choose among the various economic schools of thought which currently vie for the attention of economists and policy makers around the world.

SCHOOLS OF ECONOMICS

Modern economic theory – far from being unified under the aegis of Keynes' Revolution – has developed along five different analytical, philosophical and political slants. Table 1.1 classifies the various shades of analytical views into five relatively homogeneous – though not watertight – schools of thought. Going from extreme right to left on Table 1.1 these schools are

(1) *The Monetarist–Neoclassical School.* A narrow, monolithic view of the economic system whose major base was originally the University

1

TABLE 1.1 A Table of Political Economy

	Socialist–Radical	Neo-Keynesian	Keynes	Neoclassical Synthesis–Keynesian	Monetarist–Neoclassical
Politics	Extreme left	Left of centre	Centre	Right of centre	Extreme right
Money	Real forces emphasized – money merely a tool for existing power structure	Real forces emphasized, money assumed to accommodate	Money and real forces intimately related	Money matters along with everything else	Only money matters
Wage Rate and Income Distribution	Wage rate basis of value. Income distribution the most important economic question	Money wage is the linchpin of the price level. Income distribution very important	Money wage rate fundamental. Income distribution question of less importance	Wage rate one of many prices. Income distribution is the result of all the demand and supply equations in a general equilibrium system. Income distribution a matter of equity, not of 'scientific' enquiry	
Capital Theory	Surplus generated by reserve army	Surplus needed over wages	Scarcity theory (quasi-rents)	Marginal productivity theory and well-behaved production functions	
Employment Theory	Any level of employment possible. Assumes growth in employment overtime. Full employment creates crisis for capitalism	Growth with any level of employment possible, although growth at full employment emphasized	Any level of employment possible. Full employment desirable	Full employment assumed. Unemployment is a disequilibrium situation	Full employment assumed in long run. No explicit short-run theory of employment
Inflation	Primarily due to money wage changes, but can also be due to profit margin changes	Due to money wage or profit margin changes	Due to changes in money wages, productivity and/or profit margins	In long run primarily a monetary phenomenon being related to money supply via portfolio decisions. In short run may be related to Phillips curve	Primarily a monetary phenomenon in the sense of being related to the supply of money via portfolio decisions

Post Keynesian

of Chicago and whose writings almost always bear the imprimatur of Professor Friedman. In recent years, Monetarist disciples have appeared as a vocal – but still minority – voice in academia, governments, and Central Banks. The basic analytical cement bonding this school together is some variant of the Quantity Theory of Money's famous equation of exchange (i.e. $MV = PY$ where M is the quantity of money, V is velocity, P is the price level of newly produced goods and Y is real GNP) *plus* the Walrasian equations of general equilibrium.

Simply stated a general equilibrium (hereafter GE) system is one which demonstrates that there exists a set of relative prices for all goods and services (including labour and capital) which will bring about the simultaneous clearing of *all* markets. Thus it is logically impossible to have involuntary unemployment (i.e. an uncleared labour market) in a GE system as long as prices are flexible; hence in such logical systems unemployment develops only because money wages are 'too high' and will not decline in a recession. Keynes, however, specifically denied that reduction in money wages would automatically assure a full employment solution.[1] Thus Keynes' analytical framework is logically incompatible with all GE systems including Monetarism and 'supply-side' economics.

(2) *The Neoclassical Synthesis–Keynesian School.* A much broader spectrum of views is represented in this school *vis-à-vis* the Monetarists. Neoclassical Keynesian models range from (a) the capital and growth theories (based on the marginal productivity) of Samuelson and Solow, to (b) the portfolio balance and GE views of J. R. Hicks, Patinkin, Tobin, Arrow, Hahn and Malinvaud, as well as (c) the recent Clower–Leijonhufvud attempt at reinterpreting Keynes within a broad Walrasian GE framework. A majority of the 'Economics Establishment' tend to come from this school and therefore, not surprisingly, a majority of the economics profession as well as intelligent lay readers still believe the view of this school is 'Economics'. The 'neoclassical synthesis' in the title of this school refers to the claim of Samuelson that they have been able to demonstrate that some form of a Walrasian GE framework is the logical micro-basis for Keynes' macroeconomic analysis.

Recently some investigators (e.g. Malinvaud, Grandmont, Hahn, etc.) have tried to introduce *ad hoc* constraints to the fundamental GE system of equations in order to foster a 'temporary equilibrium' analysis. None of these economists seems to have grasped the fundamental realization that the schism between GE and the monetary analysis developed by Keynes is as deep and irreparable as the difference between Euclidean and non-Euclidean geometry.

Just as the axiom of parallels is banished from non-Euclidean geometry, so, as I have indicated elsewhere,[2] must one of the fundamental axioms of GE analysis – the *axiom of gross substitution* (hereafter GS) – be cast aside as irrelevant for liquidity analysis, if the workings of a monetary, production, entrepreneurial economy are to be grasped. Whether the resulting monetary equilibrium system (without the GS axiom) should be labelled GE is mainly a semantic problem. (Would it be wise to call geometry without the axiom of parallels Euclidean?) The intellectual auxiliary baggage of gross substitution, optimality of reconciled choices of all agents via the price system, Clower's Say's Principle and Patinkin's Walras Law, etc. is so closely identified with the concept of GE, while these paraphernalia are so incompatible with a monetary economy, that to apply the term GE to any monetary equilibrium analysis would be a semantic travesty. Semantic confusion and obfuscation can only result from throwing out the intellectual but useless baggage of GE, while retaining the label.

Others, however, while recognizing the recent failures of GE theory to provide a microfoundation for macroeconomies are not yet ready to throw out their (non-monetary) systems and/or the GE nomenclature. Roy Weintraub argues, for example, that although an Arrow–Debreu world is based on a full-employment assumption and is therefore logically incompatible with underemployment equilibrium, such an incompatibility 'ought not to preclude our search for perhaps more sophisticated Arrow–Debreu type systems that are consistent with unemployment'.[3] But the full-employment assumption is inevitably related to Walras' Law! Thus to avoid this Walras' Law stigma, Weintraub states that GE should 'not be considered as bearing a necessary relationship to the theories of Walras; a general equilibrium model is simply some specification of states of the world and a set of rules that structure the manner in which those states change over time'.[4] To me such a definition throws away the baby of GE while keeping the bathwater.

A truncated macro version of the orthodox GE analysis is the 'IS–LM' framework (what Bronfenbrenner has called the Islamic religion of economists). This IS–LM analysis was first presented by J. R. Hicks.[5] If expanded to include a Phillips curve (which shows a trade off between the rate of unemployment and the rate of inflation), this Hicksian system becomes a typical Neoclassical Synthesis–Keynesian system. If instead, this Hicksian analysis is expanded to encompass some variant of the equation of exchange $(MV = PY)$, it becomes a typical Monetarist Model.

(3) *Keynes' School.* The members of this group are few in number and less well known to the public. They have worked to develop and advance Keynes' original views on employment, money, and inflation. Leaders of this group have included Harrod, Shackle, Weintraub, Davidson, Minsky, Wells, and Vickers. Members of this group, like Keynes, reject the Walrasian general equilibrium framework as 'strictly in the classical tradition'.[6] Consequently, they do not utilize the IS–LM system as a basic analytical framework (except perhaps as a means to attempt to communicate with the other right-of-centre schools).

(4) *Neo-Keynesian School.* A small but important group originally centred in Cambridge, England, who have attempted to graft aspects of Keynes' real sector analysis onto the growth and distribution theories of Ricardo, Marx, and Kalecki. The leaders of this school are Mrs. Robinson, Kaldor, Pasinetti, and Sraffa. Younger members include Eichner, Kregel, Harcourt, and Roncaglia.

(5) *The Socialist–Radical School.* The members of this residual category span a vast spectrum of views from left-of-centre liberals such as Galbraith through to Marxists and 'radical' economists. Despite the vast diversity in this category, members share two common characteristics, namely that (a) their ideas are typically dismissed as 'non-scientific' by the majority (groups to the right of centre) of the Economics Establishment and therefore unworthy of significant serious discussion in the learned professional literature,[7] and (b) they all advocate socialization of those productive sectors of the economy whose faults are perceived as non-correctable by any market process.

Table 1.1 can be termed a 'Table of Political Economy', for it attempts to associate the various schools with different positions in the political spectrum from extreme right to extreme left. As the entries in the various cells of the table suggest, the position taken on various key economic issues by the different schools of thought will tend to vary with their position in the political spectrum. Obviously the five columns are not watertight; views of individuals in any one school tend to be very close, and may, on certain issues, overlap with the views of those in schools of close proximity. Thus, for example, Galbraith may find easy compatibility with the Neo-Keynesians on some issues, little to conflict with in Keynes, but very little common ground with those schools to the right of centre.

In recent years, there has developed a 'Post Keynesian' literature and even a *Journal of Post Keynesian Economics.* As the printer's brace at the bottom of Table 1.1 indicates, Post Keynesian economists[8] are an amalgam of those primarily from the Keynes and Neo-Keynesian

schools, but they are also joined by some of the right leaning members of
the Socialist–Radical Group such as Galbraith. Moreover, certain left
leaning members of the Neoclassical–Keynesian school have exhibited
considerable sympathy for Post Keynesian analysis in recent years (e.g.
John Hicks' writings since the late 1960s). Thus Post Keynesians do not
represent a monolithic or puristic approach to the study of either micro-
or macroeconomics. The analytical framework utilized by Post
Keynesians does, however, share certain common features and concepts
(which tend to be downgraded by the other schools if they are noticed at
all). These common features are described in detail *infra*.

Post Keynesians also share the common view that Keynes provided a
revolutionary new *logical* way of analysing a *real world* economy; and,
like Keynes, Post Keynesians believe that only models which are
relevant to the contemporary world are worthy of economists' attention.
Hence, in a chronological sense, the economists who share these features
and views are the only Post Keynesians among the various schools of
economics listed in Table 1.1. The other schools rely primarily on
analytical foundations which were developed before Keynes and hence
represent regression and not progress in economic science, despite a
veneer of modern mathematical and econometric sophistication.

THE DEMISE OF NEOCLASSICAL ECONOMICS

During the 1950s and early 1960s the Neoclassical Synthesis–
Keynesians reigned all but supreme in the American economics
profession. Although members of the other schools continued to
develop their own views, while warning all who would listen about the
logical faults in the analytical framework of Neoclassical Keynesians,
their professional admonitions were generally ignored both by the
majority of economists and the public. In large part due to the
charismatic quality of Professor Friedman, however, (and perhaps his
willingness to associate the Monetarist school origins to one of the most
famous American economists of an earlier era, Irving Fisher), Monetarism was able to maintain a slight public visibility during the 1950s, and
even greater recognition in the 1960s as Neoclassical Keynesianism
began to falter.

The growing inflationary tendencies of the late 1960s and the
worldwide stagflation of the 1970s led to the collapse of Neoclassical
Keynesianism's dominance of economic theory, as belief in the stability
of downward sloping Phillips Curves (which these Keynesians had used

to buttress their neoclassical synthesis) was shattered. Stagflation ended all hope of a predictable trade off between inflation and unemployment. Monetarists, led by Friedman and his unerring sense of the deficiencies of Neoclassical Keynesians, easily savaged their Keynesian framework and rushed in to fill the partial vacuum in the professional spotlight caused by the exposure of Neoclassical Keynesians' flaws.

Monetarists, however, were soon overwhelmed by real world occurrences such as OPEC oil price increases, droughts in food producing areas, frosts in Brazil, the disappearance of anchovies off the coast of Peru, and other episodic events which seemed to induce permanent fillips to domestic price levels in all industrial capitalist systems; these price movements could not be readily explained solely by exogenous changes in domestic money supplies in each nation. Further erosion of confidence in the Monetarist approach followed the adoption of floating exchange rates in 1971 by the major industrial countries. The Monetarists had decreed that such an arrangement would insulate the domestic economy from the international transmission of inflation.[9] Events since 1971 have shown, however, that flexible exchange rates are not the panacea Monetarists had claimed.

Thus the tide of events has rapidly diminished the stature of economists of both the Neoclassical Keynesian and Monetarist persuasions in the eyes of the public. The corpus of orthodox neoclassical theory lies in shambles, and there appears to be a crisis in Economic Theory.[10] Even more importantly, the 'Second Great Crisis of the 20th Century for Capitalist Economies' is being precipitated by policy advice derived from irrelevant neoclassical economic schools of thought.

The Neoclassical Keynesians bear the responsibility for having aborted Keynes' fundamental revolutionary way of analysing real world economic problems before it could ever establish roots in the economics profession. The flavour of some of Keynes' specific economic policy recommendations to fight unemployment remained, but the logic of Keynes' economic theory was derailed. This permitted pre-Keynesian logical systems (e.g. supply-side economics) to be used in developing economic theory. Since these earlier systems were inadequate for analysing the real world economic problems of the 1930s, it is not surprising that they should be found impotent for dealing with the more complex problems of the 1980s. Post Keynesians are therefore currently engaged in picking up the shattered and often disregarded pieces of Keynes' logical system and attempting to restore economic theory to a state where it can again provide practical solutions for the real world economic problems of our times.

THE POST KEYNESIAN OVERVIEW

> Economics is a science of thinking in terms of models joined to the art of choosing models which are relevant to the contemporary world. . . . Good economists are scarce because the gift for using 'vigilant observation' to choose good models, although it does not require a highly specialized intellectual technique, appears to be a very rare one.
>
> *–J. M. Keynes*

Post Keynesians recognize that the choice of model to be used depends on the current problem at hand in the economic system under study. One general model cannot resolve every conceivable economic problem for all times and all situations. In other sciences we have different models for different problems. In mathematics, for example, we have Euclidean and non-Euclidean geometry: for some problems the former is appropriate but for others it would be disastrous. Similarly in physics there is a model of an electron as a particle and a model of an electron as a wave. By using a classification method to decide when to use one model or another, other sciences have made progress; economics should not be ashamed to follow this path.

There are two basic types of economic models, namely (a) timeless general equilibrium systems or (b) historical and humanistic systems. The former proceed by specifying a sufficient number of equations to determine *all* the unknowns in the system simultaneously (and endogenously). Such systems are timeless in the sense that all decisions and actions that can affect the solution are taken at the initial instant; in essence all contracts are signed in the Garden of Eden without any false trades. This 'initial instant' decision process completely determines the future history of mankind for every conceivable trick of Mother Nature. In the future course of events, economic actors merely read their agreed upon lines and the economic play is performed even though all know (or expect with actuarial certainty) that Hamlet and the others will die in the last act! For particular questions that can be intellectually raised (e.g. the optimal allocation problem), equilibrium models could (if anything really could!) provide an answer.[11] Unfortunately the logic of general equilibrium models implies that such systems *cannot* provide practical answers for policy makers facing hard decisions involving economic events which have important ramifications in the uncertain future. As Hahn has shown, general equilibrium models can only demonstrate that leaving allocation problems to market forces will *not* guarantee an optimum solution.[12]

General equilibrium systems were not (and logically cannot be) designed to provide positive guides to resolving the macro-political and economic problems of inflation, unemployment, economic growth, or even the 'energy crisis'. These horrendous economic problems are, however, the perfect grist for the Post Keynesian mill. Post Keynesians use historical and humanistic models into which such problems easily fit.

WHAT IS POST KEYNESIAN ECONOMICS?

Post Keynesians do not represent a puristic approach to the study of either micro- or macroeconomics. Nevertheless, there are a number of distinguishing features which separate them from Monetarists, Neo-classical Keynesians, and some Socialist–Radical economists.

The first and foremost distinguishing feature is that Post Keynesians reject the notion that any general equilibrium system is the basic logical structure for the comprehension of real world monetary economies. Of course, Post Keynesians recognize that all theories represent abstractions and simplifications of reality. The problem is to develop a framework to tame the real world so that a comprehensive realistic analysis can be undertaken. All Post Keynesians are united in the view that any logical system which defines equilibrium as uniquely synonymous with the simultaneous clearing of all markets and the prereconciliation of the plans of all economic agents in a world of uncertainty cannot provide a realistic guide to solving real world problems.

There are six concepts that all Post Keynesian models are based upon:

(1) *The notion that the economic system is a process moving irreversibly through calendar time (i.e. the economy is a process in history).* Time is a real world device which prevents everything from happening at once! The production of commodities takes time, and the consumption of capital goods and consumer durables takes time. In a Post Keynesian world, time is an asymmetric variable, and the economy is moving irreversibly and unidirectionally (forward) through time. The past may be knowledge but the future is unknown—yet, economic decisions taken in the present will require actions which cannot be completed until some future day (or days). In such a world, economic decision makers are continuously involved in sequential decisions and actions which are coloured not only by their expectations of the unknowable future but also by the inherited stocks (which embody correct previous guesses as

well as past errors) which they possess. Consequently decisions rarely if ever are made on a clean slate. Thus Post Keynesians will emphasize the role of heterogeneous expectations and the importance of non-fully anticipated events. As Hicks has recently noted, 'One must assume that the people in one's models do not know what is going to happen, and know that they do not know what is going to happen. As in history!'[13] In a neoclassical world, on the other hand, all decisions involving present and all future actions are taken at a single initial instant in time; errors are, by assumption, (at least in the long run) impossible. Thus neoclassical economics explicitly denies the old maxim 'To err is human . . .'

Sir John Hicks, who provided much of the impetus for modern neoclassical (general equilibrium) theory and who is the progenitor of the IS–LM equilibrium model (which is *the* macroframework for the Neoclassical Schools) recognized more than a decade ago that his framework was a 'potted version' of Keynes' theory.[14] More recently, under the prodding of some Post Keynesians who have stressed where mainstream economics has gone wrong, Hicks has recanted on the usefulness of the IS–LM framework: 'The IS–LM diagram, which is widely, but not universally accepted as a convenient synopsis of Keynesian theory, is a thing for which I cannot deny that I have some responsibility . . . I have, however, not concealed that as time has gone on I have myself become dissatisfied with it'.[15]

Hicks has stated that, unlike general equilibrium concepts which 'signal that time in some respects at least has been put on one side', Keynes' monetary framework was an 'in (calendar) time' approach where the recognition of an uncertain future (and not just a probabilistic one) shaped economic behaviour. The lack of recognition of the concept of 'in calendar time' by Neoclassical Synthesis–Keynesians meant, according to Hicks that

> The 'Keynesian revolution' went off at half-cock. The (general) equilibrists did not know that they were beaten . . . they thought that what Keynes had said could be absorbed into their equilibrium system; all that was needed was the scope of their equilibrium system should be extended. As we know, there has been a lot of extension, a vast amount of extension; what I am saying is that it has never quite got to the point . . .
>
> I begin (as I am sure you will want to begin) with the old IS–LM (or SILL) diagram . . . I must say that diagram is now much less popular with me than I think it still is with many other people. It reduces the

General Theory to equilibrium economics; it is not really a question of time.[16]

Marshall, in the Preface of the first edition of his *Principles* however, had stated that the 'element of Time . . . is the center of the chief difficulty of almost every economic problem'.[17] Keynes, in his analytical framework, clearly recognized that money matters only when we wish to analyse the 'problems of the real world in which our previous expectations are liable to disappointment and expectations concerning the future affect what we do today'.[18] Keynes' Revolution is in the Marshall tradition of emphasizing time at the centre of economic problems, while the general equilibrium IS–LM approach emasculates the concept of time as a historical process.

(2) *The role of expectations in an uncertain world.* Neoclassical theorists assume that uncertainty can be represented via probability statements in an economic world that is in a state of statistical control; hence all future variables can be reduced to actuarial certainty (present value) equivalents in the present instant of time. Moreover, in an equilibrium world, *all expectations must be realized by events*; surprises and disappointments are logically incompatible with the logic of general equilibrium. Post Keynesians on the other hand emphasize the difference between uncertainty and predictable risks. Post Keynesians deal with the expectations of economic decision makers in a world where there are what Shackle has called 'crucial experiments', i.e. where the carrying out of economic decisions permanently alters the economic environment (the parameters) in a non-predictable manner. Thus the economic system is not in a state of statistical control and, hence, the mathematical laws of probability do not apply. In such a world, decision makers recognize that *errors, surprises and disappointments* are part of the human condition. This perception affects the feasible options considered, and often, economic agents in a Keynes world will take actions that would be considered 'irrational' in a neoclassical world, e.g. the holding of money over periods of calendar time for liquidity motives. Monetarist economists such as Laidler and Parkin, in their survey of the economic literature on inflation, have noted that in neoclassical theory

expectations – even if erroneous – are usually treated as if held with certainty, or it is assumed that any variance in expectations does not influence behaviour. There exists a well-developed analysis, based on probability theory, of individual behaviour in the face of risk elsewhere in our subject and there surely are gains to be had from applying this analysis to aspects of the problems of inflation. This at least would be our view, but there are many economists, notably Davidson (1972) and Shackle (1955), who would presumably regard the application of such analysis as misconceived (though possibly better than assuming all expectations to be held with certainty). They would stress that *uncertainty* in the Knightian sense as opposed to risk lay at the root of the problem. Certainly an analysis of behaviour of this kind would provide an interesting alternative to the approach based on probability. There can be no guarantee *ex ante* as to which line of work will prove more fruitful, as a means of replacing the widespread assumption (often unstated) that people's actions are the same as if their expectations were held with certainty.[19]

Replacing the concept of certainty with known probability distributions merely replaces the assumption of perfect foreknowledge by economic agents with the assumption that they possess actuarial knowledge. In such a situation actuarial costs and benefits can be calculated and the economic agent can act 'as if' he possessed absolute prescience [or in modern Monetarist parlance, expectations are 'rational' and 'fully anticipate']. This semantic legerdemain permits Neoclassical economists to develop sophisticated theories which replicate the solutions of pre-Keynesian perfect certainty models while providing the specious appearance of dealing with time and decision making by economic agents facing an 'uncertain' (but fully anticipated!) future. Such literary deceptions are the necessary foundations for Neoclassical economists' precise and invariable long run conclusions that government intervention to improve employment via fiscal policy or to fight inflation via incomes policy is bound to be ineffective. (The motto of such Neoclassical models is, after all, '*laissez-faire*'.) The futility of government intervention in 'rational expectations' models, for example, rests on the concept of a *natural rate of unemployment* (which is the equivalent of full employment in a world of perfect certainty). As Monetarist economist Laidler has stated

We have argued that any rate of inflation is consistent with a state of zero excess demand in the economy provided it is *fully expected*. If to this we add the proposition that there is a unique level of unemployment in the economy associated with a situation of zero overall excess demand then we have it by implication that *this so-called 'natural' unemployment rate is consistent with any fully anticipated rate of inflation*.[20]

Is there really a difference between 'fully anticipated' events and perfect certainty?

Modern neoclassical analysis has developed expectational formation models to try to shore up their collapsing analytical structure. Such models are, as even their advocates have admitted, 'naive', 'arbitrary', or 'inconsistent'.[21] Thus 'The simplest lesson to be learned from consideration of the rational expectations hypothesis,' Laidler concedes, 'is that there is likely to be far more to the formation of expectations than the blind application of some mechanical formula to a body of data . . . [Moreover] we must face the implication that heterogeneity of expectations at any moment is more likely to be the rule than homogeneity.'[22]

Of course, heterogeneity of expectations means that people have differing expectations about the future. This guarantees that the uniqueness of tomorrow's events will prove that most of those holding today's expectations will find, as events unfold, that their expectations were quantitatively (if not also qualitatively) incorrect. Consequently mistakes, false trades and changing economic parameters are unavoidable in the real world. Yet the fundamental Monetarist concept of a 'natural rate of unemployment', upon which elaborate Monetarist policies for fighting inflation are developed, requires, as even Monetarists admit, a 'fully anticipated' future – a future which 'can only be perfectly anticipated in any actual economy if *all* people hold the same expectations since otherwise some expectations are bound to be wrong'.[23]

Post Keynesians, in sharp distinction to this neoclassical approach, build upon the fact that the future is uncertain and, as Hicks states, people know they do not know the future when they undertake economic actions. The economic future will be created by man, rather than discovered! Consequently, as opposed to neoclassical systems, Post Keynesian analysis aims to be roughly right when discussing possible future events, rather than precisely wrong.

(3) *The role of economic and political institutions in the economic system.* In the logical world of general equilibrium there are no significant real world economic institutions – not even commodity or financial markets. (This is true despite lengthy neoclassical discussions of market forces.) In a Post Keynesian world, on the other hand, economic and political institutions are influential and prominent in determining output, employment and the money price level. These institutions include (a) the banking and monetary systems, (b) time-oriented markets for goods, factors of production, and financial

assets, (c) the institution of money contracts for spot and forward transactions, and especially (d) the money wage contract as a necessary condition for liquidity over time for a market-oriented, monetary, entrepreneurial production economy.

Money only matters in a world – our world – where there are multitudinous catenated forward contracts in money terms. (A forward contract specifies the future calendar date(s) of delivery *and* payment.) In such an economy it is necessary that there be some continuity as to that thing which by delivery settles the resulting obligations. The existence of market institutions which permit (and encourage) contracting for future payment creates the need for money and liquidity. This is an essential aspect affecting the performance of all real world market-oriented monetary economies where the activity of production requires the passage of calendar time.

In a market-oriented entrepreneurial economy, most production transactions along the non-integrated chain of firms involve forward contracts. For example, the hiring of factor inputs (especially labour) and the purchase of materials for the production of goods will normally require forward contracting if the production process is to be efficiently planned. The financing of such forward production cost commitments (i.e. taking a 'position' in working capital goods) requires entrepreneurs to have money available to discharge these liabilities at one or more future dates *before* the product is sold, delivered, and payment received and the position is liquidated. Since the logic of general equilibrium theory requires all payments to be made at the initial instant, it neglects the concept of contracting over calendar time in organized markets for future delivery *and* payments. This ubiquitous liquidity problem of entrepreneurs in capitalist economies is left unattended by mainstream Neoclassical economists who consequently are deserving recipients of the businessman's traditional gibe: 'They have never had to meet a payroll!'

For a decentralized entrepreneurial economy moving irreversibly through calendar time (where the future is uncertain), forward contracting for inputs to the production process is essential to efficient production plans. Moreover, in such an economy, where slavery is illegal, the money wage contract is the most ubiquitous forward contract of all; and since labour hiring and payment precede in time delivery of newly produced goods, it is the money wage relative to productivity which is the foundation upon which the price level of new goods rests.

As Arrow and Hahn have noted

The terms in which contracts are made matter. In particular, if money is the good in terms of which contracts are made, then the prices of goods in terms of money are of special significance. This is not the case if we consider an economy without a past and without a future. Keynes wrote that 'the importance of money essentially flows from it being a link between the present and the future' to which we add that it is important also because it is a link between the past and the present. If a *serious monetary theory* comes to be written, the fact that contracts are indeed made in terms of money will be of considerable importance.[24]

Furthermore, Arrow and Hahn have concluded that in 'a world with a past as well as a future and in which contracts are made in terms of money, no [general] equilibrium may exist'.[25] In other words, the presence of time and forward money contracts is a sufficient condition for the possible *non-existence* of *full* employment equilibrium. Hence, economies organized on a contracting basis over time may settle down to equilibrium at any level of employment; that is, they may exhibit an unemployment equilibrium *in the long run as well as the short run*.

If Arrow and Hahn are correct, it therefore follows that a 'serious monetary theory' must be based on a money-wage contract view of the economy. It is the stickiness of money wages and prices (i.e. the absence of rapid movements) guaranteed via the law of contracts which permits entrepreneurial economies to engage in time-consuming production processes and provides a basis for a sticky price level of producible goods. Accordingly, forward contracting can be considered as the way entrepreneurs in a 'free market' environment attempt to maintain wage and price controls! Such cost and price controls are fundamental in obtaining financing of production processes. Bankers and businessman abhor what Neoclassical economists love – namely recontracting.

The existence of fixed money contracts for forward delivery *and* payment is fundamental to the concepts of liquidity and money. It is the change in contractual money wage rates – Keynes' wage unit – which, *ceteris paribus*, determines changes in the costs of production and the price level associated with the production of goods that profit oriented entrepreneurs are willing to undertake. The view that inflation (i.e. a rising money price level of newly produced goods) is a monetary phenomenon makes logical sense only in an economy where time-oriented money contracts (especially for labour hire) are basic to the organization of production activities. As long as the time duration of fixed money wage contracts exceeds the gestation period of production, entrepreneurs can limit their liabilities in undertaking any production process. If, however, the institution of long duration fixed money contracts begins to break down, then a 'social contract' to limit wage and price movements over long periods of calendar time must be developed to buttress the private institution of lengthy forward contracts, if production processes which require lengthy periods of time are to be maintained.[26]

(4) *The relevance of the distribution of income (and power).* The distribution of income and power is a basic aspect of Post Keynesian theory, but it is virtually ignored in logically consistent neoclassical models. When neoclassical economists have attempted to 'explain' macro-income distribution phenomena, their logic has been proven faulty (e.g. the reswitching controversy). In fact, in a general equilibrium neoclassical world, problems of income distribution over time (e.g. due to unanticipated inflation) cannot arise because the future is logically predictable, at least in an actuarial sense. Hence, non-fully anticipated inflation cannot be analysed in a general equilibrium model despite Neoclassical economists' statements about the desirability of 'indexing' to avoid unanticipated inflation. Since the logic of neoclassical theory does not permit an analysis of macro-income distribution and inflation, it is no wonder that 'income policy' discussions are an anathema to logically consistent members of the neoclassical schools.

(5) *The concept of capital in an economic system.* Here the distinction between neoclassical and Keynes' views hinges on two facets (a) whether capital is malleable or non-malleable (and therefore embodies past errors and wears out slowly over calendar time), and (b) whether there is an important difference between real and financial capital. Keynes and his followers emphasize the non-malleability aspect of real capital as well as the difference between financial and real capital and the markets for each. Neoclassical Monetarist and Keynesian portfolio and financial theory is purblind regarding the distinction in the latter case while it assumes malleability in the former case.

(6) *Post Keynesian analysis emphasizes income effects as being more dominant than substitution effects in creating, and resolving, real world economic problems.* Although Marshall developed the principle of substitution in Book v of his *Principles*, this maxim was associated with the planning period when there were no contractual commitments or existing capital facilities to bind the entrepreneur to a particular course of future action. Throughout the rest of the *Principles*, however, Marshall stresses the importance of income and its relationship to

capital and investment. Keynes, of course, tended to emphasize the income effects of Marshallian analysis. Orthodox neoclassical theory, on the other hand, is based on the axiom of Gross Substitution, i.e. that everything is ultimately a substitute for everything else. Primary reliance on the principle of gross substitution leads neoclassical economists to suggest that all economic problems can be resolved by substitution effects induced by freely-flexible relative price movements. Since substitution effects are always positive, these in tandem with assumptions of the universality of the laws of diminishing returns and diminishing marginal utility are, in the absence of income effects, sufficient to assure that free markets 'optimally' resolve every problem. Once income effects are permitted to affect the outcome, however, (as they do in the real world and in Post Keynesian Theory), the beneficence of free market solutions is put in doubt.

It would be fatuous, for example, to evaluate incomes policies from a neoclassical perspective which basically ignores income effects, and whose prices (including factor prices) provide signals about allocative efficiencies via substitution effects in some (instantaneous) decision period. If, on the other hand, different choices occur in different calendar time sequences over different Marshallian time periods where income effects can substantially affect decisions *and* outcomes, as inventory adjustments, short run profits and losses, unemployment, and changing lengths of queues all provide signals regarding past (income affecting) errors, incomes policies can be more properly evaluated.

Post Keynesian Monetary Theory follows Keynes' 'essential properties' definition of liquidity.[27] The attribute of liquidity entails that money (and all other liquid assets) possesses certain 'essential properties', namely a zero (or negligible) elasticity of production and a zero (or negligible) elasticity of substitution between such liquid assets and goods that have a high elasticity of production, i.e. that are readily producible via the exertion of labour.[28]

To denote that the elasticity of production is zero is merely to recognize, in the language of economists, the old adage that 'money doesn't grow on trees'; and hence money cannot be harvested (i.e. produced) by the use of labour. Because the elasticity of production is zero, if households, for example, decide to buy fewer autos (or space vehicles) and buy more time (liquidity) vehicles (for moving purchasing power over time, i.e. for liquidity) out of current income, while no-one else concurrently spends more on the producible goods of our industries, then employment will decline in the auto (space machine) industry while the unemployed resources cannot be deflected into the production of liquidity time machines. Moreover, since the unemployed auto workers will buy less goods, additional or secondary unemployment (through the multiplier) will occur in other industries which ordinarily sell goods to auto workers.

Since the elasticity of substitution is also zero (or negligible), as the hypothesized demand for money (or similar financial assets) increases, households will not substitute *other producible items* for these desired time machines. The demand for liquidity is a bottomless sink, and when the demand for liquidity increases at the expense of the demand for goods, there is no price at which this demand will be diverted back to the products of industry.

These salient elasticity properties, it should be noted, do *not* mean that the money supply is unalterable. The money supply can be expanded exogenously (i.e. by the deliberate actions of the Central Bank) or endogenously when the banking system responds to an increased demand for money; in the latter instance, when part of the public wishes to enlarge their 'positions' in capital goods and other durables (the 'real bills' doctrine).

These essential properties mean that underemployment equilibrium can occur whenever there are, as Hahn says, 'resting places for savings other than reproducible assets'.[29] Since the second elasticity property of liquid assets is logically incompatible with the axiom of gross substitution, a world where liquidity is important (as it is in the real world) is a system that operates under different principles than one specified by neoclassical logic. Consequently neoclassical theorists resemble, as Keynes noted

> Euclidean geometers in a non-Euclidean world who, discovering that in experience straight lines apparently parallel often meet, rebuke the lines for not keeping straight – as the *only* remedy for the unfortunate collisions which are occurring. *Yet, in truth, there is no remedy except to throw over the axiom of parallels and to work out a non-Euclidean geometry. Something similar is required today in economics.*[30]

The axiom that Keynes and Post Keynesians throw over is that of the universal applicability of gross substitution and hence income effects are given a more important role.

NEOCLASSICAL RESPONSES TO POST KEYNESIAN VIEWS

It should be obvious to the astute reader that the Post Keynesian emphasis on the aforementioned features and concepts does create at least a paradigm's worth of difference between Post Keynesian Theory and neoclassical general equilibrium analysis of either the Keynesian or Monetarist persuasions.[31] Elsewhere,[32] I have elaborated in detail how the Post Keynesian approach can resolve the problems of inflation and unemployment by analysing the importance of the institution of markets involving money and contracts in a closed economic system moving from an immutable past to an unpredictable future.

Friedman has characterized my own Post Keynesian approach as 'He [Davidson] appears to *start* from the position that there does not exist a long-run equilibrium position characterized by full employment, and then try to *deduce* the empirical characteristics of money (and other elements of the economy) from that proposition.'[33] If the word 'necessarily' is inserted before the word 'exist' and the words 'real world' before 'long run', then I believe the amended statement is a reasonable representation of my position (and it is supported by the above quotation from Arrow and Hahn). Furthermore I believe the amended statement is a preferable starting point (as opposed) to the position that *all* general equilibrium theorists *must* begin with, namely that full employment is the necessary (inevitable?) long run position of modern production economies. Unfortunately, if the neoclassical view is adopted as the starting point of any economic theory, then the observed real world unemployment and stagflation phenomena can only be explained as 'temporary' phenomena due to frictions, or price and money wage rigidities, or to (adaptive? rational?) expectational reactions, while in the long run a state of economic bliss will be attained by unfettered market processes. (The latter is, of course, not a conclusion of the analysis but merely a reiteration of the initial supposition of neoclassical analysis.)

The object of such neoclassical modelling is an 'idealized state', i.e. the long-run equilibrium solution, whereas Keynes believed that from the outset economists should model the actual state of the real world. As Keynes noted, however, 'this long run is a misleading guide to current affairs. *In the long run* we are all dead. Economists set themselves too easy, too useless a task if in tempestuous seasons they can only tell us that when the storm is long past the ocean is flat again.'[34]

2 The Conceptual Framework

Clear thinking which must *precede* good policy decisions requires the use of a precise language regarding the economic system in which we live. Thus, the foundation of any scientific study of real world phenomena (which are always vaguely expressed in the vernacular) involves a method of discovery via the use of an unambiguous set of definitions of the fundamental economic concepts. Often what appear to be disagreements among economists really involve semantic confusions resulting from opponents in the debate using the same words to convey different and often ambiguous meanings.

The fundamental concepts must be precisely specified and the logical relations among these notions developed from some basic axioms. Since axioms are merely self-evident propositions, Post Keynesian economists believe that these same maxims should be developed inductively if they are to be relevant to the real world.[1] Thus, for Post Keynesians, propositions such as

(1) monetary, market-oriented, entrepreneurial production economies do not possess any homostatic mechanism which ensures that they tend toward a full employment of available resource equilibrium over time and among nations;

(2) underemployment equilibrium and non-stable money price levels often occur in such money using economies, and

(3) the existence of unemployment and purchasing power instability must be associated with the characteristics of money, its related human institutions, and how production is organized in such real world economies, are fundamental to the development of a theory applicable to modern real world developed economies.

The neoclassical schools of economic thought, on the other hand, use only deductive axioms as the basis of their analytical system, e.g. (a) all economic agents are utility maximizers and (b) a full employment of resource equilibrium for *any* economy *exists*, where the plans and expectations of *all* economic agents for *all* time are prereconcilable and

shed light only on past behaviour and the dominant forces *in the past* which shaped human actions. To use such econometric relations to forecast the future requires, in Hicks' view, the heroic and unwarranted assumption that the fundamental relation will continue to be invariable in the future, i.e. that potent forces that prevailed in the past will *persist* into the future. If a relation held for 50 years in the past, Hicks believes, we might guess it would hold for one or two years into the future. (But we could not be sure!) 'But we cannot even reasonably guess it will continue to hold for the next fifty years. In the sciences such guesses are reasonable; in economics they are not.'[6] In other words, econometric evidence of historical predominant factors affecting economic affairs does not necessarily imply any extrapolative endurance of such forces.

Hicks' view, of course, is similar to that expressed by Keynes in his criticism of Tinbergen's and Schultz's early econometric work. Keynes believed that the use of regression analyses of time series data involved a pseudo-science which should be rejected for economic data which are 'not homogenous through time'.[7] As Keynes noted

> It seems to me that economics is a branch of logic; a way of thinking . . . One can make some quite worthwhile progress merely by using axioms and maxims. But one cannot get very far except by devising new and improved models. This requires, as you say 'a vigilant observation of the actual working of our system'. *Progress* in economics consists almost entirely in a progressive improvement in the choice of models.[8]

Thus, if one is going to make progress in economics, it will be through the development of the theoretical models based on a clear, unambiguous set of definitions and some basic axioms based on 'vigilant observation of the workings of our system'. In the previous chapter, it was noted that Post Keynesians have identified, via vigilant observation, six aspects of the real world which they believe are crucial for the development of 'good' economic models. These involve

    (1) the economic system as a process moving through calendar time;

    (2) the role of expectations in an uncertain (as opposed to risky) world;

    (3) the importance of economic and political institutions;

    (4) the importance of the distribution of income and power;

    (5) the distinction between financial and real capital and between malleable and nonmalleable facilities;

harmonious.[2] Since these axioms are entirely *deductive*, the neoclass
system is a profession of faith.[3] Moreover, under the fervour
the neoclassical schools, the idea of a *deductive axiomatic* value the
has often been proclaimed 'the' microfoundation of macroeconon
and trade theory and the touchstone of all serious (!) econor
analysis.

Post Keynesians, of course, demur from this view. Consequen
communication between Post Keynesian theorists and neoclassi
economists on the proper theoretical basis for practical policy has b
very difficult. In order for economists to end the stalemate in theoreti
and policy development of recent decades, it is necessary that (a) we
to what extent we can get agreement on axioms among economists a
(b) we ensure that all are using the same definitions and language
formulate policy.

WHAT IS A GOOD ECONOMIC MODEL?

Unlike the physical sciences, there does not exist in economics sor
crucial empirical test which will decide once-and-for-all betwe
conflicting theories as to their falsity or veracity. Moreover, one c
have no assurance that there are unchanging parameters or relatio
ships over time in economics. General equilibrium analysis, on the oth
hand, since it is completely deductive, must assume that, given the stat
initial instant conditions, there are unchanging parameters (or at lea
the rate of change in such parameters is predetermined) for the econon
system as it moves through calendar time. For example, Solow in his E
Lecture indicated that all the theoretical relations in economics ha
been discovered and the only remaining task left for future generatio
of economists is the estimation of the fundamental parameters in t
system.[4]

In contrast, Sir John Hicks has written that there are 'no su
constants in economics'.[5] Perhaps 200 years ago when economic affa
changed less incessantly over time, neoclassical (timeless) causati
theories could be used as a rough approximation of reality. But becau
of the deductive nature of *all* its axioms, neoclassical theories cann
deal with unforeseen events within the time period of their analys
hence Hicks insists that unanticipated changes (which are fundam
tally unavoidable in a modern, production-monetary economy) cann
be dealt with by neoclassical schools of thought. Empirical estimatio
past econometric relationships between economic variables can, at b

(6) the greater importance of income effects over substitution effects. With these features in mind, we can devise a useful set of definitions.

A CLASSIFICATION SCHEME

Harrod has noted that the Keynesian revolution 'consisted in essence in a set of new definitions and a re-classification . . . It was Keynes' extraordinary powerful intuitive sense of what was important that convinced him that the old classification was inadequate. It was his highly developed logical capacity that enabled him to construct a new classification of his own.'[9]

Book II of *The General Theory* is entitled 'Definitions and Ideas', for Keynes noted that among the 'perplexities which most impeded my progress in writing this book'[10] were the questions of definitions and units appropriate to analysing macroeconomic problems. Only after getting the definitions and units 'right' was Keynes able to move on to develop 'The Propensity to Consume'[11] in Book III, 'The Inducement to Invest' in Book IV and the relation between 'Money, Wages and Prices' in Book V. Moreover, in the Preface to *The General Theory*, Keynes indicates that although this work is related to his earlier *Treatise on Money* via 'a natural evolution in a time of thought', he felt 'compelled' to make certain changes in terminology in order to make progress and emancipate himself from 'traditional lines'.[12]

New conceptual classifications and definitions were therefore essential to the Keynesian Revolution for they are the primary tools of the economist for separating and analysing the multifarious phenomena we identify as economic life. In fact, Shackle has claimed that progress in economic theory can only be made via a taxonomic approach. Shackle claims that economic 'theory ought explicitly to be a classificatory one, putting situations in this box or that according to what *can happen* as a sequel to it. Theories which tell us what *will* happen are claiming too much.'[13]

Accordingly, in this volume our emphasis will be on developing a taxonomy and a set of definitions which provide a more adequate basis for analysing the problems of real world monetary economies engaging in production and in external trade and monetary relationships with other regions and nations. In the following chapters we shall distinguish between a closed and an open economic system based on a system of national (or regional) double entry accounts for production and expenditure, *and* between a unionized (hereafter UMS) and non-unionized (hereafter NUMS) monetary system based on whether a single monetary unit (a UMS) is used to denominate all production, expenditure and financial contracts, or whether different monetary units (a NUMS) are utilized in denominating different contracts between transactors at any point of calendar time.

In his *Treatise on Money*, Keynes developed concepts to deal with open, NUMS economic systems. As part of his simplification in *The General Theory*, however, he focused his definitions and analytical classification on a closed UMS instead, for the latter avoids complications inherent in the operations of any open NUMS. These complications can divert attention from the basic problem of insufficient effective demand which can exist independently of the intricacies of an open NUMS.

In Chapter 3 we start by resurrecting and updating many of the classifications and definitions of the UMS of *The General Theory*[14] so that they can be used to analyse an open UMS. Unfortunately, although some aspects of Keynes' policy were readily adopted by neoclassical synthesis Keynesians, and his emphasis on expectations and use of the word 'uncertainty' adopted by Monetarists and others, the precision of his language and concepts was bowdlerized and bastardized in order to achieve the famous neoclassical synthesis and IS–LM framework. Thus, it is necessary to briefly redevelop the original Keynesian concepts in order to make any progress.

3 Definitions for a Closed Economy: Illustrated via the Shortage of Saving Hypothesis

Unlike physical scientists who, with the aid of modern technology, claim to observe phenomena beyond the recognition of the average layman and therefore are free to invent language (e.g. the quark) to describe the hypothetical causes of observable events, economists are destined to discuss phenomena which all but the youngest among us have observed and experienced. Thus, as soon as we are out of our infancy, we all (including the most feeble-minded among us) are 'economists' able to discourse on what are the causes of inflation, unemployment, etc. with ease and expertise. After all, everyone knows what money is; all have experience with inflation; from childhood on, we are taxed on our purchases and are recipients of government services, etc.

With such widespread 'knowledge' about the basic building blocks of economics, why then, the reader may ask, do we need one or more chapters devoted to definitions? Moreover, chapters devoted strictly to defining and classifying common everyday objects of experience may seem not only to insult the intelligence of the *cognoscente*, but also tend to make for extremely boring reading for all but the most devoted linguist, taxonomist and/or methodologist. For 'practical men of affairs', as well as for the 'applied economist' interested in the study of economics primarily for its ability to shed light on the pressing problems of the day, or to demonstrate to the public and to the legislators that pursuit of one's vested private economic interests improves the general welfare, niceties of economic language are often perceived as mere hindrances in reaching one's objectives. Fastidiousness in terminology is often dismissed as merely personal affectation of 'ivy-covered' theorists about common sense economic objects.

25

Thus, the author who wishes to attract the attention of 'practical men' as well as of theorists, and who plans to devote one or more chapters to definitions is faced with the prospect that his desired readership may either (a) skip the essential definitional material and, instead, render its own pre-conceived and often ambiguous 'practical' interpretation of basic terms confronting it in the rest of the volume, or (b) put aside the volume in the belief that the discovery of the author's message cannot be worth the effort of learning a new, more precise but uncommon terminology.

Faced with this dismal prospect, most authors of economic treatises decide to accept the terminology and classification currently in vogue, no matter how ambiguous they might be, and to define as few necessary new concepts as possible as they go along. Unfortunately, as long as authors utilize imprecise accepted classifications and definitions, they can at best provide only slight variations in accepted doctrine; they cannot provide a fundamental challenge to current views. No great progress or breakthrough can therefore be made, for the difference between such works and previous material must be, at the most, marginal, as long as much of the story can be told with the same old obtuse terminology. At best then, an author can develop only an overlooked nuance about a basic concept, or claim that some parameter has a different qualitative or quantitative value than has previously been suspected.

In the present volume, however, the author is attempting to jar loose the grip of conventional theory from the reader's mind. Consequently, there is no choice but to develop a non-orthodox classification scheme and set of definitions from the very beginning. The challenge is how to provide this necessary dictionary *up-front*, while still keeping the reader's attention and interest.

One possible approach is to just dump, without apology, the taxonomic material on the reader at the very beginning, and trust that the prestige and/or the controversy surrounding the author will encourage the reader to slog through, or accept the author's use of terms as an article of faith. This was the approach taken by Keynes and, in more recent times, Friedman.[1]

In this volume, a different tack is adopted. In this chapter, some basic definitions are developed while attempting simultaneously to analyse a pressing current economic question, namely, whether the observed 'shortage of private saving' in the United States was a *cause* (*not an effect*) of the economic stagflation of the last decade. Much has been made of the declining saving ratio (i.e. personal saving as a fraction of personal income) in the national income accounts of the U.S. compared to Germany and Japan during the decade of the 1970s to explain the weakness of the U.S. economy and dollar *vis-à-vis* the strength of the German and Japanese economies and currencies. In this chapter, we develop concepts to analyse the shortage of saving (hereafter SOS) hypothesis in order to develop practical policy responses to stagnation tendencies in the United States, as well as to focus on Post Keynesian definitions of economic concepts to be utilized later in our analysis of the relationship of international money and the real world.

SAVING, CONTRACTS, MONEY AND LIQUIDITY

In an economy where market-oriented entrepreneurs organize the production process on a forward-money contract basis, i.e. hiring inputs and purchasing raw materials by entering into contractual agreements to pay money sums for delivery at specified future dates, and look to their recoupment of these money outlays by selling the output for money on either a spot or forward contracting basis, then the earning of income is directly associated with the existence of these money contracts which 'control' the inputs into production activities. In other words, the *income* which a household or firm obtains in a monetary economy comes primarily from the money payments which are made to it by the discharge of a buyer's contractual commitment involving the production process. These contractual money payments give the recipient claims on the products of industry.[2] *Consumption* is defined as spending by households of a portion of these monetary claims on the current flow of products (or resources) of industry. *Saving* then can be defined as *not* exercising a portion of the flow of current money income claims on the current flow of products (or resources of industry).

Since consumption is (by definition) restricted to households, how are we to identify saving by business firms? The gross income of any business is the excess of the monetary value of the current products sold during the production period over the contractual payments for labour, material supplies, and contractual interest payments associated with the flow of current products. A portion of this business income may be transferred during the period to households via dividends. The remaining income is equal to retained profits and capital consumption allowances; and this is defined as *gross business saving*, since it is not immediately *or necessarily* spent on the current (domestically produced) products (or resources) of industry.

How, one might enquire, would the situation be accounted for if, in the same period, firms purchased newly produced capital goods equal to (or more than, or less than) the value of gross business saving as defined above? Analytically, this should be looked upon as two separate and independent decisions, namely (a) a decision to not spend (i.e. to save) all corporate revenues on labour, raw materials, interest and/or dividends to produce the current flow of output, and (b) a decision to purchase (invest in) newly produced plant and equipment. If, in the aggregate, the current purchases of capital goods by business firms are equal to gross business saving, then this saving can be used to internally (i.e. within the business sector), 'equity' finance[3] these investment expenditures. If investment exceeds business saving, then external debt and/or equity finance will be required (in the simple two-sector case[4]). If investment is less than business saving, unless households consume more than their current income, unemployment and recession may result.

In a modern economy with a well developed financial and banking system, there is however no necessary fixed relation in the aggregate involving (a) the flow of business saving and the flow of planned business investment and/or (b) decisions to change the rate of flow of business saving or planned investment. Thus the analytical separation of these different decisions by firms to save and invest was essential to the clear thinking and analysis which was the basis of the Keynesian revolutionary way of analysing the workings of a monetary entrepreneurial economy.

In sum, gross business saving is equal to retained profits plus capital consumption allowances. A planned increase in either of these components of gross business saving *does not automatically* increase planned current expenditure on plant and equipment. Consequently it follows from our definitions that the household *and* entrepreneurial decisions to save are, in themselves, decisions *not* to purchase the current products of industry.

While this saving concept is *not* the same as that adopted by some other economists (e.g. Professor Friedman), our definition has two distinct advantages, namely (a) the concept is unambiguous – any decision to increase saving must always mean a decision to buy less of the products of industry out of any level of income and (b) this saving concept conforms to what the intelligent layman means when he describes saving, namely spending less of his income receipts.[5]

An act of saving in the private sector means, in essence, a decision not to have dinner today; it does *not* however require the saver to make a decision to purchase a specific product of industry in lieu of today's dinner at a specific time *either today or at any future date*. What the saver desires is a 'time machine' for transferring this saved purchasing power to an unspecified date in the future when he may wish to exercise a claim on production. At the moment of saving the typical saver need not be certain as to what resource (or product) he will want delivered to him at what specific time and place in the future; and, hence, the saver may be currently unwilling to enter into a forward contractual commitment for the purchase *and* delivery of any resource-using product at a specific future date. Thus, as long as the law of money contracts is expected to determine future resource commitments and allocation, then either money, or any liquid (readily resaleable) durable with low carrying costs, are eligible time machines worthy of the savers' consideration. The income recipient who decides not to exercise all his current claims out of today's income, must also necessarily decide in which form of time machine to embody today's saving. Such time machines are called liquid assets.

Time is a device which prevents everything from happening at once. Production takes time. Thus an entrepreneurial system which attempts to organize production (as well as the exchange of goods and services) via the market place requires the human institutions of money and time-specific money contracts.

CONTRACTS IN ECONOMIC MODELS[6]

The initial step in constructing an economic model involving time-oriented contracts and market organization requires a simplifying classification scheme for all contracts. An *elementary contract* is one where the date of payment and date of delivery is the same specified date. Thus, there are only two types of elemental contracts; an *elemental spot contract*, when both (immediate) payment and delivery is specified for the initial instant of contractual agreement, and an *elemental forward contract*, when the same future date for delivery and payment is specified.

Actual real world contracts are often more complex but they can always be analysed as a combination of elemental contracts. Thus, if deliveries (and/or payments) are to be made at a specified sequence of dates in an actual contract, it can be analysed as a series of elementary contracts each of which call for delivery (and/or payment) at a specified date. Accordingly, we need focus only on two dates of each elementary contract, the date of contractual agreement and the date of delivery and payment.[7]

Most consumers tend to buy the basic necessities of food and clothing (but not necessarily shelter) in retail spot markets, while the production of these goods takes considerable time. Entrepreneurs along the non-integrated chain from raw materials to finished products must initiate forward purchase contracts with labour and other input suppliers at (say) Easter in order to have the retail shelf inventories available for the spot purchases of the ultimate consumers at (say) the following Christmas. Thus, as a stylized fact, we may assume that all developed monetary entrepreneurial economies, whether open or closed, possess markets for labour, raw materials and semi-finished goods which are organized on a 'produce to (forward) contract basis',[8] while retail markets tend to be organized on a spot market basis.[9] Thus, liquidity, i.e. the ability to meet contractual obligations as they come due, is an intricacy of any economy organized on a contracting basis, i.e. in any economy where agents organize their income receipt and purchase activity on a spot and forward contracting basis.

Since production takes time, as long as entrepreneurs organize production *and* exchange on a money contracting basis – hiring factors of production on forward money contracts in anticipation of obtaining more money from the sale of the output – then claims on the resources available for current production (or on the products of these resources) will always be in the form of money. *Money* is therefore defined in terms of its function, so that *money is the means of contractual settlement*.

In a capitalist, market-oriented economy, although exchange can occur under spot or forward contractual agreements, most production transactions between firms must involve forward contracts (e.g. labour hire, raw material purchases) if production is to be planned efficiently over the production period. The *production period* was defined by Keynes as the calendar 'time which elapses between the decision to employ labour in conjunction with capital equipment to produce output and the output being "finished"'.[10] If a production period spans any significant length of calendar time, it would be foolish for any entrepreneur to undertake such a production process without some cost controls via forward contracts over the monetary costs of production. For the entrepreneur to purchase all labour and/or raw materials *spot* at the moment of beginning the production process would not only be physically impossible in terms of labour (since the abolition of slavery), but it would also be cost inefficient, for it would require the incurring of warehousing and other carrying costs for many materials not needed until well into the production period. Thus, the institution of forward money contracts is the *sine qua non* of efficient entrepreneurial production economies.

Since in monetary economies resource owners and entrepreneurs are willing to freely enter into forward money contracts, money will not only be the means of contractual settlement but it will also possess the capability of acting as a vehicle for moving generalized (non-specific) purchasing power for resources over time; i.e. *money is also a one-way* (present to future) *time vehicle or time machine*. As long as the economy organizes its production on a forward money contract basis, money will be the thing in which future liabilities (e.g. the money cost of future production, the future cost of living, etc.) will fall due. Hence, today's money can always be held to pay for these future purchases, as long as the carrying cost in the shape of storage, wastage, etc. of today's money is low.[11] Money is, as far as the private sector is concerned, a time machine *par excellence*.

Of course, durables other than money can possess this time machine (liquidity) function in various degrees, depending on their carrying costs and resaleability. Since any durable besides money can *not* (by definition) be used as settlement of future contractual obligations, then in order for any other durable to be a liquid asset (time vehicle) for moving generalized purchasing power, it must be readily resaleable at any time in a well-organized, orderly *spot* market. The degree of liquidity associated with any durable therefore depends on the degree of organization and orderliness of its spot market. If a spot market for a specific durable is thin or non-existent, then the purchase of such a durable is 'permanent and indissoluble, like marriage, except by reason of death or other grave cause'.[12]

It is often claimed that during periods of inflation, money, as well as savings deposits and bonds, lose their value as time machines as their *real carrying costs* increase. Thus, Monetarists argue that nominal interest rates must rise in order to attract wealth holders to hold financial assets such as deposits and bonds rather than other more preferable (real) time machines. This view, however, ignores the query as to which alternative resaleable assets will not suffer a compensating increase in initial spot price in an economy with inflationary expectations *vis-à-vis* a money economy without such expectations.

As long as the institution of forward money contracts does not break down as a method of organizing production *and* exchange, then the liquidity of all durables except money requires resaleability on spot markets to obtain funds to discharge a contractual obligation at some future date. If, as is usually assumed in monetarist economic models, everyone has the same expectations about the future decline in the purchasing power of money *vis-à-vis* a world where everyone expects no change in purchasing power, then such inflationary expectations must *already* be exerting their influence on the spot prices of all such liquid assets; so that there is no current advantage for money holders to switch from money to other liquid time machines in this inflationary environment. An individual can search out and therefore speculate on which resaleable real assets are better liquidity time machines than money in the face of expected future inflation *only* if there is sufficient doubt about the degree of future inflation for different people to take significantly different views.[13]

FINANCING ASSET HOLDING AND CASH FLOWS: WHY MONEY MATTERS

Marshall warned in the preface of the first edition of his *Principles* that the 'element of Time is the centre of the chief difficulty of almost every economic problem',[14] and hence it should not be surprising that economic man has developed different markets for dealing with the transactions for immediate 'spot' delivery and payments and for forward delivery and payment at a specified future date. Spot markets are equivalent to Hicks' flexprice markets because the existing stock supply is, by definition, perfectly inelastic, and hence any change in the public's demand will be immediately and completely reflected in a change in the spot prices.[15] Forward markets are (because of their fixed terms of contracts) equivalent to Hicks' fixprice markets in a calendar time setting. Flexprice and fixprice markets coexist in the real world, despite the logical impossibility of this occurring in the general equilibrium microfoundations used by some macrotheorists.

In a neoclassical world such as described by Debreu, *all* prices (for either factors of production or products) are paid simultaneously at the initial instant of time.[16] Accordingly, no economic agent need worry about his ability to meet future contractual payments when they fall due since all payments and receipts are instantaneously done and recorded in each agent's balance sheet. Since this initial instant accounting process occurs in the (assumed) absence of false trades, there can be no future payment obligations and consequently rational agents would not worry about solvency; hence inhabitants of a neoclassical world would not demand liquidity. By defining prices as those which are paid at the initial instant *for all transactions over time*, neoclassical theory has removed the flow of payments from the time dimension!

This neoclassical treatment of payments is the same even in a world of uncertainty where the latter is defined as 'uncertainty of the environment . . . [which] originates in the choice that nature makes among a finite number of alternatives'.[17] In an 'uncertain' neoclassical world 'a contract for the transfer of a commodity now specifies, in addition to its physical properties, its location and its date, an event on the occurrence of which the transfer is conditional'.[18] The payment for the commodity however is instantaneous and non-conditional since the price of any commodity is 'the amount paid . . . initially by . . . the agent who commits himself to accept . . . delivery of one unit of that commodity. *Payment is irrevocably made although delivery does not take place if specific events do not obtain.*'[19]

Thus the basic concept of prices in neo-Walrasian analysis requires the removal of both money and money income receipts and outpayments from any historical time setting; instead the flow of all payments is in real goods and, more importantly, all payments are firmly and 'irrevocably' made at a timeless 'initial instant'. In the real world, on the other hand, payments and receipts are primarily in the form of money and occur in a sequential time setting as buyers and sellers make contracts in both spot and forward markets. In such a world the threat of insolvency leads to a demand for liquidity. It is only in this world that the institutions of money and money contracts have an essential role to play.[20] It is only in this world that cash flows over time are essential to asset holding positions.

Real capital assets are either working capital goods which have a useful life of one production period, or fixed capital goods which have a life span of two or more production periods. Financial assets, on the other hand, have temporal lives which are normally specifically spelled out in the contractual base of the asset. To take a 'position' in an asset is to purchase and hold stock of the asset over time. The purchase price of the stock must be financed. The position is held until the 'date of realization' when the asset is converted back into money; at the realization date, the position is liquidated.

TYPES OF ASSETS

There are three types of assets[21] in which positions can be taken.

(1) *Illiquid Assets* are durables whose spot market is poorly organized, disorderly, thin or even notional. Illiquid assets are held by

firms primarily for their expected money income stream, i.e. for the expected 'dated' cash flows or yields over their useful life. Fixed capital, consumer durables and most working capital goods can be considered in this category. (Consumers hold illiquid assets for the expected stream of dated services.) If an asset is illiquid, then realization (liquidation) occurs only on dates of expected net cash (sales) inflow (i.e. dates when the finished output made using the capital goods are sold). Working capital goods normally have a single realization date, while fixed capital goods are liquidated in small segments over many future realization dates.

(2) *Liquid Assets* are durables which are traded in well-organized and orderly spot markets. They are held for the dated stream of cash inflows the asset is expected to yield (net of carrying costs) including any sales revenue from liquidating the asset in a spot market at the expected realization date prior to the end of its useful economic life. If an asset is resaleable, it has some degree of liquidity.

(3) *Fully Liquid Assets* include money or any other asset which can immediately be converted into money in a spot market where the market maker 'guarantees' a fixed and unchanging net spot price. Thus, fully liquid assets represent directly or indirectly the availability of a specific quantity of undated cash which can be used for the discharge of contracts at any time.

Obviously, the boundaries between these classes of assets are not absolutely distinct, hard and fast, or unchanging over time. The degree of liquidity depends on the degree of organization and orderliness of the relevant spot market. Depending on social practices and institutions, the degree of liquidity of any asset can change from time to time as the spot market for various assets changes. The smaller the transaction costs and the greater the stickiness of the money spot price of the asset over time, the greater the degree of liquidity of any asset. These factors depend, in large part, on the functioning of a market maker who maintains orderliness. Money is fully liquid because the spot price of money in terms of itself is certain and unchanging (no capital gain or loss in nominal terms). As long as money has this store of value characteristic plus the fact that it is commonly used in the discharge of contracts for the purchase of things that most members of the economy want, then money will be the basic fully liquid asset in a monetary economy.

ENTREPRENEURS, INVESTMENT SPENDING AND FINANCE

Entrepreneurs are economic agents who as managers of business firms are willing to invest, i.e. to contractually commit themselves today to the purchase of working and/or fixed capital goods in order to provide an expected flow of produced goods for sale at specific dates in the future. Production takes time, and in order to organize the production process efficiently, contractual commitments must be entered into at the start of the production process, so that delivery of components, etc. can be made as the good in process (working capital) is fabricated from basic raw material to finished product by the use of instruments of production and labour.[22]

Fixed capital are instruments of production which are, by their very nature, very durable and therefore are expected to yield money revenues from the future sales of products over a very long period of time; i.e. fixed capital are not expected to be used up in a short period of time, equal to a single production period. *Working capital* are goods-in-process, that is, durables which will provide their expected yield in the course of a single production period (e.g. a bushel of wheat). Most discussions regarding investment expenditures for capital accumulation (increasing productivity) involve the demand of fixed capital goods. In what follows, unless otherwise noted, we shall therefore concentrate on fixed capital. Hence, gross investment will be used to describe the gross output of the fixed capital goods producing industry over a period of time, while net investment (or new capital formation) is gross investment less replacement of fixed capital goods that actually 'wear out' during the period. (Nevertheless, it should be recognized that the holding of both fixed and working capital goods – which are both necessary for production to occur – requires financing.)

Entrepreneurial investors must undertake contractual commitments to hire resources to increase their stock of instruments of production many weeks, months, or years in advance of consumers actually committing their income claims (i.e. contractually agreeing to pay) for the additional output which will flow from these facilities. Since today's saver is unwilling or unable to make today specific forward contractual commitments designating which future products he will buy with his current savings and at what future dates he will make these purchases, there is no market mechanism that can coordinate today's investment plans of investors in order to make facilities available to produce specific goods in the future to meet the future consumption demands of today's savers. Consequently, in a market economy investors must take 'positions' in fixed capital goods a long time before they have received forward contractual commitments by the ultimate buyers (consumers) for the products produced by utilizing these fixed capital goods.

Moreover, since a significant passage of time is required not only to produce these capital goods but also – especially for fixed capital items such as plant and equipment – to use up (or wear out) these goods in the production of items for the ultimate consumer, positions in fixed capital goods are typically financed twice during their lives. The first financing can be termed *construction funds finance* while the second *investment funds finance*.

In the construction funds finance stage, while fixed capital goods are being fabricated they are considered working capital (goods in process) items for the capital goods producing industries. These capital goods in process are often financed via short-term construction or working capital loans obtained by their producers from the banking system. The construction funds finance so provided to entrepreneurs is used to pay their workers (payrolls) and material suppliers during this construction period.

When the capital goods are finished, delivery is made, and full payment by the buyer on the forward contract ordering the fixed capital goods is required. These purchase payments cannot usually be made entirely out of the current income receipts of the buyer. Rather they are viewed as capital account purchases. The buyer-investor must finance the purchase price of these capital goods via some investment funds financing arrangement which will span most if not all of the future production periods when these long-lived goods are in place and aiding in the production of other goods. At the date that the investor in fixed (instrumental) capital goods takes delivery of these items from the producer, the investor is typically required to make a money payment to the producer. This payment is used by the fixed capital goods producer to pay off the short-term construction funds finance loan (often made from the banking system) and to yield a profit to the producer of the investment goods. (The short-term loan, remember, was used to pay for the resources – labour, raw materials – that were required to produce the capital goods.) Of course, once the short-term construction loan is paid off, it is available from the banking system to finance another capital goods-in-process commitment. Thus the funds for construction fund finance become a 'revolving fund' which can maintain the existing rate of construction (in value terms). If construction rates are to increase, however, the banks must *pari passu* expand available finance for these additional construction flows.

The investor in fixed capital is required to finance his delivery day payment via either equity or debt *investment funding*. Arrangements for these capital account financial transactions will normally have been made prior to the delivery date. Because most fixed capital goods are *illiquid* assets, i.e. durables whose spot market is poorly organized, thin or even notional, investors recognize that profitable resaleability of fixed assets during their useful lives is virtually impossible. Hence, unlike the relatively short-term financing arrangement which was used to undertake the position in these assets while they were being built,[23] a longer term 'funding' of the position, via either by equity or debt, must be arranged for before delivery can be accepted. Of course, over the useful life of the capital goods, the investor expects (a) that goods produced from these facilities will be sold at fairly definite dates in the future and (b) the revenues remaining from these sales of finished products after paying for labour-and-raw-materials working capital loans (which are used to make input payments) will be sufficient to liquidate (pay off) the long-term equity or debt position in plant and equipment, plus earn a rate of return which will have made the taking of this position worthwhile. In a private, profit-oriented market economy, it is only the *expectation* of these sufficient quasi-rents[24] which induces the investor to take a position in fixed capital goods in the first place. In other words, it is the expectations of profitable future sales which induce entrepreneurs to invest currently in new plant and equipment – as long as there is no difficulty in financing this increased 'position' in fixed capital goods. If in the aggregate, investors' 'positions' in real fixed capital are increasing, capital accumulation must be occurring.

In the case of equity finance, the buyer of fixed capital goods has at the purchase date already amassed sufficient liquid purchasing power via money *savings* out of either previous or current income and/or the sale of other assets (including new issues of equities)[25] to pay the entire money purchase price upon delivery. In the case of debt financing, the buyer must borrow all (or some) of the purchase price via a *debt contract* (i.e. a contract for forward delivery of interest payments and the future return of principal) in order to meet the delivery payment obligation to the fixed capital goods producer.

(1) *Equity Financing*. If equity financing is used, the capital goods buyer is operating as an Equity Fund which, in essence, is a body to which a certain amount of funds has been entrusted without any specific contractual obligation for the return of these funds. There is only a hope that the return on these funds will be made as large as possible, and that some time over the useful life, the equity funds can be, if desired, returned (the position liquidated). The equity fund works solely on the asset side of its balance sheet – in a manner of speaking, 'its liabilities are asleep'.[26]

(2) *Debt Financing*. In the case of debt financing, the investors' liabilities are not asleep. Most businessmen use debt financing to hold

some, if not all, of their illiquid assets. Working capital goods are typically debt financed via short-term bank loans (the duration of which is normally related to the period of production), while investment in fixed capital assets is often financed via long-term debts. Hence, the production flow of goods and services which make up the GNP of any economy depend in large part on the ability of entrepreneurs to (a) initially debt finance their production and capital cost contractual commitments and (b) to maintain sufficient liquidity to meet the resulting debt liabilities as they fall due. In any entrepreneurial production economy which tends to use long-lived capital goods and to produce output via lengthy, technologically complex processes, financial institutions such as organized securities markets, investment bankers, and the banking system play an involved and unique role.

FINANCE AND FINANCIAL INSTITUTIONS

Financial institutions, when functioning properly, permit entrepreneurs to increase the rate of installation of additional illiquid capacity and the attendant expansion of output while simultaneously caring for the liquidity desires and needs of the private sector by creating various liquid assets (time machines) and organizing ('making') continuous markets for the purchase and resale of these time machines. It is the existence of these financial institutional arrangements which rupture any direct link between the saving desires of the private sector (and its accompanying liquidity demands) and the investment demands (and related liquidity needs) of entrepreneurs. In fact, in a simple two-sector (consumption and investment goods) model of the economy, where the major form of money is bank deposits (liabilities), increasing the quantity of money is the way in which the financial community looks after that portion of the increase in the real wealth (fixed capital) of the economy which wealth-owning households do not desire to hold legal title to (equity own), or even directly lend investment funds for (i.e. hold evidence of debt claims against investors). Thus, even if aggregate planned savings by households plus firms equals aggregate planned investment by entrepreneurs at a given rate of interest, the actual sales of GNP output can fall short of expected (warranted) GNP planned for (and expected) by firms. This will occur if firms in the aggregate plan to spend on investment in excess of what they can internally finance from gross business saving, while households plan to allocate their savings between new issues of securities and money (or other liquid stores of value). In this case, household savings, though equal to planned external finance of firms, will not purchase all the new issues at the going rate of interest. Hence, unless the banking system increases the supply of money sufficiently,[27] actual investment orders will be less than planned. This deficiency in aggregate demand will be due to a shortage of liquidity and finance, and not due to a shortage of savings!

The banking and financial system plays a key role at two separate stages in aiding the expansion of the capital accumulation process of a monetary, entrepreneurial, production economy. Firstly, at the initially specified money rate of interest, any planned expansion of the pro- duction flow of capital goods should be financed via the provision of additional construction fund (working capital) finance resulting in an expansion of the money supply (the real bills doctrine) or overdraft commitments *before* any additional real investment activity is actually undertaken; and therefore, before any increase in real aggregate saving can occur. Secondly, when current gross business spending on fixed capital exceeds current gross business saving and, therefore, *external* investment fund finance is required, banks should supply the necessary additional money stock whenever households, in the aggregate, do not plan to purchase out of current household saving (at the initial rate of interest) all the new issues offered. Then the value of these new issues sold (at the initial rate of interest) will yield a cash sum to investing firms equal to the amount by which gross investment spending exceeds gross business saving.

If banks play their proper role at these two stages, then they will have provided sufficient liquidity, *ceteris paribus*, to validate entrepreneurial expectations of future sales *provided that entrepreneurs have correctly guessed consumers' future spending plans*. If, on the other hand, the banking system does not provide enough liquidity for the economic system in a manner consistent with the justification (or validation) from hindsight of entrepreneurial sales expectations, then even though *ex ante* investment plans were warranted in the sense they were consistent *at the time* with *ex ante* household savings plans, sufficient investment spending will not be forthcoming.

A SUMMARY VIEW OF THE ARGUMENT SO FAR

Today's investors contractually order[28] long-lived capital goods be- cause of the *expected* dated stream of future *money* receipts net of expected future operating costs which the investors believe will accrue to them by exercising managerial control over these real capital goods. Investors, therefore, are not motivated by the same desires as savers. Investors are not primarily interested in obtaining a time machine to move generalized purchasing power to the indefinite future. Investors (by definition) desire to acquire the future services of real fixed capital assets as inputs in a time-consuming technical production process, for they believe they possess the skill, knowledge, and time required to (a) foresee future market demands (even before the buyers in these markets) and (b) coordinate efficiently future production decisions in their pursuit of an expected future dated stream of cash inflows. Thus, 'the prospective yield of the marginal new investment depends on the expectation of a demand for a specific article at a specific date'.[29]

Investors recognize that in taking a position in readily reproducible real capital goods, they are purchasing essentially *illiquid assets* – durables whose spot markets are poorly organized and discontinuous or even non-existent. Illiquid assets are not readily resaleable (liquidated) at short notice; consequently investors realize that if the future differs from their expectations, they may have to take large capital losses if they are forced to liquidate when they cannot meet their contractual obligations. Investors, however, believe that the liquidation of their positions in such assets will essentially occur only at planned particular dates of expected cash sales of output produced over the useful life of the equipment. Thus, fixed capital goods will never be purchased strictly for use as liquidity time machines (for precautionary and speculative purposes) as long as other durables, i.e. money and financial assets, with lower carrying costs and significantly easier resaleability are available.[30]

Since fixed capital goods are illiquid, entrepreneurial investors do not necessarily want legal title to the stock of capital; what they want is possession (or control). Similarly, entrepreneurs do not care whether they own their labour force (slaves) or allow others to hold title to the factor called labour. What is relevant is the magnitude of expected money sales revenue in the future from the finished output produced relative to the money costs involved in obtaining control of the services of the factors of production.

With the development of spot markets in legal titles to capital goods (organized security markets) where possession of title does not require delivery of the goods owned (and even fractionalized titles can be bought and sold), an institution has been developed in advanced economies which provides liquid time machines for individual savers, while the underlying position in fixed capital is illiquid and irrevocable for the community as a whole.

It is the flexibility of organized spot security market prices which permits each household unit to hold as many titles to real capital as it desires as liquid time machines and to alter its portfolio of securities as often as it desires; while in the aggregate the public holds exactly the quantity of securities and money which the financial system makes available to the public.

The existence of well-organized spot markets in securities has not only created liquidity machines for savers out of the illiquid fixed capital goods of society, but in so doing it has severed the link between ownership (portfolio balance) and control (the demand for real capital goods). This schism and its potential for conflict and anti-social behaviour has long been recognized by some economists (e.g. Berle, Keynes, Galbraith) while neoclassical economists have assumed a confluence of interest between owners (savers) and managers (investors).

MONEY AND CLEARING

Payment processes become more efficient as the economy develops a systematic clearing mechanism. In a hypothetical barter or commodity money economy without any clearing institutions, sellers would be required to acquire commodities in exchange even though they merely wished to use these as store of value intermediaries to be given up in future purchases of other economic goods. Such a cumbersome system of storing and transferring intermediary commodities for future exchange can be expensive and wasteful. With the invention of legal titles to property, it is possible to abstain from taking physical delivery of intermediary goods while possessing the 'value' of the property.[31] Thus, the ability to pass paper titles and to 'clear' such titles against off-setting obligations greatly facilitates the settlement of transactions. The further discovery that the transference of claims to bank debts themselves is just as serviceable in settlements as the transference of titles to commodity money in terms of which the debts are expressed has led to the use of bank money and its clearing institutions.[32] Such developments in payment systems, which permit the transferability of bank debts (provided 'confidence is felt in the prompt convertibility of the debt into money'),[33] has so enhanced the efficiency of market-oriented, entrepreneurial production economies organized on a forward money contracting basis, that it is impossible to discover any developed economies in modern times employing a different payment process despite great political differences in the organization of modern governments.[34]

Any debt clearing mechanism used for contractual settlements relies on the public's belief that titles to such debts can be readily convertible into the money in which they are denominated. Confidence in convertibility is the *sine qua non* for anything, except legal tender, to become a customarily acceptable means of payment. Confidence in the use of a bank debt clearing system therefore requires a mechanism which purports to prevent abuse of debt creating facilities so that the private debt issuers cannot *inordinately* expand their debt position to finance additional purchases. Assurance against abuse of debt facilities normally requires the appearance of 'something like a court of justice to make it work'.[35]

The appearance of law abiding conventionality is an oft overlooked *essential* element of any well functioning monetary system. Thus, any practical proposal for the improvement of the working of the monetary settlement system, and also *the monetary earnings system*, must be garbed in the cloak of justice and even-handedness *under the law*.[36]

INSUFFICIENT PRIVATE SAVING: CAUSE OR EFFECT OF STAGFLATION?

A recent article in *Business Week* (December 11, 1978, pp. 90–8) provides a useful vehicle for focusing our discussion involving the claimed cause and effect relationship between a shortage of savings (hereafter SOS) and stagflation. The fundamental conclusion of the SOS thesis is that the current economic ills of the American economy can be ameliorated, if not completely eliminated, by reversing US fiscal policy in those ways in which, it is claimed, policy is currently biased against private sector (mainly household) saving. SOS advocates propose such changes as (a) reducing income taxes rates for the upper income classes (who tend to save the most), (b) reducing capital gains (leaving more after-tax purchasing power to the rich), (c) substituting a general expenditure tax such as VAT (value added tax) for a portion of the income or payroll taxes (thereby discouraging spending and again providing tax relief to higher income classes) and (d) reducing welfare transfer payments to the elderly and the poor (who tend to save less) so as to provide economic incentives for the poor to spend less and save more, rather than encouraging the poor to rely on governments to finance their (extravagant?) consumption habits.

Business Week, noting that higher rates of investment are the key to greater growth in the economy, quotes Professor Modigliani of MIT as stating 'To some extent high growth produces high savings but high savings also create growth. In the long run, it is saving which limits investment and not vice versa.' (p. 91). And Professor Feldstein of Harvard and President of the National Bureau of Economic Research is quoted as saying 'Over the long term, the real problem is saving and how to stimulate a high rate of saving (p. 91) . . . The system should be tilted towards taxing spending and not income' (p. 92). Professor Solow of MIT is even more specific when he states 'you need to sacrifice current consumption to create the productive capacity to gain further consumption' (p. 91). Thus these SOS advocates appear to argue that if the US government would only create additional tax incentives to discourage consumption and increase saving activity out of current income, all other things being equal, aggregate real investment in the US must increase and the tendency for the American economy to stagnate will disappear. (Apparently the SOS advocates contend that this is true whether this 'shortage of saving' merely contributes to stagflation or is the sole cause of it!) Nevertheless, *Business Week* noted a caveat in the SOS advocates' position:

No one is advocating that government policy move headlong into pushing the private saving rate up sharply overnight. . . . If that were to happen, the economy would surely go spinning into a recession. Rather, what seems to be called for is a reversal of a system of incentives that has pushed the public toward spending and away from saving (p. 92).

Thus, it seems, in the short run if the government significantly raises private saving out of current income the economy will tumble into a recession (or even a depression!). Apparently however, in the long run a higher private saving *rate* (i.e. less consumption out of current income) is desirable and even necessary, according to the SOS view, if the GNP is to grow more rapidly.

The apparent conflict between the short run and long run conclusions of this SOS thesis is due, in large part, to a lack of precision in the language and analysis of SOS advocates. This semantic muddle in which the long run effects of a change in policy are claimed to be desirable while the short run results are clearly disastrous makes Keynes' gibe that 'in the long run we'll all be dead' particularly appropriate for the implications of the SOS doctrine.

Taken at face value, the SOS hypothesis suggests that Congress should drastically alter fiscal policy. Before making such a fundamental change in policy direction which during a period of over forty years provided the citizens of the United States with an unprecedented growth in prosperity and personal security, a fundamental logical assessment of the validity and applicability of this SOS hypothesis to current economic conditions is in order. If such an analysis demonstrates that much of the current stagnation is *not* directly due to a tendency of the private sector to undersave, then the SOS hypothesis and its policy implications should be abandoned.

SOS advocates have based their analysis on a confusion between the role of finance and that of savings in stimulating capital accumulation by the private sector. To a large extent it is the misdirection of Monetary Policy in a vain attempt to prevent inflation in the last decade which has led to a shortage of finance and consequent lower investment activity which has ultimately lowered savings. This deliberately restrictive money policy created financial obstacles for optimistically expansive entrepreneurs (i.e. those with tremendous vision, enthusiasm and 'animal spirits'), which in turn, often led to their displacement in executive suites by conservative, short-sighted timid managers who in times of credit restraint were bound to be successful by limiting the contractual commitments of their firms and hence reducing the rate of capital accumulation in the economy. A market-oriented entre-preneurial economy based on a forward money contract method of organizing production can grow rapidly *only* when entrepreneurs are willing and eager to expand their contractual liabilities over time and the banking system provides them with the finance to do so.

Finance is primarily bookkeeping entries and does not, in itself, use up any resources (except for the services of those employed in the financial sector – which is very small relative to the amount of finance provided each year, and hence, as a first approximation, can be neglected in the following discussion). Hence the ready availability of finance permits (without significant real costs) private entrepreneurs to marshal all the resources they desire to expand productive capacity. Con-versely, lack of finance (i.e. a tight money policy) in itself does not save real resources that would otherwise be utilized automatically elsewhere in an entrepreneurial economy. Instead a shortage of finance prevents plans for capital accumulation from becoming operational. Lack of finance causes the idling of resources in the capital goods producing industries, thereby limiting the economy's ability to provide capacity for growth in future consumption. Moreover, financial constraints not only limit entrepreneurs' ability to provide for future consumption by engaging in capital formation now; but by destroying potential effective demand for current goods and services, restrictive monetary supply policies also squelch the profit opportunities and cash flows which are necessary to validate past entrepreneurial plans. Hence after a period of tight money which results in recession (or a slowing of growth) and its attendant increase in entrepreneurial cash flow problems and bankruptcies, the surviving entrepreneurial-investors are likely to be more cautious and less willing to undertake additional capital expansion commitments when finance again becomes available. Thus monetary (and fiscal) policies designed to limit spending (encourage private saving) in any given expansionary phase of the business cycle will create a conservative psychology among investors which will, *ceteris paribus*, cause the next expansionary phase to be more sluggish than otherwise. In such an environment, a permanent change in government policies designed solely to encourage additional savings out of income will exacerbate any tendency in an entrepreneurial economy towards stagnation by creating an atmosphere which destroys the 'animal spirits' of private investors.

HOW WOULD A SHORTAGE OF SAVING POLICY AFFECT PRIVATE INVESTMENT?

If the SOS thesis is correct, then the federal government should deliberately adopt policies geared solely to reduce the private sector's consumption spending out of current income.[37] Specifically this means that the government must encourage the private sector to cancel some orders (which would otherwise be forthcoming) for today's production of consumer goods (without encouraging any substitution by the private sector to place additional forward orders today for specific additional consumer goods to be delivered at a specific future date). Accordingly, to the extent that 'free enterprise' business firms gear their decision to hire workers today to their current (and prospective) near term orders for finished goods, a deliberate government policy to lower consumption spending *must* decrease employment today in the consumer goods industries without providing any direction to investors as to where to increase their orders for specific pieces of *additional* plant and equipment so that this (hoped for) prospective increment in the capital stock will be on-stream when, at some unspecified date in the future, savers decide to increase their orders (*more than otherwise*) for consumer goods. (Of course, for as long as the government maintains its specific policy of increasing saving by reducing consumption out of current income, investors should expect fewer orders for consumer goods in the future, not more!)

A government policy which seeks *only* to reduce private expenditure on new goods and services (which is, by definition, an increase in private saving), merely reduces the total orders for the products of industry as long as the policy is in force. In a market-oriented economy, however, it is the volume of actual orders and the expectation of *near* future orders which is the 'invisible hand' which directs businessmen's decisions into the quantity of resource-hiring contractual commitments to be undertaken to produce finished consumption *and* investment goods (where the latter depends on the expected volume of orders for consumer goods in the further future). If consumer demands decline today as a result of deliberate government policy *and* no specific orders are simultaneously placed to offset the consumer decline, why should businessmen expect sales in the future (as long as the policy remains) to increase *more rapidly* than their expectations of sales before the policy to reduce consumer spending was inaugurated? Yet it is just such expectations of even greater (near) future orders which are necessary (*but not sufficient*) to induce businessmen to expand their contractual orders for capital goods today. The installation of a government policy to reduce consumption (i.e. increase savings), however, means that already existing plant and equipment is immediately made less scarce (or even redundant) and hence it can be conserved for future consumer demand when, *and if*, this arrives. Consequently there is permanently less need for entrepreneurs to place orders for *additional* capital equipment *for two reasons* if the government adopts a *permanent* policy whose sole objective is to reduce consumption spending out of any level of GNP! Firstly, such a policy if successful, immutably reduces expected sales to consumers out of any level of GNP. Secondly at the time the policy is initiated it will make the existing stock of capital facilities more redundant than otherwise and hence more readily available if demand expands in the future; hence expansion or even replacement of existing fixed capital is postponed. As a consequence, if a government policy which encourages private savings is effective, not only will it release current resources from the consumer goods industry, but simultaneously it will lower the need to expand capacity, thereby reducing the rate of capital accumulation and economic growth.

In sum, to the extent that a deliberate government policy against current consumption is successful, it will encourage the private sector to spend less on such things as space vehicles (cars) which are produced *today* by labour and capital and to put this saving into liquid assets (time vehicles), which cannot be produced by labour and existing capital facilities. As long as such liquidity time machines exist, savers cannot be encouraged to order more real goods (produced by labour and capital) as a store of value for their planned increase in savings. Hence, the increased demand for time machines, *encouraged* by deliberate government policy, cannot and will not be directly and automatically translated into an increased demand to possess and control *additional* real fixed capital. Of course, if only the demand for real capital were to increase concomitantly with the increased demand for liquid forms of saving stimulated by the SOS policy, then the labour and facilities released in the consumption goods industries could be re-employed in the capital goods industry. This, of course, is the wish (assumption) underlying the SOS hypothesis, but in a monetary, market-oriented economy where savers desire liquid time machines as a repository for their saving, there exists no direct mechanism (except via a possible lowering of interest rates and improving financial conditions) for stimulating capital accumulation. Unfortunately, with the development of a modern monetary and financial system, savers (e.g. households) do not desire (or need) to store their 'temporary' generalized purchasing power into readily producible durable things (i.e. real wealth or capital) which are produced by the use of labour and equipment, for the aforementioned essential properties of liquid assets preclude the use of *easily reproducible* durables produced by private enterprise as liquid time machines.[38]

Yet, the only logical sense that can be made out of the SOS hypothesis is that any policy which creates direct incentives for increasing private saving must simultaneously cause 'savers' to desire to hold their additional saving directly in the form of additional capital goods. Otherwise the financial system will intervene between the savers and the investment goods buyers, and the financial system is not merely a 'veil' on the real activities of the economy. Instead the financial system permits the formation of investment spending plans independent of the saving plan makers in the private sector and vice versa.

Any government policy which successfully increases aggregate private savings propensities out of income must however ultimately reduce entrepreneurial incentive to produce consumer goods today – thereby rendering a portion of existing plant, equipment and labour force unnecessary, and therefore must cause entrepreneurs to lower their current purchases of capital goods. To the extent that this decline in orders today causes entrepreneurs to lower their expectations of future sales, an even greater decline in the demand for capital will occur thereby exacerbating the stagnation problem. The inevitable logical conclusion of a government policy to reduce current consumption out of income in a period where the economy is already stagnating is that such a policy will merely bring forward in time the long run when we will all be dead!

But as the SOS advocates might parry, will not the private saving be put to use via the purchase of securities thereby reducing the cost of finance (i.e. lowering the rate of interest) and hence stimulate additional investment expenditures?

Such a question implies *it is ultimately the ability to lower interest rates and provide additional finance* which is the slender reed upon which the SOS hypothesis is relying on to bring about more rapid expansion. Simultaneously SOS advocates are implicitly assuming that the concurrent reduction in consumer sales and increased excess capacity created out of existing facilities will not depress entrepreneurial expectations of *future* profitable sales and thereby lower the demand for real capital. If the goal of the SOS advocates is to improve financial conditions, why not state this specifically and advocate 'easy financing' policies directly? Then, at least, the discussion can focus on the crux of the problem, namely, the shortage of finance, rather than debating the results of the stagnation problem, i.e. the shortage of saving.

To stimulate capital expansion during a period of stagflation, it is necessary (a) to increase the availability of finance at reasonable terms rather than reduce consumption out of income, and (b) to assure that the resulting aggregate demand for goods is sufficient to encourage entrepreneurs to employ all who are willing and able to work. This second necessary condition implies that it may actually be necessary to *increase private consumption* (or social investment) in order to encourage entrepreneurs to increase their rate of capital accumulation. As long as there is idle capacity and unemployed workers, increasing the availability of finance *need not create inflationary pressures*.

Only if the economy were already at full employment *and* orders for additional capital goods were increasing at a rate which led to long (and increasing) queues of buyers and lengthy delays in promised delivery dates could there be some justification to *temporarily* tilt government policy towards private saving. Even in this case, however, financial arrangements rather than the lack of private saving can be the basic constraint and hence financial policy must be the centrepiece of any policy to increase the rate of capital accumulation by the private sector.

WHAT WILL A VALUE ADDED TAX DO?

It should be obvious from the preceding analysis that the institution of a tax on spending, e.g. a value added tax or VAT (either as a substitute for a tax on income and capital gains or to finance welfare payments) will not, *in itself*, stimulate additional expenditure on real capital goods. VAT cannot be justified on the basis that it will *per se* increase capital accumulation. Nevertheless, since Congressional committees do consider the possibility of instituting such a tax, it might be useful to indicate what the effects VAT could have on the U.S. economy.

Two decades ago, I demonstrated that the *ceteris paribus* effects of the imposition of a general excise tax such as VAT[39] would be (a) if money wages are downwards sticky, to increase the general price level of producible goods at any level of employment while simultaneously reducing employment and output by driving a tax wedge between market prices and the costs of production and by encouraging buyers (domestic and foreign[40]) to avoid tax payments by attempting to reduce consumption of domestically produced goods; while (b) even if it is assumed that the incidence of VAT falls entirely on the price of inputs so that money wages and other costs of production fall proportionately to the tax rate, and hence there will be no change in the price level at any output flow, employment of labour and capital will still be reduced to the extent saving out of current incomes is stimulated. In either case, to the extent that VAT is perceived to be a *permanent* tax which reduces consumer spending out of income, entrepreneurs should expect, *ceteris paribus*, consumer demand for domestically produced goods in the future to be permanently lower than it would be in the absence of VAT. Since, in an entrepreneurial society, it is the expected increase in consumer spending which is the ultimate determinant of the entrepreneurial desire for capital accumulation, entrepreneurs should order less plant and equipment than otherwise, i.e. the institution of VAT will, *ceteris paribus*, tend to aggravate rather than ameliorate stagflation tendencies.

To reiterate, in a capitalist market-oriented economy, the sole reason entrepreneurs will spend more on plant and equipment today is their expectations that sales of consumer goods (or goods to government or foreign buyers) at specific dates in the near future will be sufficiently larger, so that the output from the existing stock of capital *plus* the increment in plant and equipment being contemplated can all be sold at a price which will cover the present cost of the newly ordered equipment plus earn a sufficient return to make the effort worthwhile. If, government policy is instituted which deliberately discourages current consumption via VAT etc., entrepreneurs will not order additional equipment today and incur the high carrying costs of holding these facilities idle. On the contrary, entrepreneurs are likely to lower current capital expenditures as VAT makes some portion of existing plant less scarce than otherwise.

Of course, if VAT were to be announced as only a temporary tax with a specific termination date *and* a government guarantee is given to reverse policy and stimulate consumption to an even larger extent than if VAT had not been installed, then some additional investment spending could be induced currently. In this case, however, it will be the guarantee of larger consumption spending at a future date and not the discouragement of consumer expenditures today that is the stimulus to more investment today; therefore, VAT is an unnecessary adjunct. At some date between today and the announced date of government stimulation of additional consumer demand, entrepreneurs will increase their orders for capital goods provided the credit conditions for financing of an expanded position in fixed capital (which is not the same as private saving desires) were appropriate.

Thus, whether the nation was in a period of stagnation or one of full employment, a tilt towards saving policy might, *ceteris paribus*, stimulate additional investment *only* if

(1) the government restrictions on consumption were specifically limited as to duration, while

(2) entrepreneurs believed the government could 'fine tune' private sector consumption expenditures *and* that, at the announced termination date of the tilt towards saving policy, consumers would expand their spending on domestically produced goods at a rate which would greatly *exceed* what they would have spent in the absence of the tilt towards savings policy in the interim;

(3) the termination date on such a policy was close enough in the future so that entrepreneurs would have to place orders almost immediately in order to have the new facilities on stream by the termination date so that the expected increase in future consumer demand could be met;

(4) entrepreneurs do not go bankrupt or suffer severe financial losses during the period when government deliberately discourages consumption sales;

(5) financial facilities are readily available.

Conditions (1) to (5) are all necessary for achieving higher investment rates today if the government tilts policy towards encouraging private saving. Explicit recognition of these conditions expose the logical weakness of the SOS hypothesis. Ultimately in a market-oriented production economy, it is the entrepreneurs' expectations of greater consumer sales in the near future, and not the constraint on consumption purchases today, which lead to greater rates of capital accumulation by capitalists.

SHOULD WE REDUCE CONSUMPTION OR EASE FINANCE AND ENCOURAGE CONSUMPTION?

A *long run* policy of reducing consumption out of current income each year is antithetical to the only justification for economic activity in a capitalist economy – namely to ultimately satisfy the consumer. Those who advocate stimulating a higher rate of saving by sacrificing 'current consumption' are arguing on the basis of a variant of the old butter v. guns analogy (substitute capital goods for guns) which they believe is applicable to the current state of stagnating Western capitalist countries such as the U.S. Since it is admitted even by economists of the SOS persuasion that the butter v. capital goods analogy is only applicable to a fully employed economy, those advocating SOS policy current must claim that the U.S. is either at or very close to full employment and hence expanding capital goods output requires reducing consumer goods production. In a money economy, however, simply reducing the employment of resources in the consumer sector will *not* automatically increase output in the capital sector. Even at full employment, such a reallocation requires (a) expectations of higher rather than lower consumption out of current income in the near future (if not today), and (b) finance arrangements which provide entrepreneurs and savers with sufficient liquidity so that the banking system will take title (indirectly) for that portion of the capital stock that the households do not wish to hold (own) at the current rate of interest. If these conditions are met, then entrepreneurs can go ahead with their plans to enhance the stock of capital independent of the saving plans of households while the actual volume of private saving will always be brought up to the requisite sum.

As long as we rely primarily on private entrepreneurial decisions to accumulate real capital, the most important factor increasing the demand for real capital is the infusion of decision makers with the expectations of higher (not lower) consumer demand. (Keynes called such expectations 'animal spirits' – 'the desire for action rather than inaction'.) If animal spirits can be created and if sufficient construction and investment fund finance is provided by the banking system, then via the tried and true rules of the capitalist game, entrepreneurs will increase their positions in long-lived capital goods *today*. In a capitalist monetary economy, however, demand means 'want *plus* the ability to pay', and hence entrepreneurs cannot demand more plant and equipment unless they can pay more. This increased ability to pay, however, involves primarily the availability of finance via the banking system. If such finance is created and provided to entrepreneurial investors, then private households will – and must – adjust their aggregate saving accordingly. Conversely, *even* if private saving plans of households are coincidentally equal to the needs for externally financing larger investment positions by firms, if the banking system is not accommodating, the increased investment plans of entrepreneurs may be aborted![41]

The essential role of a modern banking system and the financial institutions which permit and encourage (or discourage) debt and/or equity financing of 'positions' in long-lived real capital goods is ignored in the logical analysis of the SOS hypothesis. Because there is no important role for these financial institutions and money in the SOS analysis, its advocates have confused the existence of a shortage of finance which can constrain the rates of capital accumulation with the apparent current shortage of private saving in the U.S. economy; but the perceived saving shortage is a *result* of the deliberate shortage of finance policy of the Federal Reserve whose primary objective is to induce lower demand for capital goods, thereby creating slack markets and thus fighting inflation! Yet, monetary policy is singularly ill-adopted for preventing inflation in the prices of the producible goods which make up GNP in a modern entrepreneurial economy.[42]

In recent years what has been in short supply in the United States is finance and not the rate of private savings (including foreigners' savings – as defined in footnote no. 4). Private saving rates were more than sufficient to free all the resources necessary to expand the rate of capital accumulation significantly. If financial conditions had been better, tilting policy towards increasing consumption out of current income would prove favourable to increasing the rate of growth of the capital stock in a private profit-oriented economy.[43]

OUTPUT CONCEPTS ELABORATED

Several output concepts should be developed in order to provide further clarity in the exposition. Most readers are familiar with the national income accounts which relates the Gross National (GNP) to the value of the gross production or output of industry during a specified period of time. Although the GNP consists of literally millions of different goods and services, it is desirable for our purposes to categorize all these goods as belonging to two basic groups, namely *available output* (AO) and *nonavailable output* (NAO). AO is defined as currently produced goods which are fabricated into a form available for immediate purchase by households. Thus AO equals all household purchases in the period net of the change in inventories of consumer goods held by industry at the retail level; nevertheless as a first approximation we can associate AO with current consumption spending by households. NAO, on the other hand, is currently produced goods which, by their very nature, are in a form which is not available for purchase by households. In a simple two-sector model NAO is the gross investment output of the economy.

In a market-oriented capitalist economy where production precedes sales, the quantities of AO and NAO respectively which are already produced and ready *for delivery today* are the result of yesterday's entrepreneurial decisions regarding the desired size of their positions in fixed (plant and equipment) and working (goods in process) capital. In general, in a mass production (as opposed to a produced-to-order only system) entrepreneurial economy, these illiquid entrepreneurial positions have to be financed for a significant period of time before consumers are willing to contractually commit themselves to purchase either today's AO or tomorrow's AO which will be produced, in part, by utilizing today's NAO. Thus in order to induce increased gross investment by the private sector (NAO today *and* tomorrow), government policies must encourage 'position' taking in NAO by (a) stimulating optimistic expectations of future specific consumer demands for AO and (b) permitting ready financing of such entrepreneurial positions. Given entrepreneurial views of the future, it is the lack of adequate finance and not a profusion of orders for consumer goods (a shortage of private saving!) which is the prime constraint on expanding capital accumulation by the private sector.

The SOS advocates are implicitly and incorrectly postulating that, in a modern bank-money economy, *before* investors can order new plant and equipment, savers must give up liquidity by transferring their money claims on resources (earned from current income) directly to the investors. In other words, SOS theorists assert that additional capital goods production merely requires the transfer of claims on resources from economic units who spend less than their income (savers) to units who wish to spend in excess of their current income (investors). The existence of a modern financial system, however, permits but does not require such specific claim transfers between savers and investors in order to facilitate an expansion in capital goods production.

Moreover, if savers decide (or are encouraged) to execute less claims on current AO, then investors may be discouraged by the decline in sales (recession) from exercising even the current level of orders for plant and equipment, *even if savers are eager to transfer their unused claims to investors*. (Why should an entrepreneur increase spending on plant and equipment when he cannot sell everything that he can produce via current capacity?)

Finally, even if investment demand is assumed to be unchanged by the increase in private saving and the resulting decline in potential sales, unless the financial system not only expedites claims transfers but simultaneously *creates* additional claims, the economy will be unable to increase its GNP – even though there exist idle resources which could be employed to *expand* the current flow of total output.

It follows from the well defined conceptual analysis presented above that no volume of GNP which is directed by entrepreneurs into NAO (capital formation) can exhaust or exceed the supply of saving out of current income. In a capitalist economy where inputs in the production process are hired on a forward money contract basis, when entrepreneurs are given the financial facilities to 'command' resources to produce capital goods, then the private sector has no choice but to limit its spending out of current income on consumption to that portion of GNP which is AO. Only when the demand for AO *plus* the demand for NAO currently exceeds, and is expected to continue to exceed the potential total output of the economy, should the government consider a temporary tilt towards private saving – as long as such a tilt does not cause the demand for NAO to come crashing down with that for AO! (*This latter caveat is ignored at one's peril.*) Even if the government does not adopt a policy tilt towards saving in a full employment situation, however, the greater rate of investment and productivity growth *will be maintained* as long as the banking system does not limit credit availability. Such financing would lead to a windfall *profits inflation* for those who are holding inventories of NAO which can readily be converted into AO; but such a profits inflation *if expected to continue* will in itself (a) encourage an increased demand for more NAO (capital goods) and (b) provide additional internal finance by tilting the income redistribution towards entrepreneurs.[44] As long as the *windfall profits* inflation does not spill over into an *incomes inflation* (i.e. higher money wages relative to productivity and/or higher expected 'normal' profits) then the windfall profits inflation will be temporary. A windfall profits inflation is simply the way a market system brings about the higher rate of capital accumulation (*at full employment*) and higher private savings without any specific government policy to stimulate savings.

It is 'Enterprise which builds and improves the world's possessions . . . If Enterprise is afoot, wealth accumulates whatever may be happening to Thrift and if Enterprise is asleep, wealth decays whatever Thrift may be doing'.[45] Hence the role of government in an economy which relies on the private sector to accumulate capital is

(1) to provide ground rules for the capitalists' game which permit entrepreneurial income to permanently increase *only* if output expands (i.e. larger permanent profits are directly geared to greater output not larger profit margins) and labour income to permanently increase only with productivity gains;

(2) to encourage the purchase of products of industry by households as quickly as industry can expand, and

(3) to have the banking system provide all the finance for entrepreneurs to put their planned investment projects into execution (the real bills doctrine) and to provide all the liquidity the private sector desires.

If the government plays such a role, then when idle plant and unemployed workers are present, any increased demand for NAO will not only create jobs and additional income which induces further increases in consumption spending, but any resulting lasting price increases will be relatively small and will only reflect rising real costs (if any) due to diminishing returns associated with the increased production flows.

It is the lack of financial facilities due to deliberate policy decisions to limit the growth of the money supply, and/or deliberate policy constraints on the growth of demand for output which can limit capital accumulation either by hobbling the most optimistic entrepreneurs' ability to finance additional investment and/or by creating an inadequate demand which can quickly turn optimism to pessimism.

From the entrepreneurial viewpoint, any expected profitable project will be undertaken if there is (a) sufficient short term construction finance (bank loans) available to finance the production of the real capital during its period of gestation, and (b) sufficient investment fund finance when the capital goods are installed so that they can be funded via a long term issue of debt or equity finance. Since the fabrication of all capital projects must precede (in time) the installation and use of the equipment as an input to the production process, the short term financing over the gestation period of long-lived capital must be forthcoming before any funding (and saving availability) problem can even be considered. The supply of finance for planned (*ex ante*) additional investment projects depends on the banking system (given the liquidity propensities of the public). If investors are to increase their orders for fixed capital goods today they (or their suppliers) must obtain an increased supply of liquidity (finance) *before* any additional employment hiring and income generation can occur in the economy, no matter how thrifty the private sector may plan (*ex ante*) to be out of the additional income when it comes (*ex post*). The entrepreneur needing additional finance today cannot borrow the additional future planned saving of the private sector, for 'the *ex ante* saver has no cash [today] but it is cash [today] which the *ex ante* investor requires'.[46]

If the saver is forced to increase his saving today in order to transfer claims to the *ex ante* investor, then some AO which otherwise would be bought today will go unsold (or be sold at a loss); the resulting loss of sales will make the *ex ante* investor immediately more cautious than otherwise. In the face of increasing slackness in today's markets for AO, *ex ante* investors are likely to be less willing (even if finance is readily available) to contractually commit themselves to ordering capital goods whose additional output will have to find profitable market outlets tomorrow.

Once made, a contractual commitment to purchase capital goods and make payment at a specified delivery date in the future involves the investor in a cash commitment which if not honoured can lead to substantial legal penalties and even bankruptcy – a situation which even Adam Smith recognized was to be avoided if at all possible. As Adam Smith noted: 'Bankruptcy is perhaps the greatest and most humiliating calamity which can befall an innocent man. The greater part of men, therefore, are sufficiently careful to avoid it. Some indeed do not avoid it; as some do not avoid the gallows.'[47]

Legal commitments which can result in such misfortune – no matter how low the subjective probability – are not readily undertaken. Before signing contractual purchase contracts, any prudent investor will require a greater balance in his bank account, and/or a large commitment from his banker than otherwise so that payment at the specified delivery date can be virtually assured. In the absence of the availability of this additional finance, buyers and sellers of additional capital goods recognize that the shadows of the bankruptcy gallows covers such audacious forward contracts. If, on the other hand, the additional finance is made available by the banking system, forward contracts can be signed *in good faith* and capital goods producers can, *in good conscience*, enter into additional contracts for the hiring of labour and the purchase of materials and hence the NAO will, *ceteris paribus*, increase, *even if the private sector does not reduce current consumption plans out of current income.* As long as idle resources are available, real GNP will increase. With the expansion of NAO, the private sector's real saving (out of its increased real income) must increase concomitantly!

Finance and the commitment for finance are bookkeeping entries which must be increased if the investment activities of entrepreneurs are to expand. Since the creation of additional bookkeeping entries does not require utilizing significant additional resources (i.e. the elasticity of production of finance is zero or negligible), a reduction in planned current consumption out of income which frees real resources is *neither* a necessary nor sufficient prerequisite for increasing the market demand for capital goods, and *it is only by increasing the market demand for capital goods (NAO) that stagnation can be avoided.*

In the absence of the creation of additional bookkeeping entries, *ceteris paribus*, no prudent businessman would commit himself to expanding his illiquid position in fixed capital, and hence no additional investment can be forthcoming, even if the private sector were planning to save a sum out of future income just equal to the increment in NAO which entrepreneurs would undertake to produce if the finance were available.

Hence, a heavy demand for NAO (capital goods) can be held up by a lack of financial facilities on reasonable terms. This is especially likely to occur if the government relies on monetary policy rather than on an incomes policy to fight domestic inflation. It is the limitation of available finance by government policy rather than any bias against private saving out of current income which is the potent and very dangerous weapon which has restricted the rate of investment in the U.S. in recent years. As long as the banking system makes available at reasonable terms *all the finance* that entrepreneurs desire, investment will be at the greatest rate that private investors desire. If this is still deemed too slow a rate of investment, then as long as businessmen are motivated by the profit system to respond to consumer demands, *the cure for the slow rate of accumulation is to stimulate current and near future consumption out of income, not to stifle it by tilting the system towards additional saving.*

The great capital accumulations of history – the building of the pyramids in Ancient Egypt, the cathedrals of the Middle Ages, the discovery and exploration of the New World, the railroads and the de-velopment of the American West – were never constrained by the desired personal saving ratios of households. It was the ability of the entrepreneurs of these magnificent ventures to obtain ready finance (often via questionable financial manipulation) which permitted these vast capital accumulations of their time!

APPENDIX: MONEY AND GENERAL EQUILIBRIUM[1]

In order to have a meaningful discussion of whether the concept of money can be given a meaningful role in any general equilibrium theory, it is essential to explain specifically what is meant by 'money' and what is meant by a 'general equilibrium' (hereafter GE) system. Much of the confusion in professional discussions occurs because these terms are often used differently by different economists – and unfortunately even by the same economist to mean different things at different times and places.

MONEY

Modern Monetarists mistakenly believe that the use of illustrative examples of money can provide a definition of a concept; hence, modern monetary theory abounds with so-called 'definitions' of M_1, M_{1-A}, M_2, M_3 . . . M_7, which are exemplifications rather than explanations. Imagine the confusion and chaos that would occur if astronomers defined 'planets' by using the name of specific heavenly bodies (how would one tell a planet from a moon?), or even worse if some chemists defined the term 'molecule' in terms of specific inorganic salts, while a second group included specific inorganic acids with the salts, and a third group included inorganic bases etc.

Scientific communication and progress can only occur when de-finitions are cast not in terms of specific illustrations but are formulated in terms *of essential* features and properties. Then if a specific item possesses these essential properties and features, it is an example of the defined object no matter how strange this may appear to the layman, e.g. a whale is a mammal, or bamboo shoots are grass, not trees.

In this spirit of scientific definition, I shall insist that the concept of money in existence in a modern production, market-oriented economy involves two fundamental, concomitant features. These features in turn require two necessary properties. Money is that thing which by delivery permits economic agents to discharge obligations that are the result of spot and/or forward contracts. Thus the first definitional feature is that *money is the means of contractual settlement*. Money is also capable of acting as a vehicle to move generalized (non-specific) purchasing power over time, i.e. the second feature involves *money as a one-way* (present to future) *time machine*.

In modern monetary economies, this second feature which is known as liquidity, is possessed in various degree by some, but not all, durables. Since any durable besides money can*not* (by definition) be used as a means of settlement of future contractual obligations, in order for a specific durable to be a vehicle for moving generalized purchasing power over time, it must be readily resaleable at any time in a well organized orderly *spot* market. The degree of liquidity associated with any durable is a measure of its capability as a 'liquidity time machine' and that depends on the degree of organization of its spot market.

The means of contractual settlement or payment feature of money, on the other hand, is *not* possessed by any other durable except money. If some 'liquidity time machine' was suddenly to also possess this means of settlement feature (or to lose it), at that moment the durable would become (would no longer be) money. Thus, for example when in the 1930s the U.S. Supreme Court upheld the abrogation of the gold clause in business contracts, gold was no longer money in the United States – even though it may have retained a degree of liquidity to the extent it was saleable for money in spot markets.

It therefore follows that exemplifications of money in any economy (e.g. M_1, M_2, etc.) can only be identified in relationship to the existing law of contracts in the particular economic system under observation, and the market organization and institutional arrangements which permit contracting in money terms over short (the initial instant or today) and longer periods of calendar time. Obviously therefore, some Monetarists have abused the concept of money in their extended 'definitions' which include corporate securities, bonds, etc. (e.g. M_3, M_4, etc.) for they have improperly identified the time machine aspect as the essential feature of money and have basically ignored the means of contractual settlement feature – while the latter is the essence of anything which deserves the title of money.

Money plays an essential and peculiar role only when contractual obligations span a significant length of calendar time. If the economic system being studied only permits *spot* transactions, i.e. contracts which require payments at the immediate instant, then even if its members utilize a convenient medium of account (the numeraire) and/or exchange, such a numeraire is *not* money in the full sense of the term. Spot transaction economies (which are equivalent to Hicks' flexprice economies) have, as Keynes insisted, 'scarcely emerged from the stage of barter'.[2] In other words, a world in which economic activity never involves contracts for payment at specified future dates that are weeks, months or even years in the future is an economy in which both the settlement concept of money and its related notion of liquidity are vacuous.

Money only matters in a world – our world – where there are multitudinous catenated forward contracts in money terms. In such an economy it is necessary that there be some continuity as to what will be the thing which by delivery settles the resulting obligations. The existence of market institutions which permit (and encourage) contracting for future payment creates the need for money and liquidity.[3] This is an essential aspect affecting the performance of all real world market-oriented monetary economies where the activity of production requires the passage of calendar time. Any economic model which ignores these time related monetary contractual obligations and associated liquidity concerns will be a misleading guide to practical affairs and any economists who use such a defective model will be deserving recipients of the businessman's traditional scoff 'They have never had to meet a payroll!'

The attribute of liquidity requires that money possesses certain 'essential properties', namely a zero (or negligible) elasticity of production and a zero (or negligible) elasticity of substitution.[4] (Since I have developed this 'essential' elasticities property theme at great length elsewhere,[5] it will be assumed in what follows, that the reader is familiar with that analysis.)

Arrow and Hahn in their monumental study of general equilibrium analysis have recognized that money, contracts and time are inevitably and untimely related. If money matters, then the 'terms in which contracts are made matter. In particular, if money is the good in terms of which contracts are made, then the price of goods in terms of money are of special significance. This is not the case if we consider an economy without a past and without a future.'[6]

This crucial theme, which was the foundation of Keynes' monetary equilibrium analysis, has been developed at length in my *Money and the Real World*, especially in the second edition where the Arrow and Hahn conclusion that 'if a serious monetary theory comes to be written, the fact that contracts are indeed made in terms of money will be of considerable importance', and therefore, in 'a world with a past as well as a future and in which contracts are made in terms of money, no [general] equilibrium may exist'[7] is put in perspective. This motif is basic to the examination of what economists mean by the concept of GE and its relationship to money.

GENERAL EQUILIBRIUM

Despite the pervasive use of the term GE in the professional literature, a search for a unique, unchanging definition to be shared by all proponents can prove difficult if not futile. Until recently, Walras' Law, i.e. the simultaneous clearing of all markets, was thought by most to be the *sine qua non* property of GE. Recently however, some have claimed that 'general equilibrium will *not* be considered as bearing a necessary relationship to theories of Walras',[8] and, by extension one assumes no necessary relationship to Walras' Law. Thus in recent years a plethora of different interpretations of GE have been developed – some apparently only tenuously related to its original Walras' Law meaning – as GE proponents were confronted by the logical inadequacies of the original Walrasian theory to provide a well formed microfoundation for macroeconomic theory which deals with production, money, and expectations about an uncertain future.

Confusion persists, however, even among those who still adhere to the Walrasian foundation of GE. Some believe that Walrasian equilibrium was applicable to the short run;[9] others have insisted that it represented only a long run norm.[10]

In his admirable survey of *General Equilibrium Systems*, Bent Hansen has recognized that the 'nature of equilibrium has not always been clear to the economists who used the concept'. Hansen suggests that equilibrium has been defined differently by different economists.

The most common definition of equilibrium is equality of demand and supply. A market is said to be in equilibrium if the quantity in demand is equal to the quantity in supply. An alternative definition states that demand price and supply price must be equal. . . . These definitions or, rather, conditions of equilibrium, thus presume some law of motion for prices and quantities. A third definition of equilibrium . . . states that equilibrium prevails if all plans and expectations of all economic subjects are fulfilled so that, at given data, no economic subject feels inclined to revise his plans or expectations. This definition of equilibrium obviously calls for laws of motion governing the revisions of plans and expectations.[11]

Despite these differences in definition of equilibrium and the laws of motion involved, it is normally believed that the simultaneous clearing of *all* markets is a necessary and sufficient condition for GE – a result which Patinkin summarized via *Walras' Law*.[12] Of course, if Walras' Law is a necessary condition for equilibrium, then Keynes' *General Theory* which demonstrated the possibility of less than full employment equilibrium (when the labour market does not clear) would be a contradiction in terms. Those who maintain the importance of Walras' Law therefore have concluded either 'Keynesian economics is the economics of unemployment *dis*equilibrium',[13] or else Keynes' claim was the boast of a charlatan theoretician, i.e. if Walras' Law holds, Keynes' contribution to equilibrium theory was either ill conceived or negligible.

In 1939 Hicks had proclaimed

> I believe I have had the fortune to come upon a method of analysis which is applicable to a wide variety of economic problems . . . The method of General Equilibrium . . . was specially designed to exhibit the economic system as a whole . . . [with this method] we shall thus be able to see just why it is that Mr. Keynes reaches different results from earlier economists on crucial matters of social policy.[14]

Thus, Hicks encouraged a line of development of macro-monetary theory which was carried through to fruition by Lange and Patinkin.

Initially it was assumed that Walrasian theory and GE were synonymous. The research programme initiated by Hicks was, starting with a fully articulated preference schedule of economic agents and initial endowments, to demonstrate that there existed an equilibrium price vector which could pre-reconcile the independent desires of all agents, and to demonstrate that this equilibrium was unique and stable. The formal theory of GE turned out to be for economists exceedingly difficult, but by the early 1960s most economists believed that Patinkin had finally resolved Hicks' 1939 enquiry as to why Keynes reached different results from orthodox theory.

Patinkin's Model and Walras' Law

Patinkin has probably done as much as any other economist to propagate the notion that GE models can provide a proper microfoundation for macroeconomics and thereby permit the integration of monetary and macrotheory within the framework of a market clearing GE system. Of course, had Patinkin successfully done what he claimed, there would be no need for this symposium on 'Money and General Equilibrium', for the problem would have been resolved more than two decades ago. The existence of this symposium implicitly recognizes that economic theory was shunted onto a wrong track by Hicks and Patinkin. Hence, it will be useful to look at Patinkin's model to see where he went wrong.

Basic to Patinkin's model is his view of equilibrium which he characterizes as 'only at the price E_n – where the amount of excess demand is zero, where, that is, the amount people want to buy is equal to the amount people want to sell – can equilibrium prevail'.[15] Moreover

> The corresponding concept of equilibrium in the market as a whole . . . is defined as the existence of equilibrium in the market for each and every good. A set of prices which brings the market as a whole into equilibrium will be called an equilibrium set . . . The term 'equilibrium prices' must also be expressed or tacitly qualified by the phrase 'at a given array of initial endowments.' . . . In equilibrium, the amount of excess supply in each commodity market is, by definition, zero. Hence the amount of excess demand for money must also be zero. Thus . . . it suffices to show that this set of prices establishes equilibrium in each of the commodity markets alone. This relationship, which is a particular form of what is known as Walras' Law, is basic to the following analysis.[16]

Since Walras' Law requires that the existence of excess supply in one market involves excess demand in one or more other markets, Patinkin has made market clearing synonymous with GE. Furthermore, by imposing 'well behaved' demand and supply functions (the latter is vertical at the full employment level[17]) and a law of motion via the tatonnement pricing system and the gross substitutability of all excess demands, Patinkin ensures existence, uniqueness, and stability of the equilibrium solution of his model. Patinkin claims his equilibrium is short run, an equilibrium which exists only on the Monday of a Hicksian week; long run equilibrium would require the same short run solution to prevail week after week.[18]

Patinkin's model involves economic agents who, possessing perfect certainty as to future prices and interest rates, engage solely in spot transactions for all commodities on the Monday of a marketing period.

All trades are at the equilibrium price vector which makes trading plans reconcilable, i.e. no false trades. Since such a spot market economy is essentially a barter system, how could Patinkin claim he had integrated money into this GE non-monetary economy?

In true Alice in Walrasland fashion, Patinkin claims to develop a demand for money function in this timeless perfectly certain GE world by imposing a stochastic payments process. In this payments process, the date of settlement of all contractual obligations for goods ordered on Monday is not part of the terms of the contract.[19] Instead the settlement is determined by a lottery during the marketing period so that there is *uncertainty* as to the hour of actual settlement (i.e. the probability of having to make payment at x hours is < 1) although all payments must be made before the following Monday.[20] It is the risky, but statistically predictable timing of payments which is, in Patinkin's world, the fundamental *and only* reason for a demand for money.

Patinkin deserves kudos for having recognized that the demand for money is essentially related to uncertainty, the passage of time, and the need to discharge contractual obligations at a future date, *and* that no GE system could provide a role for money without all these aspects. Unfortunately, Patinkin's solution via a stochastic payments process still need not generate a demand for money by the public during the marketing week. Since the actual hour of payment is statistically determinable in Patinkin's scheme, the risk of default is insurable and all economic agents could buy *and* pay for insurance against default 'on the spot' on Monday morning. Hence, in equilibrium, all Monday morning markets (including the insurance markets) will clear. The public can make all payments spot so that no money need be demanded by the public for payments during the rest of the marketing week.

What Patinkin and others did not fully comprehend is that Walras' Law ensures that since goods essentially trade for goods, money as conceptualized in section 1 *supra* can never play a unique role in the system. Only by introducing the most artificial and contrived devices (e.g. a stochastic payment scheme) can a system based on Walras' Law obtain what appears to be a role for money, but even such *ad hoc* theorizing can, with further analysis, usually be shown to violate some logical relationship. In Keynes' world – the real world – money plays a unique role because of its properties and features. In such an economy an excess demand for money does *not* require an excess flow supply in another market, or vice versa; Walras' Law does not apply for there is no automatic market mechanism to assure simultaneous market clearing at full employment in a monetary production economy.

Although Hicks' *Value and Capital* did encourage general equilibrium theorists into a delusive search for reconciling their system of analysis with a macrotheory involving money, production, prices and employment, in recent years Hicks has been warning that GE concepts were logically inadequate to deal with such a monetary equilibrium system. Hicks now insists that 'the use of a [general] equilibrium concept is a signal that time, in some respects at least has been put on one side',[21] Keynes' monetary framework required an 'in [calendar] time' approach which recognized 'the irreversibility of time . . . that past and future are different'.[22] This lack of recognition of Keynes' 'in time' monetary analysis meant, according to Hicks,

> The 'Keynesian revolution' went off at half-cock. The [general] equilibrists did not know that they were beaten . . . they thought that what Keynes had said could be absorbed into their equilibrium system; all that was needed was the scope of their equilibrium system should be extended. As we know, there has been a lot of extension, a vast amount of extension; what I am saying is that it has never quite got to the point . . . to look over my own work, since 1935, and to show how some aspects of the struggle, and the muddle, are reflected in it . . . I have found myself facing the issue, and (very often) being baffled by it.
>
> I begin (as I am sure you will want to begin) with the old ISLM (or SILL) diagram . . . I must say that diagram is now much less popular with me than I think it still is with many other people. It reduces *The General Theory* to equilibrium economics; it is not really *in* time.[23]

Hicks' *Value and Capital* provided the impetus for shunting economics on to a wrong line of enquiry while the development of the intellectually challenging but difficult mathematical techniques of GE made those economists who had invested so much effort into their mastery anxious to display their use in resolving the issue raised by Hicks. Part of the problem, however, was due to the fact that prior to *Value and Capital* the concept of equilibrium as used by Marshall, Keynes, etc. (and as still used by some economists today) did not require simultaneous market clearing as a necessary condition. Even in Patinkin's *Money, Interest and Prices* we find equilibrium being utilized in two senses. Although market clearing is synonymous with GE throughout most of his volume, in Appendix K Patinkin admonishes Keynes for not meaning equilibrium 'in the usual sense of the term that nothing tends to change in the system'.[24] Elsewhere I have demonstrated that market clearing may be a sufficient, but not a necessary condition for equilibrium as defined by Patinkin in Appendix K; hence underemployment equilibrium can exist, and be unique and stable, without the need to involve Walras' Law.[25]

Keynes had declared that his *General Theory* was 'chiefly concerned with the behaviour of the economic system as a whole . . . [where] the actual level of output and employment depends not on the capacity to produce or on the pre-existing level of income, but on the current decisions to produce which depend in turn on current decisions to invest and on present expectations of current and prospective consumption'.[26] Although such a claim obviously means that neither Walras' Law or Say's Principle (see *infra*) are applicable, since Keynes maintained the assumption of (Marshallian) income maximizing entrepreneurs,[27] Patinkin and others assumed Keynes was logically inconsistent in claiming to have developed an underemployment equilibrium. What was not recognized at the time was that Marshallian microtheory was logically distinct and different from Walrasian microtheory. In Keynes' Marshallian framework there are three features which permit equilibrium in the sense of nothing changing in the system, without market clearing. These are that (a) aggregate demand and/or supply functions for goods and therefore for labour are formulated in a different manner from the traditional Walrasian GE (e.g. Patinkin's) model[28] and/or (b) the Gross Substitution Theorem is not universally applicable throughout the system and/or (c) the elasticity of expectations is zero (or negligible).[29] In any economy where features (a), (b), or (c) are applicable either separately or in combination, the pricing system does not automatically reconcile the desires of all agents within the physical limits of the system. Thus, equilibrium in the sense of Walras' Law need not exist, although equilibrium in the sense of a maintained state (as defined in Patinkin's Appendix K) can persist. Moreover, if in such an economy, equilibrium in the sense of all markets clearing simultaneously occurs, it is the result of coincidence and not due to a deliberate and automatic market mechanism.

The crux of Keynes' underemployment equilibrium analysis involves Chapter 17 of his *General Theory* where money, time related monetary contracts, liquidity preference phenomena and the interrelations between the real and financial subsectors are fully developed. From this chapter it is obvious that features (b) and (c) are, in some sense, the most distinctive differences between Keynes' framework and the GE system. Nevertheless, because of the difficulty and obscurity of Chapter 17, its message has been ignored. Instead, feature (a) was developed by Clower (based on Chapters 2 and 8 of *The General Theory*) to demonstrate that 'Keynesian economics is price theory without Walras' Law'.[30]

Clower's Revolution Against Walras' Law

In 1964, unhappy with the GE research programme 'launched by Hicks in 1937 and now being carried forward with such vigour by Patinkin',[31] Clower counterattacked to protect Keynes from charges of theoretical incompetence or even quackery. Clower attempted to get 'what looked like Keynesian results'[32] from a GE model, i.e. Hicks–Walrasian microtheory by introducing income constrained demand curves via the dual decision hypothesis. This hypothesis provided a different formulation for demand curves and hence, except in conditions of full employment, did not satisfy Walras' Law.[33] Thus Clower could achieve what appeared to be an underemployment solution where Walras' Law was clearly inapplicable – while the level of employment and prices need not change in the system. Clower stated that the dual decision hypothesis demonstrated how 'effective excess demand may be insufficient to induce price adjustment, despite the obvious sufficiency of notional excess demand [to achieve full employment]'.[34]

In essence Clower's analysis assumes that since households do not know for certain the monetary values of the sale of the labour (factor) services during the period they will be purchasing goods, their consumption expenditures are constrained by their realized current income receipts rather than their desired (full employment) income receipts. Hence when workers do not sell all the labour they desire (an excess supply of labour) their demand for goods is constrained so that there is no excess demand for goods, and Walras' Law is inapplicable.[35]

For Clower (and later Leijonhufvud), the problem of unemployment was that there is no market mechanism, in a monetary economy, to coordinate full employment hiring decisions with the full employment purchasing decisions which would then be forthcoming. Apparently, in a Clower construction, if only entrepreneurs would hire the full employment level of workers, then notional and actual income receipts of households would be equal and therefore actual spending would equal desired (notional) demand at full employment. Hence there would be no insufficiency of *current* effective demand for the products of these workers; Walras' Law would apply and full employment equilibrium would be maintained.

Clower insisted that although he could not find any evidence in Keynes' writings to indicate that Keynes utilized the dual decision hypothesis, Keynes either had this 'hypothesis at the back of his mind, or most of the *General Theory* is nonsense'.[36]

Unfortunately Clower's construction, although it seems to achieve 'Keynesian results', does not get to the essence of the underemployment problem of monetary economies. In a monetary, production, market-oriented economy, even if entrepreneurs hire the full employment level of workers, there can be an insufficiency of aggregate effective demand, when all the goods currently produced cannot be profitably sold at any price-money wage level. It is the prospect of possible insufficient effective demand at full employment which clearly differentiates Keynes' analysis of a monetary economy from either a GE system or Clower's model. The possibility of insufficiency of effective demand at any level of employment in Keynes' system is a result of his definition of money and its essential properties, where money 'cannot be readily produced; – labour cannot be turned on at will by entrepreneurs to produce money'[37] nor is any other producible good a gross substitute for money as either a means of setting contractual obligations or as a time machine. Since all Walras' Law systems and even Clower's model ultimately require the gross substitutability of excess demand, such models are incapable of introducing money into their framework. To oversimplify and paraphrase Clower, *Keynes' economics is Marshallian price theory without the gross substitution theorem, Walras's Law or even Say's Principle as fundamental conventions.*

Clower's model is ultimately an inadequate representation of Keynes' framework for two reasons. Firstly, money is not explicitly introduced into Clower's model. (Clower incorrectly claims that 'a model with income and without money could be called Keynesian'.)[38] Secondly, Clower mistakenly asserts that *Say's Principle*, where 'no transactor consciously *plans* to purchase units of any commodity without at the same time *planning* to finance the purchase either from profit receipts or from the sale of units of some other commodity . . . may be regarded as a fundamental convention of economic science'.[39] If the commodities and profit receipts referred to in Say's Principle are a result of the production (using labour services) process, then Clower is mistaken about the fundamental nature of Say's Principle.

It is not the income constrained demand curves which ultimately distinguish monetary economies from GE systems (for Clower has demonstrated how income constraints can be introduced into non-monetary GE models), rather it is the existence of money that makes the difference. Keynes emphasized that the theory he wished to develop involved an economy in which money plays a part on its own and affects motives and decisions and is, in short, one of the operative factors in the situation, so that the course of events cannot be predicted, either in the long period or in the short, without a knowledge of the behaviour of money between the first state and the last. And it is this which we ought to mean when we speak of a *monetary economy*.[40]

Thus contrary to Clower's first claim, Keynes specifically denied that his analysis could be represented without explicitly introducing a specific and unique role for money.

One of the most important sufficient conditions for demonstrating both the uniqueness and stability of a GE solution is the gross substitutability of excess demands.[41] It is not an exaggeration therefore to state that Walras' Law models specifically, and axiomatic (Walrasian) value models (which most economists believe is *the only* microtheory) in general, have traditionally utilized some price mechanism or law of motion which assumes the gross substitutability of all excess demand to achieve equilibrium. Since Walras' Law asserts that 'in any dis-equilibrium situation, there is always an element of excess demand working directly on the price system to affect prevailing elements of excess supply',[42] to the extent that GE systems are identified with solving the problem of reconciling all conditional intentions of economic agents within the productive capacity of the economy, gross substitutability is a basic building block. Ultimately this means that in a GE model the only thing acceptable today in exchange for today's (or even tomorrow's) products is, in effect, some other of today's products (or the present value of tomorrow's products in terms of today's products). Thus an excess of demand in one of today's markets implies an excess of supply in another of today's markets.

In a monetary economy, however, the existence of money which can purchase today's goods *or* tomorrow's goods but which exists outside the list of products that can be produced today or tomorrow (by the application of labour), destroys the universality of Walras' Law *and* Say's Principle and gives money a fundamental and peculiar role in the system. Thus a monetary economy operates differently from either a GE system or a Clower construction.

It is, as Shackle emphasized a decade ago, because

money is that institution which permits *deferment* of specialized fully detailed choice . . . And when exchanges are mediated by money, which exists, and can be increased in existing quantity, with virtually no use of productive resources, and which is not desired for its own sake but, in the last resort, only because it will exchange for other things . . . is the identical equality broken between the total of expected [or even realized] production earnings and the total of intended expenditures.[43]

Since the real world moves through calendar time towards an uncertain (and unknowable) future, man has created the institution of money which alleviates the need for fully detailed and specific choice at the 'initial instant'. Because of the peculiar properties of this money, neither Walras' Law nor Say's Principle is applicable to a monetary economy.

Say's Principle, for example, is violated whenever the federal government plans to finance the purchase of newly produced goods with newly created money (whose elasticity of production is zero) obtained by selling bonds to the banking system. In such a transaction, the government has consciously and with impunity violated Say's Principle by planning to buy commodities without using the sales receipts of producible commodities to finance the purchase. In fact, in a Keynes framework, many autonomous expenditures, whether by the public or the government, are initially financed via the creation of money in violation of Say's Principle.[44] The expansionary effects of deficit spending are, in large measure, due to the willingness of governments to violate Say's Principle!

Clower originally avoided this obvious problem of how non-income induced spending can be financed, by (a) concentrating primarily on the aggregate demand of households where it is assumed all expenditures are, in the aggregate, constrained by actual income and (b) assuming that actual payment for the sale of labour (factor) services precedes *in time* the purchase of all goods so that the latter are constrained by the former. Implicit in all this is that actual expenditures in the goods markets are not only constrained, but also induced by income, i.e. there is no autonomous spending.

If, however, factor payments must precede product purchases, how can entrepreneurs pay for their hired labour when they have not yet sold the goods? To resolve this chicken-egg dilemma, in a 1969 revision of his paper, Clower inserted a long paragraph[45] to describe the market organization and financing mechanism of his model. In this passage, Clower, apparently unwittingly, violates Say's Principle in order to start the trading process in motion.

Clower states that a central marketing authority ensures that no purchase order 'is "validated" unless it is offset by a sale order that has *already* been executed'.[46] But he states

> It is implicit in this entire line of argument that at some 'initial' stage in the evolution of market trading arrangement, the market authority advances a nominal quantity of *book* credit to one or more transactors to set the trading process in motion (without such initial advances no sales order could ever be executed since no purchase order would ever be validated).[47]

Hence the starting purchase orders are validated by an advance of credit, not by the sales of producible commodities. This means that at the beginning of trade (each Monday morning of the Hicksian week) Say's Principle is inapplicable. Moreover, as long as in the aggregate, the outstanding volume of debts is never completely extinguished (as in the real world), then Say's Principle is never universally operative. (Patinkin, and by implication Clower, avoids this inoperative aspect of Say's Principle by assuming all bonds are redeemed on the last hour of the marketing period within a single trading week – as if refinancing debt positions or even perpetual bonds are unimportant phenomena.)[48]

In sum, the existence of money with its peculiar elasticity properties and its related contractual institutions (and not simply income constrained demand curves) means that Walras' Law and Say's Principle have as much relevance to a monetary economy as Euclidean propositions regarding parallel lines have to a non-Euclidean world. Keynes compared classical economists to Euclidean geometers in a non-Euclidean world who, observing that 'straight lines apparently parallel often meet, rebuke the lines for not keeping straight – as the only remedy for the unfortunate collisions'.[49] Similarly GE economists, who insist that flexible wages and prices alone, because of gross substitution and Walras' Law, ensure the existence of a stable and unique full employment equilibrium, are utilizing non-monetary propositions to prescribe remedies for the problems of a monetary economy. (This is also true for those who use Say's Principle.)

Instead of continuing to develop such non-monetary models in the delusive hope of ultimately being able to provide comprehension and counsel for the monetary economy in which we live, economists should follow Keynes' metaphorical research programme 'Yet, in truth, there is no remedy except to throw over the axiom of parallels and to work out a non-Euclidean geometry. Something similar is required today in economics.'[50]

If we are to understand how a monetary economy operates we must throw out the assumption of gross substitutability of *all* excess demands, Walras' Law and Say's Principle as fundamental conventions for analysing such an economy. Although Clower's income constrained demand curves can explain the problem of why a GE system will not automatically return to full employment once it is in a recession, it cannot explain why a full employment level of production once achieved may not be able to be maintained. In a monetary economy, it is the peculiar properties of money in a world where the future is uncertain that are the fundamental causes of unemployment. What a monetary economy permits, which a barter economy and general equilibrium system do not, is the existence of one or more time machines – money and other liquid assets – which can transfer purchasing power over time for future goods and future liabilities without absorbing significant current productive resources into the production of these wonderful time machines.

This does not denigrate the importance of Clower's attempt at an *ad hoc* revision of GE systems to achieve 'Keynesian results'. Nevertheless such specific case modification as the dual decision hypothesis is suggestive of a degenerate research programme *à la Lakatos*, where novel facts and anomalies (unemployment) are explained at the cost of decreasing analytical content and continual *ad hoc* hedging of theories.[51] Clower's 1964 work was an invaluable contribution in forcing economists to (a) reassess the Walrasian GE framework and (b) recognize that Keynes' results need not be relegated to the position of a disequilibrium anomaly. Within a decade of Clower's initial attack on the GE research programme, it was obvious that a number of macroeconomic issues could not even be phrased in the timeless, perfect informative Walrasian framework of Patinkin or Arrow–Debreu. Accordingly, even though as late as 1971 Arrow and Hahn could still define an equilibrium as having the 'usual meaning' in economic theory, in that it involved

a set of prices and production and consumption allocations such that each firm maximizes profits at the given prices, each household maximizes utilities at the given price and with the income implied by those prices and its initial holdings of asset and profit shares, and aggregate consumption is feasible in not exceeding the sum of aggregate production and initial endowments,[52]

equilibrium notions were already beginning to proliferate in the literature. Following Clower's lead, many economists attempted *ad hoc* modifications of GE systems in the false hope that Keynes' analysis did not 'preclude our search for more sophisticated Arrow–Debreu type systems that are consistent with unemployment'.[53] As a consequence, the current literature bristles with concepts such as 'momentary equilibria', 'temporary equilibria', 'Keynesian equilibria', and even 'a sequence of momentary equilibria', as economists realize that 'the simple stories of general competitive analysis must be recast drastically in order to model the concerns of macrotheorists'.[54] To one who has no vested interest in the research programme of GE that has developed since 1937, it appears that current GE researchers have refused to accept the findings of others that 'The General Equilibrium Model is Incomplete and Not Adequate for the Reconciliation of Micro and Macrotheory'.[55] Instead GE theorists have exhibited a blind faith that if they continue to develop multitudinous and idiosyncratic *ad hoc* modifications of their systems, an intelligent model where money can play a unique role will be developed. Let us briefly examine an example of one recent attempt at *ad hoc* modifications of GE systems to achieve Keynesian results and a role for money.

Grandmont's ad hoc Modifications of GE

Grandmont and a number of his colleagues have attempted to demonstrate that the Keynesian concept of unemployment can be explained in GE models which explicitly deal with calendar time, money, and very inelastic price expectations. In their explanation of 'Temporary Keynesian Equilibria' the typical Grandmont *et al.* model has the following features:[56]

(1) the absence of any financial system (no borrowing and no spot market for selling or reselling securities);

(2) non-storable consumption goods are the only producible items (no capital goods). It therefore follows that the only buyers of goods are consumers and hence all spending is induced (and constrained) by income. Thus there is no autonomous spending and implicitly all goods purchases follow Say's Principle;

(3) fiat money is the only store of value and the only thing that can be carried over from one period to the next;

(4) all transactions take place in spot markets, but some markets are assumed to adjust via price changes, while others are assumed to adjust via quantity changes.

In reality, feature (4) means that Grandmont *et al.* are merely applying the techniques of GE analysis to the now largely discredited neoclassical synthesis findings that price rigidities are the sole cause of unemployment.[57]

By adopting Hicks' 'fixprice' system, Grandmont demonstrates that a 'temporary competitive equilibrium' can exist due to downward rigidity of money wages (or price) and a zero or negligible price elasticity expectations, so that excess supply in the labour market (or the product market) does not alter entrepreneurial hiring and production plans for future periods.[58] In sum, Grandmont *et al.* achieve temporary Keynesian equilibrium with unemployment by making rigid money wages and/or monopolistic competition (fixprices) 'a central feature of the Keynesian model'.[59] This state can be maintained if current results do not affect future plans.

Although Grandmont's results are achieved by assuming *ad hoc* restraints on the typical GE law of motion (price adjustment), features (2) and (3) above are worthy of note for they introduce into the system (without acknowledgment) Keynes' essential elasticity properties of money. Grandmont's money has a zero elasticity of production (since it is fiat, while all producibles are assumed non-storable) and a zero elasticity of substitution since it is the only store of value available. Nevertheless, Grandmont's framework is still not a model of a monetary economy, for the analysis is limited to a world of spot transactions with no contracts in money terms over time.

In sum Grandmont gets a 'Keynesian' underemployment solution because of downward wage and price rigidities – a result the neoclassical synthesis achieved decades ago and which led Patinkin to label Keynes' theory as disequilibrium economics. Keynes would not deny the existence and importance of monopoly power and money wage rigidities, but he argued that a reduction in money wages (or prices) would not, *ceteris paribus*, have a direct tendency to increase employment.[60] For Keynes it is the existence of money and not monopoly power which invalidates Walras' Law for a real world monetary economy.

WHAT SHOULD WE MEAN BY GE?

Although Grandmont *et al.* have introduced some essential monetary properties into their models, their systems remain faulty for they rely on *ad hoc* constraints to the fundamental GE price adjustment process to achieve 'temporary' equilibrium while they do not emphasize the role of money. None of the GE researchers seem to realize that the schism between GE and monetary analysis is as deep and irreparable as the difference between Euclidean and non-Euclidean geometry and that, as I have already indicated, the fundamental conditions or axioms of GE analysis must be thrown out if monetary equilibrium is to be analysed.

Whether the resulting monetary equilibrium system analysis should still be labelled GE is partly a semantic problem. (Would it be rational to call geometry without the axiom of parallels Euclidean?) The intellectual auxiliary baggage of gross substitution, Walras' Law, Say's Principle, optimality of reconciled choices of all agents via the price system, etc. is so closely identified with the concept of general equilibrium, while these paraphernalia are so incompatible with a monetary economy that to apply the term GE to monetary equilibrium systems would seem to me to be a semantic travesty. Semantic confusion can only result from throwing out the intellectual baggage of GE, while retaining the label.

Others, however, while recognizing the recent failures of GE theory to provide a microfoundation for macroeconomies are not yet ready to throw out their (non-monetary) systems and/or the GE nomenclature. Weintraub argues, for example, that although an Arrow–Debreu world is based on a full-employment assumption and is therefore logically incompatible with underemployment equilibrium, such an incompatibility 'ought not to preclude our search for perhaps more sophisticated Arrow–Debreu type systems that are consistent with unemployment'.[61] But the full employment assumption is inevitably related to Walras' Law! Thus to avoid this Walras' Law stigma, Weintraub states that GE should 'not be considered as bearing a necessary relationship to the theories of Walras; *a general equilibrium model is simply some specification of states of the world and a set of rules that structure the manner in which those states change over time*'.[62] To me such a definition throws away the baby of GE while keeping the bathwater.

One pre-eminent worker in the field of GE spent his Inaugural Lecture at Cambridge University trying to explain the *Notion of Equilibrium in Economics*. Hahn uses the Arrow–Debreu paradigm as the touchstone concept because

(1) It is precise, complete and unambiguous, (2) it has been much maltreated by both friend and foe . . . [and] because it so happens that all serious work which is now proceeding to recast the equilibrium notion is being undertaken by those who have been most active

in building the [Arrow–Debreu] paradigm in the first place and who consequently understand it.[63]

Thus Professor Hahn recognizes that the Arrow–Debreu general equilibrium system, although precise and unambiguous, is also defective and needs recasting and he, like Weintraub, believes the resulting system can still be called a GE. It is, however, precisely when it comes to the role of money that the GE deficiencies are most obvious and, I reiterate, if the role of money is to be properly identified, the recast analysis will bear so little resemblance to the traditional GE concept that it will be a mockery to maintain the GE nomenclature.

At the risk of some repetition of our earlier argument, let us follow Hahn's lead and proceed by starting with the precise and unambiguous concept that any GE system involves the existence of a stable and unique market clearing solution to the problem of pre-reconciling *all* conditional intentions of *all* economic agents in the system when each agent is operating under rational inter-dependent choices of action in the light of informed reason – the information having to include the choices made by others at the same point in calendar time as the agent. Any such GE system must be able to demonstrate that existing markets can achieve such pre-reconciliation by establishing a set of prices which (a) gathers all information including that on conditional intentions of all agents for each point of time, (b) converts this information into knowledge and (c) delivers that knowledge to all economic agents equally and simultaneously. Thus the GE concept *assumes* in its most rigid form that there are no false trades, i.e. no transactions which provide misleading information about the conditional intentions of others; or in its weak format, that even if transactions occur at false (or non-equilibrium) prices they do not either (a) mislead economic agents about the 'true' nature of the economic system or (b) alter the 'true' nature of the system or (c) prevent the time trajectory of the economy from converging towards the equilibrium state.

As Hahn has already noted, in this touchstone GE system 'money can play no essential role'.[64] In fact such an equational system can be utilized only in the negative sense of demonstrating why the real world 'economy cannot be in this state'.[65] Thus the Arrow–Debreu system 'must relinquish the claim of providing necessary descriptions of terminal states of economic processes'.[66] In other words, even in the longest of long-run, the equations of a Walrasian or Arrow–Debreu world will never describe the norm or trend towards which the real economy is groping![67] More specifically Hahn notes that what should be required of any equilibrium notion is that 'it should reflect the sequential character of actual economies . . . in an *essential* way. This in turn requires that information processes and costs, transactions and transactions costs and also expectations and uncertainty be explicitly and essentially included in the equilibrium notion. This is what the Arrow–Debreu construction does not do.'[68]

But as soon as conditions of a sequence of time and uncertainty are pressed on the system, GE concepts simply will not do! For example, Perroux argues that as soon as information is unequal among all economic agents, as it must be in an uncertain world where all agents do not have equal access to information and some information may be unknowable when the future does *not* yet exist, then 'general equilibrium is no longer constructable, nor mathematically formalisable'.[69] Attempting to reduce uncertainty to a Markov process, a tree of events, or subjective probabilities so that a decision strategy can be decided once and for all at the initial instant is an 'ingenious procedure for formally constructing an equilibrium but it does not tackle the problem of uncertainty'.[70] Once it is recognized that all agents do not and can never know the true states of the world, then even this probability construction collapses.[71]

Despite the millions of man hours economists have already spent in a vain search for a monetary GE theory that can deal with uncertainty (in the sense of the unknowable), calendar time, prices, production, money and employment, many still hope that such a theory can be developed. Hahn believes that the technique of GE can be salvaged if the concept of equilibrium is redefined such that 'an economy is in equilibrium when it generates messages which do not cause agents to change the theories they hold or the policies they pursue'.[72] Thus agents are still assumed to have responses conditional on the actions of others, and the price system can reconcile these responses as the market provides information to all agents, but this definition of equilibrium Hahn suggested 'implies *almost* the missing traditional complement that markets are cleared . . . short enough and rare enough episodes of uncleared markets would on my definition be consistent with equilibrium'.[73]

Hahn, therefore, permits equilibrium to exist even if Walras' Law is violated as long as the action of agents are not 'systematically and persistently inconsistent'.[74] It is gratifying to know that inconsistencies can be ignored as long as they are sufficiently uncommon and random occurrences so that they can be neglected; but that is hardly the solution to the problem at hand. The Great Depression and recent worldwide experiences of stagflation cannot be dismissed so readily.

Hahn admits that his concept of equilibrium is 'not at all clear' and is an 'ill-specified hypothesis',[75] and he has avoided the essential question as to whether we can analyse a monetary economy with a conceptual system which does not provide a special role for money.

CONCLUSION

Traditional General Equilibrium axioms and laws are incompatible with a monetary system. GE concepts involve non-monetary systems; such systems cannot be recast to give money an essential role without losing their non-monetary essence. Thus to speak of monetary GE models is a contradiction in terms.

The concept of money in its full sense can only be developed in a monetary equilibrium model which rejects Walrasian microtheory for Marshallian price analysis. In his *Treatise* and *General Theory*, Keynes developed such a monetary model in which the concepts of time, uncertainty, catenated spot and forward contracts, market organizations, institutions and money play fundamental roles affecting the behaviour of economic agents. I have elaborated and developed this model in my *Money and the Real World*. This analytical framework rules out many of the basic GE propositions, and consequently a monetary model functions quite differently from one described via the techniques and laws of GE.

If GE economists continue to recast their models often enough, they may, by accident, ultimately rediscover Keynes' great wheel of money mechanism – but the resulting model will bear as much resemblance to what is commonly understood as GE systems as non-Euclidean geometry does to Euclidean systems.

4 The Taxonomy of International Money

A CLASSIFICATORY APPROACH

With a great deal of cogency, Shackle has argued that economic theory should adopt a 'classificatory method' of an analysis, i.e.

> theory ought explicitly to be a classificatory one, putting situations in this box or that according to what *can happen* as a sequel to it. Theories which tell us what *will* happen are claiming too much: too much of independence from their turbulent surroundings, too much capacity to remain upright in the gale of politics, diplomacy and technical chance and change, too much internal simplicity for even the world of business itself . . . The efficiency of formal codes is the efficiency of classification.[1]

In this chapter, economies are classified by various essential characteristics. Clear distinctions are made between open and closed economies (as measured by ϕ, a variable to be developed below) and between unionized monetary systems (UMS) and non-unionized monetary systems (NUMS) (as measured by θ, a variable developed below). Table 4.1 presents the four possible combinations of these features.

The closed UMS cell of this table is the equivalent of the traditional 'closed' economy model which was utilized with great success by Keynes in *The General Theory* to demonstrate the possibility of underemployment equilibrium. If in this rarefied, simple case it was possible to show why market-oriented, entrepreneurial economies could yield undesirable levels of unemployment and price instability, then it was reasonable to believe that the more complicated open economies (in the second column of the table) were even less likely to achieve a socially desirable level of output, employment and price stability without some governmental and private institutional planning and control. The open UMS cell can be associated with an analysis of a home (local) regional economy trading

TABLE 4.1   A Classification of Economic Systems by Trading Patterns and Monetary Systems

Monetary system	Closed economy ($\phi = 0$)	Open economy ($\phi > 0$)
Unionized Monetary System UMS ($\phi = 0$)	(1) no external trading partners (2) single money as the means of contractual settlement	(1) external trading partners (outside the accounting system) (2) single money as the means of contractual settlement
Non-Unionized Monetary System NUMS ($\theta > 0$)	(1) no external trading partners (2) various monies used as means of contractual settlement with no permanent exchange rate	(1) external trading partners (2) various monies with no permanent exchange rate

with other regions (usually in the same nation) where the trading regions have a legal (or customary) currency union which, either by law or by practice, uses the same monetary unit to denominate *all* private spot and forward contracts.

The closed NUMS cell would be applicable to a global analysis of all economies, where the various trading partners use one monetary unit for denominating contracts between internal residents and different monetary units for contracts between foreigners and domestic residents. Finally, the last cell of Table 4.1 (open NUMS) is applicable to the analysis of an individual real world national economy which has foreign trading partners with different currencies and variable exchange rates.

In his *Treatise on Money*, Keynes attempted to develop a model directly applicable to the last cell (open NUMS) of Table 4.1. The complications of dealing with an open NUMS economy, however, obscured his message as to the causes of both price level and output changes; Keynes strove for a more simple analytical framework in *The General Theory* to explain his views. Moreover, since *The General Theory* was written while international trading relations were collapsing and real world developed economies were approaching a state of autarky, the analytical use of a closed UMS seemed applicable, at least as a first approximation. It is therefore understandable that in his 1936 book

Keynes should emphasize policy prescriptions that would be directly applicable to closed UMS economies. Today, on the other hand, with the 'Second Great Crisis of Capitalism in the Twentieth Century' facing the non-Communist world, and with the major capitalist economies operating as open economies under some form of floating exchange rate system, it is essential that attention again be focused on the analytical structure of an open NUMS economy.

The four-way classification scheme of Table 4.1, which defines precise theoretical constructs, depends on

(1) the theory of Aggregate (National) Accounting used for the data generation involving economic activities of production, bank finances and trade to distinguish between open and closed economies; and

(2) the laws and customs of society which determine the medium of contractual settlement to distinguish between UMS and NUMS.

AGGREGATE ACCOUNTING AS A BASIS FOR THE CLOSED–OPEN DIVISION

For the most part, aggregate economic variables (e.g. GNP) can have no meaning outside of the manifestations assigned to them by Aggregate Accounting Theory. The aggregate (or social) accounts do not measure conventionally existing items – rather, they are a way of accounting for particular abstract theoretical phenomena.[2]

In theory, a closed economy is one where all economic transactions are among residents of the economic system under observation. There are no transactions between individuals in the domestic economy and others *outside the accounting system*. There are no external trading partners who either (a) sell domestic firms and residents raw materials, labour, finished goods or (b) purchase the products of domestic industries, or (c) buy and/or sell assets from/to domestic economic agents. In such a closed system, the aggregation of the accounting records of *all* transactors are included in the aggregate or national accounts and all payments (except currency transactions) are entirely recorded in the books of the closed banking system. A double-entry record keeping system[3] of Aggregate Accounts ensures that, in a closed system, the total money expenditures of domestic residents equals the total money receipts of residents. Thus in a closed economy, the total expenditures of domestic residents on final goods and services must equal total receipts obtained from the sale of such goods by domestic enterprises.

It therefore follows from the definition of *income* developed by Keynes in *The General Theory*[4] that the flow of aggregate income earned over a period of time *in a closed system* must equal total expenditure on final goods and services spent by domestic residents. By definition, each person's purchases of final goods must be someone's income (i.e. every price of a final good becomes someone's income). This famous *accounting* identity which *requires* the market value of gross national product to equal the market value of the gross national income earned by residents of a closed economy is, of course, the basis of the famous savings equal investment *definitional* identity which was the key for many in comprehending the message of the Keynesian Revolution.[5]

In a closed economy, the system of aggregate accounts does not normally distinguish between groups of residents, and therefore such an accounting framework traditionally does not draw attention to the distribution of income (or wealth) among groups of economic agents. In fact, net asset transfers are deemed so unimportant in a closed economy context that aggregate accounting statistics on such activities are rarely collected. A closed economy analysis is, therefore, more likely to emphasize the size and growth in aggregate income over time rather than the distribution of aggregate income among transactors (although of course, because of Keynes' *General Theory* definition of income, the functional distribution, i.e. factor costs, can be ascertained from aggregate income statistics).

In an open economy, however, accounting practices highlight income and wealth distributions among trading partners, and therefore aggregate statistics on income and wealth distributions over time are collected and carefully analysed by international trade experts. By its very nature, an open economy involves a significant volume of transactions between domestic residents in (say) A and inhabitants of other economies. Accordingly, the accounting system for open economy A must highlight the division of income and wealth between A and its trading partners, as well as indicating the size and growth of the aggregate income of A.

In the aggregate accounting system of an open economy, all the simple, neat, tight equalities between aggregate payments and receipts of domestic residents no longer hold, e.g. the market value of production of final goods by domestic enterprises need not equal either the gross income earned by domestic residents, nor the total expenditures of domestic residents on final goods and services. The following accounting relationships are useful in sorting out the differences between closed and open economies where

V_C = the market value of domestically produced final consumer goods for domestic use net of the value of foreign components

V_I = the market value of domestically produced investment goods for domestic use, net of foreign components

V_G = the market value of domestically produced government-purchased goods for domestic use, net of foreign components

V_X = the market value of domestically produced goods for export net of foreign components

V_M = the market value of all foreign produced goods imported into the domestic economy, i.e. the sum of imported final consumption goods (V_M^C), imported final investment goods (V_M^I), imported final government goods (V_M^G) and imported elements (or components) of all domestically produced goods (V_M^E).

All values are expressed in terms of the domestic monetary unit. The value of *aggregate expenditures* on all final goods by domestic residents (E_D) is

$$E_D = V_C + V_I + V_G + V_M \tag{4.1}$$

The value of *aggregate domestic product* (V_{DP}), i.e. production originating and emerging from domestically *located* enterprises (or domestically generated income) is

$$V_{DP} = V_C + V_I + V_G + V_X \tag{4.2}$$

It should be noted that the traditional definition of GNP is

$$V_{GNP} = C + I + G + V_X - V_M \tag{4.3}$$

where

V_{GNP} = the market value (in value added terms) of all final goods produced in the economy during the period,

C = total expenditures by households on consumer goods including imports of consumer goods and components,

I = total expenditures of domestic residents on investment goods including imports,

G = total government expenditures on goods and services including imports. Thus, although V_{GNP} must always equal V_{DP}, the consumption, investment, government and export components of these two sums need not be equal. For example, V_C will equal C only if the value of imported final consumption goods (V_M^C) during the period is zero and the value of imported elements or components in domestically produced consumer goods is also zero.

The difference between the value of domestic product (or GNP) and aggregate expenditures is equal to the excess of merchandise and invisible exports over imports, i.e.

$$V_{DP} - E_D = V_{GNP} - E_D = V_X - V_M \equiv B \tag{4.4}$$

where B is the balance of merchandise (and invisibles) trade.

It follows from Keynes' definition of aggregate income in *The General Theory* that the value of aggregate domestic product must, *by definition*, equal the value of aggregate income generated domestically (Y_d^g), i.e.

$$V_{DP} \equiv Y_d^g \tag{4.5}$$

To Y_d^g, one must add foreign generated income earned by domestic residents $(Y_{f \to d}^g)$ and subtract the domestically generated income earned by foreigners $(Y_{d \to f}^g)$ in order to obtain *aggregate income earned by domestic residents* (Y_d^e), i.e.

$$Y_d^e = V_{dp} - Y_{d \to f}^g + Y_{f \to d}^g \tag{4.6}$$

(Y_d^e is sometimes misleadingly referred to as Gross Domestic Product or GDP.)

In a closed economy, $V_X = 0$, $V_M = 0$, and $Y_{d \to f}^g = 0$, and $Y_{f \to d}^g = 0$, so that

$$Y_d^g = V_{DP} = V_{GNP} = E_D = Y_d^e \tag{4.7}$$

In an open economy, on the other hand, where $V_X \neq 0$, and $V_M \neq 0$, equation 4.4 indicates that the difference between the value of aggregate domestic product and aggregate domestic expenditures on final goods is equal to the balance of trade. Moreover, since income is defined as payments for productive services rendered, the difference between aggregate domestic income earned and aggregate domestic expenditures will equal the balance of trade in goods and services – if *services include not only final, but also productive, services*. That is

$$Y_d^e - E_d = V_X' - V_M' = B' \tag{4.8}$$

where the index ' indicates the inclusion of the value of productive services (as well as final services) in exports and imports.

Thus the difference between the value of aggregate income earned by decisions of MNCs' comptrollers to take advantage of different re-generated domestically) is obtained from equations (4.2), (4.6) and (4.8) as

$$Y_d^e - V_{DP} = B' - B \tag{4.9}$$

where $(B' - B)$ is equal to value of the excess of productive services exported over productive services imported during the period.

Finally if to Y_d^e we add transfer incomes to domestic residents from foreigners and subtract out incomes transferred abroad we obtain the aggregate income available (Y^a) to the domestic resident. The difference between aggregate income available and aggregate expenditures is equal to the balance of payments on current account (B_{CA}) as normally reported, i.e.

$$Y^a - E_D = B_{CA} \tag{4.10}$$

In theory it is easy to visualize the trade balance in terms of B, the excess of merchandise and invisible product exports over imports. In fact, however, it is often very difficult to distinguish from accounting records between the importation of invisible final services (e.g. waiter services for a tourist in a foreign country) and the importation of a productive service (such as the use of foreign capital in a domestic industry) and often B' rather than B is used as the measure of the trade balance. Rather than either B or B', the trade balance on current (or income) account (B_{CA}) is often cited since it is the latter which is an indicator of payments imbalance which may be putting pressure on the exchange rate. B_{CA} includes the value of home *owned* output of goods and services *whether actually produced domestically or abroad* placed at the disposal of foreigners minus the value of foreign *owned* output *produced at home or abroad* placed at the disposal of domestic residents.[6]

In these days of vast multinational corporations,[7] the measurement of the trade balance from this last viewpoint involves practical complications which, while fitting the definitions, may not be immediately obvious. For example, let us analyse a hypothetical situation for Volkswagen which has an auto assembly plant in the U.S. Even if all parts, etc. are produced in the U.S. and all cars sold to U.S. consumers, the market value of these Volkswagen cars includes a profit margin which is owned by foreigners and hence that portion of the value of each VW should be counted as $Y_{d \rightarrow f}^g$ and is equivalent to an import of similar value for the services of a factor of production.[8] In other words, the existence of *multinational corporations* (MNCs) who maintain production and trading activities in many nations, can affect, via decisions which are internal to the firm, the accounting magnitudes which measure the balance of trade of any nation during any period. These decisions involve accounting transfer pricing transactions among subsidiaries which are chartered in various nations. These transfer prices need not have any equivalent value magnitude in real world markets. Hence, extreme caution must be exercised before interpreting any balance of trade statistics as symptomatic of a fundamental national disequilibrium, rather than an accounting imbalance due, in large part, to decisions of MNCs' comptrollers to take advantage of different regulations or tax laws in various national jurisdictions.

As a simplification, economists often associate imports with goods produced by foreign workers and exports with the use of domestic labour. In these days of MNCs, however, things are more complicated. For example, assume that a MNC increases production at its facilities located outside the U.S. but owned by a U.S. chartered affiliate, and the MNC sells the increased output outside the U.S. Some portion of the value of the increased production must accrue to an American corporation and is therefore counted as an increase in American exports without necessarily directly creating, *ceteris paribus*, any additional jobs for American workers. Despite such complications which are becoming more important with the growth of MNCs over time, for the theoretical discussions which follow such problems will be ignored at leàst until Chapter 12.

Finally, foreign lending can be defined as financial contractual commitments by domestic residents which places the domestic currency or claims to it at the disposal of foreigners in return for some form of either an IOU from a foreigner, or a title to foreigners' existing property. Net foreign lending which might be called 'the unfavourable balance of transactions on capital account'[9] is equal to the excess of foreign lending by domestic residents over the value of similar transactions by foreigners in their purchase of domestic IOUs, titles, etc.

MEASURING THE DEGREE OF OPENNESS

Weintraub has suggested that the degree of 'closed-ness' of any economy can be empirically measured by a variable n, which is the domestic component content of each money unit of final product making up aggregate domestic production during a period.[10] In Weintraub's analysis as $n \to 1$, the economy becomes more closed.

For our purpose, it is more desirable to measure the degree of openness, $\phi[= f(1-n)]$. Where ϕ is equal to the ratio of the market value of imports denominated in local currency terms to the total amount of domestic expenditures on final goods and services,[11] i.e.

$$\phi = (V_M/E_D) \tag{4.11}$$

If $\phi = 0$, the economy is closed. The greater the value of ϕ, the more open is the economy. At the limit, when $\phi = 1$, the economy is completely open and residents buy *only* imported products.

Table 4.2 presents estimates of ϕ for a number of nations for selected years from 1970 through 1979–80. This table indicates the relative degree of openness in modern economies and their trend over the decade of the 1970s.

THE PRICE LEVEL IN AN OPEN ECONOMY: AN INTRODUCTION

A complete discussion of inflation must await Chapter 8. Nevertheless, it is important to emphasize that the magnitude of ϕ has important implications involving the origins of and the magnitude of the rate of inflation facing residents of the domestic economy. As far as domestic citizens of any economy are concerned about inflation, the price level which is important to them is that of the things they buy, and not necessarily of the things they produce, except to the extent that the latter overlaps with the former.

It follows from equation 4.1 that

$$E_D = P_D Q_D + P_M Q_M = PQ \tag{4.12}$$

where P and Q without subscripts equal the price level in terms of the domestic currency and the quantity of all final goods bought by domestic residents, while the subscripts D and M respectively refer to domestically produced and foreign produced (imported) goods bought by domestic economic transactors. P is a weighted average of P_D and P_M, where the weights represent the importance of domestic goods and imports in the total purchases of the local inhabitants, i.e.

$$P = (P_D)(1 - \phi) + P_M(\phi) \tag{4.13}$$

Thus, the greater the openness of the economy the greater, *ceteris paribus*, the potential for importing inflation. For example, if $\phi = 0.2$, then a 10 per cent rise in the price level of imports (P_M) in terms of domestic currency will lead to a 2 per cent increase in the average price level (P) of things residents buy.[12] In this case, if no change is to be observed in P, then the price level of domestically produced goods (P_D) would have to decline by 2.5 per cent to offset the imported inflation. If P_D is directly related to unit labour costs and if domestic productivity was rising by, say, 3 per cent per annum, then price stability for domestic

TABLE 4.2   Degree of Openness (ϕ)

Country (in order of increasing openness)	1970	1973	Year 1974	1975	1979–80*
United States	.06	.07	.09	.08	.11
Mexico	.11	.10	.11	.11	.14
Japan	.10	.11	.15	.14	.17
Australia	.16	.14	.17	.15	.19
France	.15	.17	.22	.18	.21
Greece	.16	.22	.23	.23	.23
Philippines	.19	.19	.24	.24	.23
Venezuela	.20	.22	.26	.28	.24
Indonesia	.15	.20	.22	.22	.25
Italy	.18	.19	.25	.22	.26
Ecuador	.19	.20	.30	.28	.27
New Zealand	.25	.25	.30	.29	.27
Canada	.22	.23	.25	.25	.28
F. R. Germany	.20	.20	.24	.24	.28
South Africa	.25	.24	.29	.30	.29
United Kingdom	.21	.25	.31	.27	.29
Denmark	.31	.30	.34	.31	.32
Finland	.28	.27	.31	.29	.32
Sweden	.25	.26	.33	.30	.32
Portugal	.28	.30	.36	.29	.33
Switzerland	.33	.31	.33	.28	.34
Austria	.31	.32	.36	.33	.38
Iceland	.46	.40	.41	.44	.46
Norway	.43	.44	.48	.46	.46
Saudi Arabia	.41	.44	.53	.52	.51
Netherlands	.48	.48	.55	.51	.52
Belgium	.42	.46	.53	.47	.56
Israel	.42	.50	.50	.52	.56
Ireland	.40	.42	.50	.47	.61
Jordan	.32	.41	.50	.57	.64

*Calculated for the latest period in 1979–80 for which data were available.

SOURCE   International Monetary Fund, *International Financial Statistics*, October 1977 and February 1981.

residents would require that money wages rose by no more than 0.5 per cent per annum. In other words, if import prices rise over time, domestic money wages must rise by less than the growth in productivity if domestic residents are not to experience inflationary price changes in the things they buy!

Although a complete discussion of inflation in an open economy must be postponed until Chapter 8, the implications of imported inflation (equation 4.13) for the domestic economy can readily be illustrated via the following example.

During the twelve months of 1979, the price of imported Saudi marker crude oil in terms of dollars increased approximately 65 per cent.[13] The value of imported oil into the U.S. was approximately equal to 2.3 per cent of U.S. aggregate domestic expenditure during this period. Assuming the increase in Saudi prices is representative of the price of all imported crude, then, *ceteris paribus*, the price of domestic goods (P_D) would have had to decline by 1.5 per cent during 1979 if the price level of all things bought by U.S. residents (P) were to remain unchanged in 1979. This means that if labour productivity had been rising at its 'traditional' 3 per cent per annum during 1979, domestic money wages would have been able to rise by no more than 1.5 per cent on average if inflation in the U.S. were to be avoided.

According to estimates, labour productivity actually *declined* by approximately 3 per cent in 1979. Consequently, if the inflationary impact of the OPEC oil price increase in 1979 was to be offset in the United States, money wages would have had to *decline* by approximately 4.5 per cent. Even if it were possible to convince American workers that an 'across the board' reduction of 4.5 per cent in their money wages would have eliminated inflation and hence would not affect their real wages (other than the adverse effects of lower productivity and the adverse change in oil terms of trade *vis-à-vis* OPEC, both of these factors being taken as parameters in this case), American workers would not have accepted a decline in their money wages. This refusal to accept lower money (not real) wages is not due to a money illusion, i.e. to workers confusing their money wage decline for a further decline in real wages. Instead, it is due to the fact that entrepreneurial economies organize production *and* the purchase of long-lived durables on a forward money contracting basis. Consequently most American workers have long-term cash outflow commitments in terms of mortgages on their houses, rental leases on their apartments, consumer loan obligations on autos, furniture and appliances, and even loan obligations to finance children's college education. Any reduction of workers' cash (wage) inflows, therefore, even if it did not imply a further reduction in money wage purchasing power, would immediately create a serious cash flow problem, thereby threatening many families with insolvency. Hence, lower cash inflows even when they do not mean less real purchasing power will be unacceptable to economic agents operating in an entrepreneurial economy which organizes its production and consumption activities on a forward contracting basis,[14] and which does not permit recontracting without capital or income penalties.

In sum, equation 4.13 implies that the price level of goods and services which make up domestic aggregate expenditure is a function of several factors

(1) the rates of money wages (w) to labour productivity (A) in domestic industries,

(2) the profit margin or mark-up (k) of these domestic industries,

(3) the price of imports (P_M) in terms of domestic money, and

(4) the degree of openness (ϕ) of the economy.

In other words,

$$P = f(w, A, k, P_M, \phi) \tag{4.14}$$

where

$$\left(\frac{\partial P}{\partial w}\right) > 0, \left(\frac{\partial P}{\partial A}\right) < 0, \left(\frac{\partial P}{\partial k}\right) > 0, \left(\frac{\partial P}{\partial P_M}\right) > 0, \left(\frac{\partial P}{\partial P_M \partial \phi}\right) > 0.$$

THE UMS–NUMS DIVISION

Money is a human institution that is directly related to the law of contracts and the customs established in the economic system under investigation. Money is that thing that discharges legal contractual obligations. Money, however, need not be limited to legal tender; in modern nations it will include anything else 'the State or the Central Bank undertakes to accept in payments to itself or to exchange for compulsory legal-tender money'.[15] Thus, in practice, if things other than legal tender are customarily accepted in discharge of debts to the State or the Central Bank, they will be accepted to discharge private contractual obligations, and hence are money.

There are two basic types of monetary systems – a *unionized monetary system* (UMS) and a *non-unionized monetary system* (NUMS). If *all* spot and forward contracts between transactors (in either a closed or open economy) are denominated in the same nominal unit, such a contracting system is a pure UMS. The system is still a UMS even if various nominal units are used in different contracts between different transactors, as long as the exchange rates among the various nominal units are (a) fixed (and the cost of conversion negligible) *and* (b) are expected to remain unchanged over the life of the contracts. Such a system of contractual arrangements with various nominal units can be considered a modified UMS where the various currencies are *fully liquid assets*. (The definition of a fully liquid asset is any asset which itself is the medium for discharging contracts (money) or can be converted into the medium for discharging contracts in a spot market where the market maker 'guarantees' a fixed and unchanging spot price.) If there is more than one fully liquid asset and if law or convention permits contractual settlement of any contract with any available fully liquid asset at the option of the payer, then the system can be considered a pure UMS. If, however, law or convention requires fully liquid assets to be actually converted into the money of contractual settlement at the option of the payee, then the system is one step removed from a pure UMS where the size of the step depends on the cost of conversion.[16]

Where different contracts are denominated in different nominal units, expectations of fixed exchange rates are therefore a necessary requirement for any system to approach UMS status. Moreover, since forward contracts for production, hiring, investment, and other economic activities do not have any uniform duration, and since a going economy is always operating under a myriad of existing catenated spot and forward contracts, the exchange rate must be expected to remain unchanged for the foreseeable (contracted for) future!

One can conceive of, for example, the State of New Jersey as an open economy ($\phi > 0$) dealing with the rest of the United States in a pure UMS since all contracts between New Jersey residents and trading partners throughout the U.S. are in dollar terms. It should be noted that each district U.S. Federal Reserve Bank issues its own bank notes and that until a few years ago Federal Reserve Notes found circulating in the U.S. but outside the district of issue were sent back to the issuing bank for redemption. Nevertheless, notes from any Federal Reserve Bank were acceptable for paying contractual obligations within the U.S., as the exchange rate between Boston Federal Reserve dollars and, say, San Francisco Federal Reserve dollars was fixed and unchanging. Thus, the twelve Federal Reserve districts were part of one single UMS, even though each individual district could be considered an open economy trading with the other eleven districts in a UMS (and with the rest of the world in a NUMS).

Similarly, Scotland and England can be looked upon as open economies trading with each other (and others), where each has very different-looking bank notes circulating as currency. These two nations are part of the UMS of Great Britain and even if devolution comes to Scotland and the *political* 'openness' of the two nations increases, this should not *per se* affect either the magnitude of ϕ for England or Scotland alone, and the UMS between them should remain.

In a NUMS, regional or national contracts are denominated in local monetary units, while interregional or international contracts are denominated in various other nominal units *and* the exchange rate between units is expected to exhibit significant variability over the time period while currently negotiated contracts are still binding. In essence then, the UMS can be thought of as a limiting case of a NUMS when any domestic currency can be used as the means of contractual settlement, for the exchange rates are expected to remain absolutely unchanged during the period.

Since the degree of unionization of the monetary system depends on expectations about the fixity of future exchange rates, we cannot measure it directly. We could quantify the degree of 'non-unionization' of the monetary system θ, *ex post*, by the variability of exchange rates between trading partners over past periods, but in an uncertain world the historical record (looking back) need not reflect what past populations expected the future to be (looking forward). Of course, if the historical record showed $\theta = 0$ (e.g. for the exchange rate between the English and Scottish pounds), then it is probably true that past populations considered the two nations to be a UMS. If the historical record shows $\theta > 0$, however, it is likely that the past citizens thought they operated in less than a perfect UMS, but the degree of non-uniformity is unknown except if we make the historic (and unlikely) assumption that the historical path accurately tracked people's expectations at the time.

In sum, our classification system has been devised in such a manner that it is theoretically possible to have degrees of openness and degrees of non-unionization. Thus, an expanded Table 4.1 would have as many rows and columns as desired, with the upper left hand corner cell having the parameters $\phi = 0$; $\theta = 0$, the magnitude of ϕ increasing towards unity as we go across columns and the magnitude of θ increasing towards ∞ as we go down columns.

It should be possible to classify all real world nations for any period into one of the cells of Table 4.3. The closer to the upper left hand corner of the matrix, the more closed and more unionized will be the monetary

TABLE 4.3   Schematic Table of Openness and Non-unionization

	Degree of Openness (ϕ)					
Degree of Non-unionization (θ)	$\phi = 0$ $\theta = 0$ ϕ					$\rightarrow 1$
	∞					

system of the local economy *vis-à-vis* its trading partners;[17] the closer to the lower right hand corner, the more open and the more non-unionized the monetary system of the local economy with its trading partners.

EXCHANGE UNCERTAINTY – UMS v. NUMS

The most obvious advantage of a UMS is that there is one less uncertainty (unpredictability) that economic agents need worry about when they undertake long-term contractual commitments, namely the uncertainty of exchange rate changes (and/or conversion cost changes) which can wipe out any expected profit for an entrepreneur *vis-à-vis* the same contractual arrangement if only $\theta = 0$.

It is true that to the extent that the forward exchange market reaches far enough into the future to cover the date of contractual settlement, such markets permit the shifting (but not the elimination) of this additional uncertainty which, by definition, is *not* present in a UMS. This possible shifting of the real cost of exchange uncertainty (*a real cost which does not exist in a UMS*) is similar to the possibility of shifting the real costs of future production and marketing uncertainties from producer-hedgers to speculators that can occur in a UMS; but in either case the existence of forward contracting does not eliminate the real costs involved.

Thus the existence of a NUMS inflicts a *real cost* on to the economic system which, *ceteris paribus*, would not exist otherwise. This real cost, which is due solely to the way economies organize the medium for discharging a contract in a NUMS, must be borne by someone.[18] Moreover, since organized forward exchange markets are limited to short durations (e.g. 90 days), long term exchange uncertainties associated with contracts that are of longer duration cannot be shifted but must be willingly borne by the original transactors if they are to consummate a 'deal'.

WAS THE GOLD STANDARD A UMS?

Under the gold standard, the exchange rate between domestic currencies was basically fixed, except for the movements between the gold export and gold import points. As long as each Central Bank defined the domestic monetary unit in terms of a weight of gold and was obligated to 'make' a market in gold, i.e. to maintain two-way convertibility between domestic money and gold, the gold price of each currency could fluctuate only between the gold points, which themselves depend on (a) the difference between the buy and sell prices of gold at the Central Bank, and (b) the cost of shipping gold.[19] As long as it is possible to convert domestic currency in economy A to gold via the Central Bank and then ship it to B and convert it to B's currency to pay a contractual obligation, then the exchange rate could never fall below the gold export point in A (above the gold import point in B). So long as there is *absolute confidence* that existing parities can be maintained under the gold system (i.e. that each Central Bank had sufficient reserve assets to continue to 'make' the domestic market in gold), then as soon as the market exchange rate moved close to, say, the gold export point in economy A, commercial banks and business firms that deal in international trade and hence keep transactions and precautionary balances in each currency would move in to buy the relatively 'weak' domestic currency by selling some of the 'strong' currency. Hence, the private sector's liquidity desires and balances provide 'helpful' exchange movements *provided* 'there is a fixed rate of exchange and complete confidence that it will not be altered'.[20] Thus, the gold standard, except for the fluctuations between the gold points, did tend towards being a UMS. The closer the gold points were to each other, the more the trading partners linked into a UMS, i.e. $\theta \to 0$.

5 Trade, Money and International Payments

In order to systematically analyse the role of finance and money in any NUMS, we must restrict our vision to a single cause of payments' imbalance at any one time. Although the items in the balance of payments are, via the system of double-entry bookkeeping, interconnected so that, for example, a positive overall balance on 'current accounts' must be offset by a negative balance on the 'capital accounts', it is essential for clear analysis to deal with imbalances in one subset of accounts at a time. Traditionally, economists have delved most deeply into the problem of an adverse balance of trade, i.e. where $B > 0$. When the value of imports exceeds that of exports ($V_M > V_X$), the domestic economy has to finance a deficit in its balance of international payments with the rest of the world. This, then, is the problem which we shall analyse in some detail in this chapter.[1]

If an economy has a deficit in its trade balance *vis-à-vis* a situation where no imbalance occurs, there is created an urgent *liquidity* problem for the deficit trading partner of how to finance the deficit. The nation with the surplus balance of trade also has a liquidity problem, albeit a less pressing one to resolve, namely which liquidity time machine(s) it shall use to store the value of its export surplus.

There are two possible *ceteris paribus* causes for the emergence of a trade imbalance. The first might be termed an imbalance due to a *relative difference* (change) in the composition of exports and imports within a given sum of aggregate demand for goods of the trading nation due either to (a) an exogenous difference (change) in the composition of final demand in either trading partner, or (b) an exogenous difference (change) in the relative money costs of production[2] between trading nations. These purely relative or compositional differences (compared to a balanced trade position) can be either permanent or temporary, expected or unexpected. The second possible cause for the emergence of a trade imbalance can arise from an exogenous higher level (increase) in global aggregate demand[3] originating in one of the trading partners and impinging directly on exports or imports.

In orthodox trade theory, adjustments to trade imbalances are assumed to occur under some variant of either (a) a real wealth mechanism, (b) an elasticity of demand mechanism, and/or (c) a Keynesian trade multiplier mechanism. Our analysis, on the other hand, will focus on an adjusting process involving the theory of reserve asset holdings for open economies as derived from Keynes' liquidity preference theory for a closed UMS. We focus on

(1) the demand for transactionary and precautionary reserves in the relative difference in composition case, and

(2) the income-generating finance process (which has been developed since *The General Theory*)[4] for the higher global aggregate demand case.

Traditional international trade theory has tended to ignore this liquidity approach to adjustment processes for trade imbalances; instead it stresses 'real' adjustment mechanisms.[5] In such real processes, both surplus and deficit nations share equally in the mechanism of adjustment. In the liquidity approach, on the other hand, given the existing financial arrangements and institutions, the major onus for adjusting is placed on the partner faced with a shortage of liquidity – the deficit nation.

REAL ADJUSTMENT PROCESSES FOR TRADE IMBALANCES

Orthodox trade theory suggests there are three possible induced adjustment processes which tend to 'automatically' reduce, if not eliminate, exogenous trade imbalances. Of course, since any of these processes take time, the holding of reserve assets is implicitly necessary for regions if they are to buy time to permit these induced processes to work to reduce a trade deficit. Nevertheless all three adjustment mechanisms tend to downplay the importance of holding reserves (liquidity). These three processes are

(1) the real wealth mechanism,

(2) the neoclassical relative price (and cost) mechanism,

(3) the 'Keynesian' foreign trade income multiplier mechanism.

The Real Wealth Mechanism

Economists who emphasize adjustments to trade deficits via a real wealth mechanism argue that any trade deficit is financed by the sale of *real* assets (wealth) by residents of A, the trade deficit economy, to residents of B, the trade surplus economy. This hypothesized redistribution of wealth directly affects the demand for all goods including imports means the want plus the ability to pay) before the real wealth for the products of A while lowering A's demand for the products of B until, *in the long run*, the trade imbalance between B and A is eliminated when sufficient real wealth has been transferred from A to B. It is assumed that households in B are encouraged by the wealth redistribution to spend more (and/or earn less) while those in A are induced to spend less (and/or earn more). If these wealth effects were sufficiently large and of exactly offsetting magnitudes (as they must be by the definition of long run implied in this type of analysis), then the trade deficit is eliminated without any necessary changes in the (real) value of output (including leisure) of the two regions combined.

It is assumed in this type of analysis that during this adjustment process the assets sold by A to B to finance the trade deficit are easily marketable in both regions without loss, or as Scitovsky puts it, 'all assets are perfectly integrated'.[6] Scitovsky maintains that the perfect integration of all assets is an unattainable ideal, although under a gold standard, such integration would be possible as long as the deficit trading partner did not run out of the gold asset! Of course, if all assets are not perfectly integrated, it is possible for economy A to run out of marketable assets (liquidity) or to see the market value of its remaining assets decline over time, so that this deficit nation would have to halt its purchase of imports because of a lack of finance (since demand for imports means the want plus the ability to pay) before the real wealth effect on demand has completed its work in the two economies. As a result, employment and output can plunge in *both* trading partners with a concomitant decline in the (real) value of the global output.

The Monetary Approach to the Balance of Payments

The monetary approach to international payments problems is merely a specific variant of this real wealth adjustment mechanism for open economies. Johnson succinctly summed up the monetary approach view when he argued

> abstracting from the process of economic growth over time, and the associated increase in wealth and in the stock of money demanded that goes with growth. It follows that balance of payments deficits or surpluses are by their nature transient and self-correcting, requiring no deliberate policy to correct them. . . . The reason is simply that deficits reduce money stocks whose excessive size underlie the deficit,

and surpluses build up the money stocks whose deficiency underlies the surplus.[7]

Thus, in this monetary approach, it is the *assumed* initial 'excessive' size of a domestic asset (the domestic money supply) which, via a real (wealth) effect at the initial nominal price level, induces an excessive domestic demand for all goods including imports and thereby creates the (endogenous) trade deficit. Of course, by postulating that trade deficits are *always and only* the result of an excess stock supply of real balances and by assuming that there must exist a (Walrasian) price vector which assures the simultaneous clearing of all markets when goods trade for goods, it follows that any observed trade imbalance must be a 'temporary' phenomenon. By supposition trade imbalances are always eliminated by relative price movements between exports and imports; the entire problem and its solution is resolved by assumption. Given the hypothesized ubiquitous nature of the gross substitution axiom, such relative price movements in exports *vis-à-vis* imports ensure that, in the long run, exports 'pay' for imports, while the same relative price changes redistribute real wealth (real balances) without, it is assumed, changing the long run global real wealth total. In sum, the 'monetary approach to the balance of payments' not only *assumes* that there is only one underlying cause of any observed trade imbalance (namely excessive domestic money supply creation), but it also *assumes* that flexible prices (and exchange rates) can always resolve the problem without any significant effects on the combined aggregate real income and wealth of the trading nations. And all of this is accomplished in name of a monetary approach which analyses the operation of a *real* or *barter* economy in which (a) money has no unique role to play (other than the assumed initiating cause of the disturbance) and (b) liquidity considerations are irrelevant.

The logic of the 'monetary approach to the balance of payments' is as flawed as its counterpart. Milton Friedman's monetary framework is a misconceived basis for the analyses of real world closed monetary economies. These monetarist approaches have no analytical value in explaining the operation of real world entrepreneurial economies which organize production and exchange transactions on a forward money contracting basis. As Johnson proudly admits (see note 5), Monetarists conquer the difficulties of monetary phenomena by conceiving them as merely an extra complication superimposed upon real problems of an economy operating fundamentally on a 'barter' basis. This view is inherently incompatible with Keynes' view, and Post Keynesian monetary theory which asserts that an entrepreneurial monetary economy operates in a manner intrinsically different from a barter economy. Money is not just an extra complication imposed on a barter system! Consequently, the Post Keynesian and Monetarist approaches are incompatible and no eclectic synthesis is possible. Economists will have to choose whether they wish to model the operations of real world economies as either (a) barter systems upon which monetary phenomena are simply superimposed complications, or (b) entrepreneurial economies where money, contracts and liquidity phenomena play distinctive roles in affecting motives, decisions and actions in both the short run and the long run.

The Neoclassical Relative Price–Cost Mechanism

Neoclassical theory has always relied on some variant of David Hume's 'price-specie flow mechanism' to alleviate the problems of a trade imbalance. The financing of the deficit by an outflow of specie (gold)[8] from the deficit to the surplus nation results in a continuing change in relative prices and/or costs (in terms of a single currency) in the two regions until the deficit is eliminated.

A variant of this adjusting mechanism could occur if the fear of running out of specie (or any integrated international reserve asset) forced a devaluation in the exchange rate of the deficit nation money *vis-à-vis* the surplus trading partner's money. Such a devaluation raises the deficit nation's costs (in terms of domestic currency) of its imports relative to home production, while reducing, *ceteris paribus*, the foreigner's costs of purchasing exports of the deficit nation relative to the foreigner's own production in terms of the foreigner's money. As long as the sum of the elasticity of demand for imports plus exports in the trading partners exceed unity (the Marshall–Lerner condition), then it is averred, exchange devaluation by the deficit nation will, in the long run, eliminate the trade deficit without affecting the *long run* global real income of the trading partners combined.

Of course, this mechanism assumes that each nation's 'demand schedules for imports' in the price–quantity quadrant remains unchanged despite the large redistributions of income occurring among the trading partners and between sectors within each nation. Balogh has, therefore, criticized this view by noting that

Changes in income both shift and alter the shape of the 'schedules' which traditional analysis assumes to be 'given'; the 'elasticity-mongers' take as constant those things which must necessarily change. In fact, world demand for imports is not unequivocally determined by real factors and its price-elasticity is subject to violent fluctuations due to variations in the level of employment [and real income]. Nor does it necessarily improve with the passage of time.[9]

Both the orthodox specie-flow and the elasticities approach to devaluation ignore the influence of demand on global real aggregate income and vice versa. Exports and imports in each nation are assumed to be merely gross substitutes for each other *and* for a large mass of non-internationally traded goods which exists in each nation. If exports and imports are very strong gross substitutes in both economies, then the Marshall–Lerner conditions will always hold, at least in the long run! The Marshall–Lerner conditions are readily violated however if exports and imports are not very good substitutes for domestically produced goods and if any income effects offset or eliminate the positive effects.

If, in the real world, trade between nations does not always involve the immutable gross substitutes assumed by orthodox theory, then income (and liquidity) effects can predominate; therefore sole reliance on real relative demands or costs to alleviate trade deficits even in the long run of calendar time can be misplaced.

The Foreign Trade Multiplier Mechanism

The 'Keynesian' foreign trade multiplier mechanism assumes that in each economy the marginal propensity to import is less than, or equal to, the marginal propensity to consume. If the marginal propensity to import equals the marginal propensity to consume in each region, *and* if the same marginal propensity to spend exists in each region, then an exogenous increase in the demand for imports in A will, via multiplier effects in both countries, lead to an equilibrating demand for the imports in B (assuming a two-trading partner system). In a multilateral trading system, even with equal marginal propensities, exact offsets are, however, unlikely.[10]

Moreover, it is highly unlikely that marginal propensities to consume and/or import are equal in each trading partner. Thus, the Keynesian trade multiplier mechanism (assuming all aggregate marginal propensities exceed zero and are less than unity) merely dampens down the initial size of any exogenous trade deficit rather than eliminating it, even in the long run.

With significant redistribution of incomes and wealth occurring within each nation as well as among trading partners, however, it would be foolish to expect that aggregate marginal propensities to consume and to import remain unchanged during a period of trade imbalance and income adjustments. Consequently it is possible that the Keynesian trade multiplier mechanism may do little to dampen the magnitude of the imbalance over time. If aggregate marginal propensities are endogenous variables, changes could exacerbate the export–import flow imbalances over time.

In sum then, two of the three 'real' adjusting mechanisms assumed to be operating (by orthodox theorists) to eliminate trade imbalances require a host of unrealistic assumptions involving the predominance of gross substitution effects. These real wealth and relative price adjusting mechanisms blatantly ignore or denigrate the impact of unpredictable income effects which can destroy the implicit stability of market clearing equilibrium due to the gross substitution axiom. The Keynesian trade multiplier mechanism, on the other hand, *assumes* stabilizing (deficit-reducing) income effects resulting from assumed marginal propensity parameters whose magnitude is fixed within a given range to ensure stability.

The approach to trade imbalance adjustment mechanism which is developed below, on the other hand, follows Keynes' monetary analysis in emphasizing liquidity motives of firms and households in the operation of an entrepreneurial production economy. This liquidity adjustment process, stabilizing or otherwise, operates initially and primarily through the financial systems of the trading partners.

THE DEMAND FOR MONEY – DOMESTIC OR INTERNATIONAL

Money has been defined by its two primary functions, namely (a) a medium of spot and forward contractual settlement, and (b) a liquidity time machine, i.e. a store of generalized purchasing power. In the absence of uncertainty over time, the liquidity functions of money over time would be superfluous!

Keynes' powerful dual 'purpose' classification of money[11] led to the two essential properties of money (zero or negligible elasticities of production and substitution) which are 'significant attributes' for money in an uncertain world where 'expectations are liable to disappointment and expectations concerning the future affect what we do today'.[12] Utilizing this Keynesian approach, the demand for money (in a closed UMS) via the transactions, precautionary, speculative, and financial motives has been developed to a fine edge.[13]

The role of money and liquidity relationships in an open NUMS, on the other hand, have not been as similarly developed. Practical complications create perplexing theoretical problems especially for traditional neoclassical analysis where money is a mere 'numéraire', and international trade is treated as if it were a barter process where goods trade for goods, and monetary theory is just an 'extra complication' (to use Johnson's phrase) on a real or barter analysis. In the real world, however, each nation has its own medium for denominating and settling private contracts between domestic residents. Different monies may be used to settle private contracts between residents of one nation and residents of other nations. Central Banks may use yet another medium (often not available to the private sector) to settle claims against each other, or against other national banking systems. Financial arrangements and institutions are an essential element in the determination of the level of international flow of production and exchange of goods and services.

What determines the medium of contractual settlement that is utilized in international *vis-à-vis* wholly domestic transactions? The money in use, an essential element of all economically developed *civilizations*, depends upon both law and custom. Since in modern economies the State enforces both law and custom in the case of contractual disputes between residents of the same nation, the internal medium of contractual settlement is not only whatever is declared to be legal tender by the State, but also anything the State or the Central Bank undertakes to accept from the public in payment of obligations or in exchange for legal tender money.[14] Unfortunately, no such simple chartelist prerogatives exist to determine the money of settlement when contractual disputes occur between residents of different nations. Thus, custom and voluntary cooperation between governments are important factors in this situation.

In general, local currency cannot be directly used to settle an international obligation denominated in terms of another currency. Thus, the payer of such a foreign contractual commitment will have to sell the domestic currency in either a spot or forward foreign exchange market to obtain the means of contractual settlement.[15] Whether the exchange markets are organized by, or at least supported by, either the State or the Central Bank (as the lender of last resort), or by private agents acting without *any* State support, will be *the* major determinant of the degree of international liquidity possessed by the domestic money.

Just as it was essential to comprehend the liquidity motives of economic agents holding cash and other liquid reserve assets in a closed UMS economy facing an *uncertain* future (Keynes' theory of liquidity preference), so we must develop a parallel theory of international liquidity and reserve asset holdings for agents operating in an open NUMS.

THE NEED FOR RESERVES

In a world where the future is uncertain and the carrying out of entrepreneurial production decisions involves the passage of time – often long periods of time – the recognition of errors in expectations and the necessity of altering one's activities as time passes becomes an inevitable aspect of the human condition.

In such a world there is sequential causality of events. For example, entrepreneurs are continually examining outcomes over time to see if they match previous expectations. Unexpected outcomes at time t_0 are inspected for possible evidence of new, different, and previously unforeseen trends. If, or when, these surprising events are (correctly or incorrectly) perceived to have significantly altered the economic environment, entrepreneurs will, *ceteris paribus*, alter their expectations about the future. These revised expectations will induce agents to recast their decisions at time t_1. These changed decisions will affect economic actions and activities at time t_2.

The calendar time which passes between t_0 when 'surprise' events are discovered, and t_1 when decisions are altered, depends in large measure on how long it takes agents to collect information, analyse the resulting data, and in the context of their historical and current experiences, identify the previously unexpected pattern as a non-ephemeral event. Thus the period between t_0 and t_1 is an information collecting, processing, and identification period, and its calendar length (which cannot be specified in advance) is mainly determined by perceptual and psychological factors.

The calendar distance between t_1 and t_2 (between revising decisions and changing activities), on the other hand, is constrained by two major economic factors. Firstly, the length of time each agent is bound by previous forward contractual commitments *and* the real costs of buying oneself out of these commitments will, if necessary, limit actions which could bring t_2 closer in time to t_1. Secondly, the more uncommitted or additional liquidity one has or can obtain to meet new contractual obligations that will be incurred by any new actions undertaken at any point of time, the closer t_2 can be brought to t_1. The possession of sufficient liquidity is freedom in the sense of permitting new actions to be taken quickly, and thus often shortening the distance between t_1 and t_2 when entrepreneurs perceive their past errors and desire to embark on new and different activities. In sum, the duration and magnitude of existing contractual commitments (for any given degree of liquidity possessed) forces a posterior calendar time lag on new actions.

When a change in expectations is induced via economic evidence of surprise events occurring at time t_0, the magnitude of the endogenous change in expectations at t_1 is measured by Hicks' elasticity of expectations.[16] Of course changes in expectations may also result from the perception of change in either non-economic factors or economic factors generated by forces other than those under discussion. '*We must never forget that . . . expectations are liable to be influenced by autonomous causes* [and] we must leave it at that.'[17] In the real world, economic agents *know* that they must make decisions in a system of incomplete information. Autonomous changes in expectations of others can, in the aggregate, have surprising results in one's economic environment. In such a situation each agent is aware of the possibility that an unpredictable change in circumstances may occur at t_0. Accordingly there may be a need to change one's expectations at t_1 and one's actions as soon as possible after that. The holding of liquid reserve assets is therefore a rational protection against the buffeting of the unforeseen and unforeseeable winds of economic change.

The holding of *liquid* reserve assets gives decision makers time to sort out and interpret the myriad of market and other signals which they are continuously receiving, and then decide whether a change in plans is required while they continue to meet contractual obligations not only during the period of signal interpretation but also during the period of posterior lag while the decision maker plans alterations in his original activities. *Thus, the possession of liquidity is essential for the continuity of economic activity in a free market entrepreneurial economy where everyone recognizes that the economic future is statistically unpredictable and full of potential surprises.* Such a world bears no resemblance to the neoclassical models of Walrasian equilibrium; but in such a real world 'liquidity is freedom'.[18]

Hicks has invented a classificatory scheme for asset holdings in such an uncertain world.[19] All assets, whether real or financial, are divided into three categories.

(1) *Running Assets* are those required for the 'normal' operations of economic processes. Goods in process and currently utilized plant and equipment are the real running assets used in the production activities of business enterprises. Transactions, cash balances or other fully liquid assets currently being held to meet expected contractual obligations in the very near future are the running financial assets for the normal expenditure activities of buyers.

(2) *Reserve Assets* are assets that are similar to running assets but are *not* normally required for the current level of planned activities. Instead, reserve assets are held for contingencies which may occur during normal economic activities. Thus, spare parts and idle capacity are real reserve assets, while precautionary and speculative holdings of money and other liquid assets are financial reserve assets.

(3) *Investment Assets* are held primarily for the *expected* income they will earn at specified future dates. For example, plant and equipment under construction are, in Hicks' view, examples of real investment assets. To the extent that there are illiquid bonds or equity certificates which are being held solely for their future income prospects since there are no well-organized spot markets in which they can be resold, such holdings would be financial investment assets. Illiquid securities are relatively rare in developed monetary economies. They can be identified with the debt obligations among friends, family, etc. or the equity securities of closely held, small corporations where spot marketability is unlikely if not impossible.

In the financial sector, money holdings are usually either running or reserve assets while the holding of securities can be classified on the basis of the degree of organization of the spot market in which the asset can be sold.[20] Fully liquid securities are likely to be financial running assets. Financial reserve assets will consist primarily of liquid, but not fully liquid assets, while illiquid securities are financial investment assets. In the real world, of course, the holders of financial assets might not conceive of these categories as watertight compartments, e.g. most financial assets are not black or white (fully liquid or illiquid) but are, instead, shades of (degrees of liquidity), and the holder is not required to sharply divide his asset holdings into separate categories in his own mind. The same asset can often be held primarily for one purpose and secondarily for another.

In his perceptive analysis of *Reforming the World's Money*, Harrod noted that the management of international financial assets is 'the most important problem confronting those responsible for economic affairs in the free world'.[21] The need to manage and maintain adequate levels of international running and reserve assets are essential aspects in promoting economic prosperity in developed trading nations.

Just as for each individual there is a level of transactions and precautionary balances which is perceived as necessary to hold to meet upcoming contractual obligations, so for each nation there is a level of international asset holding ('foreign reserves' which are held by the Central Bank as running or reserve assets) which must be held as balances to bridge the gap between foreign receipts and upcoming foreign payments obligations. Individuals and nations face similar cash flow or running–reserve asset liquidity management problems. If it were possible, with perfect certainty, to coordinate exactly the time payment of all cash inflows and outflows, individuals or nations would have to hold transaction balances only momentarily, if at all. Such coordination is, of course, impossible; hence, financial assets must be held to bridge significant periods of calendar time. The greater the lack of planned coordination between contractual cash inflows and outflows, *ceteris paribus*, the greater the need to hold stocks of running and reserve liquid assets. In international transactions this need manifests itself in the need for foreign exchange holdings which are positively related to (a) the flow-level of foreign contractual obligations coming due, (b) the lack of coordination between international inflows and outflows, and (c) a need for precautionary or reserve assets to cover possible but unpredictable emergencies in foreign transactions cash flows.

In a closed UMS, any individual's cash holdings can increase at the expense of others; but, in the aggregate, any aggregate expansion of cash balance holdings by the public requires an increase in the domestic money supply (i.e. the liabilities of the banks and/or the government). Similarly, each nation can individually increase its foreign exchange holdings at the expense of others, but from a global view all countries cannot on average simultaneously increase their total holdings of running and reserve liquid assets unless new international liquid assets are created. In a closed UMS system every increase in planned expansion of economic activity requires an increase in the money supply via the 'income-generating finance' process,[22] if 'congestion' in the money market (which can constrain expansion) is to be avoided. In a similar manner international liquid assets must increase concomitantly with planned international trade expansion.[23]

There is no existing financial mechanism which assures the confluence of the growth in the supply of international reserves and the needs for such balances as the volume of international trade expands. Of course, some have argued that if exports and imports grow at identical rates, there is *no* need to expand the international reserve base – as if goods exchange for goods in international trade without the intermediation of money. Consequently, proponents of this 'barter' view of international trade proclaim that the only financing problem faced by nations engaged in international trade is that of financing a trade imbalance. There are, according to this view, no financial constraints to international trade as long as $B = 0$ for each trading partner with exports and imports growing concomitantly *over time*.

Once uncertainty and the impossibility of perfect coordination of cash inflows and outflows are recognized as an inherent characteristic of all trading relations, it is obvious however that an increase in international reserve holdings (liquidity) is a necessary condition for expanding trade even in the event that expansion does not increase the size of trade deficits. Even if expansion of trade is balanced, if cash inflows and outflows are randomly distributed over time, then Bernoulli's Law of large numbers would suggest that as trade expanded, the *absolute* discrepancy between cash inflows and outflows for each nation at any point of time would increase; hence, larger international reserves would be needed to finance these 'temporary' absolute cash flow imbalances even if in the 'long run' and on average, no nation would wind up with a trade deficit or surplus. [24]

Consequently, just as expansion of the money supply is a necessary prerequisite for expanding economic activity in a closed UMS, so the expansion of international running and reserve asset supplies is a necessary precondition for the orderly continuous growth of international economic activity. In the days of the automatic gold standard, if world gold supplies entering international asset holdings increased (due to new production) less rapidly than world trade, there was a tendency towards 'congestion' in international financial markets which constrained the growth of trade; and this limitation was in addition to the separate question of how individual nations could finance their ensuing trade deficits when international activity did not expand at an equal pace in each nation.

In the following chapters, we shall therefore attempt to analyse and deal separately with the problems of

(1) how to finance a trade imbalance, assuming no change in total international trade,

(2) how to finance global growth in international trade assuming no additional trade imbalances; and finally

(3) how to finance trade imbalances when there is simultaneous growth in international trade.

6 International Money and Liquidity

The fundamental question for monetary theory is: Why do people hold money which is barren, rather than interest bearing securities or productive physical goods? The answer must involve uncertainty about the future and the inability to precisely coordinate cash inflows with contractual cash outflow commitments.

The holding of money and other very liquid running and reserve assets provides protection for economic agents against the continual threat of bankruptcy when expected discrepancies or unexpected disruptions in the cash inflow–cash outflow process occurs. The holding of sufficient liquid assets is the only known form of preventive medicine for the otherwise fatal disease of insolvency whose incidence is highly correlated with uncertainty regarding future events. This need for liquidity to stave off potential cash flow maladies is the same whether a closed UMS or an open NUMS is under discussion, but the uncertainties (and hence the need for liquidity) are multiplied in the latter case by the incertitude regarding exchange rate variations between the time an international contract is signed and the time payment commitments come due.

It is the need for liquidity in an uncertain world which led Keynes to his analyses of the motives for holding cash – a 'study in depth of a majesterial quality not matched in the present century'.[1] Keynes' trifurcated classification of money holdings into transactions, precautionary and speculative balances, despite the fact that money is held in a single pool 'which the holder is under no necessity to segregate into three watertight compartments'[2] is an incisive analytical tool. Nevertheless it is a less exacting monetary analysis than his *Treatise* investigation of bearishness and finance, for it is in the *Treatise* that Keynes' 'views about all the details of the complex subject of money . . . are to be found'.[3] In my *Money and the Real World*, the complex monetary analysis of Keynes' *Treatise* was blended into the liquidity classification system of the *General Theory*. In this volume, the principles of *Money and the Real World* are generalized for open NUMS nations.

DOMESTIC MONEY SUPPLIES IN A NUMS

In a closed economy, the quantity of money held by the public depends solely on the liquidity demands of domestic residents, and on the quantity of reserve assets available to the national banking system *operating under the rules set down by the Central Bank and the State*. In an open economy on the other hand, the demand and supply forces for a local money are more widely dispersed geographically, and do not stop at the borders of the domestic economy. The widespread existence of well organized spot international money markets (whose transactors include multinational corporations, as well as foreign and domestic residents, and the national banking systems of the various countries) provide both an additional potential source of local money demand and a potential source of domestic money supply. These international complications may put control of the domestic money supply beyond the conventional policy actions of domestic central banks.

Under a fixed exchange rate system domestic or foreign residents who are holders of currency A can, whenever they choose, freely convert their holdings to the money of country B without any capital loss. The central banks in A and B, by pegging the exchange rate, must respond, *ceteris paribus*, by expanding the supply of money B held by the public (domestic or foreign), while concomitantly reducing the quantity of A's money held by the public.[4] With Central Banks ultimately making the market for foreign currency at a fixed rate of exchange, any individual can increase his holdings of liquid (money) balances by demanding either foreign or domestic money. Thus, for example, if the aggregate demand for money by the French increase, they have two alternative sources of satisfying this increase in total demand. Domestically the French may borrow from their own banking system, which may create additional money to meet this increased demand. Alternatively, the French can go to a foreign banking system (e.g. the United States) or even to the Eurodollar market[5] to borrow funds. In these latter foreign transactions, however, French residents initially receive a foreign currency; but since under the fixed rate system the Bank of France has fixed the value of francs in terms of foreign currency, Frenchmen can then readily convert their foreign money holdings directly into francs. The French present their foreign currencies at the Bank of France which, in turn, is obligated to give them francs. Accordingly, under a fixed rate system, foreign money running and reserve assets are direct and perfect substitutes for domestic money assets. Increased ownership of foreign money allows the individual, at his own option, to increase his quantity of domestic money held or vice versa. The Central Bank has therefore given holders of foreign monies the ability *to initiate* an increase in domestic money supply in order to, *ceteris paribus*, increase aggregate demand. By actively intervening in the exchange market to maintain a fixed price, the Central Bank makes foreign money *a fully liquid asset*, i.e. 'an asset which is perfectly substitutable for the domestic currency in meeting the liquidity needs of the domestic residents'.[6]

In a fixed exchange rate system, therefore, an individual in country A should be completely indifferent between holding his own country's money or foreign money for meeting his contractual obligations as they come due in the future, as long as he is *completely* confident in the Central Bank's ability to maintain a fixed exchange rate. From the supply side the domestic and foreign monies are transferable at will in fixed proportions, and changes in the supply of one currency will not, *ceteris paribus*, induce changes in the demand to hold another. Individual portfolio holders should not care which currency they hold as a store of value. The denomination of money balances only becomes important to them when they have to discharge a contract denominated in one currency or the other.

FIXED v. FLEXIBLE RATES AND ASSET HOLDINGS

In reality fixed exchange rates are *never* absolutely fixed. Under the gold standard, the exchange rates could fluctuate a few percentage points. Under most modern 'fixed' exchange rate systems, Central Banks agree to intervene in the exchange market only after the exchange rate moves by a specified (but usually small) per cent. For example, in the currency arrangement known as the European Monetary System or EMS, France, West Germany, the Netherlands, Ireland, Belgium and Denmark have pledged, at least in the short run, to prevent their currencies from rising or falling against each other by more than 2.25 per cent while Italy has pledged a 6 per cent margin. Thus, for example, if the Danish krone rises 2.25 per cent against the Belgium franc, the Central Banks of these two nations should be selling krone or other reserves and buying Belgium francs.

In such a fixed rate system, there is still flexibility of exchange rates within a small range, specified in advance. In the normal course of events, slight imbalances in trade due to seasonality, random causes, variations in stockpiling, or phases of the business cycle do cause some oscillations in payment inflows and outflows. Such variation will affect the demand and supplies of the currencies of the trading partners leading to some weakening of the spot exchange rate for the nation running a payments deficit. As long as this is perceived as a temporary aberration, this change in the spot exchange rate will induce comptrollers of multinational corporations (and others who engage in international trade and finance), who normally deal with cash flows involving both currencies due to contractual commitments, to buy more of the weaker currency to hold and sell some of their holdings of the stronger currency. Such transactions will reduce the trader's expectations of the real cost of meeting future commitments in both currencies, thereby creating market forces which would tend to move the price towards the original exchange rate after the 'temporary' decline.

The rationale for such transactions is easily illustrated. Suppose currency A's exchange rate declines by 1 per cent. The comptroller of the XYZ Multinational, knowing he has a contractual payment in terms of in the near future, will have to decide whether to buy currency A spot or at the future commitment date. The weaker the exchange rate *vis-à-vis* the 'normal' rate, the greater the incentive to purchase currency A on the spot, for this will mean substantial savings compared to the 'normal' exchange rate, as long as there is *complete confidence* in the ability of the Central Bank to maintain the normal rate.[7] Thus, whenever the exchange rate change is perceived to be temporary and short-lived, the elasticity of expectations will be by definition approximately zero. Thus, the institution of fixed exchange rates will normally induce expectations that tend to stabilize and restore the normal exchange rate. These private actions provide leads and lags in trade payments and help maintain a 'fixed' exchange rate with a minimum of Central Bank direct intervention in the foreign exchange market.

If, on the other hand, a 1 per cent weakness of currency A occurs in a *freely* flexible exchange rate system, no one can be sure whether, in the future, the rate will move further away from the original rate or in the reverse direction. If international transactors are on average split evenly (in terms of payment commitments) between those who think the weakness is temporary (inelastic expectations) and those who think it will worsen (elastic expectations), there will be no adjustments in the leads and lags of private trade payments. Moreover, if the preponderant view is that the current weakness in the exchange rate is a signal of still further large declines to come, then the elasticity of expectations will be elastic and the leads and lags in private sector trade payments will tend to reinforce the current decline. Elastic expectations create instability and induce a process of cumulative exchange rate decline. As Hicks has noted

> Technically, then, the case where elasticities of expectations are equal to unity marks the dividing line between stability and instability. A slight disturbance will be sufficient to make it pass over to instability. . . . Thus even when elasticities of expectations are equal to unity, the system is liable to break down at the slightest disturbance.[8]

Whenever there is a perception of weakness in the exchange rate in a flexible rate system, the *uncertainty* about the future value of the currency A increases and the elasticities of expectations are likely to become elastic. Transactors, in a multi-currency world, are likely to reduce their transactions and precautionary balances of the weakened currency and substitute (as running or reserve assets) either other currencies which are perceived as stronger or other internationally marketable assets (e.g. gold) whose value in terms of currencies in which future contractual commitments are denominated is expected to increase. The more flexible the exchange rate system is perceived to be, therefore, the more likely any apparent weakness in currency will induce perceptions of greater uncertainty about the ability of that currency to maintain its value *vis-à-vis* other currencies. Thus the more probable it is then that private sector liquid asset holders will abandon the weakened currency as a running and reserve asset. The 'gnomes of Zurich' often abandon a currency for transaction and precautionary reasons, and not necessarily for the prime purpose of speculation. The gnomes may have no idea as to whether the market is properly evaluating the possibility of further market declines in the weakened currency, but they will sleep better at night if they move their precautionary holdings to a safer liquidity time machine. The resulting movement to other currencies accentuates the weakness of the threatened currency and thus fosters a further depreciation. Flexible exchange rates in an uncertain world where unforeseen changes are inevitable must, *ceteris paribus*, increase the extent of exchange rate changes, for any given exogenous disturbance. This disturbing fact in itself should create disincentives for long-lived international commitments by international traders.

As long as the exchange rate system is perceived to be one of fixity, changes in portfolio composition tend to correct weaknesses due to 'temporary' trade payments imbalances. If exchange rates are perceived not to be fixed, however, individuals are no longer indifferent to the proportions of the various currencies they hold either as running or reserve assets. Moreover, once flexibility in exchange rates is widely expected, foreign and domestic monies become potential objects of speculation in themselves. Current changes in exchange rates *relative to expected future rates* induce portfolio shifts, in the same manner as changes in the current rate of interest *vis-à-vis* the expected future rate of interest induces changes in the quantity of money demand for speculative purposes in the traditional liquidity preference theory. Furthermore in a real world of uncertainty *and change*, flexible exchange rates must mean that the elasticities of expectations can hardly be assumed to be inelastic or approximately zero for any length of time. In the absence of financial institutions and well established practices whose explicit function it is to severely limit the time rate of change in the spot exchange rate, expectations can readily become elastic so that any current unexpected changes in exchange rate, whether ephemeral or permanent, can induce destabilizing views about the future. If the elasticity of expectations is elastic, then the existence of an equilibrating price vector which includes foreign exchange rates cannot be demonstrated. Even if existence could be demonstrated, stability is threatened. In the non-fixed exchange rate system existing since the breakdown of the Bretton Woods Agreement, Central Banks have had to increase their active intervention in spot exchange markets to achieve some modicum of stability.[9]

Yet defenders of freely flexible exchange rates implicitly *assume* that such unconstrained systems must possess an equilibrium price vector which clears all markets simultaneously and that any observed change in exchange rates would be stabilizing rather than destabilizing. These proponents of flexible rates suggest that if Central Banks removed themselves as 'makers' or supporters of the foreign exchange market, then private sector entrepreneurs – presumably international bankers – would move in and 'make' the foreign exchange market. Moreover it must be assumed, since these international bankers are motivated solely by the profit motive (as opposed to the nationalistic pride or political myopia which, it is claimed, motivates Central Bankers), the private sector exchange market makers 'know' the true parameters of the exchange market (or at least have 'rational expectations') so they can make the correct adjustments in the exchange rates over time.

Accordingly, *in the long run*, it is claimed freely flexible exchange markets would always adopt the exchange rate which maintained a general equilibrium among all trading partners; for if the original private 'market' makers did not do their job properly, they would go broke, and other international bankers would spring up and ultimately do a better job in identifying the correct equilibrium prices over time. This view assumes, as a starting point, that there exists a stable equilibrium price vector over time despite unexpected change and the potential for bankruptcy by private sector international bankers who 'make' the foreign exchange market.[10]

Only if the private sector bankers who 'make' the spot exchange markets can 'fully anticipate' the future can the threat of bankruptcies and the ensuing discontinuities that threaten the existence of a general equilibrium solution be avoided. In an uncertain world, however, there is no reason to believe that private bankers could 'fully anticipate' future economic and political events – more fully than Central Bankers, and the governments of the trading partners. Recognizing that it is humanly impossible to 'fully anticipate' the future, the question is then raised as to why private profit-maximizing bankers would be motivated to even try to identify the 'proper' long run equilibrium exchange rate. Why should profit maximizing bankers have any different motives or behaviour from the aforementioned comptrollers of multinational corporations? As has already been demonstrated, the actions of this latter group in a freely flexible exchange rate system are likely to accentuate actual movements in exchange rates induced by any random shock. International bankers should act in a similar manner, especially if these private sector bankers are aware that expectational elasticities of others are likely to be elastic in such a system. For whether we are talking about private sector dealers in security markets in a closed system, or those in foreign exchange markets in an open system, 'life is not long enough; – human nature desires quick results, there is a peculiar zest in making money quickly. . . . Furthermore, an investor who proposes to ignore near-term market fluctuations *needs greater resources for safety.*'[11]

Private sector foreign exchange market makers will therefore need more liquid assets as reserves to maintain 'long run equilibrium' (if there is such a thing!) in the face of short-term payment ebbs and flows than Central Bankers would require under a fixed exchange system.[12] Furthermore, even if any of the private bankers had sufficient reserves to swim against the short-term tide towards the assumed existent and stable long run equilibrium position, and therefore most promote the public interest, such a banker would be considered idiosyncratic or eccentric by the public and his professional colleagues and,

> will in practice come in for most criticism. For it is the essence of his behavior that he should be eccentric, unconventional and rash in the eyes of average opinion [otherwise, he would not be swimming against the tide of public opinion] . . . .*Worldly wisdom teaches that it is better for reputation to fail conventionally than to succeed unconventionally.*[13]

If private bankers are therefore to be entrusted with the 'making' of foreign exchange markets while they are motivated by profit opportunities, they will find it easier to achieve success by swimming in the lead of the tide of public opinion rather than trying to buck the short-term currents.[14] Under such circumstances instability rather than stability is likely to be the rule under any but the most stationary of economic environments.

In the absence of any institutional foreign exchange market-maker (either the Central Bank or private bankers with preferential access to the Central Bank)[15] foreign currencies could therefore lose much of their liquidity value for domestic residents in turbulent times. In these circumstances, foreign reserve holdings would provide such facilities only to those domestic residents who had planned foreign contractual obligations upcoming in the very near future. For all others, such holdings would be illiquid and hence very dangerous. Autarky and/or bilateral barter transactions would become more prevalent with the attendant losses in global real income.

It may be argued that a truly flexible exchange rate without any private or Central Bank market-maker to limit short-term exchange rate movements and thereby inspire some *confidence* in the stability of the current exchange rate, would be equivalent to operating in a closed economy where no forward money contracts could be used for organizing production and trade. The necessity for entrepreneurs to limit their future liabilities via forward money contracts (e.g. payrolls and raw material costs) before undertaking long duration productive activities has already been noted. Moreover, 'The convenience of holding assets in the same standard as that in which future liabilities may fall due and in a standard in terms of which the future money cost of output is expected to be relatively stable, is obvious.'[16] Hence, as long as there are well organized *and* orderly markets for foreign exchange, then entrepreneurs can store value in either domestic or foreign assets with the full confidence that at any moment they can convert the foreign denominated asset into the standard in which expected international liabilities are falling due. But well organized, orderly markets are, in a world of uncertainty, impossible without the presence of a market maker who is willing to swim against the tide even if it means incurring losses.

The trick of the entrepreneurial money economy game lies in the need to hold over time assets whose value can be computed in terms of the same units as future liabilities and future money costs of production are expected to be relatively stable! In a world of non-predictable change, there can be no store of value over a period of calendar time in an entrepreneurial economy, unless liabilities are fixed in some nominal unit over the time period. Whatever is the nominal unit of contractual obligation has a unique role to play in an entrepreneurial system. Since the money wage contract is the most ubiquitous forward contract in non-slave societies, the money wage plays a predominant and persistent role in the determination of employment and the market prices of producible goods. In an entrepreneurial economy, '[t]he firm is dealing throughout in terms of sums of money. It has no object in the world except to end up with more money than it started with. *That is the essential characteristic of an entrepreneur economy.*'[17]

In an open economy where multinational firms deal in production contracts denominated in different money units, the object of the firm will be to end up with more money than it started with no matter which nominal units the books of the firm are kept in. Thus expected stickiness of exchange rates over the life of the production period (for production contracts) is a desired condition for firms engaging in long-term production commitments that cross national boundaries.

MONETARY POLICY IN THE FACE OF SUBSTITUTABILITY

An important question relating to the topic of monetary regulation is whether a fixed exchange rate system or a flexible rate system enhances the ability of national Central Banks to control the domestic money supply and more efficiently execute monetary policy. With fixed exchange rates, currencies are perfect substitutes, implying that the individual wealth holder is indifferent to which form he stores his money in.[18] With this indifference between foreign and domestic money, a basic tenet of orthodox monetary theory is violated, for there is no longer a limited range of monetary assets which are clearly under the control of the local Central Bank. Domestic residents can, for instance, increase the domestic money supply by selling new debts to foreigners for foreign money and then converting the latter to local currency. Since the domestic Central Bank cannot control the quantity of money in foreign countries, the Central Bank cannot control the quantity of money potentially available to domestic residents.

Even if we assume that changes in the quantity of money can influence aggregate effective demand, the Central Bank may be unable to exploit this influence via monetary policy because it is unable to always initiate and control all changes in the quantity of money. If, for example, the Central Bank of country A via open market operations exogenously increases the money supply in order to encourage additional domestic production, then at the initial rate of interest the money supply of A exceeds the domestic demand for A. Let us assume that residents in country A can and do desire to use some of the initial increase in the money supply to purchase bonds from abroad, i.e. from country B. If an expansion of the domestic supply initiated by Central Bank A leads to an increase in lending of residents of A to residents of B, then the Central Bank in A will find that its initial expansion of the domestic money supply creates a *ceteris paribus* balance of payments deficit which is matched by a balance surplus in B. Foreigners in B could, if they wish, convert their additional receipts of currency A into currency B, thereby increasing the money supply in B. Of course, Central Bank B might return money A to Central Bank A, eliminating part of the initial increase in the quantity of money in A at the cost of a loss of international reserves by Central Bank A. The substitutability of international monies under a fixed exchange rate system makes the money supply of the countries involved interdependent. Any initiating money supply expansion in one country can lead to changes in money supplies and/or aggregate demand effects in all trading partners. (Obviously, this illustration is oversimplified as we have ignored adjustments in interest rates in both countries which will occur as well.)

It appears to follow from this illustration that one of the appealing aspects of a move to flexible exchange rates to advocates of such a system is the promise that countries can now more easily regulate their inflows and outflows of money. The presumed increase in the ability to regulate comes from two sources. Firstly, because the Central Bank no longer guarantees the value of domestic money in terms of foreign money, foreign money is no longer a perfect substitute for domestic money. Thus, holding a given quantity of foreign currency no longer means, for a wealth holder, holding a specific quantity of domestic currency. There is now risk of capital gain or capital loss as no Central Bank is willing to convert domestic and foreign currency at some unchanged rate over time. Secondly, because the Central Bank no longer intervenes in the foreign exchange market, it is often assumed that the net movements of monies among nations are zero, i.e. domestic money supply does not endogenously respond to changes in international capital flows. It is usually asserted that there are therefore no longer leakages in the money supply through official intervention and that all the effects of the domestic money policy are felt within the domestic country. To quote Milton Friedman

In effect, flexible exchange rates are a means of combining interdependence among countries through trade with a maximum of internal monetary independence; they are a means of permitting each country to seek for monetary stability according to its own lights, without either imposing its mistakes on its neighbors or having their mistakes imposed on it.[19]

Flexible rates, then, are *assumed* to provide countries with the monetary independence that permits the implementation of their own unique policies as proposed by Monetarists.

The flexible rate system of the 1970s did not produce the period of sustained monetary tranquillity that its proponents had hoped for. There were still periodic flows of 'hot' capital and inflation rates in excess of what monetary authorities desired. Governments still found that despite the greater flexibility of exchange rates, money supplies among countries remained interrelated, and the promised absolute control over the domestic money supply remained elusive. Many economists are perplexed as to why the exchange rate of some countries should depreciate significantly more than indicated by simple rules such as purchasing power parity or relative rates of monetary growth.

Obviously the flexible exchange rate system did not work as its proponents had hoped. In particular, the anticipated dominance and control of a Central Bank over domestic money supplies has failed to materialize. The behaviour of monetary aggregates and exchange rates is a clear indication that the ability of domestic authorities to regulate the domestic money supply is far from complete. But how can domestic money supplies circumvent the government's control? If only the French like to buy and sell in francs, and only the English execute contracts in pounds, must not all francs find their way back to France and all pounds to England? And if the Bank of France is the only supplier of francs (and the Bank of England of pounds) does not the Bank of France (or the Bank of England) therefore control the quantity of francs (or pounds) that Frenchmen (or Englishmen) have for buying or selling? And if the Bank of France will not support the exchange rate, how can foreign money holders affect the French money supply?

The problem with this argument is that it simplistically assumes that money is held *only* as a medium of contractual settlement; it does not recognize that as long as well organized exchange markets exist, foreign monies are potential liquidity time machines as well. In the Friedman argument that flexible exchange rates provide monetary independence between nations, there is the implicit assumption that domestic residents will not view foreign currencies as substitutes for local money and other domestic liquid assets as stores of value. It is implicit in the Friedman approach that residents will only demand the money of their own country for liquidity purposes. Of course, as long as domestic contracts for labour performance and the delivery of goods are denominated in domestic money terms, individuals engaged in domestic economic transactions will continue to require domestic money for immediate and near future planned purchases. As long as the domestic money remains by law and/or by custom the medium of contractual settlement, domestic money will and must be held to meet these transactional commitments for the short period of time before they come due. Nevertheless under certain circumstances domestic transactors might find foreign currencies more appealing as longer term liquidity vehicles.

If, for example, economic agents expect either a change in the exchange rate and/or inflation in terms of future domestic prices, several adjustments might occur involving the substitution of local and foreign currencies and the changing of the format of further contractual commitments.

Firstly, if there is a well organized market for foreign exchange, and if there are new (or growing) expectations that, compared to the domestic money, the foreign currency will have more stable purchasing power in terms of domestic labour time and domestic (or foreign) goods, then local residents will utilize more of the foreign money as a store of value during the period before expected payments from current contractual commitments come due. This will put, *ceteris paribus*, downward pressure on the exchange rate which will in turn reduce the foreign exporters' markets and thereby create unemployment abroad unless the foreign Central Bank creates additional foreign currency to take care of these liquidity and unemployment pressures.

Secondly, if inflation in domestic prices of goods and services is expected, individual sellers will attempt to shorten the length of their contractual commitments as they will be unwilling to commit their sales price over long periods of time during which they do not know what the money costs of their inputs will be. This in itself will encourage more inflationary movements in the price of new goods over time. Finally, if the transactions involve traders from various countries, sellers may not only shorten the duration of their contracts, but desire to alter the denomination of their contracts, from the domestic money supply to the foreign money supply.

In sum, if expectations grow that the domestic money will be less stable compared to foreign monies in terms of purchasing power over producible goods, then the public will shift their liquidity preferences towards foreign money holdings. This increased demand for foreign currency as liquidity time machines will cause pressure on the exchange rate and the potential for a loss of export markets for foreigners unless the foreign Central Bank expands their money supply to mop up these additional liquidity demands. Consequently as long as organized exchange markets are freely available to the general public and Central Banks feel a responsibility to alleviate liquidity pressures which can depress economic activity, the Monetarist view that under a regime of flexible exchange rates each nation can pursue its independent monetary policy is not valid.

Instead, in a world of uncertainty, where payment flows occur over calendar time and individuals must commit themselves to make money payments at specified future dates, Keynes' theory of liquidity preference, generalized for an open NUMS system, suggests that individuals will hold a diversified portfolio of liquid money assets including foreign currencies and other foreign denominated liquid assets for precautionary purposes. The liquidity demands of residents in an open system is consistent with the desire for diversity and this is especially true when various nations are expected to display differing rates of inflation. If the expected loss in purchasing power of the domestic money rises compared to that expected for a foreign currency, rational residents will increasingly rely for liquidity on foreign monies which are expected to be more stable (in terms of purchasing power of domestic and foreign produced goods and labour) than domestic money. Domestic and foreign monies are always substitutes in demand for running and reserve assets as long as well organized exchange markets exist, and movements in exchange rates can be magnified by elastic expectations in a system of flexible exchange rates, whenever unexpected changes occur.

In a fixed exchange rate system, however, since various monies are always (near) perfect substitutes as liquidity machines, the public is basically indifferent (except for a convenience factor) as to the proportion of the different monies held in their portfolios at any point of time or over time. Convenience in meeting contractual obligations rather than changes (actual or expected) in exchange rates dictate the portfolio composition of different currencies.[20] The introduction of a degree of flexibility in the system means currencies are no longer perfect substitutes in demand, and individuals' demands for holdings of various monies will be affected by expectations of future changes. In either case, however, the Monetarists' implicit assumption of a zero demand elasticity of substitution between domestic and foreign monies is false.

In the context of the current (1980) system of non-fixed exchange rates, prices of foreign currencies are significantly constrained by Central Bank intervention and rules. Hence the public's demand elasticity of substitution among major currencies may be very large but it is far from infinite. For example, multinational corporations, having strong incentives to diversify the currency composition of their cash balances in order to facilitate meeting the productive contractual commitments in various countries, will be particularly sensitive to varying the composition of their holdings as exchange rates are expected to alter. Even individuals and businesses that are clearly domiciled in a particular country will have precautionary or speculative motives for diversifying the currency composition of their money holdings as long as exchange markets permit rapid, inexpensive conversions of various currencies. Moreover, anyone who consistently makes some purchases from foreign countries has at least the same transaction motives for demanding foreign currency balances. Importers and exporters, businessmen and tourists who travel abroad, residents of border areas, etc. all have incentives to diversify their monetary balances. By holding foreign money the uncertainties in the costs of their future foreign purchases are reduced.

Accordingly, as long as various monies are perceived as potential alternative liquid time machines in an open economy with a well organized foreign exchange market each Central Bank is constrained in its ability to pursue an independent monetary policy. This limitation on the ability of Central Banks to regulate where monies are substitutes in demand has important implications for such issues as an European currency area and the proper world monetary system. For example, should or could the world system emphasize independent national monetary control for internal stability? Alternatively, should the system emphasize cooperation and coordination at the expense of monetary independence? Currency substitution provides a good criterion for resolving this issue. If the currencies of two countries are close substitutes in demand for liquidity purposes, then the monetary and other economic policies of the two nations cannot be independent. Hence two or more nations whose currencies are close substitutes should be encouraged to coordinate their monetary policies as a 'bloc' rather than move in separate directions. The more currencies that are close substitutes, the larger should be the 'bloc'.

The increasing trade among the European countries, for example, has opened new avenues of monetary movement. Money now moves quickly and easily from European currencies to determine which one is the most opportune for placing their current balances. Residents of countries such as Italy where the currency is least stable hold increasing quantities of more stable currencies. These developments all point out that European currencies are becoming closer and closer substitutes in demand. At the very least, the European countries are prime candidates for a unified currency area, either in the form of a common currency or separate currencies linked by permanently fixed exchange rates. However, the fact that empirical estimates indicate that foreign currencies in general are good substitutes for the U.S. dollar indicates that the optimal 'bloc' may be much closer to the entire world. In that case the countries of the world should consider abandoning the current regime of floating rates and return to a fixed exchange rate system that encourages the synchronization of monetary, fiscal and incomes policies.

7 Finance and Trade in NUMS v. UMS

Over two centuries ago, Adam Smith recognized that the growth of the wealth of any nation was dependent on its ability to foster specialization of production tasks in order to provide the economies of scale of a mass production technology. At any point in history the ability of entrepreneurs to introduce increasing specialization into production activities is limited by the size and the potential near-term growth of the market. Progress can therefore be purchased by trade with other nations. The obvious moral of Adam Smith's analysis is that no economy which desires the rapid accumulation of wealth for itself can remain an island unto itself.

FINANCE AND GROWTH

Keynes' finance motive analysis[1] demonstrated that, in a closed UMS, the national banking system held the key to facilitating the transition from a lower to higher scale of economic activity. As long as mass production processes must be planned ahead if they are to be efficiently organized, then entrepreneurs in non-slave or non-cooperative economies will require the institution of long duration forward contracts to ensure the cooperation of factor owners in delivering factor services and materials according to the production schedule. Since these contractual commitments require factor owner payments (cash outflows) before the product is sold and sales revenues (cash inflows) are received, entrepreneurs must be assured they can obtain sufficient finance to meet these earlier production cash outflows. Any inability to obtain sufficient financial commitments today prevents entrepreneurs from undertaking production activities today, no matter how profitable these production processes are expected to be at a later date when the product is produced and sold to final buyers. Any shortage of finance today due to the banking system's refusal or inability to expand the medium of contractual settlement to meet the enlarged contractual obligation necessarily involved in any planned aggregate expansion of production flows, will quickly squelch entrepreneurs' ability and their enthusiasm for growth.

Forty years before the Monetarists raised the question of 'crowding out', Keynes noted that if the banks do not lend more to entrepreneurs as spending plans increase, these plans will be thwarted and 'the public can save *ex ante* and *ex post* and ex anything else until they are blue in the face, without alleviating the problem in the least'.[2] If the banks

> refuse to relax, the growing congestion of the short-term loan market or the new issue market, as the case may be, will inhibit the improvement, no matter how thrifty the public propose to be out of their future income . . . The investment market can become congested through a shortage of cash. It can never become congested through a shortage of savings. *This is the most fundamental of my conclusions within this field.*[3]

In entrepreneurial systems of organizing production, economic growth requires a banking system that will provide an 'elastic currency' so that the expanding needs of trade can be readily financed. In the absence of banking institutions which can provide an endogenous money supply, an entrepreneurial, market-oriented production economy will find that its best made plans for expansion will be stymied.

Unfortunately, the same banking system which provides a mechanism for the endogenous expansion of the money supply to meet the needs of trade (the real bills doctrine), does not normally distinguish between entrepreneurial increased requirements to finance larger payrolls due to (a) increased employment (at a given money wage) associated with any enlarged production flow and (b) higher money pay per unit of labour effort (after adjusting for changes in labour productivity), i.e. higher efficiency wages or unit labour costs of production. Consequently, a banking system designed to provide a financial environment which eases the transition to greater employment and output flows, is also capable of passively supporting inflationary forces due to economic, social, and political demands from various groups for higher money incomes in order to obtain, *ceteris paribus*, a greater share of any aggregate output flow. In other words, any financial structure which is appropriately designed to provide an endogenous money supply under the real bills doctrine is simultaneously capable of creating a permissive environment for wage or profit margin inflation. Any healthy banking apparatus which meets the needs of trade can be subverted to create an elastic currency of 'inflation bills' rather than 'real bills', and any deliberate policy aimed at restricting the banking system's ability to issue 'inflation bills' will therefore concurrently limit its ability to supply sufficient real bills to maintain or increase economic activity.

In this chapter, in order to simplify the exposition, the discussion will be limited to the financing of *real* growth. Any analysis of an endogenous expansion of the money supply to meet the (inflationary) demands to finance higher money costs of production (money incomes) must be postponed. Accordingly, at this stage, it will be assumed that any increase in demand for finance is either for a planned expansion of domestic production and employment and/or a planned discrepancy between exports and imports.

FINANCE, MAINTAINING INCOME AND CASH FLOWS

If an economy is in a stationary equilibrium state where employment, money wages, prices and output are unchanged over time, then in each production period, output flows, incomes generated, and the level of effective demand must also be by definition unchanged. In such a hypothetical state, entrepreneurs are, at the beginning of each period, planning to maintain the same day-by-day working capital position as they did in the previous period. Since production takes time, even in a stationary state, and since cash outflows for factor payments precede cash inflows from sales of the final product, entrepreneurs will require, in the current period, the same financing commitments from the banking system as they have just repaid on the last day of the previous production period when they liquidated their working capital position. The finance provided by the banking system permits entrepreneurs to organize each period's production flows. Thus, in a stationary state, bank finance is a revolving fund where the current period's planned production activities are essentially financed by the funds returned to the banking system, as entrepreneurs liquidate their past period's working capital position. Schematically, in an ideal stationary state, the cash flow positions of the banks, entrepreneurs and households at any point of time *during the period* are at exactly offsetting phases, while over the period the net cash flows of all three groups are zero.

FINANCE, EXPANDING INCOME GENERATION AND CASH FLOWS

Since production takes time, expanded production activities require prior additional financing commitments as entrepreneurs enlarge their position in working capital goods. This increase in entrepreneurial position taking is an integral process of a production-forward contracting economy, where firms must meet additional hiring and material purchase contractual obligations before the enhanced flow of goods is finished, sold, delivered, *and* paid for. Consequently, planned expansion in economic activity *must* involve, *ceteris paribus*, either the prior expansion of the money supply or prearranged available overdraft facilities with the banking system.[4] Starting from a position of output flow–finance equilibrium, if there is an increase in aggregate entrepreneurial planned commitments for the purchase of additional fixed and/or working capital goods – and before the actual expansion is under way – the money markets' commitments for financing investment plans *at the initial rate of interest* will, *ceteris paribus*, exceed actual savings.[5]

In any modern monetary economy, planned expansion of domestic production which generates additional national income (ΔY_d^g) requires, *ceteris paribus*, a prior expansion of the domestic money supply to ease the problem of entrepreneurs' expanded cash outflow commitments during the gestation period of increasing output. Although the income-generating finance process is usually associated with increased investment spending in a closed economy,[6] a similar finance process would be at work in an open economy whenever the value of planned export production flows is increasing.

If current contractual cash inflows from the sales of goods and services (income) exactly match, moment to moment, contractual cash outflows on goods and services (expenditures) for *all* agents simultaneously, there would never be any aggregate cash flow problem. It might appear therefore, that entrepreneurs who plan production flow increases could finance the increased cash outflows by simultaneously increasing forward contractual sales. Even if forward sales were to increase *pari passu* with forward production commitments (as would be the case in an entrepreneurial economy which only produces 'to order' and not 'to market')[7] however, entrepreneurial economies would still require that cash outflows due to production commitments *precede in time* the receipts of sales revenue from the product. Hence, for each individual entrepreneur as well as in the aggregate, firms cannot match at the same point of time cash outflows for increased factor payments with cash inflows from the sales of larger output. Instead, entrepreneurs must rely on the banking and financial system to create finance to meet the earlier (in time) planned increase in factor income generation as they take larger working capital positions.

The banking system's role in providing additional finance for expansion in order for cash inflows to match current contractual production cash outflows is even more obvious when entrepreneurial plans are geared to expected spot market sales rather than forward sale contracts. (This is, of course, the typical neoclassical textbook case, as well as the case for most retail sales in the real world.) In this 'produce-to-spot-market' situation production cash outlays must manifestly precede in time product sales receipt cash inflows. Thus, whether markets for the sales of final products are organized on a spot market or on a forward contract basis, as long as production is organized on a forward contract basis (the essence of an entrepreneurial system), the matching of daily cash inflows with outflows requires the banking system to provide a revolving fund of finance if an economy is in a stationary state, or an expanding fund of finance if entrepreneurs plan to expand economic activity. Given the fact that production takes time and that factor owners demand payment before the end of the production period in a non-cooperative system, the ability of firms to withstand a net cash outflow due to hiring commitments during the days before the end of the production period requires borrowing for working capital finance from the banking system.[8]

Since production cost outflows are, by definition, someone's income, the financing of such production flows is simultaneously a process for generating money income.[9] Whenever entrepreneurs plan to increase production flows, they must hire more inputs, thereby incurring additional cash outflows during the production process. For any single entrepreneur, the immediate increase in his production cost cash outflow will initially be financed by either having accumulated pre-existing idle cash balances or readily marketable assets (e.g. IOUs) which can be sold to obtain cash to make up the flow deficit. If the firm had previously accumulated idle cash balances, then, *ceteris paribus*, some other agents (firms and/or households) must have been experiencing net cash flow deficits, which have to be *ultimately* financed at some point of time via the banking system expanding the money supply.

Any individual entrepreneur wishing to expand his production flow can resolve the problem of financing his ensuing cash deficit during the production period by selling new securities to other entrepreneurs who are currently running a cash inflow surplus. This avenue of finance is not available however, if in the aggregate, entrepreneurs today plan to expand production flows and hence increase payroll and other factor costs, and aggregate demand for finished goods today (which were in the process of production 'yesterday') is not to be reduced below the level sufficient to buy all of today's final output. If households lowered their demands for today's final output in order to provide additional finance for the entrepreneurs planning to expand production flows, then all of today's final available output (whose costs of production were financed by yesterday's working capital bank loans) could not be sold at profitable spot prices today. This would create an unresolvable liquidity problem for entrepreneurs today! And it would be of no use to entrepreneurs to know that households were willing to save to finance an expansion of tomorrow's production flows, when entrepreneurs found they could not sell today's final products at prices which permitted them to pay off yesterday's bank loans.

In the aggregate, if entrepreneurs wish to increase their working capital positions, they must obtain additional finance which can only be accommodated by a *pari passu* commitment of the banking system to purchase additional securities in exchange for an expansion in the money supply. This, in turn, provides the wherewithal for settling the increased volume of contractual commitments which productive expansion requires. Consequently, the banking system has an important and unique role to play in providing the required additional liquid funds whenever entrepreneurs in the aggregate plan to increase the income flow of the community by expanding output and employment flows. The importance of this liquidity–financial market method of generating income and wealth was succinctly summarized by R. F. Kahn when he wrote

the total wealth of the community (together with its National Debt) is represented by the total amount of securities in existence and by physical assets held directly. Part of the securities are held by the banks themselves; part of the securities held by the public is financed by the banks; and banks finance the holding of physical assets by business, thus reducing the supply of securities [held by the public]. The extent to which the banks hold securities, finance the holders of securities, and finance the holding of physical assets, is equal to the quantity of money. *The quantity of money is the means by which the public hold that part of their wealth which is looked after by the banking system.*[10]

Entrepreneurs, attempting to increase their aggregate position in working capital goods, will have to borrow against (expected or actual) additional future sales contracts in order to be able to meet their increased cash outflows as they expand their hiring and raw material purchases. (This process is equivalent to the *construction funds finance procedure* for fixed capital described in Chapter 3.) If we start from an equilibrium position where cash outflows are being matched by inflows, and production flows are unchanged, and then hypothesize an aggregate expansion of planned production requiring increased payroll payments, etc., then the banking system endogenously expanding the money supply to meet the immediate financial needs is an essential requirement for carrying out expansion plans in any entrepreneurial system.

CASH FLOWS AND BANK CLEARING

As a first approximation, assume that all contractual payments are processed through the banking system of a closed economy (rather than via hand-to-hand currency disbursements). Whenever the current level of production is in equilibrium with sales, agents are, *over the period*, in a matching cash flow position. Finance is a revolving fund flowing around the banking system, while all banks are on average, over the production period, in balance at the clearing house and the aggregate bank deposits held by the public are *ceteris paribus*, unchanged.

Since any planned expansion is unlikely to be equally dispersed over all sectors and regions of the economy, any increased spending on production will immediately throw some banks into deficit at the clearing house during the period when additional production is being fabricated and inputs paid for, but before the finished product is available for sale. If the Central Bank is sensitive to these expansionary financial problems, additional reserves will be provided for these deficit banks, permitting them time to tide entrepreneurs over the production period until purchases by other sectors (due to higher incomes) create a return flow through the clearing house.

This time lag for clearing the flows via the necessary expansion of bank reserves is even more apparent when expansion of production involves interregional and international trade. During a period when there are no trade imbalances and trade flows are neither increasing or decreasing, contractual settlements occurring at the interregional (and international) clearing house are such that on average all regional and national banking systems are in balance. If on the other hand any trade payments deficit develops, it will immediately lead to interregional (and international) bank clearing problems which can be resolved either by the loss of reserves by the deficit banks, or by the creation of additional reserves for the deficit banks, or the borrowing of reserves from surplus banks by the deficit banks. The ability of the combined interregional and international banking system to resolve these clearing house payment difficulties will be a measure of the capacity of trading partners to overcome any obstacles to growth which, by the very nature of an entrepreneurial economy, must begin with some changes in net cash flows.

FOREIGN LENDING AND FINANCE

Whether an economy is open or closed, planned expansion of domestic production processes to meet expected or actual forward orders of either domestic or foreign buyers will require the domestic money supply to increase in proportion to the increase in domestic factor input and material production costs. (Of course, if some factor owners or raw material suppliers are foreigners, then, *ceteris paribus*, foreign money supplies will have to increase *pari passu* with the increase of these foreign inputs into the expanding aggregate working capital unless the foreigners are willing to hold domestic money as a liquidity time machine.)

Similarly, a planned increase in country A's expenditure flows on imports from country B, which is in addition to the total flow demand for goods produced in nation B, will require B's banks to increase the supply of B's currency to finance the expansionary plans of B's entrepreneurs to meet A's increased demands as they are manifested today in either additional forward contract contractual orders or expected future spot sales. During the production period needed for B's entrepreneurs to increase export output, additional finance is needed in B to facilitate additional hiring in B's export industries. When, at the end of the production period, increased finished output flows are available for export to A, then A's residents will require additional liquidity from holders of B's currency in order to finance the hypothesized trade deficit caused by the increased flow of orders for B's exports.

The foreign lending balance (L) is a variable which reflects the net differences in loan (and equity) transactions between residents in B and the rest of the world. In the absence of unilateral international transfers (or gold movements), an excess of the amount of B's money loaned to its trading partner A, over the amount of A's money lent to B's residents at the current exchange rate, i.e. a positive net foreign lending position by nation B, is a necessary *ceteris paribus* condition for B to finance an export surplus to A.

Foreign lending is always expressed as a 'net' figure. It involves financial contractual commitments between domestic residents and external agents (over a given period) which places domestic currency or claims to such currency at the disposal of a foreigner (in return for either title to a foreigner's property, or a foreigner's promise to pay) in excess of corresponding contractual obligations which put foreign currency at the disposal of domestic residents. (Keynes had noted that net foreign lending might be termed 'an unfavourable balance on *capital account'*.)[11] Any expansion of world trade must, *ceteris paribus*, initially involve some increase in net foreign lending by those nations whose exports are expanding more rapidly as the world's aggregate liquidity increases concomitantly.

FINANCING TRADE DEFICITS WITHOUT A CHANGE IN GLOBAL AGGREGATE DEMAND

An increase in L due to an increase in A's demand for imports from B *at the expense of home produced goods*, would simultaneously increase A's demand for foreign currency as a running asset while lowering A's transaction demand for domestic money. In this case where the increased demand for imports is solely a substitute for domestic production, there would be no change in A's total demand for money (domestic plus foreign).

In a closed UMS system, the absence of change in the aggregate demand for cash balances would be obvious. As region A merely substituted imports from B for its own regional production there would be no change in the public's cash holdings, only a redistribution between the regions. To the extent that residents of A had idle balances (reserve money assets), they could draw these down to finance the trade deficit. Over time, however, this interregional redistribution of domestic bank balances via a change in clearing house patterns would threaten some banks and their customers with running out of cash. Assuming no policy actions by the Central Bank or the State to recycle funds at that stage (or before), asset holders in the deficit region (or their bankers) would have to sell 'fully integrated' marketable assets to the surplus region in order to reflux money to A's banks so that A can continue to purchase the products of B. Ultimately over time, if there is a persistent trade deficit and offsetting asset selling pattern (B's net foreign lending being positive), then A will run out of marketable assets and/or promises it can pledge to gain replenishment of its money holdings for transaction purposes.

Most orthodox economists would argue that net interregional trade deficits and offsetting net foreign (regional) lending on production and income accounts cannot go on indefinitely. In the 'long run', some adjustment mechanism must end the persistent trade deficit. This 'long run' view that trade deficits and net foreign lending (refluxing of funds) cannot endure *assumes* the absence of either

(1) a government fiscal policy which deliberately recycles income (and money balances) from the surplus to the deficit region, or

(2) unilateral grants (private or governmental) as a reflux mechanism, or

(3) the continuous creation of additional bank reserves for the deficit region's banks by the Central Bank.

It is true that in the absence of one or more of the aforementioned mechanisms to reflux money, the deficit region's banks will find that they are having increasing difficulty in meeting their clearing house obligations that are being incurred at current rates of economic activity and trade. Because of their clearing house problems, A's bankers will reduce their level of lending to their customers, who in turn will be forced to lower their expenditures including those on the products of region B. Due to the resulting shortage of liquidity in A, it will become a depressed economic area. Nevertheless, as long as regions A and B are in the same UMS, there will be no change in the exchange rate between the money used to denominate contracts in region A and the money used as the basis of contracts in B.

In sum, even if aggregate spending and economic activity are unchanged, the occurrence of trade deficits (and therefore cash flow problems) between regions in a UMS can create important liquidity problems. Trade deficits between regions cause interregional cash flow payment difficulties, with the trade deficit region spending more on foreign production than it earns on foreign sales. If the banking system is responsive, these cash flow imbalances will initially induce a liquidity finance process between residents of the deficit region (and their bankers) and residents of the trade surplus region (and their bankers). Deficit region residents and their bankers will continually finance the region's trade imbalance of imports over exports by either (a) selling pre-existing *liquid* reserve assets to residents or bankers in the trade surplus region, or

(b) by borrowing funds from the surplus region by selling foreigners either a new debt contract or a title to property.

The deficit region must either have (a) sufficient saleable *reserve assets* to weather the expected period of the deficit or (b) sufficient expected *promising future prospects* to finance the deficit. The deficit cannot be expected to continue indefinitely through calendar time. The surplus region, it is assumed, will be economically 'rational' about its economic relations to the deficit region and, therefore, will not continuously give up current real goods indefinitely into the future for promises (to pay back real goods) which are never redeemable. In other words, there is a presumption that the deficit will not be financed indefinitely by unilateral transfer payments, gifts, or promissory notes which are never called.

If, however, both regions are encompassed within the same national boundaries, the central government's taxation and spending policy can act as a transfer device, and help finance at least some or all of the deficit *indefinitely*. The magnitude of finance thus provided depends on the tax burdens of each region *vis-à-vis* the central government's propensity to spend in the deficit region compared to the surplus region. (If, for example, the deficit region is either undeveloped or an area of high unemployment, modern central government taxing and spending patterns are likely to permit the financing of deficits as long as these economic discrepancies between regions persist.)

In the absence of government fiscal policy or private unilateral transfers, the primary private sector mechanism for financing regional deficits involves the banks or the residents of the deficit region selling assets to the surplus region. This requires that the assets held by residents of the deficit region and/or their bankers are readily marketable in the surplus region. Consequently, any institution which makes regional assets more widely marketable will ease the difficulties in providing finance for interregional payments. The willingness of a Central Bank to either directly and continuously 'make' a market in the local commercial paper and other debt instruments of deficit regions, or to act as lender of last resort for such financial instruments can therefore ease interregional payment pressures and avoid liquidity problems at the interregional clearing house. The need to sell securities by the deficit region's banks can be offset, *ceteris paribus*, by the desire to buy liquid assets by the surplus region's banks, public, or Central Bank. Hence, deficits due to regional imbalances in export–import flows can be, if the Central Bank is perceived to be willing to support local financial asset markets, readily offset by reverse deficits in net interregional lending. In the short run, activity or support by a Central Bank in spot markets for regional financial assets can prevent any interregional liquidity problems due to interregional balance of trade deficits from depressing economic activity.

Of course, if the Central Bank is not sufficiently active in supporting the market for local financial assets, then the market value of these assets will weaken as their stock is continually liquidated to finance a recurring deficit. The deficit regional banks will see that their reserves at the Central Bank relative to their business activity are declining over time. This reduction in value of reserves to turnover will cause some banks in the deficit area to worry that their liquidity positions are being impaired, and cause them to restrict credit availability to their customers in order to regain liquidity.[12] This in turn will reduce the region's aggregate demand for goods and services. If the Central Bank is not sufficiently active in the regional markets, there will not be sufficient liquidity for the current level of interregional activity, and each bank in the deficit region will have to reduce its lending operations, forcing a decline in employment activity and a reduction in the region's imports.

On the other hand, if the Central Bank supports (directly or indirectly) the market for such assets, then the resulting liquidity creation will permit the planned aggregate demand to remain operational despite the trade deficit. The result will be to provide a higher total level of income and wealth of *both* trading partners (as otherwise idle resources are employed) *vis-à-vis* the situation where there is no financial intervention by the Central Bank. The development of national banking systems headed by *pro bono publico* Central Bankers has therefore often served to offset or at least limit the deflationary forces which interregional trade deficits can generate.

FINANCING TRADE DEFICITS BETWEEN NATIONS IN A NUMS

There are two important additional complications to financing trade deficits if regions A and B are in different nations using different monies and possessing independent banking systems and non-fixed exchange rates. Firstly, there is no central government authority which can provide taxing and spending policies to provide recycling fiscal actions at an interregional clearing house to offset trade deficit-induced losses in liquidity. Secondly, in the absence of a prior agreement between the governments of the trading nations that each will be willing to purchase liquid assets from the other at a fixed price without limit, trade deficits can unleash market forces which may change the exchange rate between the national currencies. This will, *ceteris paribus*, reduce the market value of the deficit region's marketable assets in terms of the foreign currency, and cause a further reduction in liquidity (value of reserves to turnover) for those banks in the deficit region who finance trade between the nations in the NUMS.

Neither of these complications are inevitable! Governmental grants and loans can prevent either or both. For example, the United States' Marshall Plan for Western Europe in the late 1940s and the U.S. Lend–Lease Agreement with England a decade earlier were *planned* programmes for government to recycle liquidity in order to balance the otherwise unfinanceable (under the traditional rules of the game) huge trade deficits of England and Western Europe. This liquidity refluxing was done for political reasons; nevertheless it impressively illustrates that there is no natural *or* national law which prevents authorities in trade surplus areas from redistributing (recycling) purchasing power and assets for as long a period as they wish – *with obvious and widespread economic* benefits to residents of both the surplus and the deficit region.

Even if the possibility of intergovernmental unilateral transfer payments to resolve the financing of interregional trade imbalances is ignored, as long as the banks of each region are members of a single banking system with a Central Bank at its head, then this interregional (international) Central Bank operating as *the* monetary authority can continue to create sufficient balance sheet reserves for the banks of the deficit region by acting as a 'market maker' for the assets (including debt pledges) that residents of the deficit region wish to sell. These created balance sheet items can finance the trade deficit.

If the deficit region's banks are experiencing interregional clearing house difficulties, the Central Bank can readily replenish their clearing reserves by buying the 'loan, discount and advances' debt instruments of the banks' customers. By thus acting as a 'lender of last resort', the Central Bank can always liquify, *if it so wishes*, any assets the region's bankers (or their customers)[13] want to sell. If the Central Bank is willing to 'monetize' the debt obligations of trade deficit regions, it can create sufficient liquidity to finance each period's deficit for as long as the residents of the trade surplus region (and their bankers) are willing to hold the 'money' of the Central Bank for liquidity time machine purposes, and as long as the Central Bank believes it is reasonable to do so without jeopardizing the 'confidence' of its customers in the 'soundness' of its policies.[14] In so doing, it will, *ceteris paribus*, increase global real income and wealth!

In the modern world, national Central Banks are *not* members of a well-organized international central banking and clearing house system. Consequently, the ability of any national Central Bank to provide liquidity for its citizens in the face of an external trade deficit is closely circumscribed by its initial holdings of gold and other foreign reserve assets which foreign Central Banks (or foreign private citizens) are willing to buy. Thus, the ability of the nation's Central Banker to accommodate its clients is often less than that of regional bankers in a modern national banking system where the nation's Central Bank actively aids the 'making' of markets for regional commercial paper. In the absence of such local activity, deficit regional bankers (like the 'independent' national Central Bankers on an international scale) would only be able to finance clearing house deficits due to interregional trade imbalances as long as they (or their customers) hold widely marketable assets whose values would not be readily depressed by significant sales. National Central Banks must hold significant quantities of internationally marketable assets if they are to help their clients – significantly more than they would need if there was a supranational Central Bank willing to help 'make' markets for local (national) assets.

Furthermore, in an NUMS system, the 'liquidity' of any marketable asset used to finance international transactions is subject to an additional complication, namely the uncertainty of exchange rate changes. This is in addition to the market price uncertainty of any liquid asset in terms of domestic money. Consequently, in an open NUMS economy, because of the multiplication of uncertainties about the value of running and reserve financial assets (which must be held to manage international cash flows as a result of spot and forward contractual obligations), any region requires, *ceteris paribus*, a larger stock of reserve assets for any given volume of trading with external partners than a similar region operating within a UMS.

When the nations of the world operated under an automatic gold standard, then gold and the direct holdings of foreign currencies were the running and reserve assets which bought the time to make whatever economic adjustments were deemed necessary while sustaining a trade deficit. Except for minor fluctuations between the gold points, the exchange rates were fixed and therefore nations could operate *as if* they were (nearly) in a UMS system with (near) fixed market values for gold and foreign exchange in terms of either local currency. Under such a scheme, given the magnitude of trade flows, each nation's international running and reserve asset holdings could be lower than if the exchange rates were not fixed; or larger trade flows could be financed given the global holdings of gold. For any country running a given trade deficit, its holdings of reserve assets determined the length of calendar time in which adjustments and policy changes could be phased to minimize disrupting dislocations. In a NUMS on the other hand, whenever any nation runs a trade deficit, uncertainty regarding the international value of its reserve assets are increased and therefore, *ceteris paribus*, the time frame for phasing-in orderly adjustments and avoiding wrenching changes is reduced. Thus, trade deficits (which are inevitable in a world of change) occurring in a NUMS tend to encourage hasty and potentially destructive financial reactions relative to the adjustments to similar circumstances occurring under a UMS.

REPLENISHING RESERVES IN A UMS

In the present state of the world, any attempt to form an international UMS (for at least some of the more developed nations) requires 'contractual' agreement among the Central Banks of these nations.[15] The Central Banks must agree on 'rules of the game' which permit fixing of exchange rates and then must accept or invent a common 'reserve' asset which each Central Bank agrees, *in advance*, to 'buy' with domestic currency under pre-specified rules. This advance obligation of the Central Banks ensures that if any national banking system gets into trouble at the international clearing house, the deficit banking system or its Central Bank can sell (*at its own option*) its 'reserve' assets to cure its clearing imbalance.

As long as reserve assets are well distributed among the participants, the game of international trade can continue and flourish, with obvious real gains to all who play. But, as in the famous Parker Brothers board game that children play named 'Monopoly', if any participant runs out of the means of settlement when he lands on a square which requires a payment to another participant, then that player defaults and is forced out of the game. In the 'Monopoly' board game, play can continue for long periods of time because there are pre-existing rules for replenishing liquid assets, e.g. 'When you pass Go, collect $200.' Such an inflexible rule does not ensure that a player will never become insolvent and have to default; it merely ensures the possibility of $200 excess of cash outflows over revenue inflows for each trip around the board. This rule of the game ensures that the medium of contractual settlement in the hands of the public (players) can expand as players move more actively around the board, in turn ensuring that the game can go on longer than if the money supply were constrained to a zero or small fixed rule of growth per unit of time, independent of the performance of the players. This rule for expanding the money supply as players pass 'Go' is not ideal in terms of providing for an elastic currency, for ultimately the game does end when some players overextend their investments and some unexpected action creates an obligation which they cannot finance (i.e. when a liquidity shortage occurs). Nevertheless, this rule for increasing a player's liquidity is indirectly associated with the player's activity in obtaining and developing properties which can be financed through the increase in the payments' medium.

In the real world game of an entrepreneurial economy, it is socially desirable that development continue forever, that is that the game never end. This goal of a perpetual game in which players' activity promotes continuous growth and property development would require a more flexible rule for costlessly expanding liquidity than that in the game of 'Monopoly'. In the real world game of international trade and finance, any agreement to form a UMS must have some rules for replenishing reserve asset holdings in general, and redistributing such assets from surplus to deficit banking systems if the game is to grow, rather than come to an end – ending the enjoyment of most, and perhaps all of the participants. In the real world, ensuring that the international trade game and finance availability continue to grow over time, under rules which treat all players fairly, is a necessary condition for improving the welfare of all. Mankind can surely devise financial rules and institutions which encourage nations to produce goods up to their maximum full employment level and trade with each other.

To keep the game going and growing, an international UMS would require each Central Bank to relinquish its desire to engage in a completely independent domestic monetary policy. This perceived fear of loss of national autonomy due to joining a supranational banking and clearing system is largely a bogus anxiety. The loss of complete economic self-determination is the cost of any permanent trading relationship. Economic autonomy means complete economic isolation, for trading partners can affect a nation's economic health. Autarky can be purchased only at the cost of a lower level of aggregate real income. International trade, on the other hand, means unavoidable interdependence and feedback effects among the trading partners – and potentially higher real income. Trepidation over the loss of the current degree of national autonomy has been a fundamental factor preventing 'rational' nations from instituting some form of supranational Central Bank to coordinate more efficiently the liquidity–finance methods for generating additional income among trading partners. Nevertheless, it is obvious that a well designed supranational Central Bank, staffed by a management that comprehends the need for additional liquidity as a prerequisite for generating additional income for open entrepreneurial economies, could contribute significantly to the more rapid global growth of real income and employment. Until national governments recognize this elemental truth, private sector banking interests will, on their own, continue to develop makeshift institutions (e.g. Euro-currencies) which do provide additional international liquidity for the expansion of world trade. Unfortunately, these temporary expedients often tend to fail at the least propitious time as they are unable to weather a liquidity crunch when cash flow imbalances inevitably develop with expansion.

Some Monetarists have argued that if nations adopted a freely flexible exchange rate system where national Central Banks *never* interfered in exchange markets and never provided a means of replenishing international reserves, then private sector bankers would 'make' the market in foreign currencies. Such privately made currency markets, it is claimed, would be more efficient in that they would promote *more* trade at lower real costs than any internationally agreed fixed exchange rate system. Under such a flexible rate system however, private national banking systems could continue to finance clearing imbalances only as long as the deficit nation's bankers had marketable reserve assets to sell to the residents of the surplus region. As soon as the private bankers observed a decline in their holdings of reserve assets, they would operate as prudent bankers under the conventional rules of conservative banking. The deficit region's bankers would reduce their loans to customers thereby reducing their need to hold as large a stock of running and reserve international assets. Bankers would then change relative interest rates in the two regions and/or the exchange rate to induce domestic residents of the deficit region to reduce their demand for foreign goods and foreigners to lend more and buy more domestically, and the deficit nation's net foreign lending is assumed to decline. (This assumes that any current devaluation does not induce expectations of further exchange rate declines in the near future, i.e. it assumes that elasticity of expectations ≈ 0.) Foreigners, under the axiom of gross substitution, will buy more imports and lend more abroad. In sum then, the Monetarist argument requires a belief in the universality of gross substitution and a zero elasticity of expectations, for it to be claimed at least that a *freely* flexible exchange system will encourage rapid changes in relative prices ensuring *after perhaps some 'short run' disruptions*, a sufficient substitution mechanism to yield a long run full employment equilibrium.[16]

Unfortunately, freely flexible exchange rates encourage elastic expectations whenever unexpected events occur, and therefore they possess the potential for the collapse and devastation of all entrepreneurial systems in turbulent times. The real world cannot rely upon assumed large and rapid positive substitution effects and zero elasticities of expectations to cure unexpected trade imbalances in the long run without killing the patient.

A freely flexible exchange rate system need not imply instability as long as there is little or no unexpected change over time, as in a stationary state, or even in a 'steady-state' growth model. In these cases although the exchange rates are theoretically flexible, they either do not change or their rate of change is known to be small and normally less than the *known* rate of interest. Thus, exchange rates are assumed to be *sticky* over time. Of course, entrepreneurial economies can live with flexible exchange rates *provided* it is known with perfect certainty that they will not become unhinged. Professor Friedman, in his debate with me, claims there is

> a confusion between flexibility and instability that has done so much to impede understanding of the desirability of flexible exchange rates. A price may be flexible, in the sense that it can and does change promptly in response to changes in demand and supply and that there are no institutional obstacles to its changing, yet be relatively stable, because demand and supply *are relatively stable over time* (e.g., this was the case with the exchange rate of the Canadian dollar in 1950s). Violent instability of prices in terms of a specific money would greatly reduce the usefulness of that money; however flexibility of prices in terms of that money has no such effect.[17]

It may be reassuring to some to know that flexibility does not imply instability as long as the exchange rate is relatively stable over time, because supply and demand forces are (assumed) stable over time. Keynes' description of Ricardo's analytical approach is, in my view, more appropriate for portraying Friedman's panache, for he

> offers us the supreme intellectual achievement, unattainable by weaker spirits, of adopting a hypothetical world remote from

experience as though it were the world of experience and then living in it consistently. With most of his successors common sense cannot help breaking in — with injury to their logical consistency.[18]

In his bold assertion that flexibility does not imply instability as long as market forces are stable over time, Friedman has removed (by assertion) the fundamental problems of uncertainty and change that plague real world systems. Yet he continues to suggest policy prescriptions for modern economic systems that are currently and continuously rocked by precipitous and unexpected shocks.

In the real world, established patterns of trade are necessary prerequisites for low cost exchanges of goods and services. Established trade patterns require long lived investments in distributive channels and facilities. These, in turn, require long-term contractual arrangements *and* confidence in a sticky rate of exchange, so that money prices and the resulting contractual commitments are 'sticky' over time for both parties involved in long-term international contracts. In the absence of such 'confidence', for example, how could a farmer in country A 'know' at planting time what his revenues will be from the harvest of his crop, if a significant portion of his historical market has derived from the residents of nation B? Yet, without some confidence (at harvest time) in expected future revenues in terms of domestic currency, a farmer would be foolish to take a large position in the working capital of seed and fertilizer at planting time. Similarly, should the farmer take a position in fixed capital such as vines or fruit trees which take many years to mature, if he is not reasonably *confident* at the time of investing in these facilities of future revenues from foreign as well as domestic markets?

The development of forward foreign exchange markets can shift the burden of exchange rate uncertainties from the entrepreneurs of export and import industries to a class of speculators; but the real cost of such uncertainties is an *additional* burden to society which cannot be completely eliminated by forward markets. Moreover, in the real world, long duration forward exchange markets (e.g. in excess of 270 days) do not normally exist, so that position taking by entrepreneurs in production or investment activities whose gestation period exceeds this span of calendar time cannot be hedged via financial transactions. Thus, in an uncertain world with freely flexible exchange rates, long-term contractual commitments are less likely to be undertaken, and the resulting level of production and trade will be less. Moreover, any attempt to move from a position of some fixity in exchange rates to one of more flexibility, unless done during a period of long-term stability in exchange rates, is likely by itself to depress all trade by inducing an increase in the elasticity of expectations itself. Since the demand for change in the system is most likely to occur only when (under the existing system) there are pressures for change in exchange rates, any recommendation for greater flexibility will encourage greater expectational elasticities and thereby greater instability. Only in a world where there is no pressure for exchange rate changes would it be possible to institute a system of freely flexible exchange rates, i.e. we can have flexibility only if we do not need it! If we start from a position of balance at the clearing house and if demand and supply are relatively stable over time, then exchange rates will be, *ceteris paribus*, stable. Flexibility is unnecessary! The test of any system's value is whether, in turbulent times, it adds to disorder or maintains at least a modicum of stability so that mollifying adjustments can occur. Freely flexible exchange rates, by adding exchange rate uncertainties – an additional real cost of trade which would not occur in a UMS – must retard Adam Smith's process of the growth of the wealth of nations via the specialization of productive activities.

TRADE DEFICITS, WAGE COSTS AND REAL WAGES IN A NUMS

Given current economic institutions there is no supranational authority which can recycle finance from trade surplus nations to trade deficit nations via a deliberate policy of taxing the former and spending more in the latter. Nor is there any international monetary authority which can readily recycle and/or replenish the running and reserve assets of trading partners. Thus, each nation must jealously guard and husband its international reserves. Each nation enhances its international liquidity position by attempting to accumulate additional international liquid assets which could be used to finance a trade deficit if one should occur. (Of course, all nations cannot concurrently build up their holding of international reserve assets unless the global total of such reserves is growing.) Enhancing liquidity can also occur by arranging in advance for international overdraft facilities to be used if a payments' problem develops and existing reserve holdings are perceived to be inadequate.

If successfully engaged in, these international liquidity augmenting activities will provide freedom and time for the nation to analyse the causes of international clearing house problems and to devise plans to cure the malady if necessary. Acceptable policies to reduce or eliminate trade deficits if international liquidity cannot be replenished might include

(1) tariffs and quotas to reduce domestic private sector spending on imports,

(2) discriminatory taxation on private sector purchases and/or holdings of foreign assets *vis-à-vis* domestic liquidity holdings, and

(3) direct control of the rate of foreign lending and long term investment, i.e. direct control of capital outflows.

If these direct actions are effective in stemming the international cash outflows and thereby preventing an international liquidity problem for the nation, and if the f.o.b. price of foreign exports (and domestic exports) remains unchanged, then the nation will have successfully maintained its existing terms of trade. Consequently, changes in domestic real earnings will be directly related to productivity changes in domestic industries.

If, on the other hand, national authorities were to permit complete *laissez-faire* in the foreign sector, and *if* freely flexible exchange rates prevailed, and *if* the national economies could withstand the short run disruptive reverberations of any trade imbalance, and *if* lending were perfectly mobile, and *if* the money wage in each nation were completely flexible and endogenously determined (as it is assumed to be in neoclassical theory), *then*, in the long run, *real wages* would tend towards equality in all nations. In this neoclassical long run wonderland, workers in any one sector or nation of the global economy could not improve their real wages except at the expense of workers in other sectors. Workers of the world could never unite to improve their common lot!

In the real world, where wages and profit margins are controlled largely by social, political, and monopolistic forces, such a long run neoclassical solution, even if possible, would occur only long after the 'capitalist' entrepreneurial system and its economic institutions had collapsed. The traverse from the current system of sticky wages, prices, exchange rates and long-term contracts, to one of flexible exchange rates, money wages and prices and *only* spot payments for all economic transactions would be so horrendous that even if the operation were to succeed, the 'capitalist' patient would be dead!

In any monetary market-oriented production economy, the real wage of domestic workers depends on the money wage, productivity, the domestic degree of monopoly *and* the terms of trade with foreigners. The struggle by each group of workers for higher domestic money wages must (given productivity, the degree of monopoly and the terms of trade) involve a quarrel over relative real wages in the domestic economy. To the extent that higher money wages favourably alter the international terms of trade, then the struggle is widened to the effort of *all* domestic groups of workers to improve their real income at the expense of the rest of the world.

If nations which were formerly related via a NUMS were to join together in a UMS, the existing relative real wage rates (per unit of human effort) and the existing 'degree of monopoly' or mark-up in each industry would be 'locked in' at the moment of acceptance of a common monetary unit. Until that point in history, the wage and profit structures that have developed in each nation would be the result of historical processes which were evolving at least somewhat independently in each region.[19] Once each nation agrees to enter a UMS, the national economic structures become so enmeshed that, given the terms of trade with the rest of the world that remains outside the UMS, significant alterations in relative real wages (or profit margins) can only occur via either (a) a social agreement on a policy to coordinate income claims throughout the UMS system, or (b) a market and political struggle among groups in the various regions of the UMS utilizing every form of social, political and monopoly power within their grasp. This struggle will continue (and therefore cause instability in the purchasing power of money), until either a large enough number of groups acquiesce to significantly lower their real incomes so as to satiate the appetite of the more monopolistic, and/or politically strong groups demanding higher real income, *or* there is a complete breakdown of the monetary system of the UMS as inflation continues and everyone loses confidence in the money as a satisfactory medium for settling contractual obligations.

If a group of nations currently organized in a NUMS agreed to form a UMS, then in order to achieve full employment throughout the UMS system, the current money costs of production in terms of the UMS's nominal unit would have to be at just the right level to match the aggregate demand for products from within the UMS plus the demand of the rest of the world. Once a common nominal unit is adopted, if the nations tried to stabilize the purchasing power of their common currency in terms of some internationally 'produced commodity' market basket, then money wages in each nation (in terms of the common currency) would have to vary with productivity changes in each nation, while the terms of trade with the rest of the world remained invariant; otherwise there would have to be offsetting movements between the terms of trade within the rest of the world and the money wages in each nation within the UMS.

8 The Stability of the Purchasing Power of Money

Production in entrepreneurial market-oriented economies is always organized on a forward-money contractual basis. The efficient planning of time-consuming mass production processes by entrepreneurs, in a world where slavery and peonage are illegal, requires contractual commitments for the hire–purchase of inputs before the production activity is undertaken. Such contracts not only ensure regular (non-casual) employment and fair treatment of labour over time,[1] but they also provide entrepreneurs with the necessary controls over factor services and costs, thereby limiting the money liabilities involved in undertaking any planned production activities.

The ubiquitous existence of forward money contracts not only forms the backbone of the organization of productive activity and sales, but these contractual arrangements are at the same time the basis for generating most of the flow of aggregate money incomes earned by engaging in such production processes. Income cannot be properly defined for an entrepreneurial economy unless this relationship between productive activities and contractual payments is understood.[2]

The stability of the purchasing power of the monetary unit in which forward production contracts are denominated is therefore of prime importance. The willingness of both contracting parties to enter into contracts for forward payments (which is an essential characteristic of entrepreneurial economies), depends on the belief that there is some measure of stability or stickiness in the purchasing power of money over time. The widespread use of the human institution of forward contracting is therefore evidence of the stickiness of price expectations, while at the same time the *existence* of a myriad of overlapping forward contracts provides the basis for such expectations.

Society's recognition of the uncertainty of future events would appear to be incompatible with the almost universal belief that the purchasing power of money to be delivered at the contractually agreed future payment date bears some anticipated discernible relation to the purchasing power of money at the date of contractual agreement.

Yet, punctilious acceptance of the law of contracts is basic to civilized behaviour in an entrepreneurial economy. As long as production is organized via long duration forward-money contracts, then social convention dictates that the contractual *money costs* of future production are to be accepted as datum over the life of such contracts. Consequently, decorum, decency and propriety of market behaviour evolve from the belief that the purchasing power of money over the goods to be produced in the near future is discernible from today's contractual cost relations. The opportunity for all to enter freely into forward contracts if desired and the existence of multitudinous overlapping forward production and purchase contracts provides all with a strong degree of confidence in the stickiness of the money costs of future purchases in an otherwise enigmatic future.

Of course this conventionality of economic life does not guarantee that current money contractual relations will ensure that prices will continue to be sticky into the indefinite future. People merely know that existing contracts limit the costs of goods currently being produced for sale in the near future. Expectations of price stability and the use of existing long duration contracts reciprocally reinforce psychological factors promoting, *ceteris paribus*, the adoption of time consuming production activities in entrepreneurial economies.

If there is no conventional belief in the stickiness of the purchasing power of the money used in settling contractual obligations, then no one would enter willingly into long-term contracts fixed in terms of that monetary unit – and hence that money would lose all its attributes of liquidity![3] If there is little or no expected stickiness in the purchasing power of money over time, then by definition price expectations will be elastic.[4] Hicks has demonstrated that the existence of elastic price expectations will result in 'a complete breakdown' of capitalism whenever current prices differ from what was previously expected.[5] Consequently, the only protection that an entrepreneurial economy possesses against destructive elastic expectations is 'price rigidities and ultimately beyond price rigidities . . . people's sense of normal [i.e. sticky] prices'.[6] It is the ubiquitous use of long duration forward-money contracts which provides the framework of money price rigidities necessary to perpetuate continued belief in the stickiness of money prices of newly produced goods. Since this psychological belief in sticky prices over time is a *necessary* condition for the continuing operation of an entrepreneurial economy, any policy which has as its objective the encouraging of greater flexibility (over time) in crucial contractual prices (e.g. policies to promote 'flexible' foreign exchange rates) will severely undermine the basis for entrepreneurs to organize long duration production activities. Any books, articles, etc. which claim that freely flexible prices, or a very rapid price speed of adjustment to changes over time $\left(\text{i.e. } \dfrac{\mathrm{d}P}{\mathrm{d}t} \gg 0 \right)$, will improve the functioning of an entrepreneurial economy are not only wrong, but are also a pernicious threat to capitalistic systems.[7]

THE MEASURE OF PURCHASING POWER

The purchasing power of money can be measured in terms of the inverse movement of three conceptually different types of price indices. These are

(1) an index of spot prices of pre-existing (secondhand) goods, including such non-reproducible goods as land, old masters, etc.;

(2) an index of the flow–supply prices of currently produced goods and services, i.e. the items that make up the current national product; and

(3) an index of the price per unit of factor services being used in today's production activities, e.g. a money wage-unit index.

If money's purchasing power is related to either a spot price or a flow–supply price index, then a *commodity* (*basket*) *standard* is being utilized as the yardstick for comparing purchasing power over time. If a factor price index is used, then an *earnings* (*labour*) *standard* is the basis of comparison. Purchasing power stickiness in terms of one standard does not necessarily imply stickiness in terms of another.

Inflation is defined as the decline over time in the purchasing power of the money of contractual settlement. The actual rate of inflation is typically measured in terms of a commodity price index which normally combines spot and forward commodity prices and often includes some factor prices (e.g. interest rates) as well. For policy purposes, however, it is clear that it is neither the rising spot price of most non-reproducible goods (e.g. antiques) nor the price of secondhand securities as traded on the New York Stock Exchange which is the focus of public concern regarding inflation. This does not mean that all spot prices are irrelevant. The spot price of land as well as those of many reproducible commodities (e.g. crops, minerals), can play an important role in the inflation process, while the spot price of non-reproducible liquid assets are often looked to as havens for protecting the purchasing power of 'savings' from the ravages of inflation.

As a stylized fact however, we may claim that inflation becomes a major cause of public concern only when it is the money flow–supply price of producible goods (mainly those that bulk large in consumers' budgets) which are increasing over time. Hence a price index composed primarily of flow–supply prices of goods, where each article's price is weighted by its relative importance in the average consumer's market basket, is conceptually the most appropriate barometer of the public's worry over inflationary tendencies. Nevertheless other price indices do exist and their use for specific purposes and contexts may be appropriate.

There are three types of commodity price indices as well as one type of earnings index which are traditionally used as measures of inflation. If the money price index of a consumer market basket is used (e.g. the Consumer Price Index or CPI), then purchasing power is being measured in terms of a *consumption standard*. If some price index of an aggregate basket of domestically produced goods is used (e.g. the GNP deflator or the Producers' – or wholesale – Price Index), then a *domestic commodity standard* is being used to measure purchasing power. If an index of domestic prices for a market basket of internationally traded goods, adjusted for changes in tariffs and transportation costs, is used, then the local money's purchasing power is being measured via an *international standard*. Finally if an index of the domestic prices per unit of human effort (or factor services) is used, then money's power is being measured via an *earnings standard*.[8]

Most published commodity price indices are averages of spot *and* forward price movements of the various goods comprising the standard market basket. Since spot prices rise (or fall) more rapidly than forward prices in times when rapidly unforeseen changes are occurring,[9] any actual commodity price index will therefore exhibit greater volatility than one composed solely of flow–supply prices whose average movements are constrained by existing forward contracts. Nevertheless, to the extent that prices in pre-existing forward contracts are geared to current changes in some actual index of spot prices (e.g. 'cost-of-living' adjustments in labour contracts, or fuel adjustment clauses in public utility rates), then initial changes in spot prices can, *ceteris paribus*, induce rapid changes in forward contract factor prices and the resulting flow–supply prices of output. Thus it is possible for a hypothesized increase in a spot price to induce increases in newly produced commodity prices and/or earnings if the latter two are institutionally geared to the former.

Table 8.1 compares the movement in the various domestic prices indices over the period since 1960 for the U.S.

TABLE 8.1   U.S. Price Indices (1960 = 100)

Year	CPI	Money Wage Index	GNP Deflator	Wholesale Price Index
1960	100.0	100.0	100.0	100.0
61	101.0	103.1	100.9	100.0
62	102.1	106.5	102.8	100.3
63	103.4	109.6	104.4	100.0
64	104.7	112.5	106.0	100.4
65	106.5	116.3	108.3	102.1
66	109.6	121.6	117.8	105.4
67	112.7	127.6	115.1	106.7
68	117.5	135.5	120.1	109.7
69	123.8	144.4	126.5	113.8
70	131.1	154.0	133.2	117.7
71	136.8	164.8	139.7	121.3
72	141.3	175.4	145.6	125.1
73	150.1	186.2	153.9	136.5
74	166.5	200.9	167.3	157.4
75	181.7	217.6	182.8	174.4
76	192.2	233.4	192.3	181.8
77	204.6	251.0	203.5	192.7
78	220.3	271.6	218.3	207.7
79	245.1	293.1	237.0	230.6
80 (prelim)	279.4	319.7	258.4	261.2

SOURCE   *Economic Report of the President*, January 1981. Tables B–3, B–36, B–80, B–55.

The stickiness of purchasing power, according to Table 8.1, will vary according to which domestic commodity or earnings index is used as the yardstick. If an international standard is used to measure the local money's purchasing power, then stickiness depends in part on the proportion of the international commodity market basket which is produced abroad, and on factors which affect the movement of the prices of these foreign goods *vis-à-vis* the prices of domestically produced goods in the standard international commodity basket. Hence even if a local money is stable in terms of a domestic commodity standard, its international purchasing power may change due to changes in foreign economies.

Each nation will be able to stabilize the purchasing power of its money in terms of both the international and domestic standards only if two conditions are simultaneously met, and international capital flows or changes in demand do not alter the exchange rate. These conditions are

(1) that the efficiency wage (i.e. the money wage rate relative to labour productivity or unit labour costs) in both domestic and foreign industries producing goods in the international standard market basket is unchanged; and

(2) that the average degree of monopoly (as measured by the gross profit margin as a percentage of unit labour costs) is unchanged in these industries. Unless these conditions are met, or changes in efficiency wages are just offset by the degree of monopoly changes in specific industries, any attempt to stabilize the purchasing power of a local money in terms of an international commodity standard will involve decreasing (or increasing) the purchasing power in terms of the domestic commodity standard.

The efficiency of local labour at any point of time as well as the rates of change in labour productivity over time differ widely (a) in various regions of the world, (b) in different industrial sectors, and (c) even in the same industrial sector in different nations. If the purchasing powers of various local monies are all to be stabilized in terms of some internationally traded market basket of commodities, then differential rates of change in domestic money earnings over time in each industry will have to be geared to productivity growth in each industry that produces goods for international trade. Money wages per worker will have to increase most rapidly for those nations (regions, industries) where labour productivity is rising most rapidly.[10] If in some nations export industries are experiencing the most rapid growth in productivity and money wages and if the relative wage structure in each nation is fixed or sticky over time, then such nations will experience the most rapid decline of purchasing power in terms of *the domestic earnings standard.*[11] Nations with slow productivity growth rates will experience relatively little growth in money wages, while any nation experiencing a decline in labour productivity (e.g. the United States in 1979–80) will require that money wages decline in order to avoid inflation. Thus, if nations are to be successful in stabilizing the purchasing power of their respective domestic monies in terms of an international commodity standard, then the money earnings per worker in the various nations will have to *diverge* as long as labour productivity trends among nations diverge.

It will be impossible for all local currencies to be simultaneously stabilized in terms of an international commodity standard, if the average degree of monopoly (profit margin mark-up) is increasing in industries that produce the international market basket unless (a) the degree of monopoly increase is equally distributed among the trading industries of all nations, and simultaneously, (b) the money wage rate falls (or rises less than local productivity growth) sufficiently in each nation to offset profit margin increases. The smallest wage declines will be in those nations displaying the greatest relative growth in labour productivity.

The creation of an oil cartel such as OPEC, whose industrial base is concentrated in a few nations and whose specific objective is to redistribute real income from oil consumers to oil producers by increasing the mark-up over labour costs on crude oil, threatens the purchasing power of the local currencies of oil-consuming nations in terms of any international commodity standard in which energy is an important component.[12]

RELATIONS AMONG VARIOUS PURCHASING POWER STANDARDS

In any open NUMS, if a local currency possesses significant stickiness of purchasing power in terms of an international commodity standard, then its stability in terms of a domestic commodity standard will depend upon both (a) the relative importance of internationally traded goods in domestic production and consumption activities, and (b) the average domestic efficiency wage and degree of monopoly in all domestic industries (including those which do not produce for exports). Thus if all nations successfully pursue domestic incomes policies which gear money wage changes in each domestic industry directly to changes in labour productivity in each industry – or a policy where, *on average*, domestic wage changes are geared to domestic productivity changes – and if there are no changes in the average degrees of monopoly, then purchasing power stability in terms of either an international or a domestic commodity standard may be attainable.

Of course, international stability of purchasing power may, under some circumstances, give rise to the possibility of simultaneous trade payment imbalances. If these imbalances are permitted to affect the exchange rate (or if the exchange rate is deliberately altered in an attempt to eliminate these imbalances), then international purchasing power stickiness is jeopardized. If international stability of purchasing power is considered desirable but is achievable in unfettered markets only at the cost of continuing trade deficits and surplus, then there can be justification for policies designed to eliminate the payments imbalances via (a) the use of tariffs or quotas; (b) programmes which encourage surplus nations to import more goods; and (c) programmes which recycle the surplus payments back to the deficit nations via either loans (if the imbalance is thought to be temporary) or by automatic grants (if the imbalance is permanent despite efforts of type (a) and (b) above).

Whenever any important trading nation pursues a policy which will secure an improvement in its own terms of trade, i.e. to increase the purchasing power of the local currency in terms of an international standard, then except by a fortuitous offsetting of many factors, there can never be a stable international standard for all the various domestic monies. Exchange rates will, *ceteris paribus*, have to alter as relative labour productivities and relative degrees of monopoly power vary over time among nations.[13]

Each nation, of course, does have it in its power, if it can secure the agreement of its residents, to stabilize the local currency in terms of a domestic commodity standard. To achieve stability in terms of both a domestic and international standard, however, requires the coordination of income policies among trading partners. This coordination includes an agreement to maintain constancy of the terms of trade at their initial ratio, if future international purchasing power stability is to be achieved. If such an agreement on fixing the terms of trade is impossible (as is the current situation between oil consumers and OPEC), then any consuming nation wishing to stabilize its money in terms of a commodity standard including international goods must either (a) be willing and able to guarantee two-way convertibility between the commodity market basket and the domestic money;[14] or (b) control domestic efficiency wages in such a manner as to cause unit labour costs plus mark-ups in domestic industries to offset, on average, changes in the domestic money prices of foreign produced goods (as indicated by equation 4.13 in Chapter 4).[15]

Assuming no change in the degree of openness of a nation and that no nation can afford to maintain a stock of important international goods for the purposes of two-way convertibility, then any nation facing a situation where the terms of trade are becoming adverse has to make a choice of which path of adjustment to follow. Such a nation can attempt either to

(1) maintain the purchasing power of money in terms of a wholly domestic commodity standard via a domestic incomes policy which

gears money wage increases to domestic productivity increases while permitting an erosion of purchasing power in terms of any commodity standard which includes imports; or

(2) maintain purchasing power in terms of an international standard by developing an incomes policy which limits money wage increases to less than domestic productivity growth by an amount sufficient to offset the effect of imported inflation (as calculated by equation 4.13 of Chapter 4); or

(3) permit unfettered markets to enforce money income constraints on domestic residents. The process through which this occurs will differ somewhat in each nation, depending on how imported inflation affects existing domestic labour and product markets and brings about domestic liquidity problems that reduce employment, output and real income.

Policies (1) and (2) involve direct, explicit incomes policies where all residents can be informed, in advance, as to the real costs of adverse change in the terms of trade in relation to their specific economic position. Policy (3) indirectly enforces a Darwinian incomes policy where each resident is uncertain about the personal incidence of the real costs of change in the terms of trade. Under policy (3) each resident is encouraged to, and required by the rules of the 'free' market game to try to push off as much of the burden on to others in the economy. Since the real costs cannot be avoided by all, the effect is to exacerbate inflationary tendencies. These pernicious tendencies not only gravely weaken the operation of any entrepreneurial economy, but they can destroy the social fabric which holds every society together, as every citizen is locked in a Darwinian struggle for economic survival with each other as a result of economic hardships imposed by external sources. Policy (3), therefore, should be everlastingly prohibited as a legitimate course of action by all enlightened governments.

Policies (1) and (2) involve different paths for money wage rate changes over time (given productivity growth). Neither policy need involve unemployment if successful domestic money wage (and profit margin) controls can be pursued. Moreover, policy (2) offers the potential for stable exchange rates despite the adverse change in the terms of trade. Exchange rate stability will reduce exchange rate uncertainties, and thereby enhance the willingness of entrepreneurs in each nation to enter into long-term international contractual relations.[16]

Although international contracts of, say, 90-day duration or less can be readily hedged by both parties via the forward exchange market, this adds a real cost to transactions – one which would not exist if the trade occurred within a UMS. (This real cost must be borne by someone – namely, the speculator who takes an open position in forward exchange.) Consequently, any NUMS imposes a *real* cost on society, a cost that a similar system organized on a UMS basis would not impose on trade between nations (or regions) as long as the local monies were not stabilized in terms of an international standard. There is, therefore, a real and substantial cost savings possible for large trading partners who simultaneously pursue policies which stabilize their local currencies in terms of an international commodity standard.[17]

In a world where there are differential rates of productivity change, it will be impossible to maintain simultaneous stability in terms of an international standard, a domestic commodity standard, and a domestic earnings standard. Purchasing power stability in terms of all three standards cannot be maintained simultaneously – except in a system where no change occurs. Nor can absolute stability in terms of any one commodity standard be maintained unless one can predict with absolute certainty the course of future events. Recognition that unforeseen change is endemic to real world economic activities means that absolute price stability is an impossible goal. At best, policy should be designed to support and encourage arrangements which enhance the 'stickiness' of purchasing power over time in terms of one or two of the afore-mentioned standards, while allowing price adjustments in terms of the third standard to absorb the major impacts of changes that occur in the real world.

Which standards then should be chosen by governments as measures to which to link money's purchasing power, and which should be free to vary? The response depends on what is perceived as the greatest economic and political evil: inflation (or deflation) in terms of (a) an international commodity standard, (b) a domestic commodity standard, or (c) an earnings standard. This will, in turn, depend on economic factors such as the relative economic importance of foreign *vis-à-vis* domestically produced goods in consumption and investment patterns as well as sociological and political factors involving the power of trade unions and other groups who wish to protect and/or expand the purchasing power of their own money earnings. In modern entrepreneurial economies where the distribution of income and power is a fundamental factor in the inflation process, the resolution of such issues cannot be achieved by appeal to some fundamentally unchanging rule of monetary or fiscal operation. Political and economic forces interact and political cooperation purchased by astute compromises (which in democratic societies is certainly more desirable than political and economic coercion) may have to be made in pursuing any anti-inflation incomes policy. It is possible, for example, that the most desirable solution, socially and politically, would be to aim for purchasing power stickiness in terms of some sub-global international commodity standard. For example, if some nations trade primarily with only a handful of others, it might be desirable to pursue stickiness of a sub-global international standard geared only to the goods exchanged between the major partners, i.e. goods traded within this international common market. If stickiness can be achieved in terms of this 'common market' standard, then this group of common market nations would have the choice of operating with separate local currencies whose exchange rates in terms of each others' currencies could not vary (except for variations in transportation costs, changes in tariffs or large financial capital movements over time), or the choice of adopting a common currency unit which would convert these trading partners from a NUMS to a UMS. In either case, however, relative changes in productivities among these common market nations will require offsetting relative changes in money earnings per worker in each nation.

In sum, in any (national or international) entrepreneurial system where production is organized on a forward-money contracting basis, it is essential for the efficient operation of the production and trading processes that expectations of the stickiness of money's purchasing power, in terms of some international or domestic commodity standard, should prevail. Expectations that purchasing power is freely flexible, that is potentially unstable whenever an unexpected change occurs, signifies very elastic price expectations. Such expectations, as Hicks has demonstrated, imply the potential destruction of any capitalist system. In developed interdependent economies where production takes time and contractual commitments are essential, expectations of the lack of any anchor in terms of one of the major standards for the purchasing power of money would be a catastrophic breach in the continuity of the system – as destructive to society as we know it as any nuclear war.[18]

UMS, EFFICIENCY EARNINGS AND INFLATION

In any UMS, all contracts are denominated in terms of the same money unit. Accordingly, the existence of an international standard for measuring the purchasing power of the money of the nations in the UMS, is merely the equivalent of a domestic standard for the entire

UMS. If the flow–supply prices which underly any commodity standard are to be sticky, then the efficiency money wage or unit labour cost and the degree of monopoly must possess the property of viscosity. Thus, inflation analysis in a UMS is equivalent to the study of inflation in a traditional, closed system.

Since the money efficiency wage is defined as average money earnings per unit of human effort used in the production process divided by the average flow of output produced per unit of human effort utilized in productive activities, then in the aggregate, (money) efficiency earnings can be conceived of as the average (money) earnings of all factor inputs per unit–flow of production or the flow–supply price of a unit of GNP denominated in terms of money. In an entrepreneurial economy all factor money incomes, *except profits*, are determined by contractual factor hires before production is begun, and since such contractual hirings would not be undertaken without some entrepreneurial expectation of future output forthcoming from such hirings, the efficiency earnings of *contractually* employed factors are fundamental to short-term production decisions. Entrepreneurs must expect sales revenues from new production when it is marketed to at least equal the efficiency earnings of the contractually employed factors associated with any expected output flow.

Profits, however, are not normally contractually determined; hence the gross and net profit components of the efficiency earnings level are not easy to identify *ex ante*. In his *Treatise on Money*, Keynes implicitly using Marshall's concept of supply price as 'the price required to call forth the exertion necessary for producing any given amount of commodity',[19] therefore excluded unexpected or 'windfall profits' from entrepreneurial income. Thus, normal remuneration of entrepreneurs (or normal profits) is similar in nature, if not in law, to other factor incomes in that it is that remuneration which will leave entrepreneurs just satisfied with the production decisions they made; (windfall) profits and losses occur when the realized sales price (*ex post*) differs from the sales price (*ex ante*) expected when the entrepreneur undertook the production decision.[20] Using this definitional view, *ex ante* efficiency earnings are equal to the flow of contractual earnings plus the normal earnings of entrepreneurs for any given flow of output divided by the specified output flow. If entrepreneurs' actual earnings differ from the *ex ante* efficiency earnings then

> entrepreneurs will – in so far as their freedom of action is not fettered
> by existing bargains [contracts] with the factors of production which

are for the time being irrevocable – seek to expand (or curtail) their
scale of operations . . . The fact that entrepreneurs have generally
entered into long-time contracts with the factors of production . . . is
indeed of great importance.[21]

In the *General Theory*, Keynes, while not conceptually altering his
definition of the income that entrepreneurs endeavour to maximize,[22]
did slur the distinction between expected and realized sales revenues[23]
and therefore obliterated the difference between *ex ante* or expected
profits and realized profits. Moreover, in the system of national
accounting used in the real world, realized and not expected profits are
counted as the aggregate income category of entrepreneurs (non-
contractual factors). Since this latter accounting terminology is currently more familiar than Keynes' concept of income, realized gross
profit margins rather than expected profits margins will in our
discussion be used as a component of the non-wage portion of the
efficiency earnings of GNP.

There are three basic reasons why efficiency earnings for domestic
production may increase over time. These are

(1) diminishing returns, i.e. when the productivity per worker
declines as the rate of flow of output increases in response to an increase
in demand;

(2) increasing profit margins, i.e. when either the wedge between
market price and labour production costs rises *ex ante*, or the wedge
between the spot and forward price increases; and

(3) increasing money wages relative to productivity.

For more than a century economists have taught that every expansion
in the flow of output will normally involve diminishing returns as some
input such as land or managerial talent becomes increasingly scarce.
Moreover, similar results can occur if expansion involves employing less
efficient inputs, i.e. what I have labelled elsewhere *hiring path diminishing
returns.*[24]

Inflation, if it is due to diminishing returns, involves a once-only rise
in prices for any increased production flow and cannot be avoided in the
short run. No society has a vested interest in low prices by maintaining
low output merely to avoid diminishing returns. (Policies to mitigate
this type of inflation include (a) paying piece rates rather than time
rates – which shifts the entire burden of diminishing returns on to the
labour force in industries exhibiting diminishing returns, and/or
(b) training and research programmes to upgrade skills and enhance
productivity.)

Increasing profit margins and excessive money wage increases (relative to productivity increases) involve *incomes inflation* as various groups attempt to obtain more of the national product for themselves. These uncoordinated, inconsistent and competing claims for rising income put us all on a treadmill where we must all run faster – demand more money income – merely to keep in the race. For modern production market-oriented economies, incomes inflation is the 'Second Great Crisis for Capitalism in the 20th Century'. If there are strong political and social forces which are prompting increases in profit margins or unit labour costs, then purchasing power stability in terms of any domestic standard cannot be maintained. The economy will then suffer an incomes inflation.

Two competing anti-incomes inflation policies are currently advocated. Each suggests a different means to the same end, namely to create an economic environment where powerful sub-groups in our economy cannot expect to extort income increases at the expense of the rest of society. The traditional remedy for incomes inflation is a restrictive monetary and fiscal policy, so that the economy becomes so impoverished it cannot be held to economic blackmail by powerful sub-groups. Actual (or threatening) severe unemployment dislocations and significant business losses are the missiles with which traditional monetary and fiscal policies hope to restabilize the money value of domestic commodity standards during a period of incomes inflation.

The alternative is a *national policy to coordinate incomes claims*, that is, some form of *permanent incomes policy* (PIP). The stated objective of PIP is to limit movements in the level of efficiency earnings over time. A properly designed PIP will require some agreement about an equality of sacrifice when economic events are unfavourable, and an equality of sharing the gain in prosperous times. On the other hand, any restrictive policy which is based on inflexible rules which limits the growth of the money supply and/or government expenditure to pre-specified rates must involve an inequality of sacrifice, as Peter's pay rise may bankrupt Paul's employer – efficient or inefficient – when the banks are forced to turn off the taps and the government cannot offset the resulting weak markets for goods.

NUMS, EFFICIENCY EARNINGS AND INFLATION

If foreign social, political or market forces are raising foreign efficiency earnings *vis-à-vis* domestic efficiency earnings when both are calculated in terms of a single currency, then the *terms of trade*, i.e. the quantity of home produced goods which must be given up to obtain a unit of foreign goods, have turned against the domestic nation. Thus, an adverse change in the terms of trade which is due to a relative increase in foreign efficiency earnings when measured in terms of domestic money, will induce a decline in the purchasing power of local money in terms of any commodity standard which directly contains foreign components, unless domestic efficiency earnings decline sufficiently to lower the prices of domestic components of the commodity price index sufficiently to offset the increasing price of the foreign produced components. If, however, the domestic earnings standards (i.e. domestic money wages and profit margins) have institutional barriers which limit or prevent their decline, then an adverse change in the terms of trade (i.e. in foreign efficiency earnings in local money terms) will reinforce inflationary tendencies in terms of any commodity standard in which foreign goods are large elements.

For example, a rise in the dollar price of a barrel of oil by OPEC must increase the Consumer Price Index or GNP price deflator in the United States unless U.S. money wages (relative to productivity) and/or profit margins decline sufficiently to offset the energy cost increases. Thus, in 1974–5 and 1979–80 when OPEC prices were increased, any attempt to prevent inflation in terms of the CPI or GNP deflator via the use of traditional monetary and fiscal policy could be successful only to the extent that the induced unemployment drastically limited (if not reduced) domestic efficiency earnings increases. Such stagnating anti-inflation policies were attempted with little success during these periods. Stagnation due to such restrictive policies could have been avoided and inflation limited if a coordinated incomes policy (based on equation 4.13) would have been adopted.

If each trading nation is to engage in a coordinated attempt to prevent inflation in terms of the international standard, then the (weighted) average international efficiency wage level and degree of monopoly must be sticky over time. This will require, as already suggested, a coordinated international incomes policy gearing national money wage increments to productivity increases in each nation as well as keeping profit margins constant.

A coordinated incomes policy to maintain international purchasing power for local monies will still have to deal with possible situations of *ceteris paribus* trade payments imbalances between nations. The adjusting mechanism will depend on the cause of the imbalance. If, for example, nation A exogenously and permanently increases its demand for the exports of nation B, while A does not have the productive capacity to increase domestic production flows to sell more goods internationally and thereby obtain the means to pay for these additional imports demanded, then the existing terms of trade must turn against A. A reduction in A's standard of living is unavoidable (assuming B does not make a gift of its exports via continuous grants to A). The change in the terms of trade and lowering of the living standard can be accomplished without any inflation in the things A's residents purchase if there is a sufficient decrease in A's efficiency earnings. If, however, A's inhabitants refuse to willingly accept lower money wages (relative to productivity) and profit margins, then inflation and/or a change in the exchange rate which forces a decline in the purchasing power of A's money in terms of the international standard is inevitable.

If, on the other hand, A possesses the productive capacity to produce more goods which could be utilized by inhabitants of B or other nations, but this additional output will not be purchased because of the lack of demand due to restrictive policies in B or elsewhere in the world, then the remedy lies in expanding the opportunities for A's exports and not forcing a reduction in the standard of living on the inhabitants of A.

THE ALL SAINTS DAY MANIFESTO

The problem of coordination of incomes policies among trading partners in order to achieve stability of purchasing power in terms of an international standard (or in terms of a unionized money for the entire group of nations) has not been clearly recognized by Monetarist economists who often advocate either a return to an international gold standard or some other form of UMS. For example, in 1975, *The Economist* reported that 'nine prominent European economists have come together to recommend that EEC central banks should issue a Europa, which should be a European money of constant purchasing power. It should be purchasable by nations of EEC countries with their national money, at a variable exchange rate.'[25]

The nine economists, all members of the Monetarist school, published their analysis and recommendations in a document called the All Saints Day Manifesto. In this document, these economists recognize the tremendous value of eliminating exchange rate uncertainties, so that a resulting increase in economic activity and productivity can be expected from the growth of international markets which would follow. The authors of this Manifesto recognize that forward exchange markets beyond a few months are not well developed, and even if these longer duration forward exchange markets could be organized, the real resources devoted to them could be saved by use of a single currency.[26]

These economists also believe, as an article of faith, that as long as the rate of unemployment is not driven below the 'natural rate' by means of an expansionary monetary policy, the price level of domestic producible goods in terms of local currencies would not increase. Thus, they claimed that the transition from the existing (1975) European economic situation to one of a European monetary union would require those nations with 'high' rates of inflation to institute restrictive policies to induce 'a recession lasting several years' while 'inflationary expectations' are eliminated.[27] Of course, the squeezing out of inflationary expectations via a recession of several years' duration involves creating sufficient long-term unemployment, low profits and threats of business losses and bankruptcies, in the hope of stabilizing efficiency wages in terms of local currencies. This requirement of restrictive policies to limit efficiency wage increases embodies the typical Monetarist view that an implicit money wage–incomes restraint policy must be garbed in the explicitly respectable cloak of limiting money supply growth sufficiently to create slack markets. In the face of weak demand, it is assumed, workers and entrepreneurs 'voluntarily'[28] limit their wage and profit margin demands to non-inflationary levels. The level of long term unemployment which secures this voluntary money incomes constraint is, in Monetarist terminology, the 'natural rate of unemployment'. What is not explicitly specified is the actual rate of unemployment (and business bankruptcies) which is the 'natural rate'.

The Europa, it is claimed in the All Saints Day Manifesto, will be a European money of constant purchasing power that would circulate side by side with existing local monies. Residents of any nation would be free to exchange Europas for local currencies and vice versa, i.e. there would be two-way convertibility. The Europa would be made inflation proof, these economists claim, because the exchange rate between the Europa and each domestic national money would be altered every time there was a change in the local money's purchasing power, so that 'the price level of a representative commodity basket is constant in terms of Europas'.[29] For example, if the Italian lira was suffering 20 per cent inflation as measured by a price index of internationally traded goods, the Europa would increase its lira price by 20 per cent. The exchange rate between the Europa and each national currency, although not freely flexible, would be adjusted via some crawling peg mechanism or dirty float in order to avoid ephemeral fluctuations.

After a transitional period (i.e. in the long run) the authors see the Europa finally replacing national monies. At that stage the Europa's 'supply should be controlled according to a monetary rule that would guarantee it purchasing power stability'.[30] Thus, they foresee a UMS for the common market nations. The authors also recognize that unless specific actions are taken, the creation of an Europa monetary system will create a tendency towards eliminating regional wage differentials in terms of the Europa, thereby raising money costs of production more in low productivity regions and nations within the UMS. This would induce firms to migrate to high productivity regions causing low productivity nations to become depressed areas. To maintain a regional dispersal of the population of firms and economic activity throughout Europe, the authors of this manifesto recommend a 'vigorous regional policy which raises productivity in low productivity (poor) regions and transfers income to these poor areas'.[31] This general regional policy recommendation is made without any suggestion for an apparatus to enforce tax and expenditure policies to execute these transfers across national boundaries in Europe.

This All Saints Day Manifesto, the creation of nine 'prominent' European economists, which recommends the creation of a single European currency the Europa, with *mandated* stable purchasing power and two-way convertibility with local monies, is overwhelming corroborative evidence of the purblindness of Monetarist economists to the role of money in a modern entrepreneurial economy. Their myopia involves their failure to recognize the crucial role of contracts for forward delivery of goods and services, and especially long duration money wage contracts, in endowing *any* money with purchasing power and liquidity.

If the Europa were free to circulate alongside national monies and if European workers expected the Europa to be more inflation proof than their national currency, then would not rational workers insist on setting their wage contracts in terms of the Europa? Once the institution of wage contracts in Europa units become widespread, then if, over time, money wages in Europa units rose more rapidly than productivity,[32] the Europa would not be able to maintain a stable purchasing power in terms of goods and services purchased by Europeans. What is required for the stability of purchasing power of the Europa is an incomes policy which stabilizes unit labour costs and profit margins in Europas in a manner to offset any change in prices of non-Common Market goods imported into European nations. Thus, assuming no import price changes for a UMS system such as that proposed for the European Common Market, purchasing power stability in terms of producible goods and services requires the stickiness of money wages (relative to productivity) and profit margins in Europa units over time.

For democratic monetary entrepreneurial economies, the existence of either a social contract able to maintain compatible functional and regional income claims in nominal units geared to output flow and resource availability, or a deliberate policy of keeping labour and management in their place by inducing slack markets (in the hope of bringing competing claims for the products of industry in line with available supply) are the *only* alternative general policies which have been offered by economists to policy makers desiring purchasing power stability in periods where money efficiency earnings are rising due to a struggle among various economic groups over the distribution of available income. In the absence of either repressive stagnation or coordinated incomes policies, as long as European nationals are free to choose between the Europa and local currencies, fiddling with exchange rates between the Europa and the local European currencies will not provide for stable purchasing power in terms of a commodity standard for either the Europa or the local currencies.

Of course, if the Europa's circulation were limited to, say, the mode of settlement among Central Banks, while the Europa was not legally enforceable as the mode of contractual settlement of private agreements,[33] then of course, even if regional efficiency earnings specified in terms of local currencies changed rapidly, it would be possible to stabilize the purchasing power of the Europa by agreement among national governments (or their Central Banks) to vary the exchange rate between the Europa and the local currency in response to the measured inflation in terms of the local currency. In the aggregate, as far as the private sector of each nation was concerned, however, the Europa's purchasing power stability could not affect their situation, for there would be no way to make compatible all the incompatible income claims which cause incomes inflations in terms of local currencies by trying to transform them into Europa claims. The Europa would simply be legally unavailable for settling contractual claims in the private sector. It would merely be the clearing currency among Central Banks. Each nation would have to get (a) its domestic 'income claims' house in order for domestic standard stability and (b) coordinate domestic income claims with those of foreigners if international price stability is to be obtained.

In sum then, purchasing power stability in terms of an international commodity standard can be achieved only via differential, domestic income policies (i.e. varying labour standards over time) among nations or regions in tune with productivity trends and terms of trade patterns. If, on the other hand, a uniform labour standard for money is desired over time, then there will be differential rates of inflation in terms of a commodity standard by region or nation (or differential tariff–subsidy policies and/or unilateral income transfers). The failure of Monetarist economists to recognize the fundamental impossibility of ensuring stability in the purchasing power of money in terms of either a commodity standard or an earnings standard in modern entrepreneurial economies, without either an explicit agreement on income distribution as a result of either a social contract or a protracted and injurious (to all) Darwinian struggle over said distribution, is more of a tribute to their mental stubbornness than their intellectual prowess.

PROFIT MARGIN DIFFERENTIALS

Most of the preceding analysis has assumed that uncoordinated differential changes in efficiency wages will create disequilibrating tendencies in exchange rates. If such disturbances are merely of a temporary nature, then the availability of reserve assets plus borrowing power for the deficit region will help ride out the storm while permitting offsetting factors to restore the initial relationship. If, however, the disturbance proves to be large and protracted, a second line of defence for the deficit nation can be found in the imposition of quotas and taxes to offset the (assumed) transient forces.

Finally, with reserves providing the necessary time to interpret market information, if the disturbances are determined to be permanent and not readily correctable in 'free' markets without severe economic dislocations, then permanent action in terms of an explicit differential incomes policy to adjust the efficiency wage levels in the two nations will be required.

What should be the sequence of response if the disturbance is due to a permanent change in the relative degree of monopoly (e.g. OPEC) among the trading partners? In the case of OPEC, the tremendous increase in gross profit margins in the oil industry was validated by the worldwide market structure in the energy industry, which permitted mineral rights' owners and producing companies to enrich themselves at the expense of others. In a closed economy with a single monetary system, such a redistribution would reduce the real income of workers and others in the more competitive sectors, but as long as the more monopolized sector's income recipients had a strong demand for the output of the workers and equipment in the more competitive sector, the aggregate level of employment could be maintained. All that would be required is a redistribution of aggregate income, not a reduction. If, however, the monopolized sector's demand for output from the more competitive sector is less income elastic than the demand of the latter sector's income recipients, or if the income inflation resulting from the income redistribution process induces Central Bankers or governments into instituting restrictive monetary and fiscal policies, then unemployment and stagnation will develop with the monopolists living as a pocket of wealthy among the poverty of the rest.[34]

In modern democracies, with a strong central government monitoring the level and distribution of national income, restraints on domestic monopoly power or, failing that, taxation on the basis of ability to pay, coupled with government investment projects and welfare expenditures in the poor sector, can recycle a sufficient amount of purchasing power (liquidity and finance) to maintain 'decent' income and employment levels in the competitive sector, and hence support employment and output levels in the face of the incomes inflation and any domestic redistribution struggle.

In the open economy of the oil consuming nations, however, the significant increase in the monopoly power of OPEC coupled with the limited OPEC demand for foreign goods (relative to their income growth) has the potential to create mass poverty, unemployment, stagnation and the retardation of investment in the rest of the world. In the absence of a central authority to force the recycling of the purchasing power received by OPEC to the oil consuming (more competitive) nations, or of the power of a single central monetary authority to recycle (or create) additional bank reserves in order to prevent regional banks in the deficit areas from difficulties in meeting contractual commitments to the bankers of the monopolists, the idling of resources in the competitive sector is inevitable!

The only alternatives to continued stagnation would be to break the relative power of the Cartel by either

(1) creating competitive alternatives to the products of the Cartel, or

(2) taxing imports from the Cartel to redistribute monopoly rents to domestic governments,[35] or

(3) negotiating an international social contract for some equitable distribution of total world income at maximum output between oil consuming nations and oil producing nations.

9 Can We Have an International Standard when there is an OPEC Cartel?

As long as oil is one of the more important internationally traded commodities, the existence of the economic power of the OPEC Cartel threatens any proposal for the operation of a stable, efficient international monetary system. OPEC's major goal and pre-occupation is to continually redistribute the world's income and wealth from oil consuming nations to oil producing nations via market pricing policies. As long as the OPEC Cartel members believe it is possible to improve the distribution of world income and wealth in favour of the Cartel, then they will continually attempt to force adverse changes in the oil terms of trade of the consuming nations. To the extent that the Cartel is successful in altering the oil terms of trade in its favour, the purchasing power of any specific money under study must change in terms of the international standard, unless the degree of monopoly and/or the efficiency wage involved in the production of the other goods in an international standard market basket fortuitously decline *in terms of a specific monetary unit* by the exact same proportion as the increase in the price of OPEC oil (weighted by its importance in the standard). The continued existence of OPEC, therefore, makes it extremely unlikely, if not impossible, to avoid some minimum rate of inflation in terms of *any* major oil consuming nation's money. This does not mean that domestic inflationary tendencies set off by imported inflation in terms of oil prices could not be limited via a domestic incomes policy. On a social and political level, however, the difficulty of successfully pursuing any domestic incomes policy is exacerbated by OPEC's relentless drive for more income at the expense of the rest of the world. Unless the oil consuming nations can in some way limit OPEC's economic power, the

167

continued rapid growth and evolution of entrepreneurial economies in oil consuming nations will be severely jeopardized.

If OPEC is permitted to continue to follow its behaviour pattern of the 1970s and uses its devastating market power in international trade, then the oil consuming nations will have to choose between three alternatives.

(1) The development of some cooperative international structure which adopts or accommodates to whatever real income demands OPEC makes on the oil consuming world, and then provides some acceptable international *incomes policy* mechanism which equitably shares the losses in some manner among the remaining income claimants in all non-OPEC nations.

(2) Each nation independently attempts to be quasi self-sufficient in energy *and* other imports from major oil importing nations. The less open an economy becomes, *ceteris paribus* the more it can limit the inflationary effects (of OPEC's demands) on the price level of the things its residents buy. This move towards autarky would not eliminate the need to institute a *national* incomes policy to share out the remaining real income (after deducting the unavoidable losses to OPEC) among the internal income claimants.[1] To the extent that foreign trade with non-OPEC nations continues, in the absence of some international coordination of incomes among these non-OPEC nations, each oil consuming nation will try to improve its terms of trade with the other oil consuming nations in the hope of shunting some of the loss of real income to OPEC on to its trading partners. Such attempts can only exacerbate the difficulties of international trade.

(3) Each nation can subscribe to a free market, *laissez-faire* philosophy and do nothing to limit OPEC demands on domestic real income. Alternative (3) implies passively accepting whatever the rate of inflation that results from the loss of real income to OPEC plus the inflation due to the resulting global struggle among income claimants for the remaining income as each group tries to push the burden of OPEC on to others. Inflation and stagnation therefore becomes a way of life, 'freely' chosen by economic agents.

Alternative (3) is ultimately a lethal process for any monetary system, for it leads to a complete breakdown in the public's confidence in the monetary system and hence, to an unwillingness to enter into long-term forward money contracts. Alternative (2) leads to a collapse of foreign trade as the terms-of-trade objectives of the non-OPEC nations are incompatible; the only stable solution under (2) will be one of almost complete autarky.

Thus, as long as petroleum remains a major internationally traded commodity, world oil consumer nations have only two *practical* alternatives, namely to either break the grip of OPEC or adopt alternative (1). It is therefore essential to understand the unusual features and properties of crude oil and its markets, in order to comprehend the basis of the OPEC Cartel's economic power. Only then can it be determined whether (a) consuming nations can develop policies to dismantle some of the Cartel's power or (b) they must cooperatively accommodate OPEC's demands via alternative (1) in order to avoid setting off destructive trade wars among themselves.

The analysis of OPEC's oil terms of trade and the basis of the Cartel's power is developed in this chapter from the viewpoint of the United States economy. Ultimately, it will be the United States who decides on consumer strategy (a) or (b) for dealing with OPEC's threat to international monetary relations, for the United States is the only *consumer* economy currently strong enough (and also such a large potential producer of fossil fuel energy sources) that it could, if it so chose, effectively weaken the oil Cartel.

THE ENERGY PROBLEM

In order to formulate rational policies to alleviate the tremendous strains that OPEC prices and the resultant changes in the volumes of U.S. goods that must be exchanged with OPEC governments for each barrel of oil (the oil terms of trade) have placed on the U.S. economy, it is necessary to analyse the fundamental cause of the so-called 'energy crisis'.

The sudden quadrupling of world crude oil prices in 1973–4 was in large measure responsible for the severity of the worldwide economic dislocation and stagflation which followed. By 1976–7, the OPEC Cartel was receiving in monopoly revenues well over $125 billion a year from consumers, with U.S. consumers paying approximately one quarter of this sum.[2]

With the Iranian dislocation in January 1979, this monopoly tribute escalated dramatically. The effects of such rapid and large increases in transfers of income from consuming nations to members of the oil Cartel magnify the existing worldwide inflationary and recessionary tendencies. The result could be disastrous for capitalist nations unless direct action is taken to break the OPEC Cartel's domination of energy markets. It will therefore be very costly should the consuming nations decide not to adopt a direct and forceful programme to severely limit the power of the Cartel, and instead attempt to reduce their dependence on low resource cost oil from OPEC and other nations by either (a) developing higher real cost energy sources within the domestic economy or (b) permanently depressing their economies to force less energy consumption. Developing higher real cost alternatives means diverting scarce resources to less productive activities, thereby indirectly lowering the potential for productivity growth, while purposeful recession achieves such a slowdown directly.

The OPEC Cartel's successful attempt to drive up energy prices and limit oil production has reduced the real income available to U.S. consumers for three reasons. Firstly, the greater volume of exports the U.S. pays to OPEC nations for each barrel of oil imported (an adverse change in the oil terms of trade for the U.S.) means that less GNP per capita remains in the U.S. Secondly, the induced slowdown in U.S. oil production due to 'user costs' (see *infra*) and wrongheaded governmental policies such as phased decontrol of oil and gas wellhead prices, encouraged U.S. refiners to increase imports of OPEC oil at the more adverse terms of trade. Thirdly, the use of recession inducing policies, while reducing oil imports and encouraging 'conservation', wastes precious resources via unemployment, discourages the accumulation of capital, hence constraining the growth of real income.

In sum then, it is in the vital self-interest of U.S. consumers of energy to break the Cartel, simply in order to reduce the loss of real income going to the Cartel.[3] If, however, further adverse changes in the oil terms of trade for the U.S. lead to a further balance of payments deficit, then, as after the 1973–4 episode of OPEC price increases, the dollar could be devalued *vis-à-vis* foreign currencies, leading to a further loss in real income for U.S. consumers. Such a devaluation will mean that U.S. consumers will be giving up more U.S. produced goods for each unit of import from the entire rest of the world. The lower the U.S. price elasticity of demand for imports and the world's elasticity of demand for exports, the greater, *ceteris paribus*, will be the loss in real income for U.S. consumers because of the devaluation.

Consequently, it is essential to analyse the fundamental causes of the energy crisis so that rational policies to alleviate the potential burdens of adverse changes in the oil terms of trade can be formulated.

IS ENERGY SCARCE?

In 1973, the onset of an energy crisis, in a world that for a century had been plagued by a potential oversupply of fossil fuels at existing market prices, caught many knowledgeable observers by surprise. The energy shortage immediately generated a search for a scapegoat or a rational explanation of the predicament faced by the highly developed capitalist economies heavily based on energy resources, such as the United States, Western Europe, and Japan.

Orthodox economic theory has taught that businessmen's single-minded pursuit of profit opportunities, tempered by competition and the absence of externalities, would result in an optimum allocation of resources and the maximization of the community's welfare. Thus if orthodox theory is to be believed, executives of multinational energy companies should not be pilloried for failing to meet the needs of any one selfish nation, for in their pursuit of profits they are unwittingly maximizing the economic welfare of mankind. As for the evidence showing the lack of competition at the various stages of the vertically integrated oil industry, some students of the industry, such as Hartshorn, claim that the international supply of crude oil is 'the same as what might be expected to arise from the operation of the law of comparative costs in a freely competitive international market'.[4] After all, the consumer seemed to be plentifully, and cheaply, supplied with oil.

Again according to orthodox neoclassical theory, the problem of depletable natural resources such as oil is one of determining, in Solow's words, the 'optimal social management of a stock of a non-renewable but essential resource'.[5] An immediate consequence of conceptualizing the problem in this manner is that it presumes that if the market is 'workably competitive'[6], market prices reflect 'true scarcity' of the resource and hence higher market prices signal that the economy is running out of oil, or at least of low cost oil.

There have been a number of studies, however, which question whether the price of oil is representative of the state of depletion of this natural resource. Professor Adelman, for example, has concluded that the world price of oil 'has no possible relation to scarcity present or future, known or feared'.[7] My own studies[8] of energy supplies indicate that there is little danger of a Malthusian shortage in either the U.S. or the Western hemisphere for decades to come even if present demand trends continue. The energy crisis, whatever else it may mean, does not mean that the age of cheap fossil fuels is over – at least, not in terms of cheap economic real costs of finding oil.[9] Nor does it mean, on either a worldwide or North American basis – at least if history is a basis for judgment – that increases in current market prices are necessary to meet any growing petroleum consumption demands. For example, during the years 1962 to 1972 (when until the very end of the period prices were not rising) world consumption of petroleum increased by 107.4 per cent, and whole world crude oil *proved* reserves increased by 108.5 per cent during the same period. In other words, the world was not facing any greater threat of running out of crude oil in 1972 than it was in 1962. What had happened was that the North American *proved* reserves increased by only 18 per cent from 40 to 47 billion barrels, while Middle Eastern reserves climbed spectacularly from almost 200 billion to over 350 billion barrels. This modest rise in North American reserves *vis-à-vis* the Middle East should not be interpreted as meaning that the continent is 'running out' of oil. During this period however, all rational producers who could afford it preferred to invest their time and money in finding cheap reserves in the Middle East (10 to 50 U.S. cents per barrel) rather than more expensive reserves in North America ($2 to $4 a barrel).

Of course as long as the U.S. market was partly insulated from cheap foreign oil by import quotas, and the domestic wellhead price was supported at a profitable level by state prorationing regulations and the Federal Connally Hot Oil Act, there was still a profit incentive to continue to find some additional U.S. reserves to meet the growing U.S. demands; indeed reserves did increase during the period; but it was the explosive growth in demand by Western Europe and Japan, together with the apparent cornucopia of cheap Middle East oil, that led to the drastic reallocation of investment by oil companies from North America to the Middle East and elsewhere.

With the institution of domestic oil price controls in 1971 and their continued enforcement on a 'temporary' and ever (upward) changing basis, expectations of decontrol and rapid escalation of domestic prices were encouraged, while at the same time everyone expected ever higher OPEC Cartel prices. The decline in domestic reported proven reserves[10] since 1972 (despite increased domestic exploratory activity and higher domestic prices since 1974) would, on a cursory view, appear surprising. One would have suspected that higher prices meant that more of the oil-in-place underground would be profitable to produce, since even 'old oil' prices skyrocketed since 1972. The analysis here, however, implies that underreporting of proved reserves would be the rational behaviour of profit maximizing firms who desired government to firstly decontrol oil prices more rapidly and permit U.S. wellhead prices to reach world levels, and then move with the OPEC governments' controlled world price.

USER COSTS AND OIL INDUSTRY MODELS

The exploration, development and production of oil take significant time and hence this economic activity is by its very nature future oriented. Once it is recognized that future market conditions for energy are uncertain *and* unpredictable, then many of the orthodox neoclassical economic theory tenets regarding an optimal intertemporal allocation path for natural resources such as oil are not applicable. Such optimal paths can only be rigorously defined for known future conditions.[11] Economists therefore should avoid Delphic Oracle-like statements on optimal energy production and use. Instead they should analyse alternative market conditions and policy proposals for their effects on production flows, prices, income, and the distribution of wealth and economic power.

The recent development of a Post Keynesian school of economic analysis based on the writings of J. M. Keynes emphasizes this latter approach. Post Keynesians begin with the fundamental axiom that the future is uncertain. Hence it is expectations about a future which can*not* be predicted in a probabilistic manner (like the drawing of chips from an urn i.e. the economic universe is not in a state of statistical control) which drive entrepreneurial actions regarding production, investment, and pricing. These expectations about the future generate action (or inaction) which creates the future; that is, the economy adapts to widely held expectations and not vice versa.

One of the basic Post Keynesian conceptual tools for analysing the use of natural resources is the concept of 'user costs' for, as J. M. Keynes emphasized in *The General Theory*, 'In the case of raw materials the necessity of allowing for user cost is obvious.'[12] (Keynes borrowed the term 'user cost' from Marshall but was the first to develop the concept and apply it to the question of intertemporal production from any depletable properties.) User costs constitute one of the major economic links between the current situation and the future, because they involve weighing expected future profits against current ones. The concept of user costs can be illustrated as follows.

For any particular property, the fossil fuels in the ground are a fixed inventory, or an exhaustible resource. The more of these fuels that are used today, *ceteris paribus*, the less will be available for future delivery. Consequently, a rational entrepreneur will compare the present value of expected profits for a forward contract sale at each possible future date with the profitability of selling that amount today. If profit maximizing entrepreneurs are to produce for current sale, current marginal revenue must be expected to cover not only the current marginal production costs associated with that barrel of oil, but also the user costs inherent in all depletable resources, namely, the highest present value of marginal future profits given up by producing that barrel of oil currently rather than in the future. If well organized forward markets existed in the real world, producers of natural resources could readily use the forward prices to estimate user costs. However, forward markets for oil and other natural resources for days, months, and years in the future do not exist. Only if such forward markets already existed *and* only if they truly represented the demand that future consumers would have (and not the views of today's speculators regarding the future demand), could entrepreneurs then employ the concept of user costs to obtain an efficient intertemporal production programme by following the guidance of free market prices. Instead, the only information available to producers is the history of the industry, the current situation, and the individual's hopes, fears, and expectations about the future prices of resources. Thus current production plans depend in large measure on unfounded expectations about the future where waves of propaganda, optimism, or pessimism can overwhelm 'rational' entrepreneurs and make oil bearing properties objects of speculation. Most ultimate consumers of oil and other natural resources do not know, nor can they predict accurately, their demands for the products of natural resources weeks, months, or years into the future.

It therefore follows that in a world where the future is uncertain, with producers 'free' to make any production decisions they think most profitable, we are left with a bootstrap theory of the time rate of exploitation of fossil fuel-bearing properties. Current expectations of producers about future prices relative to costs play the pivotal role. Accordingly, relative stability over time in prices and production of energy resources requires that most producers believe that tomorrow will not be significantly different from the recent past, although the market can perhaps accommodate some divergence of views among producers as long as they expect stability on average.

Competition in such markets will provide intertemporal stability of prices and production flows only if the views of the competitors either coalesce in the belief that the future will not be significantly different from the recent past, or differ as to whether user costs are positive or negative in such a way that the 'average' view is that user costs are zero. If, even with competition, most producers expect a significant change in prices relative to costs in the future, the current rate of exploitation will be accelerated (that is, if average user costs are negative) or retarded (if average user costs are positive).

Thus, in the 1930s the discovery of the huge East Texas fields touched off expectations of large negative user costs (in other words, expectations of wellhead price declines) in an industry that at the time was relatively competitive – at least in the state of Texas at the wellhead stage. The result was a disastrously rapid rate of exploitation of domestic oil fields, which then brought about the fulfilment of those expectations of rapidly declining wellhead prices relative to costs. (The moral of this historical episode is that expectations of rapidly changing prices relative to costs in this industry can actually encourage behaviour which will make the prophecy self-fulfilling, if the expectations are widely held and not readily altered.) State government-enforced market prorationing (proportional cutbacks in wellhead production), supported by the 1935 Federal Connally Hot Oil Act, was required to alter these negative user cost expectations of competitive producers and stabilize the domestic industry. In later years, as foreign oil became important in world supplies, the operation of import quotas plus state market prorationing effectively eliminated any strong negative user cost expectations by domestic producers. At the same time, user cost speculation in the international market was restrained by the ability of the 'Seven Sisters' to maintain an orderly market.

Most sellers of energy resources have, however, been led to expect rapidly rising prices by the events of the seventies. The most important of these include the relaxation of prorationing arrangements in Texas and other oil producing states, the growth of the power of the Organization of Petroleum Exporting Countries (OPEC) at the same time that import quotas were being removed, and the unsettled politics of the Middle East. These events stimulated speculative proclivities and consequently retarded current production of fossil fuels and other energy sources such as uranium.

Current events have created an environment where most domestic energy producers and property owners expect rapidly rising wellhead prices of natural gas, old crude oil, and coal (as conglomerates 'require' equal returns from each division). The price of domestic crude is expected to rise, as OPEC turns the cartel screw a little tighter and tries to 'catch up' to some extent with the world inflationary forces that it itself released in the recent past, and all controls from wellhead prices are removed, thereby permitting U.S. prices to rise to world levels. In 1980 wellhead prices in the United States were below what the market could be forced to pay (that is, demand was in the price inelastic range), while competitive fuels were controlled by both growing monopolies such as OPEC, and separate but not independent divisions of the same 'energy companies'.

Tremendous investments are necessary to bring alternative energy sources on stream at costs that might be profitable today. Nevertheless, producers of these alternative energy sources know that OPEC has tremendous reserves of crude oil which could be profitably marketed at prices well below today's. Hence, producers of alternative fuels fear that any threat on their part of encroaching on a very large share of the OPEC market could induce short period price cutting by OPEC to underprice the alternatives *and* make the necessary large capital investments unprofitable. These large positive costs expectations associated with investment in non-OPEC alternative sources of energy imply that 'unfettered' energy market forces are unlikely to significantly weaken OPEC's power.

All these factors encourage producers to expect, at worst, no major lowering in the existing real price of energy, and at best, a further substantial increase. In other words, monopolistic control of supply is validated by events and governmental policies – and hence speculative expectations can have a significant impact on diminishing current supply offerings. User cost considerations currently dominate discussions as to the rate at which energy resources should be exploited.

Keynes once pointed out that economic progress depends on the spirit of *enterprise*, which in this context refers to the activity of producers motivated by a desire for action rather than inaction, and operating under reasonably stable conditions in an uncertain world, to produce a steady flow of output for the economy. Keynes recognized that in an uncertain world some men's proclivities would always influence them to try making speculative profits via supply manipulations, and he noted that 'Speculators may do no harm as bubbles on a steady stream of Enterprise. But the position is serious when Enterprise becomes the bubble on a whirlpool of Speculation.'[13] The current critical supply situation for natural gas and oil in the United States, and the cartelized supply of all fossil fuels in the world, are due in part to Enterprise becoming engulfed in Speculative practices. Underlying the situation are the positive user cost expectations generated by the power of a worldwide energy cartel.

Recognition of the existence of user costs means that during some periods such expectations can dominate production and investment decisions of entrepreneurs, and hence lead to supply results which differ from the traditional neoclassical textbook case. Hence the traditional analytical model used by many neoclassical economists can be very misleading. For example, a traditional neoclassical model of the natural gas industry by MacAvoy and Pindyck[14] (who would claim it is also applicable to the oil industry), assumes that the bringing forth of 'reserves' is a reproducible process which occurs under conditions of increasing real costs or diminishing returns to factor inputs. No-one will deny that in a given state of technology, a natural resource industry may operate under the law of diminishing returns and therefore exhibit increasing costs. Where these textbook models err, however, is to assume that increasing real resource costs are the *only* component of the supply price necessary to pay for production, and therefore these models assume that the elasticity of the real input cost function is the same as the supply price elasticity. For example, MacAvoy and Pindyck state that 'An equation for marginal development costs [is] the "supply curve" for production in field markets.'[15] This could be true only if user costs were zero,[16] a condition that has not characterized the situation in the United States since 1970.

If increasing resource costs are an inevitable outcome of increasing the annual offerings of new reserves, *and if user costs are excluded*, then it follows that if the current wellhead price is just sufficient to bring forth the current flow of annual reserves, then the price will have to increase in order to encourage the profitable development of larger annual reserves. If, as the traditional model assumes, the *only* factor holding back greater reserve offerings is that of increasing real resource costs, then in a competitive market the quantitative relationship between the percentage change in wellhead price required to bring forth a percentage change in the quantity of reserves offered, i.e. the supply price elasticity, is equal to the elasticity of real factor input costs. For example, if to produce ten per cent more reserves per annum requires an increase in resource costs of five per cent, then the resource cost elasticity (which by assumption is the supply price elasticity) is equal to two.

Figure 9.1, which is a reproduction of a diagram appearing on p. 463 of the MacAvoy and Pindyck paper, shows a rising marginal resource cost curve (R) which is assumed to be, in the traditional textbook models, the supply curve(s) of the industry.

The elasticity of the supply curve is the crucial measure of the response of producers to market price incentives. If the supply response is infinitely elastic, no price increase is required to stimulate additional offerings. If the elasticity is less than infinite then, all other things being equal, the price must increase if additional annual reserves are to be brought to market. If the elasticity is elastic, i.e. if its magnitude is

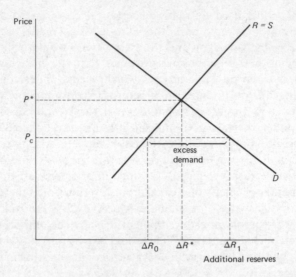

FIGURE 9.1   Traditional Supply and Demand of Reserves Model

between unity and infinity, a large proportion of the price increase goes to stimulate additional offerings and only a small proportion of the price increase goes to increase the windfall economic rents of producers and landowners. If the supply response is inelastic, i.e. if its magnitude is less than unity, then the additional offerings called forth by any price increase will be relatively small and the economic rents of producers and landowners will increase substantially if the price is permitted to rise. Finally, if the supply price elasticity is less than zero or negative (a case not normally handled by the traditional model but one which a realistic alternative model as developed below suggests) then higher prices *reduce* supply while increasing earnings of producers and property owners. Consequently the magnitude of the supply elasticity is crucial to the issue as to whether and by how much an increase in wellhead prices will increase supply offerings or merely provide economic windfalls.

As has already been indicated, the traditional model, of which the MacAvoy–Pindyck analysis is an example, assumes that supply elasticity only reflects real resource costs. User costs, that is the expectations about future changes, are ignored. Thus in the MacAvoy–Pindyck analysis of Figure 9.1, 'Under conditions of shortage, the regulated ceiling price P_c prevails rather than the market demand price P^* . . . [and] the quantity realized (ΔR_o) is on the supply but not demand function',[17] and according to MacAvoy and Pindyck, there is an excess demand for reserves or an energy shortage. In this model, the apparently obvious solution is to permit the price to rise to P^*; at this price demand and supply are equal and the shortage has been eliminated by the free market.

In the real world, however, both expectations about future prices and market conditions have changed drastically since 1972 when reported proved reserves of natural gas peaked. U.S. wellhead prices of gas and oil have been under a variety of 'temporary' government control programmes while world energy prices have skyrocketed, thereby creating universal expectations for all producers that as the government gets out of the 'controls' business, U.S. wellhead prices will rise substantially and will continue to 'track' future OPEC price increases. Such strong positive user cost expectations create a negative supply elasticity. This possibility has on occasion been recognized. For example, Alfred Kahn alluded to this phenomenon in his testimony in a Federal Power Commission case when he stated that 'the holding of supplies off the market in anticipation of rising prices . . . imparted a negative elasticity of supply'.[18]

When such user costs are prevalent, it is not proper to assume that the marginal resource cost function (R in Figures 9.1 and 9.2) is the industry supply function. Rather, expectations about the higher future prices involve positive user costs which must be added to resource costs so that the supply curve (S in Figure 9.2) will lie above the resource cost curve (R), and as Kahn suggested, it may even display a negative elasticity as shown in Figure 9.2.

Thus, if P_c is the current wellhead price, then Figure 9.2 shows (as did Figure 9.1) that ΔR_o reserves will be forthcoming and that there is an excess demand or shortage of oil in the market at that current wellhead price. But unlike Figure 9.1, Figure 9.2 shows that because of the negative supply elasticity any increase in the ceiling price can exacerbate the shortage.[19] What is needed is a policy which would make it unprofitable for producers ever to speculate on future price increases. One such policy is to insist that any increase in the regulated wellhead price is phased in at an annual rate which is less than the current rate of interest, so that the discounted value of the additional profit obtainable from holding reserves off the market in order to sell at expected higher future prices is always less than zero. Under such a situation, user costs would be negligible and the marginal resource cost curve would approximate to the supply curve, and according to Figure 9.2, a lower P^* could alleviate the shortage.

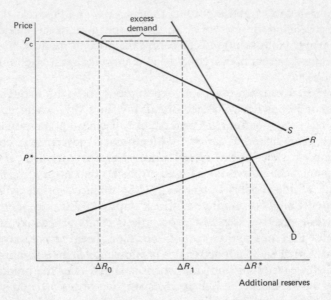

FIGURE 9.2   User Cost Supply and Demand of Reserves Model

Another similar policy would be to increase the carrying costs of oil being held underground via a per-barrel tax on oil that is *not* produced. For example, any property in the U.S. which is producing less than MER[20] can be taxed on a per-barrel per-day basis difference between actual daily production and MER. Similarly a daily tax level could be placed on all oil leases in the U.S. currently held if the property is not producing anything. This would encourage the more rapid development of leases and production of oil in the United States and discourage speculative withholding of domestic underground energy sources which is likely to be a prevalent industry practice while entrepreneurs and energy property owners are motivated by self-interest.

THE ENERGY QUESTION

The fundamental energy question is at what price will American consumers get their energy needs filled. Neither oil industry spokesmen nor most academics will deny that there is plenty of domestic energy, as well as Western hemisphere and foreign sources of hydrocarbons which could take us well into the twenty-first century even if there were no further technological progress in developing new energy sources or in lowering the real costs of exploiting existing sources.

Of course, 'If we speak frankly, we have to admit that our basis of knowledge for estimating the yield ten years hence of a railway, a copper mine . . . amounts to little and sometimes nothing; or even five years hence.'[21] To this list of unknowables we might add the ultimate limits of the world's reserves of fossil fuels. Yet, since the OPEC price jumps of the early 1970s, many economists, businessmen, and government officials have attempted to estimate the potential yield of oil and other fossil fuels from the earth's crust over the next few decades or even centuries.

Since we must apparently make predictions regarding available supplies of oil at distant future dates in order to rationalize current energy policy decisions, it should be made clear to the unwary reader that there are only two ways to forecast the distant uncertain future. Either we interpret history (the facts) and assume that future patterns are related to past patterns, or we appeal to the simple beauty of the pure mathematics of geometric v. arithmetic progressions.

Professor Harkin, for example, cites an MIT study which provides various 'scenarios' where demand always grows geometrically (growth rates between 0.5 and 6.2 per cent per annum are assumed) while reserves are added to oil supplies on an arithmetic basis each year (between 3 billion barrels and 20 billion barrels per year). Inevitably each scenario shows that at some future date the world runs out of oil. Thus Harkin concludes 'with an outlook such as this it does not seem appropriate to characterize OPEC pricing as extortion'.[22] Apparently, just as Malthus found that war, disease, pestilence, and famine were to be desired for putting positive checks on population and protecting man from his own folly, so Professor Harkin implies that consumers should thank OPEC for preventing us from running out of energy by extorting sufficient wealth from us so that we cannot afford to use up energy sources.

If, on the other hand, one attempts to forecast the uncertain future by extrapolating from historical patterns and existing facts, as I do, the picture is not dismal in the Malthusian sense. My judgment of this is based on my reading of the historical facts and current information including (but not limited to) the following.

1. Throughout recorded history, no economy has ever run out of a major so-called 'depletable' energy source (coal, peat, or oil, for example), while history indicates that it is possible for demand for 'renewable' energy sources to outrun supplies – Europe ran out of wood

twice (being saved from a disastrous energy shortage one time by the plague!). Moreover, there are good economic reasons for this. For so-called 'renewable' energy sources, the existing stock at any given time is limited, while replacement and/or growth of supply depends on biological and physical processes. Thus, the availability and rate of exploitation (production) of renewable energy is constrained by bio-logical and physical laws which cannot be relaxed merely because economies develop greater needs. Major 'depletable' energy sources, on the other hand, have tremendous stock supplies available at any time, and their rate of exploitation (flow–supply) depends on economic forces which are governable by man.

2. Over the years, the world has tended to find more oil than is produced, and hence the long-term trend has been for world oil reserves to continue to rise even though demand has grown rapidly and real costs per barrel have declined. (Is this compatible with a Malthusian shortage?)

3. Documents published by the Church Committee Hearings on Multinational Corporations (1974) provide dramatic evidence that publicly-announced proven reserve statistics often understate the actual situation. For example, an Aramco document indicated that in 1973 the company conservatively estimated proven reserves at 245 billion barrels while publicly announcing reserves of 90 billion.[23] Moreover, this estimate was made while Aramco had been leaving 55 out of 85 known oil reservoirs in Saudi Arabia undeveloped.[24] Similarly, the hearings presented a 'secret intelligence report' revealing that Iraq had at the time 'fantastic' quantities of untapped oil reserves which were not being exploited because the Iraqis had a 'surplus of oil'.[25]

4. Even if we accept as accurate the publicly announced estimates of remaining world proven reserves of oil, the resulting 750 billion barrels is 50 per cent more than the oil required to meet all demand until the year 2000 at present growth rates of demand.

5. Very conservative estimates of future reserves of conventional oil (not tar sands, shale, etc.) put additional reserves at 2000 billion barrels (while some estimates suggest up to 11000 billion at current wellhead prices).

6. Non-conventional oil reserves should supply at least as many reserves again as conventional reserves do.

7. Large new oil field discoveries in drilled areas cannot be ruled out. In 1972, for example, the Mexican oil company PEMEX probed more deeply into oil fields which had been thought to be thoroughly and even wastefully exploited by the private oil companies before nationalization.

PEMEX found very large new reservoirs of high quality, low sulphur crude. Apparently, in this 'new' oil field the wildcat success ratio was an astounding 82 per cent, and drilling has shown one single field to be at least 58 square miles with an average pay thickness of over 3300 feet. The potential supply bounds of the Mexican fields are still to be discovered.

In the face of these facts, and recognizing the difficulty of forecasting decades ahead, one should be very sceptical of basing energy policy on scenarios which rely solely on the Malthusian race of a geometric progression in demand against an arithmetic progression of supply. This is especially true when such scenarios encourage consumers to passively pay homage (and a good deal of income) to the OPEC Cartel as if they were the saviours of mankind. Since current supply conditions are dominated by the expectations (user costs) of energy producers, then Persian Gulf States will, for the foreseeable future, continue to manipulate oil supplies so that oil prices more than keep up with inflation (i.e. oil in the ground is better than money in the bank), and increasing the current domestic wellhead price via decontrol will *not* allocate significant additional resources into increasing domestic production.

In fact under President Carter's May 1979 Decontrol Order, in the 28 months of phased decontrol (1 June 1979 to 30 September 1981), 'old' oil prices will have increased by approximately 70 per cent per annum even if OPEC did not raise prices during that entire period. Thus, old oil in the ground would be better than money in the bank in that it would yield 70 per cent merely by holding it for 28 months. If producers of old oil are rational, therefore, then during the period of decontrol, *ceteris paribus*, the flow of old oil should be sharply reduced, thereby further contributing to more foreign purchases and higher prices than if there were no decontrol.[26] In January 1981, President Reagan ordered immediate decontrol, thereby encouraging some additional production of 'old' oil and contributing to a temporary glut.

U.S. GOVERNMENT POLICY FOR SOLVING THE ENERGY CRISIS

Immediately after the huge run-up of oil prices by OPEC in 1973–4, many prominent economists proclaimed that the operation of the free market would soon cause the demise of the oil cartel. For example, in his column in *Newsweek* magazine of 4 March 1974, Nobel Prize winner Milton Friedman proclaimed

> The world crisis is now past its peak. The initial quadrupling of the price of crude oil after the Arabs cut output was a temporary response that has been working its own cure. Higher prices induced consumers to economize and other producers to step up output. It takes time to adjust, so these reactions will snowball.
>
> In order to keep prices up, the Arabs would have to curtail their output by even larger amounts. But even if they cut their output to zero they would not for long keep the world price of crude oil at $10 a barrel. Well before that point the cartel would collapse.[27]

Unfortunately, much of U.S. government policy was based on a philosophy similar to Friedman's. There was an inherent belief that although some controls of energy markets were needed in the short run, it was only a matter of time until energy markets would again settle down into a competitive-like equilibrium. By the end of the 1970s, however, even most fervent free marketeers were willing to admit that the Cartel would not collapse of its own accord. At that stage, adherents of market solutions often suggested that OPEC was doing a great favour to oil consumers by raising prices. Consumers, it was suggested, did not realize that oil was a depletable asset and hence would use it 'wastefully' if not forced to conserve by higher prices. Government officials finally realized that there were only two ways of resolving the energy crisis. One was to decontrol domestic oil and permit its price to rise in step with the price of OPEC oil, so that some of the income currently being lost by consumers to foreigners would instead be transferred to oil producers within the U.S. while U.S. consumers were forced to 'conserve' because of their lower real income. The second solution involved adopting policies which attempted to limit OPEC's economic power[28] by involving the U.S. in an economic war – using market forces and laws, not gunboats – against the Persian Gulf States who declared all-out economic war against the U.S. in 1973.

In 1979 the U.S. Government opted for decontrol to resolve the crisis. In 1979 the Department of Energy optimistically forecasted that even by 1984, decontrol would lead to less than an 8 per cent increase in domestic oil production, while the Congressional Budget Committee forecasted less than a 5 per cent increase. Since at the time, the U.S. was importing about 50 per cent of the oil it used, the resulting reduction in imports would be small and still leave the U.S. price of energy under OPEC control for decades to come. There may be ways to stimulate significant non-OPEC energy production and make us less dependent on the Persian Gulf States, but decontrol is clearly not the way.

What about conservation? Higher prices will encourage conservation only via a substitution effect and/or an income effect. A substitution effect occurs when the price of oil rises relative to substitutes and thus consumers voluntarily use more of the less expensive energy source. But the *New York Times* (5 April 1979) reported that when the price of domestic oil rises, the price of substitutes rises 'sympathetically'. There are good logical reasons for this 'sympathetic' rise in the price of substitutes over time.

The existence of market conditions for raising prices and increasing income to the OPEC Cartel and deregulated oil producers depends on the existence of an exploitable market situation involving the present and future price elasticity of demand for oil in the relevant price range. As far as the OPEC Cartel is concerned, therefore, it depends in large measure on the current price in consuming countries and ultimately on the supply price at which alternative sources of energy will become significant substitutes for OPEC oil. As has already been indicated, however, many suppliers of a substitute energy source also have an economic interest in OPEC petroleum reserves, because they are either conglomerate energy companies with an OPEC concession or they have other large oil reserves. Others will recognize the futility of entering into a war for free market shares of energy with OPEC when the latter has access to vast quantities of oil producible at a real cost equal to a tiny fraction of the necessary market price which makes its product profitable to produce. Thus, producers of substitutes for OPEC oil, in the absence of government policy to eliminate OPEC power, must take into account the positive user cost in providing any substitute fuels. This positive user cost will raise the supply price above resource costs, while the expected carrying costs of underground inventories of energy supply are zero or negative in real terms as long as it is expected that OPEC will continue to increase the real wellhead price of oil.

The positive user cost of substitutes produced by energy conglomerates internalizes a cost that in a competitive economy would be external to the firm. Independent producers of domestic oil, shale, tar sands, coal, uranium, and so on (provided they were not permitted to share the monopoly returns of the major energy companies) would not care if they inflicted capital losses on the value of foreign underground reserves of petroleum by providing a cheaper energy source. The existence of rational, multi-source, energy producing conglomerates, however, constrains production of substitute fuels, makes monopolistic control of energy markets easier, and reduces consumer welfare. The ability of conglomerates to maintain high prices for substitute sources of energy tends to reinforce their monopoly power in marketing their OPEC oil.

If, at the current price, consumer demand for OPEC oil is therefore still in the exploitable range, a strong cartel of oil producing nations can allow multinational energy conglomerates and others to continue to raise prices relative to real resource costs. The continuous revenue increases of OPEC nations since 1970 seem to be attempts to search out the points at which demand for OPEC oil becomes so elastic that monopoly rents are fully exploited. (Higher prices require production restrictions, however, and hence market-sharing arrangements have been worked out to prevent one member of the Cartel from increasing its gains at the expense of others.) Since the multinational energy companies also have vested interests in the price of OPEC reserves, they are willing to support the OPEC Cartel by maintaining an 'orderly' production market in all fossil fuels. Thus, monopolistic and speculative withholding reinforce each other and merge into one. Accordingly, from both a logical and empirical basis, it appears that under the current energy market structure, sympathetic price rises are inevitable. Hence, even if domestic oil prices increase, there will be little or no conservation due solely to a substitution effect.

The primary way in which increasing domestic oil prices will induce conservation is via an income effect, i.e. by increasing energy costs faster than consumers' incomes so that they cannot afford to buy as much energy or any other goods. Since higher domestic prices also mean higher domestic incomes for those engaged in some aspect of the energy industry, however, whether any given individual conserves as energy prices rise depends on the proportion of his income spent on energy *vis-à-vis* the proportion of his income and wealth derived from the production of oil and its substitutes. Thus U.S. energy consumers with no economic interest in the energy industry will suffer the greatest loss in real income while some with extensive energy income and/or energy property wealth might actually find their real income rising and hence tend to use more energy than otherwise.

Accordingly higher domestic oil prices to the extent that they stimulate any conservation do so mainly by impoverishing some but not all U.S. energy consumers; decontrol promotes regional and sectional conflict when what is needed is cooperation against an external economic enemy such as OPEC who declared economic war on the U.S. almost a decade ago.

THE OIL TERMS OF TRADE AND U.S. STAGFLATION

The rapid increases in world oil prices since 1973 has exacerbated recent U.S. inflationary and recessionary tendencies. Moreover, the energy sector will continue to aggregate these U.S. proclivities in the future unless the economic relationships involving the oil terms of trade are understood and strong positive action is undertaken to reduce the power of the OPEC Cartel.

Table 9.1 presents an index of the oil terms of trade for the U.S. since 1972. The oil terms of trade are defined as the units of U.S. exports which claims have to be given to, to pay for each barrel of imported oil. Since there are many grades of oil and many different sources, and since the price for each type of oil does not move always proportionately or simultaneously, Table 9.1 is in terms of a specific and important quality oil – Saudi Arabian marker crude. Since the Saudi crude imported into the U.S. is produced (at least until 1980) by a U.S. chartered corporation (Aramco), and since a portion of the purchase price of Saudi crude is returned to the United States via Aramco dividends to its U.S. stockholders (Exxon, Mobil, Texaco, and Socal), the numerator of the terms of trade calculation was an index of the Saudi Arabian Government's 'take' or revenue per barrel[29] rather than an index of the actual posted wellhead price. (The denominator was an index of U.S. export prices as determined by the Department of Commerce.)

TABLE 9.1   Oil Terms of Trade (1972 = 100)
(U.S. Exports to Government take per barrel of Saudi Marker Crude)

Year	All Exports (1)	Capital Goods (2)	Industrial Supplies (3)	Food (4)	Autos (5)	Other Consumer Goods (6)
1972	100	100	100	100	100	100
1973	112	125	113	85	123	118
1974	396	492	345	275	484	505
1975	432	505	377	346	509	535
1976	448	487	405	409	503	538
1977	451	487	406	432	484	557
1978	410	425	388	420	430	493
1979	516	603	444	501	517	626

SOURCES   U.S. Department of Commerce; Adelman (1977, p. 11).

Table 9.1 indicates that since 1972 there has been basically an adverse change in the oil terms of trade whether computed on the basis of 'all exports' or on the basis of specific export categories more likely to be purchased by OPEC nations such as Saudi Arabia. In terms of 'all exports' this adverse trend first peaked in 1977 when the U.S. gave up 4.5 more units of exports per barrel imported relative to the export cost of similar imported oil in 1972. The terms of trade did however improve slightly in 1978 as only 4.1 as many units of exports were given up, and of course 1978 was a year where U.S. real income per capita improved significantly. In 1979, with the Iranian oil crisis and the consequent jump in oil prices, the oil terms of trade again turned against the United States rising to a new high of 5.16.

Interestingly, the oil terms of trade relative to U.S. food exports (Column 4 in Table 9.1) actually improved in 1973, but have since become adverse and followed the trend of all U.S. exports. (The 1973 decline is a statistical result due to the fact that U.S. food exports showed a price rise in the latter part of 1972 and through most of the year 1973, while other U.S. exports did not climb significantly in price until 1974, while oil prices did not begin their rapid climb until late in 1973.)

As far as Saudi Arabia is concerned (and this is generally true for all the OPEC nations) capital goods make up the bulk of their imports with food second in importance in the import sector. Other consumer goods including autos are, however, becoming increasingly important in the last few years as the wealth of the OPEC nations grows. Thus, as Columns 2, 4, 5, and 6 of Table 9.1 suggest, with the exception of food, the oil terms of trade *vis-à-vis* specific exports have become more adverse to the U.S. than the 'all exports' category. Thus Column 1 probably underestimates how badly the oil terms of trade have turned against the U.S. since 1972.

Table 9.2 indicates that the annual volumes of crude oil imported into the United States increased to more than 300 per cent in 1979 compared to 1972 volumes, while imports from OPEC nations rose to a peak of 431 per cent in 1977 but since then have been reduced to approximately 400 per cent of 1972 volumes. The OPEC share of U.S. crude oil imports which was 59 per cent in 1972, peaked at 86 per cent in 1977 and has since slid to 78 per cent. In 1978 and 1979, due to increasing supplies from mainly Mexico and a very slow growth in U.S. demand for crude, U.S. dependence on OPEC in terms of volumes of imports did decline, but the U.S. was still giving up more of its GNP to OPEC.

Using the estimated change in the 'oil terms of trade' index of Table 9.1 in conjunction with the growth in the 'imported OPEC oil' index of

TABLE 9.2   United States Crude Oil Imports

Year	Total Crude Imports (1972 = 100)	Imports from OPEC (1972 = 100)	OPEC's Share of U.S. Imports (%)
1972	100	100	59
1973	146	161	65
1974	157	196	73
1975	185	247˙	78
1976	239	350	86
1977	299	431	86
1978	298	403	82
1979	305	398	78

SOURCES   U.S. Bureau of Mines; Economist Intelligence Unit.

Table 9.2, it is calculated that the U.S. gave up *claims* to 1944 per cent more total goods annually in 1977 to obtain a 430 per cent increase in OPEC oil relative to what it gave up in 1972. In 1978, with an improvement in the oil terms of trade and a slight lowering of U.S. demand for OPEC oil, the U.S. gave up claims on 1652 per cent more goods for 410 per cent more OPEC oil than in 1972. With the renewed escalation of oil prices in 1979, however, the U.S. gave up claims for 2054 per cent more goods to OPEC in 1979 (even though we slightly decreased our imports of OPEC oil from 1978) relative to 1972. (During the period 1972–7 the annual cost in terms of claims given up to *all* oil exporting countries increased by approximately 1200 per cent for all the crude oil the U.S. imports; by 1979 it was almost 1600 per cent.) Thus, the annual transfer of purchasing power from residents in the U.S. (and obviously similar transfers from consuming nations elsewhere) to OPEC nations and other oil exporting countries is staggering.

The actual transfer of real goods from the U.S. to OPEC is somewhat less than the 1944 per cent (in 1977), or the 1632 per cent (in 1978) or even the 2054 per cent (1979), since many of the Cartel members, and especially Saudi Arabia, found it difficult to spend all the dollar claims they received for their oil. Table 9.3, for example, indicates that the Saudi Arabian trade surplus (exports minus imports) increased dramatically from $5.5 million in 1973 to $25.7 in 1977, while the export surplus declined to approximately $20 billion in 1978 when the oil terms of trade for the U.S. improved, and the Saudis absorbed much of the excess productive capacity of the Cartel by actually reducing oil exports by approximately 10 per cent in order to maintain the Cartel price.

TABLE 9.3   Trade and Current Accounts Surplus
(Billions of Dollars)

Year	Saudi Export Surplus	Total OPEC Export Surplus
1973	5.5	18.9
1974	26.4	86.6
1975	21.1	58.6
1976	25.0	69.8
1977	25.7	63.0
1978	19.9	38.9

SOURCE   IMF International Financial Statistics Yearbook, 1979.

As Table 9.3 suggests, the Saudi (and all OPEC nations combined) trade balance was very favourable for each year since 1973. International reserves for OPEC nations have grown rapidly as their excess purchasing power has piled up. The International Monetary Fund indicates that the international reserves of Saudi Arabia had grown to over $30 billion by 1977. The IMF estimates that Saudi international reserves declined in 1978 as oil prices were stable, while worldwide inflation increased the cost of Saudi imports and the U.S. oil terms trade improved by approximately 10 per cent.

Saudi Arabia particularly and the OPEC nations generally do not or cannot spend all their rapidly increasing claims on exports of the consuming nations such as the United States. Over the six years 1974–9 the current account surplus of the OPEC nations was $224 billion. The growth of these export surpluses means that during and immediately following periods of rapidly rising OPEC oil prices, the aggregate marginal propensity to save out of income by OPEC nations is much higher than that of oil consumers in the U.S. and elsewhere. Consequently any large redistribution of income from U.S. consumers to OPEC nations resulting from an adverse change in the U.S. oil terms of trade will significantly limit the growth of demand for the products of U.S. industries, thus creating a slowing of growth or even recession.

Even if the U.S. had not had restrictive anti-inflationary, monetary and fiscal policies since 1973, the U.S. would have suffered from stagflation because of the adverse change in the oil terms of trade. To the extent that OPEC nations are willing to hold financial claims and not buy U.S. goods with the income and wealth the Cartel has extorted from U.S. consumers since 1973, the loss in real income due to the change in the oil terms of trade and the increasing volume of oil imports takes the form of higher unemployment rather than a transfer of goods. (Thus if the U.S. could have controlled inflation in these years, the idle resources could have produced more goods for U.S. consumers.) It therefore follows that in any period when the OPEC Cartel forces a rapid deterioration in the U.S. oil terms of trade (e.g. 1974–5 and 1979–80), the U.S. economy will quickly slide, *ceteris paribus*, into a severe recession. Thus as long as U.S. policy towards the 'energy crisis' is one of primarily permitting the market price to escalate over time because of the domination of the OPEC Cartel in energy markets and hoping for conservation and even recession due to the income effects of higher energy prices (adverse terms of trade *vis-à-vis* foreign oil exporting nations), the U.S. Government is ensuring the continuous weakening of the U.S. and other oil consuming economies. As long as consuming nations permit the OPEC Cartel to exploit the market for energy, energy prices will continue to outrun inflation (while simultaneously contributing to inflationary pressures) until the energy consuming nations are so impoverished that they have little income left to be extorted by the oil exporting nations. The only alternative to this dismal scenario of continuous impoverishment of energy consumers is for the U.S. (which is the third largest oil producing nation and has potentially abundant alternative energy sources available domestically and from non-OPEC sources) to actively adopt government policies which break the Cartel's grip on energy markets.

OPEC PRICES AND INFLATION

The increase in the dollar price of OPEC oil since 1973 and the subsequent rise in domestic prices (even though the latter was ostensibly under government price control programmes) has created what in the 1920s was called a *commodity inflation*. A commodity inflation must *not* be allowed to spill over into an *incomes inflation*,[30] since the former (i.e. a rise in the value of an existing stock of basic raw materials) can, with proper policies, be limited and perhaps even reversed, but the latter (i.e. a wage and profit margin inflation) is almost inevitably irreversible.

Inflation is a device for redistributing income. A commodity inflation will, as long as it lasts, redistribute real income from consumers of commodities to producers and owners of property from which the commodity comes. The current world and domestic oil price inflation is a symptom of the real income redistribution that has occurred from energy consumers to the OPEC nations, to multinational companies, and to domestic producers and property owners. The major impetus for this redistribution was the growing power of the OPEC Cartel supported in large part by the lack of countervailing efforts in recent years by the multinational oil companies, the U.S. State Department, and the federal and state governments.

American consumers must ultimately be educated about inevitable economic realities of the recent world oil price increases, namely that there has been some reduction in the available total real income of the U.S.[31] and a considerable reduction of the real income of U.S. energy consumers (although some U.S. residents whose income is derived primarily from energy have received an increase in real income). Until and unless the U.S. breaks the Cartel, the only question which U.S. society can control is how it divides the burden of this lower real income among its members. Unfortunately in a world of unfettered markets each group of workers and energy using industries will refuse to accept a fair share of the lower standard of living which this income loss entails. Instead each group tries to maintain the former purchasing power of its income share by raising its wages or prices, thus pushing the burden of the loss on others. These uncoordinated, inconsistent and competing claims for higher money income to offset higher commodity prices result in a rampant wage–price spiral, i.e. an incomes inflation, that puts all members of the economy on a treadmill where all must run faster (demand more money income) merely to try to catch up. But since there are less goods and services to be shared in the U.S. per unit of effort by capital and labour, all U.S. income recipients cannot catch up to our pre-commodity inflation shares of the national product. The Cartel has removed too much of the national product by its manipulation of the oil terms of trade.

The traditional remedy for an incomes inflation is sufficient stringency in monetary and fiscal policies ('bullet-biting') so that the economy becomes so impoverished that it cannot be held to economic blackmail by powerful subgroups in the economy who take action to maintain or improve their well-being at the cost of others in society.[32] The high levels of inflation and unemployment that the U.S. experienced since 1974 were in large measure the result of (a) 'free' market forces attempting to distribute the loss in real income (due to the Cartel oil price rise) to the economically weak sectors of the U.S. economy, and (b) deliberate Administration policies to at least nibble on, if not bite, the bullet. With little or no change in foreign oil prices in 1977–8, the terms of trade began to improve slightly for the U.S.; and although the ripples of domestic incomes inflation continued, the real income per capita, on average, began to improve. Unfortunately with the renewed surge in

OPEC oil prices in 1979–80, the U.S. experienced another large recession and decline in per capita real income as the oil terms of trade have become more adverse than ever. The economic ripples of each increase in oil prices will most adversely affect the real income and wealth of the U.S.'s vulnerable energy using industries (transportation, utilities, etc.), its northern cities, its public sector employees, and the last-in first-out members of the U.S. labour force (i.e. the working poor).

As the U.S. wellhead price is permitted to rise to, and move with the OPEC oil price level, then U.S. domestic producers (and U.S. oil property owners via royalties) will find their terms of trade improving *vis-à-vis* the rest of the U.S. economy. Of course, if domestic producers expect their prices to increase and track those of OPEC, there must be currently substantial positive user costs associated with domestic oil production; hence current and future U.S. oil production growth will be very limited. Accordingly, it becomes essential that the U.S. Government adopts actions which prevent any further deterioration of (and which hopefully improves) the oil terms of trade. Until the U.S. adopts such activist policies to improve the oil terms of trade by breaking the OPEC Cartel, the nation will experience a continuing and growing loss of income to foreign oil exporting nations, as well as a redistribution of income from domestic consumers to domestic energy producers and property owners.

The remedy for any enlightened society which is faced with such a massive market redistribution of income is not to adopt the free market philosophy of the 'survival of the fittest' race to push the loss of real income on to others in the economy society. Instead, the U.S. should attempt to limit the Cartel and stop the redistribution via a coordinated national energy policy. To the extent that the U.S. must accept some of the already accomplished redistribution and potential future redistribution until the Cartel is broken, an enlightened society should adopt a national policy for coordinating the income claims of various groups and equitably sharing the remaining output that would be available at full employment. Such a policy goes under the various euphemisms of 'a social contract', a 'tax-based incomes policy' (TIP) or even 'wage and price regulation and coordination', i.e. 'controls'. Such a *national policy to coordinate income claims* (NPCIC) is the only viable alternative to the Darwinism of free markets where economic power is not equitably distributed,[33] or a combination of Darwinism and 'bullet-biting' where the hope of keeping each group in society in its place is to be accomplished by so debilitating the economy that no one can afford to make any demands.

The desirability of instituting full employment monetary and fiscal policies in tandem with a NPCIC and a policy to break OPEC is clear. A *national energy policy* must be developed that is consistent with a NPCIC and the concomitant expansionary fiscal and monetary policies that would prevent the redistribution of purchasing power to OPEC to partly take the form of high unemployment in the U.S.

A NATIONAL ENERGY POLICY (NEP)

The U.S. should be very cautious regarding undertaking any policy which is likely to permanently exacerbate the problems of unemployment and inflation.[34] The national energy policy (NEP) outlined below would involve the U.S. in an economic war with the Persian Gulf States while trying to limit domestic stagflation. Such a war, however, cannot be easily won or without any economic disruption. Even though any economic war will require some temporary consumers' sacrifices, this war should not be avoided; for the only choice is between (a) incurring temporary and hopefully minor dislocations and inconveniences during the initial state of economic warfare or (b) the permanent draining of income from consumers of energy. The latter means a permanent drag on economic activity and higher inflation rates than otherwise as long as OPEC continues to control the oil terms of trade. Hence, the U.S. really has no choice but to develop a policy which has as its basic objective the breaking up of the OPEC Cartel and any growing monopolistic control of domestic energy sources.

A ten-point national energy policy (NEP) which could provide U.S. consumers with sufficient energy while allowing producers to earn a competitive return rather than permitting them to share in Cartel profits would include

(1) extensive anti-trust action to break up conglomerate energy companies and to create competitive alternative sources of energy (competitive to OPEC sources and the major oil and gas producers), i.e. divestiture (see Appendix 1),

(2) government coordination and regulation of wellhead prices of oil and natural gas so that any *necessary* price increases occur at such low annual rates as to make speculative withholding unprofitable,

(3) prohibitive capital gains taxes on oil and gas properties to catch any speculative profits which avoid other policy nets,

(4) the changing of leasing policies on federal properties in order to reduce the financial constraint of the front-loaded bonuses and permit independents to develop offshore properties,

(5) policies which encourage and require accelerated exploitation of old and new properties, even if in certain situations such policies were to encourage flows in excess of MER[35] (i.e. increasing the cost of holding oil underground),[36]

(6) policies which prohibit 'shut-ins' and other practices which permit speculative withholding,

(7) an announced increasing schedule of import taxes on foreign crude oil (perhaps only on non-Western hemisphere oil) and products. Such an import tax schedule should be phased in with growing U.S. production while U.S. wellhead prices are controlled as suggested in (2) above,

(8) a federal sponsored corporation which at minimum would aid in financing the development of new oil properties and other energy sources and might even enter into joint ventures with independents; in other words, a *federal energy corporation (FEC)*,

(9) the adoption of an import auctioning system with unidentifiable foreign sellers and long term guaranteed markets (see further explanation in Appendix 2) to supply the diminishing share of the U.S. market as we increase hemisphere self-sufficiency in the next few years. Such a programme will create a positive incentive for members of OPEC to break with the Cartel, and for other non-OPEC producers whose price rises in sympathy with OPEC (e.g. Mexico) to be more competitive;

(10) elimination of the foreign tax credit, and as has been argued elsewhere,[37] treating payments to OPEC nations above traditional royalty rates as extortion or bribery and hence not a normal cost of doing business and not therefore deductible from the U.S. income taxes. This last point would create a major economic incentive for domestic based offtakers and refiners who are buyers of crude oil to reflect consumer interests for a change rather than producer interests as they have in the past.

The implications of many of the 10 points of this NEP are obvious. The aims of such a coordinated energy policy are to

(1) create an elastic demand for imported oil by encouraging the existence of many independent domestic producers of energy who cannot share in the monopoly rents of OPEC and the multinational energy conglomerates;

(2) squelch producer speculation activities in all energy sources; and

(3) provide incentives for individual OPEC members to cheat on the Cartel by removing the international energy companies as a mechanism for enforcing OPEC price decisions.

Until the U.S. explicitly adopts policies to achieve such goals, the oil terms of trade may continue to deteriorate in the future as OPEC exploits every market opportunity energy consuming nations permit.

APPENDIX 1: DIVESTITURE AND THE MARKET FOR ENERGY

Divestiture involves two forms of corporate integration. Vertical integration involves the same enterprise in two or more of the various stages of production of oil from well through retail outlet. Conglomerate energy integration involves the same business firm in the various stages of production of two or more energy supplies (e.g. petroleum and coal). Although vertical integration normally receives the most public attention, both forms are symptomatic of the same economic malady – the desire of energy producers to obtain, maintain, and protect monopoly rents obtained from energy consumers via the market price system.

Most economists recognize that the essence of monopoly power involves suppliers whose behaviour drives and maintains a wedge between prices charged to consumers and long run competitive factor costs. Some economists, however, finding that the task of trying to obtain and analyse data to measure the long run factor costs, and hence the magnitude of the monopoly wedge, is extremely difficult, have taken the easy way out. Such investigators have taken a tremendous leap of faith without any basis in logic or fact. They assert that the ability of any industry to develop and maintain a wedge between price and long run factor costs depends primarily upon the structure of the industry, which can be measured by concentration ratios.[38] If the reader accepts this unproven assertion about a unique relationship between concentration ratios and monopoly behaviour, then the discussion of the existence of monopoly power degenerates simply into one on the statistics of concentration ratios, what magnitude of ratio is 'workably competitive', and above what ratio does monopoly begin (and the subsidiary questions as to whether the geographical market and product lines are properly defined, etc.).

No reasonable student of monopoly denies that if one or a small group of sellers can control the supply of a commodity in general demand *with no close substitutes*, then this firm or group working in consort can extract large monopoly rents from the buyers. If, on the other hand, there are very many firms selling products that are close substitutes so that no one firm or group of firms has more than an insignificant share of the market, then the ability to exercise monopoly power is extremely difficult. Starting from these two polar cases where concentration ratios should approximate to 100 and zero per cent respectively, many students cite concentration ratios as structural evidence of the monopoly power of sellers in the market even though most users of concentration ratios are well aware of the statistical limitations of this measure whose magnitude varies according to (a) the definition of the market (in terms of geographical area as well as product description), and (b) whether the ratio is based on sales, assets, proven reserves, etc. Moreover, the concentration ratio measures 'control' only as it is manifest under the legal institution of separate business firms, and it ignores (a) legal institutional arrangements between firms which may limit or even prohibit competitive behaviour (e.g. state prorationing rules, field unitization rules, joint ventures, farm-out agreements, etc.) and (b) a confluence of expectations and interests of separate firms galvanized by widely publicized news events.

There is less of a consensus as to how large concentration ratios must be before they pose a definite threat to consumers and therefore suggest the need for government action. Obviously, at 100 per cent the threat exists; but at zero per cent, the threat would be negligible. But where between zero and 100 per cent does the threat become significant?

Many investigators advocate a 50 per cent concentration ratio for the four top firms as a boundary above which there may be a need for anti-trust action. Below a 50 per cent concentration ratio, it is often asserted that 'workably competitive' markets exist. There is, of course, no logical or theoretically sound reason for a 50 per cent ratio (or any other ratio between zero and 100 per cent) as an action decision line. Fifty per cent appears to have been chosen simply because it is half way between zero and 100 per cent.

Implicit in all discussions of concentration ratios is the visceral belief that measuring the structure of any industry by the concentration ratios of its top four firms is a useful *proxy* for measuring monopoly power. Of course, everyone recognizes that we should be measuring behaviour that leads directly to monopoly wedges. Since this is a difficult task, many students have decided to measure what they believe are the 'shadows on the cave wall' instead, for it is so much easier to measure concentration ratios (by courtesy of government statistical collecting agencies) and then assume the shadows so perceived are accurate reflections of the monopoly dragon. These students assume there is a direct positive and stable relationship between monopoly power and concentration. Even worse, it is asserted without proof that a dangerous level of concentration is *independent of the industry involved or conditions affecting the industry or market under investigation.* The boundary between workable competition is assumed to apply to all times, all places, all conditions, and all industries.

In reality, a low (high) concentration ratio is neither a necessary nor sufficient condition for the absence (existence) of monopoly power. At best, one could assert that, all other things being equal, lower concentration ratios increase the *a priori* probability of a competitive market (or a lack of monopoly power), and a high concentration ratio increases the subjective probability (in the minds of the authors) of monopoly power. This does *not* mean that a low concentration ratio in a specific industry must mean that a competitive market exists, any more than the statement 'if I should toss an unbiased coin four times, it is impossible to get four heads', is applicable to a single trial of four tosses. In fact, there really is no universally accepted concentration ratio below which a market can be positively classified as workably competitive. To appeal to the opinion of authorities of previous studies who have accepted 50 per cent as the workably competitive level, is to reduce the argument to a semantic discussion from which there is little escape.

Under most measures of this concentration ratio test for the top four firms, the petroleum industry scores below 50 per cent, and many will no doubt offer this as definitive proof that there is no need for divestiture. For those who share this sanguine view, it should be pointed out that in 1976 imports accounted for less than 50 per cent of the U.S. crude market, while OPEC oil took up only one-third of this market and the Arab nations supplied much less than 20 per cent of the total U.S. market. As of 1980 imports represent still approximately half of the total crude oil market in the U.S. and hence OPEC crude (which comes from 13, not 4 producers) take up less than 50 per cent. Yet, can anyone doubt that in the absence of government price controls, the U.S. market price would be set by OPEC, and even more directly, by the Arabs, despite the fact that these concentration ratios would indicate that the U.S. market is workably competitive and therefore beyond the control of OPEC?

Thus, it should be apparent that the absolute level of a concentration ratio may not be very meaningful in terms of monopoly rents obtained from consumers.[39] Trends in concentration ratios over time can at least suggest increases or decreases in potential monopoly power and hence are more meaningful than absolute levels. For example, the concentration ratio of the top four producers of U.S. crude has increased by 55 per cent between 1955 and 1973, while the concentration ratio of the top 20 producers increased by 38 per cent in the same period. Thus this industry is becoming more concentrated overall, and especially so at the top.

From the standpoint of economic theory, the degree of monopoly power m, exercised by producers in any market can be measured by $m = (P - MC)/P$, where P is product price and MC is marginal resource costs. Such a measure implies a mark-up over marginal costs of

$$\frac{1}{1 - m} - 1.$$

This mark-up is compatible with either profit maximization (in which case m is equal to the reciprocal of the price elasticity of demand at the point where price and output maximize profit), or with a conventional mark-up over marginal resource costs in a world of uncertainty where profit maximization may be elusive. The mark-up involves a transfer of income from consumers to producers for each unit of output in excess of what would be required for producers and property owners to earn a competitive return on their resources. This excess is a monopoly rent per unit of output. The effect of monopoly is to redistribute income from consumers to producers and property owners *vis-à-vis* the distribution in a competitive environment. Ultimately underlying the current 'energy crisis' is a struggle regarding the distribution of income and wealth between consumers and producers!

The way to break this monopolistic power and its associated ability to redistribute income is to alter the demand curve facing the sellers attempting to exercise this monopoly power, i.e. to create conditions which all recognize will cause this demand curve to become more price elastic in the relevant range in the near future. Such a price elastic demand change will occur when there are potentially significant quantities of alternative sources of energy available (a) which are profitable to produce at less than the Cartel price and (b) whose production rates are not controlled by managers who have any vested interest in maintaining the current monopoly price in fossil fuels. In the current context, the Cartel is likely to be broken for economic reasons only when significant additional supplies exist, which are not under production controls of OPEC nations or companies that have a large vested interest in maintaining current high wellhead prices in order to preserve the capital value of their large underground reserves. Divestiture will help create such conditions.

APPENDIX 2: AN IMPORT AUCTION SCHEME

To help achieve the intermediate goals of breaking the OPEC Cartel with the desirable attendant reduction in Arab-country power over Western Europe and the Third World, it is necessary to eliminate the major international oil companies as direct importers of OPEC crude for the U.S. The OPEC Cartel has not broken down, as a cartel usually does (because of its members cheating on price), for two important reasons, namely because (a) the solidarity among the Arab producers, and (b) the international companies willingly policing prices and quantities in non-Arab OPEC countries. To act differently would threaten their Arab oil concessions. For example Aramco, the main producer in Saudi Arabia, is a combination of four of the 'Seven Sisters'. These four companies cannot purchase large quantities of crude over long periods at prices well below OPEC levels from sources outside Saudi Arabia, or else they will be in serious danger of losing their control of more than 9 million barrels per day of crude production in Saudi Arabia.

The establishment of a federal agency as the sole purchaser of imported crude and petroleum products via a secret auction system would eliminate the price surveillance mechanism of the internationals which is a strong prop holding the OPEC Cartel together. This federal agency should not be limited to making a zero profit or loss in each year. The agency should be able to, at any point of time, refuse any or all sealed bids as part of a strategy to prevent collusive bidding arrangements; hence, the agency may not be able to purchase sufficient oil to cover the difference between domestic demand and supply for any one period. If the agency were forced to sell this limited quantity of imports at a zero profit price, and if there were no domestic price controls, the refining companies could make a windfall profit because of the shortage. Moreover, for reasons given below, there may be circumstances where it may be strategic for the agency to operate at a loss.

The bidding duration of purchase contracts should have a built-in flexibility which encourages sellers to price at less than the Cartel price, so that the greater the discount offered from the Cartel price, the longer the purchase agreement. For example, suppose all bids submitted are at the world cartel price. The agency should be required to limit purchases to 60 or 90 days (and perhaps even reduce imports) and request another auction. If sellers are willing to undercut the world price, the purchase contract should have a longer duration. For example, if the seller's dollar price is 5 per cent below world price, a four-month contract for a specified quantity per month would be accepted; if the discount is 10 per cent, a one-year contract, and if 15 per cent, a two-year contract, etc. Such a duration–discount schedule may be extended to as long as four or five-year purchases for substantial discounts. This will increase the incentive to cheat on the Cartel if the U.S. will guarantee quantity purchases at below current Cartel prices for a number of years; especially if a Cartel member thinks that this may mean a guaranteed market in later years at a dollar price above the world price when the Cartel disintegrates. The objective is to make it so lucrative for any one member of OPEC to cheat and guarantee his income for a number of years, that each member is uncertain as to who will be the first to break, while those with the greatest reserves have the most to lose if others break first.

Of course, if the agency is successful in breaking the Cartel, it will be saddled with purchase contracts for specified quantities for a number of years which may be at a price *above* the market price. The agency should then sell the oil to domestic refiners at the world price thereby passing the gain on to the American consumer. The loss to the agency should then be subsidized from tax revenues, to be looked upon as a defence expenditure for economic warfare, and a successful expenditure at that!

10 Can Wages be Fixed in Terms of an International Standard?

Advocates of universal indexing of money wage contracts are suggesting that by changing the laws of contract money wages can be made sticky in terms of some commodity standard. If such a system were feasible, should money wages be geared to the money cost of an international or a domestic commodity standard? And, what would be the operational effects of such legal modification of the existing law of money contracts on the operation of an entrepreneurial economy?

THE REQUIREMENTS FOR A STABLE INTERNATIONAL WAGE STANDARD

Using the term 'wheat' as a euphemism for an internationally traded market basket of commodities,[1] the question can be posed as can one design a system where the 'wheat' wage per unit of human effort is sticky? For example, some might recommend setting effort wages in terms of some nominal unit but then *indexing* this money wage per man hour to the money price of 'wheat'. Could such a system work and what would be the advantages of such a system?

The claimed advantages of such a stable 'wheat' wage system are (a) to permit freedom of movement of relative money prices in response to relative 'real' changes in supply and demand, while simultaneously (b) ensuring wage earners (and other income recipients in a more general system) of the stability of real income per unit of effort over time.[2]

If all domestic money incomes and debt contracts were suddenly 'indexed' to the domestic money price of wheat, then sooner or later most people in the economy would perceive (expect) that a unit of

202

'wheat' is always a better store of value than a unit of money.[3] Once these expectations became ubiquitous, all economic agents would demand 'wheat' for store of value purposes (as a liquidity time machine), instead of money or even indexed securities denominated in money terms. This change in expectations would increase the demand for 'wheat' as a reserve asset (over and above its normal use as a running asset in the production of goods and services and the satisfaction of consumption wants). This additional demand for 'wheat' would, if the 'wheat' were not in perfectly elastic supply (i.e. if there were diminishing returns in 'wheat' production) initially push up the money costs of 'wheat' production (assuming for the moment *unchanged* money wages). The higher money costs of production (even with constant factor money prices) due to diminishing returns would increase the domestic money price of 'wheat'. This, in turn, would force an increase in all money wages due to indexing (with a lag based on the time it takes for the 'wheat' price change to be effective in altering the contractual money wage). This indexed induced rise in money wages, however, would fully increase the money costs and market prices of 'wheat' *for any given rate of 'wheat' production flow*, inducing another rise in the price index and a continuous feedback into money wages, 'wheat's' money production costs and prices, etc. Consequently, any successful attempt to maintain the commodity purchasing power of money wages, by altering the existing money–liquidity system through fully indexing all money wages (and other money contracts) to the money price of some basic commodity or commodities that are readily producible but not in perfectly elastic supply, will be self-destructive. In a world of time, change and uncertainty, it is impossible to instantaneously and universally *fix* all money wage contracts in terms of any real commodity wage per man hour as long as the 'chosen' commodity is readily producible but not in perfectly elastic supply.

Thus, it is the existence of diminishing returns (less than perfectly elastic supply) of any readily producible commodity standard which frustrates any attempt to develop a wage per man hour whose purchasing power is legally fixed to a market basket of such producible goods. Would the system be more successful if the commodity standard chosen were in perfectly elastic supply? Under these productivity conditions could an entrepreneurial economy obtain a universal stable commodity wage by switching from the current money wage system to an indexed money contract system? Moreover, would not such an 'indexed' system simultaneously provide a money of constant purchasing power in terms of the commodity standard since the latter would be produced under (hypothesized) conditions of constant returns? If the answer to these queries is positive, then universal indexing of contracts would be desirable especially if the commodity standard were one widely used by economic agents in production and consumption activities. A careful analysis, however, indicates that while it is not possible to *logically* rule out this possibility, the requirements of such a system are unlikely to exist in any real world situation.

Stability of the purchasing power of money in terms of the value of commodity output requires that the unit money costs of production (or efficiency earnings) be relatively sticky in terms of money. If money wages were indexed to the market price of a 'wheat' commodity or commodities whose production flow supply elasticity were approximately infinite, then in a world subject to unexpected change in the future, wages and the costs of future production would be expected to be more stable in terms of 'wheat' than in terms of money. Once these expectations became widespread, 'wheat' would be perceived as, *ceteris paribus*, a superior store of value *vis-à-vis* money and hence, an additional demand for 'wheat' as a liquidity time machine would be forthcoming. If 'wheat' were in perfectly elastic flow supply, the increased demand would induce a proportionate increase in quantity supplied. This increase in quantity supply would not be wanted for use in further production processes or consumption; rather, it would be held as *additional* inventories. The cost of this additional storage for any standardized producible commodity would be substantial. This increase in the real carrying cost of holding additional 'wheat' would reduce the value of wheat as a store of value.

Hence, any economy developing such an indexing system would create an incompatible situation. Indexing induces expectations that 'wheat' is a superior store of value; but increased holdings of 'wheat' for liquidity purposes involve higher additional storage costs for 'wheat' used as a liquidity time machine, thereby reducing its value for liquidity purposes.

Any entrepreneurial system utilizing an indexing scheme designed to universally fix wages *in terms of a commodity standard* would require not only that the production costs of the standard commodity be relatively constant for all relevant rates of flow of production *in the short run and the long run*, but also that any surplus production of this commodity (over current usage in further production or consumption) be absorbed into inventories *without cost* (for if production costs are expected to be constant in the long run there is no hope of holding current stocks for profit [liquidity] from higher future prices given significant carrying costs).[4] Although it is not logically possible to deny the possible existence of a commodity whose supply elasticity is infinite for any rate of production flow in both the long run *and* the short run, and whose carrying cost for any inventory level of surplus stocks is negligible, it does not seem probable that any such commodity exists in the real world.

In other words, any entrepreneurial economy in which money wages per unit of time are indexed in order to fix real earnings, would require linking money wages to the market price of a commodity (or commodities) which could be produced at roughly constant money costs of production and be stored without limit at negligible carrying costs. If, however, carrying costs per unit of time are important and/or if they increase significantly with the quantity of the commodity held for liquidity or other purposes, then the standard commodity could maintain its store of value use in the eyes of wealth holders only if these economic agents expected that the *future* money labour costs of production of the commodity would increase at a faster per annum rate than the ratio of annual carrying costs to current money production costs. (Such expectations imply that the money costs of producing 'wheat' will rise rapidly so that it is still profitable to store one's wealth in 'wheat' despite its high and increasing carrying costs.) Thus, 'we require the impossible combination of a stable labour cost of production of wheat with the expectation of a constantly rising labour cost of production of wheat'.[5]

In sum, in a world where the future is uncertain and change is inevitable, and where people desire to hold liquid stores of wealth, it would appear impossible to devise a universal system of indexing which can stabilize the real wage of labour in terms of some *producible* commodity whose elasticity of production is either perfectly elastic or significantly greater than zero but less than infinitely elastic.

WAGES AND GOLD

Of course, if a system is devised to stabilize wages in terms of a commodity with a negligible elasticity of production (e.g. gold), then that commodity would possess the same elasticity properties as money. It is, of course, always theoretically possible to index domestic money wages to the money price of a commodity such as gold, but then the stability of the purchasing power of gold in terms of a commodity standard in such an indexing scheme would be measured by the price of new producible goods *in terms of gold* where the latter would vary directly with gold efficiency wages (or earnings).[6] Gold efficiency wages would be stable over time, and hence the stability of the purchasing power of domestic money in terms of producible commodities assured, only if the ounces of gold purchased per man hours of labour relative to the productivity of labour per man hour were stable or (sticky) over time. In other words, fixing wages directly or indirectly in terms of gold may preserve and even enhance the liquidity powers of gold, but it would not stabilize either a local money's purchasing power, or gold's purchasing power, in terms of any producible standard, unless the gold efficiency wage (i.e. ounces of gold per unit of human effort relative to productivity of workers) was stable over time.

Moreover, in any system of indexing money wages to gold prices, if gold is permitted to (a) circulate side-by-side with local currencies and (b) be used as the mode of contractual settlement in the private sector, then it would be necessary to internationally coordinate changes in the gold effort wage (i.e. ounces of gold per unit of human effort) in each nation to relative changes in productivity among the trading partners, in order to stabilize gold's purchasing power in terms of some international commodity standard market basket.

Thus, each nation in a trading world is faced with an inescapable problem. In the absence of an internationally agreed upon and coordinated incomes policy which takes account of differential levels and rates of change of productivity in various sectors and regions, no nation can completely control the purchasing power of its local money or protect the real income and wealth of each citizen. Each nation could, *of course*, stabilize domestic money wages in terms of a single basically non-reproducible international commodity such as gold. Since gold has no known major human use except as a reserve asset,[7] stabilizing wages in terms of gold would, *ceteris paribus*, not necessarily stabilize the market value of other useful producible commodities in terms of either gold and/or domestic currency. In other words, without explicit international agreement on income distribution, each trading nation will be unable to develop any unilateral policy for stabilizing the real income of its citizens independent of the money wage-productivity, and the degree of monopoly development occurring within its own borders and in the other nations with which it trades.

For all practical purposes therefore, it is impossible to develop any money whose purchasing power will be sticky over time in terms of some international commodity standard unless and until each of the major trading partners is willing to scientifically manage its own domestic income distribution, while simultaneously agreeing to permit the world income distribution to be determined

(1) initially, by the existing terms and patterns of trade at the moment of treaty (contractual?) agreement for cooperation among trading nations, and

(2) over time, by the growth in overall productivity, relative changes in productivity among nations, and absolute as well as relative changes in demands at the existing terms of trade, plus

(3) an agreement to either transfer income via loans and/or grants among trading partners, or use a tariff policy to maintain the current accounts payments balance. Alternatively, an agreement to slowly and deliberately alter the terms of trade by a coordinated incomes policy *and* tariff policy, whenever differential productivity changes and monopoly trends would otherwise induce an 'undesirable' income distribution, regional population distribution, and/or power distribution among and within trading partners, can be adopted.

In the absence of an international agreement on these terms there can be no possibility of fixing real wages or of developing an international money (a) whose purchasing power over some basket of internationally traded goods can be controlled over time (except in the most static of situations), and (b) which can also be used by the public as both a mode of international contractual settlement and an international liquid store of value. The key to the establishment of such a sticky international money is an international agreement to adopt a coordinated wage and profit policy which will obviously initially 'lock-in' the existing historically developed international structure of efficiency wages and degrees of monopoly. From this initial situation it should be possible to simultaneously coordinate rates of changes in efficiency wages and profit margins over time among nations to achieve an equitable distribution of the real wealth of nations without rampant worldwide inflation. These requirements are, of course, identical to those required among sectors and regions within a single nation which adopts a national incomes policy to stabilize the purchasing power of the national currency in terms of some domestic commodity standard. Unfortunately, given the human condition, the social and political obstacles to obtaining such agreement have prevented the development of national incomes policies except during periods of war and other grave economic crises. How much more unlikely then is it to expect to achieve a modicum of international cooperation in the coordination of incomes policies, given the current worldwide distribution of income and economic power, nationalistic spirit, and social and political heterogeneity among nations?

The task of transmitting human nature towards working diligently for a more equitable distribution of income either nationally or internationally is a difficult, but not impossible one. Nor is a complete conversion necessary to combat inflation. As Keynes noted, in the real world as we know it

> there are valuable human activities which require the motive of money-making and the environment of private wealth-ownership for their full fruition. Moreover, dangerous human proclivities can be canalised into comparatively harmless channels by the existence of opportunities for money-making and wealth . . . It is better that a man should tyrannise over his bank balance than over his fellow-citizens; and whilst the former is sometimes denounced as being a means to the latter, sometimes at least it is an alternative. But it is not necessary for the stimulation of these activities and the satisfaction of these proclivities that the game should be played for such high stakes as at present. *Much lower stakes will serve the purpose equally well, as soon as the players are accustomed to them.* The task of transmitting human nature must not be confused with the task of managing it. Though in the ideal commonwealth men may have been taught or inspired or bred to take no interest in the stakes, it may still be wise and prudent statesmanship to allow the game to be played, *subject to rules and limitations*, so long as the average man, or even a significant section of the community, is in fact strongly addicted to the money-making passion.[8]

WHAT CAN BE ACHIEVED?

If nations are unable or unwilling to manage their own aggregate income level and its distribution directly, then they are unlikely to be willing to join in an international effort to manage worldwide production and income differentials. It is therefore impossible to develop a system in which there is an international money (which can be used by the general public) whose purchasing power will be sticky over time. It is, of course, possible to have a system of domestic currencies for settling local contractual obligations, and a system of exchange rates which can reflect permanent changes in efficiency wage relations between trading partners. In such a system however, all local currencies *cannot* be stabilized in terms of an international standard unless efficiency wages remain, on average, unchanged.

Since domestic banking systems must be linked via an international clearing mechanism, it is however possible to develop an international money of constant purchasing power which is used *solely* to settle uncleared balances between the various national banking systems. If rules are developed which prevent credits from being removed from this proposed international banking and clearing system, then the system can never find itself in financial difficulties. The international clearing money unit (or ICMU) can then always be stabilized in terms of some international commodity standard, provided ICMUs *cannot* be held by the general public either for the medium of contractual settlement or for liquidity purposes. Stability can be achieved via

(1) having the exchange rate between the local currency and ICMUs vary as the local money price of the commodity basket alters, while

(2) Central Banks buy and sell their own currencies (two-way convertibility) against the ICMU *only* to other Central Bankers and the international clearing agency while they simultaneously hold only ICMUs (no foreign currencies) as liquid reserve assets for international financial transactions; and

(3) each Central Bank has unqualified control over outward transactions of its nationals (including the holding of foreign exchange by them); and

(4) the international clearing agency has a lender of last resort mechanism which assures each Central Bank of a continuing sufficient reserve of ICMUs.[9]

By altering the exchange rate between local monies and the ICMU to offset the rate of inflation of a basket of goods in terms of each domestic money, the ICMU's purchasing power is stabilized. By restricting use of ICMUs to Central Banks, private speculation regarding ICMUs as a hedge against inflation is avoided. Each nation's rate of inflation in terms of its local currency would then be determined solely by (a) the domestic incomes policy (or lack of one) for stabilizing domestic purchasing power in terms of either a domestic commodity standard or an earnings (wage and profit) standard, plus (b) the change in the terms of trade between the domestic nation and the rest of the world, given the local government's policy towards the level of domestic money wages and profit margins.

At this stage of human history, such a scheme would not protect each nation from the folly of not instituting some form of rational domestic incomes policy to stabilize its money's purchasing power in terms of domestically produced goods (V_{DP}). If a nation preferred to leave its income level determination and distribution to the free market, it would be free to do so – but if it did, and the results were out of line with the growth in efficiency wages, etc. in other nations, the inflationary consequences could be, in the main, contained at the national boundary and inflationary tendencies need not readily spill over to trading partners!

If a sovereign nation does not or will not make the effort to save itself, then it is practically impossible for any supranational body to save it – except by setting an example of proper conduct. What the proposed ICMU scheme can do, however, is to encourage each independent nation to attempt to get control of the money costs of domestic production (efficiency earnings) in terms of its local currency so that the domestic money's purchasing power can be stabilized in terms of a domestic commodity (V_{DP}) standard. National inflation in terms of a commodity standard having *foreign* components might still be imported by a *ceteris paribus* change in the terms of trade unless there is concomitant offsetting reduction in the domestic money prices of domestically produced goods as suggested by equation (4.13) of Chapter 4.

Each sovereign nation will face the loss in purchasing power of its currency (but not necessarily in terms of ICMUs) if either (a) there is an increase of foreign monopoly power (e.g. OPEC) or foreign labour costs of internationally traded goods whose price (as quoted in world markets) is rising in terms of the local currency unit (e.g. OPEC oil in terms of U.S. dollars), or (b) there is an increase in domestic efficiency earnings while foreign efficiency earnings are constant, when both sets of efficiency earnings are valued in the same currency at existing exchange rates. Inflation resulting from (a) always worsens a nation's terms of trade, while inflation from process (b) can, *ceteris paribus*, improve the nation's terms of trade and trade balance especially if foreigners' demand for exports is relatively inelastic.

If the exchange rate between the ICMU and the local money is related to the rate of inflation in domestically produced goods in terms of domestic money, then each nation is prevented from favourably altering its terms of trade by permitting higher efficiency earnings in terms of its own currency. In other words, domestic incomes inflation cannot, in this system, spill over to other nations and hence process (b) will no longer be operative as a mechanism for, *ceteris paribus*, spreading international inflation. Consequently, the only remaining mechanism for spreading international inflation is when a foreign cartel is able to increase prices in terms of local currency as suggested in process (a).

Short of attempting to break or reduce the market power of international cartels, there is nothing any nation can do (except force a concomitant reduction in *domestic* efficiency earnings) to fight inflation of prices in terms of domestic currency resulting from the successful exercise of monopoly power by an international cartel such as OPEC. If, however, a nation is unable or unwilling to combat the cartel's attempt to redistribute world income, at least the nation should limit the inflationary effect to a minimum by adopting a domestic incomes policy which distributes the remaining gross product (after paying the tribute to the cartel) in a socially acceptable manner – namely one that avoids depressing the local economy and/or encouraging a prolonged struggle among nationals to push the loss of real income to the foreign monopoly power on to others, either at home or in third party nations. If a nation is unable or unwilling to limit domestic efficiency earnings to accommodate the additional real income claims of OPEC, the ensuing struggle over the remaining income should, for the global good, be limited to its own residents. Nations should not be permitted to push off the loss in real income to OPEC on to third party nations; the use of ICMUs, as suggested above, would constrain such national anti-social behaviour against trading partners.

Traditional theory, on the other hand, suggests that nations cannot (in the long run) transmit inflation due to rising domestic efficiency wages. Since it is assumed that domestically produced goods are gross substitutes for foreign goods in both domestic and foreign markets, the higher money costs of production, it is argued, will cause domestic entrepreneurs to lose their share of domestic and foreign markets – even if the domestic inflation improved the terms of trade in the short run. Of course, the success of domestic entrepreneurs in limiting future increases in efficiency wages depends on the assumed resulting short-run recessionary unemployment levels and business loss constraining future money wage demands relative to productivity growth.

It is of course true that if foreign and domestic goods are very good substitutes, local entrepreneurs will be threatened with a significant potential loss of income and markets and will have incentives to hold down wage offers. An offsetting factor, however, is that the improvement in the terms of trade may increase the truculent tendencies of labour unions and the remaining employed workers – especially if foreign products are a significant portion of the consumption standard. Consequently, it may take a tremendous increase in unemployment to weaken union obduracy and strengthen entrepreneurial bargaining positions sufficiently to permit foreign competition to reduce domestic inflationary tendencies. (On the other hand, the initial change in the terms of trade may induce foreign unions to increase their efficiency wages thereby weakening foreign competitive forces.) Thus, in the absence of direct policies to limit domestic efficiency wages, severe and costly recessions may be the only method for limiting inflationary forces domestically and internationally.

If the market demand facing domestic entrepreneurs is weakened either due to (a) a foreign competitor's efficiency wages rising at a slower rate than domestic efficiency wages or (b) deliberate government policies to induce recession, then there is some pressure on domestic entrepreneurs to slow the rise in future money costs of new production flows. If these domestic production flows are components of an internationally traded market basket of goods, then this is a factor for lessening the international spread of inflationary tendencies through trade among trading partners. Depression is the purchase price of a *market force incomes policy* in our inflationary times.

If, however, labour and/or cartels remain equally powerful in various nations, so that domestic and foreign efficiency wage increments rise in a leapfrog manner, but at approximately equal rates over considerable periods of time, then in the absence of a coordinated incomes policy, a planned recession may be an impotent anti-inflationary tool. If labour or product oligopolies remain powerful forces *despite planned recessions*, there is an additional incentive for the remaining domestic wage earners in each nation to try to force their efficiency wages up even more rapidly than foreign workers can, for the resulting improvement in the terms of trade will improve workers' real income to the extent that there are foreign components in the domestic consumption market basket. Leapfrogging of group and sector efficiency wages will become a way of life as waves of inflation are buffeted from one nation to another and the game becomes one of doing the other fellow in before he does you.

The existence of a separate and distinct ICMU for clearing obligations between national banking systems and as a money different from that used in settling the general public's obligations, can help foster, under proper management and education, a reduction in these inflationary tendencies which are the result of groups trying to push off on to others the loss of real income initiated by the international exercise of monopoly, oligopoly, or union power by others. Since the ICMU will automatically appreciate as the local currency's purchasing power in terms of a domestic standard declines whenever a nation permits its domestic efficiency earnings to rise, trading partners who must use the ICMU for settling bank clearing will be completely protected from importing the local inflation. Any nation who refuses to get its own domestic incomes distribution under control via a NPCIC will suffer from inflation, but it will no longer be able to infect others with this virulent disease.

Such monetary institutions as the ICMU, however, cannot in themselves prevent the exercise of international economic power, if the groups who possess such market domination wish to utilize it and circumvent the civilized rules of the game. In the case of an unruly cartel, however, an international clearing union can still help limit the domestic feedback effects of cartel induced inflationary tendencies and may even help the nations coordinate an attack on the exercise of such international cartel or monopoly power.

Perhaps more important, however, is the fact that the existence of a separate money for an international clearing union provides the opportunity to develop an international monetary system which provides for an 'elastic' international currency to meet the growing needs for international liquidity with the growth of international trade. One purpose of Keynes' original 'bancors' scheme for an International Clearing Union[10] was to have a medium of contractual settlement between Central Bankers whose supply was endogenously expandable (the real bills doctrine) but which had the essential elasticity properties of money. The need for an *endogenous*, readily *expandable* international money as a mode of settlement made the use of gold as a means of international settlement and reserve asset less acceptable to Keynes (except perhaps as a psychological ultimate reserve asset which would never have to be used), as long as some variant of the bancor system was available for systematic and scientific management. In its purest form, Keynes' concept of the clearing union ultimately rested upon creditor nations accepting the clearing union's bancors as final dischargers of all foreign debts, when a nation's residents have refused to buy additional exports from the debtors at the time of private settlement. In any closed unionized monetary system, of course, creditors who refuse to spend their earned claims on the products of industry on the date of contractual payment *must* accept claims on the banking system *or* liquid assets sold to them by debtors as their store of liquid wealth. Keynes' Clearing Union was an attempt to develop a similar closed international banking system which simultaneously permitted, under clearly specified rules of the game, an endogenous international money supply.

In a world of uncertainty, the possession of liquidity by entrepreneurs (either money or readily liquid assets with low carrying costs) provides time for them to read the myriad of signals occurring in the market place, judge which are irrelevant and filter those out, interpret the remaining signals, and then, when the existing contractual activities expire over time, alter their commitments to take advantage of expected future events. But every aggregate expansion of activities requires the commitment of more liquid assets into either the running asset or reserve asset categories. In the absence of the provision of additional liquid reserve assets to the system, therefore, the net cushion of liquid safety (reserves) will decline as international transactions increase. Since liquidity is freedom while the possession of liquid reserve funds 'does not oblige expansion, but always facilitates it',[11] the inability of an international monetary system to expand with the needs of international trade will ultimately always make international expansion more difficult. Even if the expectations for profitable expansion in the future might be proved correct, unless sufficient liquidity exists or is readily available initially, there may be no way that entrepreneurs can finance this expansion if the public simultaneously refuses to reduce its liquidity position (*at the initial interest rate*) or the banking system refuses to increase the quantity of fully liquid assets. A properly designed, well managed international clearing system can provide an 'elastic' international currency which endogenously expands to the needs of international trade.

In any closed system, the monetary authority has no problem creating additional liquidity, for as long as confidence exists in the system of money contracts,[12] contractual payees (creditors) will always accept as a liquid time machine (direct or indirect) claims on the monetary authority as final discharge of contractual obligations. The monetary authority can then take any necessary steps it deems desirable to assure that regional banks do not run out of reserves and into balance-of-payments difficulties with banks in the same national system but in a different region.[13]

In an open system, national Central Banks can face difficulties if they create additional liquidity to aid expansion of production and thereby get out of step *vis-à-vis* their liquidity creating counterparts in other nations, *and* if foreign nationals wish to withdraw liquidity from the national banking system. If a national Central Bank creates additional liquidity to encourage increased output flows at rates which exceed expansion in foreign nations, then, *ceteris paribus*, if the marginal propensity to import is greater than zero, the most rapidly expanding nation will run into clearing imbalance on its trade account unless foreigners ultimately are willing to hold their increases in liquidity in the domestic banking system. If foreigners withdraw their liquidity, then in the absence of an international clearing union using ICMUs, the domestic Central Bank will lose its reserve assets. Unless, therefore, there is a rule for replenishing reserves of the deficit banks,[14] that economy which is growing most rapidly (and therefore increasing its and the world's real income most rapidly) will be forced to slow down to the pace of the others. What a foolish game it is – to force financial balance by putting contractionist pressures on growth and world trade – especially if the idle resources exist which would permit more real rapid growth! An international clearing money (or ICMU) which can expand with the needs of trade and a managed international clearing agency operating under rules which encourage expansionist pressures on world trade and finance can provide a mechanism which at least removes the potential for liquidity constraints limiting entrepreneurs from undertaking commitments to achieve their expansion plans.[15]

Of course, some might argue against such an international clearing money system, persevering instead for a one world 'ideal' monetary system. This 'ideal' would be defined in terms of a single medium of contractual settlement for *all* public and banking obligations worldwide, where such a money was sticky in terms of its purchasing power in terms of some commodity market. In the absence of a static world or some coordinated international incomes restraint policy, however, a stable international money used by both the public and the international banking system is impossible to achieve. A separate medium of contractual settlement among Central Banks, which was not available to settle private contracts, is at least a desirable first step limiting international inflationary and contractionary tendencies, and therefore providing an environment favourable for the growth of trade and global real income.

11 Euromoney

In our analysis of money, we have focused on its two basic functions, those of (a) the means of contractual settlement, and (b) the vehicle for transferring purchasing power over time, a liquidity time machine.

MONEY AND DOMESTIC LIQUIDITY

Legal tender laws plus government rules and custom as to what the central authorities will accept as substitutes for legal tender in the discharge of contracts at any one time or place, limit what can be the medium for settling any specific contract. In a modern UMS system, for example, sight drafts transferring title to bank liabilities are normally as acceptable as legal tender in the settlement of contracts. Why does the public accept bank drafts as a discharge of obligations?

Bankers normally borrow short and lend long, and therefore are in the position of continually needing refinance to prevent a cash flow deficit which can be fatal to their operations. Bankers are able to continually issue their liabilities to the public because the public has a demand for these liabilities (or for legal tender). These bank liabilities are used by the public to repay their previous contracted debts to (a) bankers, or (b) other members of the public who want bank liabilities in order to pay for services and/or newly produced goods purchased from other members of the public, who in turn must pay for their prior borrowings from the banks. Thus, the circular flow of income is financed by a continued recycling of bank liabilities among employers, employees, buyers, sellers, etc. The flow of money payments which finances the circular flow of real income and output can be made via either the cycling of legal tender currency or bank liabilities. The existence of a banking system and a double entry clearing system greatly facilitate the use of bank liabilities over currency for most of the expenditures that make up the circular flow of income. The existence of such a bank clearing system minimizes transaction costs and permits the use of private debts in the settlement of transactions, as long as the public has confidence that the private debt can be promptly converted into the form of money which is legally enforceable in the discharge of contracts.[1]

As long as the borrowing of bank liabilities by the public equals or exceeds their repayment flows, there is no problem in maintaining this public confidence – for it is never tested. In these circumstances as the circular flow of income rises, the public demand for bank liabilities increases, making bank deposits scarce and hence valuable. Bankers have therefore no difficulty refinancing the liability side of their balance sheet from the public should any member of the public call for converting his deposit into legal tender currency.

If, however, the circular flow slows down, refinancing becomes difficult. Bankers, unlike other debtors, are supposed to be assured refinance and access to legal tender money if need be whenever they develop a cash outflow deficit through the 'lender of last resort' function of the national Central Bank. The Central Bank provides the assurance to the public that bank liabilities can always be converted into legal tender money if necessary since the banker can either rediscount bank assets to the Central Bank or sell certain bank assets in an orderly 'open' market where the monetary authority acts as the ultimate market maker.

Thus, the willingness of the Central Bank to support the liquidity value of bankers' assets via market operations, rediscounting, and/or repurchase agreements permits the public to have absolute confidence that bank deposit liabilities are a perfect substitute for legal tender money in the discharge of private domestic contracts.

MONEY AND INTERNATIONAL LIQUIDITY

As long as there is *no* international money *generally available* to all domestic *and* foreign residents, and *generally accepted* by all for the legal discharge of contractual obligations, then, if there is to be organized trade between residents of different nations in a NUMS, there must be an organized, orderly spot market for foreign exchange.[2] The existence of spot foreign exchange markets provides international liquidity for those needing to settle international contracts today, while forward exchange markets provide the promise of international liquidity at specific future contractual settlement dates. In a regime of fixed exchange rates, the foreign currency (or foreign banks' deposit liability) becomes a *fully liquid asset* in terms of domestic money as the domestic monetary authority guarantees purchase (if necessary) of foreign currency (or gold) at a fixed price in terms of domestic legal money. Cooperative agreements among national Central Banks to fix exchange rates give the public confidence that foreign obligations can always be discharged when they come due at a fixed cost in terms of today's domestic money.

In any well organized, orderly 'floating' exchange rate system, on the other hand, the Central Bank will still be required to intervene in the foreign exchange market to provide international liquidity.[3] Of course, in such a system, the actual cost in terms of domestic money of foreign obligations when they come due in the future are much less certain.

In any developed financial system, there exist various markets for the resale of liquidity time machines (e.g. bonds, equities, etc.). These well organized resale markets permit the public to store purchasing power in terms of the domestic money unit in a variety of durable assets – some more liquid than others. If the particular time machine asset chosen is perceived to be *fully liquid* (e.g. time deposits, government bonds whose market price is pegged by the Central Bank, etc.), its resale price (or exchange rate) in terms of domestic money (and ultimately legal tender if desired) at any *and* every possible date is explicitly spelled out and *guaranteed* by the market maker in the resale market for that particular date. If, on the other hand, the time machine is merely a *liquid asset*, then its future exchange rate in terms of domestic currency is *not* guaranteed by any institutional arrangement. Rather, the future resale prices of liquid assets are left to the forces of supply and demand in specific spot asset markets, which are well organized *with institutional market 'makers' operating under explicit rules for trading*.[4] These trading rules may explicitly limit the rate at which the price can change each day and/or they may specify a ceiling and floor for the resale price which is guaranteed by the market maker, but the rules need not require the maker to guarantee an unchanging price for all time.

Markets for the use of (to hold) any liquidity time machines other than money are often termed 'credit markets'. In all modern production economies, credit markets are organized under a system of regulations determined by governmental laws and custom. Regulations as to market operations, institutional arrangements, financial scope, size of charges levied on market participants and even size of transactions are routinely open to government scrutiny. Moreover, taxes are often levied on transactions in such credit markets (e.g. stock transfer taxes, capital gains) thereby affecting the operations of such markets. Even in the current fashionable anti-regulation milieu, no-one could seriously argue for the *complete* absence of all government regulation in domestic credit markets; yet such a phenomenon appears to exist in so-called Euromarkets.

Historically, most credit transactions between residents of different nations have been conducted in the domestic credit market of either one of the trading partners, or in a major domestic credit market of an important world trading nation (e.g. London, New York, etc.). Such practices force foreign nationals to be subject to the practices, laws, and levies of at least one nation. The 'fairness' of the judicial and tax processes enforcing the laws of contracts and property-holding in a specific nation is an important aspect of government regulation which provides domestic and foreign nationals with the confidence to hold credit instruments of a major national resale market in a 'key' currency.

In the past three decades, however, Eurocurrency markets have developed which permit buyers and sellers of open NUMSs to avoid the jurisdiction of all national authorities in their search for liquidity time machines. This freedom from authority is accomplished via the simple expedient of locating the market for liquidity time machines denominated in a particular national money '*outside*' the nation of issue of that currency and therefore beyond its legal jurisdiction. Consequently, these 'Euro' or 'offshore' banking markets are outside the control of national governments and their national monetary authorities.

EURODOLLARS AND LIQUIDITY

The Eurodollar market involves transactors who, operating in a market outside the legal jurisdiction of the United States, wish to hold or sell (for liquidity purposes) titles to dollar deposits. These Eurodollar (time) deposits represent claims to demand deposit liabilities of a bank in the U.S. which can be mobilized at a specific future date. There are three calendar time orientations involved, namely day deposits, longer term Eurodeposits and Eurodollar Certificates of Deposit.

The forward time aspect of Eurodeposits (liabilities of Eurobanks) may be as short as a single calendar day (with automatic renewal privileges). Day-Eurodollar deposits are redeemable on demand for a U.S. bank deposit liability; thus, the day-Eurodollar deposit holder has full liquidity. Although one cannot simply write drafts against 'day' Eurodollar deposits, they can be instantaneously converted to a U.S. demand deposit if the holder simply requests this of the Eurobanker. In essence therefore, Eurodollar 'day' deposits are the equivalent of day-of-deposit to day-of-withdrawal savings accounts of U.S. banks (prior to the establishment of negotiable orders withdrawal [NOW] privileges on such 'savings' accounts).[5] These 'day' Eurodollar deposits normally provide significantly less interest (but more dollar liquidity) than specific longer term Eurodollar deposits.

The longer term Eurodollar deposits are non-negotiable liabilities of Eurobankers which are associated with a specific future date of maturity; the Eurobank issuer is therefore under no liability to redeem these 'titles' to U.S. demand deposits until their maturity date. Consequently, the liquidity associated with these longer term Eurodeposits is, in principle, limited. It is however, in practice, possible to withdraw the principal prior to maturity and even, upon negotiation with the Eurobanker, to receive part or all of the interest accumulated to date.[6]

A third type of Eurodollar deposit is a Eurodollar CD (certificate of deposit), a liability of a Eurobanker which has a fixed date of maturity but is negotiable (resaleable) in an organized spot market on any date prior to maturity. The resaleability of Eurodollar CDs provides, in principle, more liquidity than the long-term Eurodollar deposit.

Eurodollar deposits, therefore, provide various liquidity time machines which, although they are denominated in U.S. dollars, are outside the control of U.S. monetary authorities and U.S. taxing authorities. Eurodollar deposits (and Eurocurrencies generally) therefore provide a possible liquidity haven for those wishing to store dollar (or other currency) purchasing power out-of-sight and out-of-reach of the regulatory and taxing powers of any national government.

In general, Eurobanks are banks (or branches of domestic banks) which are either physically located outside the nation or in a special designated 'offshore' location physically within the nation in whose currency it denominates its assets (loans to borrowers) and its liabilities (deposits). Thus, for example, a Eurobanker in London may provide a Eurodollar deposit liability by gaining control (title) over some U.S. bank's demand deposits (which is the mode of settlement for all U.S. contracts – and most international transactions in standardized commodities such as oil, wheat, etc.). The creation of a Eurodollar deposit by our hypothetical London Eurobanker could have originated by providing this Eurobank liability to some member of the international public in exchange for a draft drawn on a deposit at a U.S. bank. The Eurobanker could then lend title to this U.S. bank liability at a higher rate of interest than he is paying to the Eurodollar deposit holder to any member of the public who has a dollar denominated contractual obligation coming due today or tomorrow. (Such borrowers from the Eurobanker are labelled class A borrowers by Harrod.)[7]

It is often claimed that since Eurodollars (or other Eurocurrencies) are time deposits, they cannot be directly used by Eurodollar deposit holders (by writing a sight draft transferring title to their deposits) as the medium of contractual settlement for obligations denominated in U.S. dollars (or other local currencies for other Eurocurrency deposits). In other words, it is proclaimed, Eurodollars are not money.[8] Under this view, Eurobanks are merely financial intermediaries which simultaneously have liabilities in the form of Eurocurrency time deposits, and assets in terms of loans in a currency or currencies other than that of the nation in which the bank is physically located.[9] Thus, it is alleged that Eurodollar banks are similar to any U.S. savings banks who do not provide their depositors with negotiable orders of withdrawal on their savings accounts. The only difference, it is claimed, is that the Eurobankers' liabilities (savings bank function) is outside the control of U.S. regulatory or taxing powers.

CAN EURODOLLARS BECOME MONEY?

Since Eurodollar deposits are time deposit liabilities of Eurobanks, they appear not to have (at least at present) the characteristics of money, e.g. they cannot settle a domestic U.S. contractual obligation. Nevertheless, titles to Eurodollar deposits, to the extent that they are readily transferable, have the potential to be utilized as the medium of contractual settlement at least for international contractual obligations, just as the development of the *negotiable order of withdrawal* (NOW) accounts of U.S. savings banks has transformed savings bank deposits from a liquidity time status machine to an acceptable medium of contractual settlement via the use of existing clearing institutions.

Eurobanks have the capability to expand the volume of potentially available means of international contractual settlement among *large* international traders without in any way diminishing the domestic lending ability of domestic banking systems. Some have suggested that we 'are witnessing the period in which the clearing of international payments and the creation of international liquidity are shifting away from the National Monetary Authority and the IMF to the Eurobanks. This process is more closely analogous to the rise of bank deposits as the main circulating medium, supplanting notes and coins emanating from a centralized Monetary Authority.'[10]

The institution of Eurodollar deposits developed in response to the desire of non-residents of the United States to store purchasing power (in terms of dollars) in a fully liquid asset which was beyond the control of U.S. government and Central Banking authorities. Although the desire to avoid government surveillance of financial affairs has always existed, it was Russian agencies who, in the 1950s, held domestic U.S. dollar bank balances as precautionary (reserve) assets, but distrusting U.S. government authorities, encouraged the development of Euro-dollar markets.[11] The initial function of Eurodollar markets was merely to mobilize idle dollar balances held by foreigners via financial intermediation across national frontiers, without interference of domestic government regulation and/or taxation. Today however, much of the Eurodollar credit market trading may be due to the better returns offered to both borrower and lender in Euromarkets than those on similar transactions in a domestic credit market.

All Eurocurrency deposits are liquid assets in terms of the domestic currency they are denominated in. They have no foreign exchange quotation independent of the quotation of the exchange rate between two local currencies. Eurodollar deposits are simply quoted in terms of interest rates or annualized yields. Beside avoidance of regulation and taxation, the main advantage of Eurocurrencies lies in an efficient market organization which deals in large transactions only. Hence, the interest rate obtained by borrower and lender is better (net of taxes and transaction costs) than in domestic bond markets. (Harrod has also suggested the smaller spread between lending and borrowing rates in Eurodollars may have originated in the fact that it was marginal business for large commercial banks (at least in London) and could be segregated from domestic transactions; hence, there was the possibility of third degree price discrimination.[12] Banks can do profitable business if they can segregate customers, as long as there is a difference between average and marginal business.)

Eurodollar markets may have developed primarily to provide liquid assets to holders of U.S. dollar balances via financial intermediation. The end borrowers were originally classified by Harrod into two categories, Class A and Class B.[13] Class A borrowers want U.S. dollars in order to settle a contractual obligation to U.S. residents or to a resident in some other nation whose trade is denominated in dollars (e.g. an oil importer) and/or who have some reason to have U.S. dollars on their books. Class B borrowers, on the other hand, do not want dollars at all. These borrowers need some other national currency, say pounds sterling, *immediately* (on the spot). Class B borrowers enter the Eurodollar (or other Eurocurrency) market because of the lower interest rate *and* transaction costs. After receiving the loan, they immediately engage in a 'swap' arrangement where they sell the borrowed U.S. dollar bank deposit spot for the currency they want, while simultaneously buying U.S. dollars forward for their date when their Eurodollar bank loan comes due.[14] This spot-forward U.S. dollar exchange transaction fixes the repayment in terms of the local money used by the Class B borrower. Thus the borrower can contract out of all exchange rate uncertainties.

If the government (say in England) whose domestic money is needed by the Class B borrower of Eurodollars is tied to a fixed exchange rate (or even a dirty float), and if Class B borrowers, in the aggregate, would not have borrowed as many funds at the interest rate on domestic loans (*in either England or the U.S.*), then the aggregate effect of Class B borrowing is to initially and immediately lead to a *ceteris paribus* increase in the (pound sterling) money supply. (This assumes that, in the aggregate, users of English money are net Class B borrowers in the Euro-dollar market.) Thus, without the lower cost of borrowing in the Eurodollar market, this *ceteris paribus* expansion of the domestic pound sterling money supply would not have occurred, as fewer funds would have been borrowed.

The Eurodollar loan is therefore a *fully liquid asset* in terms of the dollar or any nation's domestic currency whenever other governments pursue a fixed dollar exchange rate policy; it is almost a fully liquid asset for those with managed floats (i.e. for all major trading nations). Hence, the development of Eurocurrency markets which are outside the control of any national government implies that, in a world where Central Bankers are committed either to fixed exchange rates or at least to maintaining 'orderly' slow (crawling peg) movements in exchange rates, there is no longer a limited supply of monetary assets which are clearly under the exogenous control of each nation's Central Bank. Thus, the *domestic* monetary authority has no direct and complete control of the domestic money supply.[15] Anyone (foreign or domestic resident) who can trade in Euromarkets can increase the domestic money supply of a nation by becoming a Class B borrower. If the resulting *ceteris paribus* endogenous increase in the domestic money supply is deemed un-desirable by the local monetary authority, it will have to undertake open market operations to drive up interest rates and reduce the available supply of finance to *other* domestic residents.

The existence of unregulated Eurocurrency markets creates, *per se*, the potential for validating an endogenous domestic money supply whenever there is an imbalance in the trade account (which must be financed). For example, importers in nations with a deficit trade balance can become Class B borrowers in say the Eurodollar market when their contractual obligations to foreign exporters come due. On acquiring a Eurodollar loan, these Class B borrowers can sell these private liabilities of Eurobankers on the spot exchange market for the currency of the surplus trading partner. This spot purchase of the domestic currency of the surplus trading nation in exchange for a Eurobanker liability can thereby validate the increase in the domestic money supply originally needed to finance the working capital position of entrepreneurs producing the products constituting the export surplus.[16]

Eurodollar markets have therefore led to the creation of an internationally recyclable liquid asset which *can* be used to indefinitely finance deficits (or surpluses) in a nation's balance of payments, *provided* only that residents in the deficit nation maintain creditworthiness in the Eurodollar market. This, in turn, implies that a temporary deficit in the trade balance can be financed *indefinitely* via constant refinancing (Floating Fund Finance) arrangements in Euromarkets as long as the borrower meets the interest payments. Moreover, a continuing trade deficit (as, for example, recently experienced by Third World oil consuming nations) is the equivalent of increased refinancing requirements (a rise in Floating Fund Finance) over time. There is nothing in the operation of these unregulated Eurodollar markets which will prevent Class B end borrowers from engaging in continual Floating Fund Finance, particularly since any exchange rate uncertainty on the repayment of the Eurodollar loan is eliminated by the initial spot-forward swap arrangement. As long as Class B end-use borrowers can meet the interest obligations,[17] Eurobankers will see such borrowers as excellent credit risks and be willing to increase the size of their loans to such users over time as they prove their creditworthiness by repaying previous commitments. Accordingly, Eurobankers have created an international liquid asset which can be continually recycled and enlarged if necessary in order to finance continuing payments deficits between nations *as long as national Central Banks function to maintain orderly exchange markets.*[18]

It is, of course, true that at the end of the initial hypothesized swap arrangement, i.e. when the forward purchase of dollars falls due, that the domestic currency (which was produced at the initial date) will have to be sold to obtain a U.S. dollar deposit to pay off the Eurodollar loan and, *ceteris paribus*, the increase in the domestic currency which occurred, say 90 days earlier, will be exactly offset so that the domestic money supply should return to its 91 day-earlier level. If, however, there is no net change in the size of Class B borrowings to be turned into a specific local currency, then when one Eurodollar loan is being paid off, another is being initiated so that there will be no further increase or decline in the domestic money supply due to this factor. If over time there is a continual net increase in Class B borrowings in Eurodollars for end use in the same domestic currency, then the local money supply will continue to grow by an amount related to the net increase in Class B borrowings over time.[19] Hence, trade deficits financed by Class B end-use borrowers in Euromarkets to obtain the surplus trading partner's money, can foster an endogenous increase in the money supply of the surplus trading partner. Thus, as Harrod noted, 'The employment of purchasing power acquired by Class B borrowers through the Euro-dollar market adds to the total purchasing power in the country in question, provided that that country is a net borrower.'[20] By net borrower it is meant that the quantity of Eurodollars lent for *end uses* of Class B borrowers exceeds the number of dollars initially placed in the market on any date. This difference should be equal to the net number of dollars entering into Class B swap arrangements at any date and hence, is equal to the potential expansion of the domestic money supply (at the spot dollar exchange rate). Thus, clearly the existence of Eurocurrency markets operating outside the control of *all* Central Bankers means that the supply of any domestic currency is beyond the complete control of any Central Bank as long as organized exchange markets are supported to any significant extent by government agencies.

BUT ARE EURODOLLARS THEMSELVES MONEY?

Money is anything which is generally used to settle contractual obligation; therefore, what is money cannot be identified independent of the laws and customs of contractual settlement in the economic system under investigation. In terms of production flows within a region (nation), the thing which is used to pay the monetary unit used to denominate payroll obligations (forward labour contracts) becomes the predominant money for the circulation of the GNP domestically as long as the money wage share is a major proportion of the GNP. Workers will be willing to accept that thing which in law and custom is specified to discharge the money wage contract (as payment for their services), for as long as they believe that the prices of goods and services which bulk large in workers' budgets will continue either to be denominated in the same monetary unit at their local supermarkets, department stores, etc. or whatever they are paid in is sticky in terms of its purchasing power of these goods and services.

On the other hand, for those goods which by value are large components of international trade and for which either

(1) wealthy intermediaries (i.e. middlemen) 'make' trading markets, using their own financing ability or their ability to cross national boundaries and borrow from any national banking system (or from the Eurobanks as a Class B borrower) to finance their positions in commodity stocks (while foreign exchange markets are well organized *and* orderly) and/or

(2) the wage share is a small proportion of the total price of the traded commodity and therefore, money wages are *not* the predominant form of money income underlying the market price,[21]

then the money used to discharge international purchase contracts for such commodities as they move along the distribution chain over time can be different from the money used to discharge the production payroll obligations. In essence, for international transactions in goods where wages are a small portion of value added, there is the potential that the main mode of contractual settlement can be a completely different 'money' (e.g. Eurodollars) than for produced large labour content (in terms of value added) goods. If, in addition, non-wage income recipients desire to *save* a significant portion of their gross income in a time machine form other than the money of payroll settlement, then the requirements for 'payroll' money to liquidate a position in working capital at the 'end' of a production period in order to pay off payroll loans or meet payrolls directly is small relative to market value. Thus, a large measure of the liquidation of a working capital position can be accomplished by directly accepting sales receipts in terms of a Eurocurrency deposit (which is a fully liquid asset fixed to the domestic currency which most future purchases out of income, if desired, will be made). As long as Eurobankers are expected to 'make' the Eurocurrency market with holdings of domestic money or other reserve assets for which the lender of last resort will provide the local currency, then Eurobankers will be perceived as able to redeem Eurodeposit liabilities in terms of domestic monies if the international public finds its holdings of Eurodeposits as reserve assets excessive. The Eurodeposit is an excellent form of receiving one's non-wage income, for it permits tax avoidance and government surveillance of one's economic activities. It avoids the possibility of government freezing or seizure of foreign nationals' assets. (The latter threat must bulk especially important since the 1979 U.S. seizure of Iranian liquid assets in U.S. banks.) Consequently, there appears to be much that can be (privately) gained by using a Eurocurrency as the medium of contractual settlement within a 'payments club' of large transactors in some commodity sectors of open economies where labour is not a major component of value added. Over time, therefore, one should expect that as Eurobanks develop, their liabilities may become (or may already be) a main medium of international contractual settlement among international transactors. As long as the value of transactions among such transactors grows, Eurobankers can create money as a multiple of their reserve base. If, however, the value of transactions should decline and the holders of Eurobank liabilities find the existing stock holdings excessive, the Eurobanks will face a cash flow deficit. At that stage the individual Central Banks will have to move in rapidly as lenders of last resort, if an international financial panic is to be avoided. At this stage Eurobanks would surely welcome regulation!

In sum therefore, as long as the international public maintain confidence in the Eurobankers' abilities to 'make' Eurocurrency markets, Eurodeposits can be used as liquidity time machines by owners of 'factors of production' (usually non-labour) engaged in the production flows of internationally traded goods who wish to avoid government and international surveillance and taxation. Consequently, settlement custom among traders in such commodities can make Eurobank deposits of, say Eurodollars (as opposed to settlement with demand deposits of U.S. banks which are the initial reserve asset underlying these Eurobank deposit liabilities), *the money* which finances that portion of the production and exchange of internationally traded goods which is attributable to non-labour factor services! This is true as long as these non-labour factor owners by custom form a 'payments club' where members are willing to accept all, or at best, most of their contractual sales receipts directly in terms of Eurobank deposits.[22]

If labour in each nation was also willing to accept (or insisted on receiving) payroll payments in terms of Eurobank deposits (and if such contractual payments were legally enforceable under the laws of the nations involved), then Euromoney would, by definition, and by common consent and practice, become the international money for all production flow transactions. Of course, even if labour were always to be paid in local currencies, if there were a well organized, orderly market for exchange between local bank liabilities and Eurobank liabilities (so exchange costs are minimal), if the labour costs of production of goods were more stable in terms of a particular Eurocurrency (i.e. the Eurocurrency is stabilized in terms of some general commodity standard) and if this greater stability were to be *almost universally expected to continue into the foreseeable future*, then that Eurocurrency would become (by custom) the 'money' of the system as (a) initially all local currency balances normally held for transactions, precautionary, or speculative purposes would be immediately converted into the Eurocurrency and (b) ultimately all transactors would insist on contracts which required payments in the Eurocurrency directly (to avoid any exchange costs). To maintain greater stability of the purchasing power of a Eurocurrency in terms of a *producible* commodity standard, however, would require that the efficiency wage (unit labour cost) and profit margin in terms of the Eurocurrency be more sticky over time than the efficiency wage and profit margin expressed in terms of any local currency. As long as it is unlikely that widespread *uniform* expectations of greater relative stability in the purchasing power of any Eurocurrency *vis-à-vis* all local monies can be developed, then the Eurocurrency (and its underlying local currency) can never develop into a truly ubiquitous international money.

In a more limited sense, however, Eurodollar deposits (and the U.S. bank deposits that are the reserves behind such Eurodollar liabilities) have the opportunity and potential to become a more limited international money for international bankers and their major (mainly MNCs) clients. If Eurodollars were (or are, or will be) used to clear outstanding balances among national banking systems, then Eurodollars could be the running and reserve asset of the international clearing mechanism.

A MAXIM

The development of the Eurocurrency banking system over the past three decades illustrates the fact that the financial community is amazingly adept and innovative in developing monetary institutions and relations which not only permit but encourage evasion of government rules and controls. Bankers always have a vested interest in expanding liquidity in step with the needs of entrepreneurs to finance either (a) the expansion of real output flows (i.e. the real bills doctrine), or (b) increases in efficiency wages (i.e. the inflation bills doctrine). As long as we leave banking functions to the private sector and profit making proclivities, bankers will, given sufficient time and the absence of vigilant control, invent devices to circumvent government and constitutional rules controlling the money supply if such restraints hamper the process of endogenous finance. For bankers are always anxious to oblige customers by increasing the costless production of bank liabilities, if this will increase bank profits. Moreover, in an entrepreneurial economy, the public is always willing to hold additional bank liabilities as long as they are scarce, while the Central Bank, as lender of last resort, ensures that any excess bank liabilities that occur should they become less scarce can be converted to legal money.

Thus, as long as we maintain an entrepreneurial system for the organization of production and exchange activities, private bankers are a double-edged sword. By providing costless bookkeeping 'finance', they can facilitate the enhancement of production flows when idle resources are available and entrepreneurs are optimistic about the future. They can, however, also provide the costless finance which endogenously feeds any social and political forces which are loose to drive up efficiency wages and/or profit margins around the world.

Bankers desire to endogenously expand the money supply whenever the demand for finance rises. They do not discriminate as to whether the increased demand for money is to finance (a) an increase in the production flow of new goods and services, or (b) an increase in the money costs (efficiency earnings) for a given level of production flow. Consequently, the desire of Monetarists to prevent the financing of (b) via an invariant 'rule' on money supply growth tied to the expected underlying long-term growth rate of real production flows cannot, *even in the long run*, eliminate inflationary tendencies in modern economies. As long as there are social and political forces leading to rises in efficiency wages and profit margin increases, inflexible rules on monetary expansion will, whenever forces are pushing up efficiency earnings, permit financing of these increased money costs of production for any given production flow, while inhibiting expansion of production activities. Any attempt to fight inflationary forces via a simple monetary rule will result either in stagnation and decline, or else bankers will invent ways to circumvent the rules and expand the modes of contractual settlement (e.g. NOW accounts, money market funds, Eurocurrencies), and thereby finance rapid inflation (stagflation) as entrepreneurs wrestle with higher costs despite the apparent restrictive monetary policy. Only a catastrophic depression and ensuing bank failures could punish bankers *and* the rest of society sufficiently to force some long-term stability on to the money costs of potential production flows; but then, who will purchase this potential production even at stable money prices in the midst of a 'great depression'?

Even if the Monetarists were correct in their proclamation that a steady hand at the money supply tiller (via an invariable rule) will prevent inflation, it is clear that such a system could work only by either creating economic chaos or by *socializing the banking system* (nationally and internationally), so that bankers could not, in effect, subvert the Monetarist rule by inventing new modes of contractual settlement,[23] whenever the private sector demand for finance increased at a rate in excess of the Monetarist rule!

Even if one could devise a system that forced bankers to obey the Monetarists' rule of the game, deflecting the rate of growth of money supply into financing higher rates of production flows rather than higher money costs of production for any given flow of output, price stability can be achieved *only* if efficiency earnings are sticky over time. Ultimately therefore, modern economies must devise a policy which constrains money income claims and limits the decline in the purchasing power of money in terms of labour effort to increases in overall labour productivity, thereby stabilizing the purchasing power in terms of some reproducible commodity standard of whatever money is agreed upon to discharge forward contractual obligations.

12 Multinational Corporations and International Transactions

Neoclassical models of international trade and monetary theory are typically constructed as if residents of one nation produced and sold goods and services to independent residents of another nation. Moreover, the economic agents in each nation engaging in production for foreign sales and in the actual conduct of foreign transactions are each conceived to be small and numerous, relative to the national governments and monetary authorities involved. Thus, neoclassical models assume 'large economies', i.e. economies with many (indeed perhaps a continuum) of agents in which all the 'agents are without economic power'.[1] This seemingly innocuous assumption of a world of multitudinous and small economic agents engaged in international trade (while the assumed number of governments are few) is necessary if rational agents are to treat prices parametrically (therefore permitting traditional General Equilibrium Theory to be applicable). In reality of course, such a conception of a legion of economic agents without economic power engaging in international trade has, at least, since Biblical Times, been demonstrably false. The trading companies of the early mercantilist and industrial eras, as well as present day *multinational corporations* (hereafter MNCs), have always had sufficient power to affect trading relations by their own actions. Hence neoclassical international trade and monetary theory analysis and its conclusions rest on a logical foundation which has no meaning for the real world. Such theories must be superseded by a more relevant and realistic logical analysis.

In Chapter 4, it was noted that the *trade balance on income account* was defined as equal to the value of home *owned* outputs of goods and services *whether produced domestically or abroad* placed at the disposal

231

of foreigners minus the *foreign owned output produced at home or abroad* placed at the disposal of domestic residents. In the simple case where economic activities in each nation in a trading situation are independent of residents of other nations, this definition of the trade balance reduces to the market value of newly produced exports minus the value of newly produced imports; but, as endnote no. 8 of Chapter 4 indicated, the measure of the trade balance becomes more complicated when MNCs are involved in international transactions. MNCs are often simultaneously residents of many trading nations, and consequently the proportion of the value of domestic output produced 'placed at the disposal of foreigners' v. the proportion 'owned' by domestic residents is often determined by corporate strategies rather than 'market forces'. Moreover, MNCs, although few in number, are extremely powerful economically and sometimes more powerful than the governments of the regions in which they operate.

PRODUCTION AND PAYMENTS OF MNCs

International production by MNCs, which can be defined as domestically generated production flows subject partly or entirely to foreign control or decision processes, and measured by sales of their foreign affiliates, has grown rapidly. By 1971 it measured \$330 billion and therefore exceeded the reported market value of total physical exports of *all* market economies which was \$310 billion.[2] By 1973, these values had grown to \$400 billion and \$350 billion respectively.[3] Thus international production is not only larger, but it is growing faster than international exports. Moreover, a significant portion of goods (in value terms) actually 'moving' across national boundaries involve sales between departments, subsidiaries and affiliates of MNCs rather than arm's-length purchases and sales between independent economic agents in each nation. As Chick has emphasized: 'At the global level, intra-company trade exceeds 10 per cent of free world exports. Intracompany manufacturing exports have roughly doubled between 1966 and 1970.'[4]

When intracompany transactions bulk so large in the total international trade, it becomes more difficult but even more important to analyse

(1) which money is used generally to settle purchase contracts, especially as such contracts that involve MNCs;

(2) the 'actual' magnitude of the balance of trade position of any nation;

(3) whether 'market' supply and demand forces in foreign exchange markets are related to those that would occur if the same real patterns of trade occurred solely among independent economic agents rather than involving MNCs;

(4) whether the same pattern of trade would exist in the absence of MNCs, given the technology, comparative advantage, etc.[5]

VERTICALLY INTEGRATED MNCs AND PAYMENT BALANCES

The international movement of goods between vertical integrated MNCs takes place at notional bookkeeping or transfer prices which do not necessarily bear any relation to the market prices that would prevail in sales to independent third parties. MNCs have a great leeway in distributing the income produced in an integrated corporate chain for the disposal of either foreign or domestic residents of a particular nation in order to take advantage of differential tax laws in various nations including 'tax havens'. The resulting distribution of notional value added along the integrated chain need never have been part of a 'rational' trade pattern except for tax sheltering legislation. Such tax legislation is often framed by lawyers of MNCs to benefit their employers and are readily accepted by small nations (who are less powerful than the MNCs) under the threat of economic retaliation and/or the acceptance of economic bribes.

Consequently the 'value added' of production flows in a vertically integrated MNC as legal titles to the working capital goods cross national boundaries (the physical goods need not cross these boundaries) in the production, and distribution process, and hence the 'income' generated within economy A by the handling (i.e. taking title to goods) by an affiliate of a MNC (e.g. a trading or tanker company of an integrated oil company) is determined by corporate policy. Thus in country A, where goods 'produced' by a MNC are physically located for a period of time, the total income or value added generated in the economy could conceivably be less than the domestic wage bill and other income payments (e.g. royalties) *actually* paid in domestic money to those (other than the corporation) who reside in country A. The MNC could have their domestic affiliate earn negative profits (losses) by selling at a transfer price (to another affiliate in a different economy) which does not cover the actual expenditures per unit of output in economy A. Such 'bookkeeping losses' permit the vertically integrated MNC to situate the 'income' that would actually be generated in A, if independent small buyers and sellers of A's exports were involved, into any other economic nation that the corporate executives desire. Hence, the location of corporate profits (or losses) among the various national affiliates of a MNC depend in large measure on corporate decisions and bookkeeping practices.

There is therefore a tremendous incentive to arrange intracompany transfer prices in order to pass profits to affiliates in tax havens, or to take advantages of national tax loopholes, or to avoid national regulations, or even to surmount exchange controls, or to reduce *ad valorem* tariff levies, etc. For example, secret documents of the United States Internal Revenue Service which were made public in Congressional Hearings,[6] indicated that the United States Government was aware that the transfer price used by integrated multinational oil companies for sales of crude oil from their Persian Gulf affiliate to their transportation affiliate exceeded the 'free' market price by anywhere from 20 per cent to 35 per cent for each and every year from 1960 to the time of the OPEC embargo in October 1973.[7] Moreover, more than 90 per cent of the sales of the Persian Gulf production affiliate (ARAMCO) in Saudi Arabia were intracompany transfers to other affiliates of the four 'American' multinational oil companies, Exxon, Mobil, Texaco and Socal. In one document made public at these Congressional Hearings, the U.S. Internal Revenue Service had engaged in an exercise 'to adjust transfer prices between the producer, the offtaker and refining entities to eliminate trading losses'.[8] Since these separate corporate entities are really affiliates or subsidiaries, etc. of the same MNCs – and each affiliate can have its principal office for accounting and tax purposes in different nations – it is obvious that oil company MNCs did move accounting profits and losses among nations for more than a decade,[9] thereby tending to alter the trade balances of the various nations involved! The IRS study demonstrated that the transfer prices for intracompany sales bear little or no relation (except that they differ) to the prices charged third parties. It is therefore apparent that with the growth in importance of MNCs in general and especially intra-MNC sales in foreign trade, the use of transfer pricing by MNCs has affected the balance of trade on income account of various nations. National balances of payments have therefore become, in some significant measure, an appendage of MNC decisions on income distribution and liquidity needs within the MNCs. As Chick notes

> Through adjustments of transfer prices, the recorded values of imports and exports can be affected by pure bookkeeping changes

having very little to do with any changes in cost or demand factors. Fluctuations in balance of payment positions or in exchange rates may reflect, not variations in the competitive positions of nations, but production patterns or even purely financial aspects of intra-firm management.[10]

Thus the growth of a MNC as a major organizing institution for the production of goods and services in international trade had induced revolution, as yet poorly understood and studied, in international monetary accounting relations.

WHAT IS THE MODE OF SETTLEMENT FOR MNCs?

As has been emphasized several times in this volume, the definition of money *must* involve the medium of contractual settlement as a feature of money. As long as nation states were larger than most enterprises, and the latter's production activities were primarily located within a single national entity, Keynes correctly noted that the state 'claimed the right to declare what thing should answer as money . . . when it claimed the right not only to enforce the dictionary but also write the dictionary. Today all civilized money is, beyond the possibility of dispute, chartalist.'[11] Since the Second World War, however, with the growing importance of MNCs in global production and exchange activities, the potential has been created for removing chartalist characteristics for the money used to settle many international contractual commitments. The world appears to be developing the potential for having two separate monetary systems to handle two different types of transactions:

Type 1. – domestic monies which are (a) almost always used to settle local money-denominated contracts between agents within the same nation, and (b) are linked by exchange rates to settle contracts denominated in one domestic currency or another between independent small agents who are residents of different nations; and

Type 2. – monies which can settle contractual obligations between affiliates of the same MNC, or even between affiliates of separate MNCs that trade with each other across national boundaries, or even between MNCs and some governments (including royal families, etc.).

Type 1 monies are clearly chartalist in nature, but Type 2 need not be. Of course, the second type of international transaction can be settled with traditional chartalist domestic currencies but this would subject the contract between the parties to the usual exchange rate uncertainties.

Such transactions can also be handled by either mere bookkeeping entries on the integrated MNC's books or in terms of transfer of titles to Eurocurrency deposits (bookkeeping entries on the books of multi-national banks). Eurocurrencies can readily be used to discharge such obligations if, at least initially, a significant proportion of total revenue received by the affiliate is destined to become gross business savings (as defined in Chapter 3). Since gross business savings are *not* necessarily spent on currently produced goods or services, the parent MNC will require a liquidity time machine to store the purchasing power 'earned' by the affiliate. Eurocurrencies, because they are useful for avoiding government surveillance, regulation, and taxation would be an excellent liquidity vehicle for MNCs.

Of course, it is true that Eurocurrency deposits can also be liquidity vehicles for business savings of small companies located entirely within a single nation. Unlike the MNC, however, the one nation small company would be limited to a Eurocurrency of the same denomination as the local currency (e.g. Eurodollars for U.S. firms), for liquidity time machine purposes, if exchange rate uncertainties are to be avoided. (It is obvious that single nation companies will need to meet future con-tractual obligations in the local currency.) Various Eurodeposits are therefore more useful to MNCs, because it is the liquidity needs of the parent MNC and not of the local affiliate which are overriding, and the MNC, by its very nature, can never totally avoid exchange rate uncertainties.

If transfer prices between affiliates of MNCs are paid by transferring titles to Eurodeposits, then the purchase contract can be analysed as a spot or forward contract for the purchase of goods in terms of a specific Eurocurrency which involves a Class B end-use only for a sum equal to the value needed to pay domestic factor owners who are external to the firm (e.g. local labour and material suppliers). Of course, any contract calling for payment in a Eurocurrency is not, I believe, legally enforceable in any nation's law courts. Nevertheless enforceability is not an issue if this payment involves a transaction among affiliates of the same MNC. The fact that titles to Eurodeposits are neither legal tender nor necessarily acceptable by any State or Central Bank in payment to itself or in exchange for legal tender, and hence the seller affiliate has no legal recourse in case of default, will not prevent the title to Eurodeposits from being the medium of contractual settlement. The parent MNC, in essence, guarantees payment between affiliates. Thus Eurodeposits can be money – at least for interaffiliate intracompany transactions. Similarly internal MNC accounting entries in the parent company's books can be utilized to effect payments of that portion of the transfer prices which equal affiliate profit or loss. The trading profits or losses due to accounting transfers on intracompany sales can, in essence, be converted into capital transfers which need not enter into foreign exchange markets at all! Given the potential arbitrariness of the level of transfer prices and the inevitable commingling of income and capital transactions in intracompany MNC transactions, and the phenomenal relative growth of such transactions in international trade, 'it may have become quite impossible to determine whether an exchange rate is under- or overvalued'.[12]

International transactions between separate MNCs are only one step removed from similar transactions between foreign affiliates of the same MNC. Of course, in the case where the transactors are affiliates of different MNCs, intracompany accounting cannot be used to settle contracts. Eurobank deposits, on the other hand, are readily acceptable as the medium of contractual settlement between MNCs, since both contracting parties and their Eurobanker are well known to each other. All are known to be trustworthy in meeting their payment obligations. Consequently the need for legal recourse in case of non-payment is unlikely, and therefore Eurodeposits are generally acceptable among the community of MNCs.

Hence, if they wish, MNCs can organize or join, with the help of Eurobankers, a 'payments club' system which functions outside of, but is expected to have entry into (if needed), the normal national banking system. These 'payments clubs' can handle contractual settlements equal to aggregate gross business savings of the participating MNCs without having to use their access to normal national banking systems. Payments club members can therefore avoid the tax and legal scrutiny and control of national governments, something which cannot be avoided when utilizing chartelist money to settle private contracts.

The growth of MNCs in foreign trade has paralleled, to a large extent, the growth of a Eurocurrency system which, under present rules, appears to be outside the control of any national government. It is not necessary to decide which was the cause and which the effect. One need merely note that the growth of one aided the growth of the other. The institution of a Eurobank system and the institution of MNCs are situated in a symbiotic relationship which threatens the ability of all national states to independently pursue any public monetary or fiscal policies which are believed to be in the best interests of domestic society, but which are perceived by the corporate executives of MNCs to be detrimental to their own interests.

MNCs AND NATIONAL POLICY

MNCs, with worldwide plants and investments, have developed important information networks; hence MNCs can be extremely sensitive to
variations in cost conditions as well as government policies, etc. in
various nations. Moreover, because of their sheer size and economic
wealth, multinational corporate decisions on expansion, contraction,
relocation, etc. can have major macroeconomic consequences on
individual regional or national economies. Thus MNCs are unlike the
traditional small competitive entrepreneurs of neoclassical theory, who
could only react to – but could not affect – macroeconomic variables
such as employment, exchange rates, and comparative advantage
conditions among nations. By changing intra-MNC structure and
geographical locations, corporate officers can significantly alter the
economic environment of the national economies in which they operate.
By use of Eurobanks which are actually multinational corporate
banking organizations, MNCs can often frustrate domestic monetary
policies. Whether this effect on policy is due solely to the absolute size of
these MNCs or to their transnational character is unimportant. All
MNCs must be large while all large corporations which produce goods
whose demands transcend national borders will have an incentive to
become multinational.

MNCs AND INTERNATIONAL FINANCE

MNCs engaging in transactions between foreign affiliates have a great
deal of leeway in determining the medium of contractual settlement –
much more latitude than would be acceptable, at any point of history, in
transactions between independent parties.

Moreover, in a world where time-oriented contracts for payments are
important, MNCs have more leeway in determining the date of ultimate
settlement. The MNC has at its disposal considerably more freedom for
determining the leads or lags in payment between affiliates so as to speed
up payments in weakening currencies. Non-MNCs can, of course,
engage in similar activities through the use of spot and forward
exchange markets, provided the corporate comptroller spots the
weakening (or strengthening) currency before the market does
(otherwise the spot–forward price relationship will instantly adjust).
The non-MNC corporation can only alter the lead–lag payment by as

much as 270 days (the length of organized forward markets) at a cost each time it enters or leaves the market! Hence forward price payments in a world where MNC international transactions are important can have significantly different impacts on short run exchange rates than would similar trade patterns done by independent, small economic agents in each trading nation.

More importantly, the existence of Euromarkets and the national governments' commitments to maintain orderly exchange markets severely limit the ability of each government to pursue independent monetary policies. Anytime a Class B end-use borrower enters the Euromarkets, he can frustrate stringent domestic monetary policies, or else force more severe credit restrictions to be forced on wholly domestic borrowers who for whatever reason (e.g. size, creditworthiness) do not have access to borrow in Euromarkets. Thus MNCs, as well as other large corporations, via the Euromarkets can virtually free themselves from the confines of restrictive monetary policies in any single nation in which they wish to operate. Restrictive monetary policy therefore has become primarily binding on borrowers who cannot use Euromarkets, i.e. on the small, domestic units within a national economy.

In sum then, Central Banks and national governments have, to a large extent, lost the power to make decisions on national liquidity and its distribution. Without any apparent grand conspiratorial design, un-controlled Eurobankers and their large corporate customers have moved in to fill this vacuum. Moreover to the extent that national Central Banks and/or national governments are themselves utilizing Eurodeposits as part of their official reserves, they are legitimizing this change in decision making power and encouraging Eurobank liabilities to be a major source of international liquidity.

If nations are to regain control of the international financial system and thereby reinstate some control over their separate as well as joint economic destiny in the hands of public officials, then some system of international monetary cooperation, coordination *and control* will have to be explicitly worked out. In the absence of direct multi-government regulation, private Eurobanking institutions who operate in the absence of any controls will continue to fill the vacuum. These Euro-institutions can play an extremely useful function in financing expansionary tendencies, but as history has shown, unregulated banking systems also have a propensity to magnify contractionary events into an avalanche of credit deflation and financial crisis which, in the absence of a central authority who can swim against the stream, can lead to economic collapse and depression.

National governments have two choices therefore if they are to regain control. They can attempt to prevent or restrict all movements of funds into and out of each country, i.e. they can limit money convertability by residents, or they can join together into a supranational organization to control international liquidity.

13 Gold: The 'Barbarous Relic' for Enforcing Coordinated International Incomes Policies

Money as we know it in an entrepreneurial economy can never be described, much less analysed, in the absence of the institution of forward contracting. The analysis of the evolution of the laws and customs under which such contracts are enforced and enforceable is fundamental to an understanding of the unique role of money and the need for liquidity. *Money can only be studied in an historical and institutional context.*

When buying and selling and lending and borrowing contractual arrangements exist between the domestic economy and the outside world, the analysis of the role of money is even more complicated than it is in a closed system. The domestic laws and customs in each trading nation need not be the same (nor be evolving in the same direction). Indeed, once national boundaries are crossed, it is almost inevitable that there will be major differences in laws, institutions, and custom. At the currently developed level of human civilization, true international law and institutions are almost non-existent. Yet, it is the thin veneer of human law and socially acceptable arrangements, conventions and customs regarding human economic and personal interactions which separates civilized systems from degenerating back to cannibalistic animal behaviour under the 'natural law' of the jungle!

Most contracts between nationals of different countries are written under the jurisdiction of the domestic laws of one or the other trading partners (and sometimes even under the laws of a third nation such as England and/or the U.S.), and are therefore legally enforceable only by the courts of that nation. In these circumstances, the enforcement of international contracts and international money settlements relies primarily on custom and the cooperation between governments of the trading nations. (Often cooperation of these governments is formalized in a government contract or treaty.) The need for custom and cooperation among nations is especially important when it comes to international payment settlements between national banking systems.

Time is a device which prevents everything from happening at once. Consequently, in a world of decentralized international trading, it is highly improbable, if not impossible, that at each moment in time, contractually due outpayments will just equal contractually due inpayments. There will, therefore, always be a need for some customary medium of settlement of the net payments flow between national banking systems who are providing the medium of contractual settlement to meet the obligations of international traders in terms of their various contractual currency requirements.

FIXED EXCHANGE RATES WITH GOLD CONVERTIBILITY

If trading nations agree to be on an automatic gold system, then the governments of such nations have accepted as a primary obligation of their respective monetary authorities to preserve external payments equilibrium by *endogenously* responding to the needs of the public to meet net payment flows (or settlements) between their national banking systems. These government obligations are met freely and automatically via two-way convertibility between the domestic currency and gold at some pre-specified price (or range between bid and ask). Since each nation's monetary authority has agreed to automatic gold convertibility (i.e. the Central Bank is the ultimate market maker of or creator of liquidity for the gold market), then the domestic money supply will, *ceteris paribus*, vary directly with net gold flows between national Central Banks.

Gold outflows will adversely affect economic activity in a deficit nation via the induced restrictions on money supplies and liquidity, which make the financing of any rate of domestic production flows and investment activities more difficult and more expensive (and vice versa in the surplus nation). This *ceteris paribus* constraint on liquidity, depending as it does only on the external payments balance, is consistent with any level of domestic productive activity from deep depression to full employment. It is, therefore, conceivable that under a gold standard the appearance of a trade deficit could induce a decline in domestic economic activities even if an economy was already in a depressed state!

To the extent that it provides an automatic method to correct external payment imbalances, an international gold system depends on the efficient operation of an adjusting mechanism which, by altering domestic money supplies, liquidity pressures and interest rates relative to the domestic marginal efficiency of capital, affects aggregate demand in each nation. This, it is assumed, alters relative money efficiency earnings and prices (in terms of a single currency) between the trading partners.

The first step of the presumed adjusting mechanism involves the relationship between the international liquidity preferences of residents of the trading partners and the 'animal spirits' of entrepreneurs. If the volume of foreign lending is sensitive to small changes in interest rates at home and abroad (i.e. the elasticity of substitution between domestic and foreign liquid assets to be held as time machines is large), then any gold outflow by the trade deficit nation induces, *ceteris paribus*, a relative increase in domestic interest rates, and the net foreign loan account will rapidly diminish. This differential interest rate mechanism will 'recycle' purchasing power to the deficit nation, permitting the latter to better maintain domestic and foreign expenditure flows if it has the propensity to do so. This recycling occurs because inhabitants of the surplus region are willing and eager to accept and hold additional titles to existing liquid assets previously owned by inhabitants of the deficit region, and/or promissory claims to the future income and wealth of the deficit region. In an uncertain world, the calendar time duration in which continuing trade deficits can be financed by recycling via international lending processes is not readily predictable. Recycling, once started, can be maintained as long as the international elasticity of substitution between liquid assets is large, and long-term expectations are not severely jarred by events into a basic reassessment of the situation.

If, on the other hand, this recycling via the foreign loan account mechanism is *not* very sensitive to relative interest rates in the two nations, then, under a gold standard, the resulting loss of gold by the monetary authority of the deficit nation necessary to meet the net clearing settlement obligations to the banking system of the surplus nation will, *ceteris paribus*, reduce the international liquidity holdings of the residents of the deficit nation as they directly, or via their bankers, scramble to meet their foreign contractual payment commitments. Unless the deficit nation's monetary authority takes deliberate action to offset the resulting domestic liquidity constraint induced by the gold outflow, the available domestic finance is concomitantly reduced.

If the gold outflow is to be staunched, this induced reduction in domestic finance and hence expenditures *must* (in the short run *and* the long run) reduce the money prices of factors of production relative to productivity and therefore, reduce the internal money costs of production (at least relative to what they would be otherwise). In other words, the classical specie-flow mechanism requires that the gold efficiency wage will be lowered in the deficit nation in order to induce the restoration of payments equilibrium. In the surplus nation on the other hand, it is assumed that the gold inflow leads, *pari passu*, to an expansion of its money supply, easing financing constraints and expanding money expenditures, thereby raising the money prices of productive inputs and the gold efficiency earnings in the surplus nation. It is usually claimed that the resulting changes in money costs of production (or gold efficiency wages), given a competitive environment, lead to relative changes in the gold prices of newly produced goods in each nation. Since the domestic nominal prices of goods in each nation are assumed fixed in terms of gold, then to the extent that there is a large elasticity of substitution between exports and imports (i.e. foreign trade is sensitive to changes in relative money prices), the relative changes in gold efficiency wages in the trading nations will eliminate the trade imbalance with only a minimum (temporary?) loss of real economic activity (due to reallocative adjustments) and *no long run loss in global real income*. In this classical analysis, there is assumed a redistribution of the global real income towards the surplus nation as its terms of trade improve and its gold efficiency earnings rise relative to earnings in the deficit nation, while any aggregate losses in real income are assumed – without proof – to be temporary and insignificant.

In sum, the classical specie-flow mechanism implicitly relies on an international redistribution of real income via coordinated factor price changes (in money terms in each nation) which change the relative money costs of production (without, it is assumed, significant global real income loss) to correct trade imbalances. In this classical analysis, the flow of gold is important only as *the mechanism* to coordinate and force the relative change in factor prices or efficiency wages in each nation. It is assumed that changes in the resulting money costs of production (the supply side) in conjunction with the price sensitivity for exports and imports (which are assumed to be good gross substitutes on the demand side) will always restore external payments equilibrium.

In other words, *the 'specie-flow' mechanism uses gold flows as the instrument to force a coordinated differential incomes policy on each trading nation!* Gold is the impersonal economic tyrant forcing sovereign entrepreneurial economies, via an intergovernmental agreement, to internationally coordinate in a logical and consistent manner, their internal incomes policies *for the global good.* Accordingly, as soon as a nation's monetary authority agrees to abide by the rules of the gold standard game, international participation in a globally coordinated monetary 'incomes' policy would be assured, *if factor prices in each nation responded swiftly and directly to change in aggregate money expenditures.*

If, on the other hand, domestic nominal factor prices are neither freely flexible nor able to respond rapidly in response to the reduction in finance in deficit nations or to the expansion of finance in surplus nations – as they are not in a money using entrepreneurial economy organized on a forward money contracting basis – then the depressing pressures of gold outflows and shortages of finance in deficit nations will directly reduce employment and national income. This in turn will have depressing multiplier feedback effects on both the domestic economy and its trading partners. Hence, in the real world in which we live, money wage contracts, the outlawing of slavery, and other institutions and customs severely limit the ability of 'barbarous' gold to impose an internationally coordinated incomes policies on nations who insist on being entrepreneurial rather than cooperative, and who therefore organize their production activities on the basis of forward money contracts. Instead, the tyrannical influence of gold flows is diverted into an internationally coordinated policy of induced depression, un-employment, and human misery without necessarily curing the initial trade imbalance except by impoverishing *both* trading partners. In the real world, gold, despite its barbaric ruthlessness, cannot impose an internationally coordinated incomes policy on entrepreneurial econ-omies except perhaps in the long run, when we will all be dead! Given real world monetary customs and institutions and the desire of nations to have market-oriented production economies, an unrestrained gold standard, as demonstrated in the period between the World Wars, can wantonly destroy economic wealth and cause tremendous human misery. Once started, this destructive epidemic cannot be contained in deficit nations; in an interdependent world it will ultimately infect all trading partners.

Those who advocate a return to the gold (or some other international commodity) standard without requiring simultaneous, deliberate, and intergovernmentally coordinated incomes policies among trading nations, are asserting that, contrary to historical experience, trade imbalances can be readily corrected via rapid relative factor price changes in entrepreneurial economies because exports and imports are excellent gross substitutes, and therefore the induced substitution will *quickly* cure the illness without killing the patient. Although this claimed adjustment mechanism may be applicable to a cooperative, barter type world economy, it is antithetical to the operations of an entrepreneurial economy.

With the recognition that entrepreneurial economics require sticky money wages rates for their efficient operation, Keynes reoriented attention from the importance of substitution effects among producible goods as an equilibrating process to an emphasis on income effects as an equilibrating mechanism. This is true even in the case of an open economy where the development of a trade imbalance is hypothesized to be an initiating disturbance to equilibrium. The adjustment process via income changes has often been labelled 'Keynesian', and 'multiplier' formulas have been derived to indicate the magnitude of income adjustment occurring in each trading nation for any given hypothesized trade imbalance.[1] Unfortunately, these multiplier formulas cannot provide any assurance that the income changes in each nation implied in this foreign trade multiplier mechanism will be sufficient, even in the long run, to completely eliminate the trade imbalance. Instead, the foreign trade multiplier processes demonstrate that, given well behaved aggregate demand and supply functions, income adjustments may only mitigate the payments imbalance.

FIXED EXCHANGE RATES WITHOUT GOLD CONVERTIBILITY

Via treaty or custom, governments may agree to some arrangement to fix exchange rates, or permit a 'crawling peg' or a 'dirty' float,[2] while ensuring two-way convertibility between local currencies (and without assuring the public of convertibility of gold into currency). If nations agree to such an international system, each participating nation is in effect committing its monetary authority to be the ultimate market maker of the foreign exchange market when certain circumstances prevail in the future. In the case of fixed exchange rates, a government is providing an assurance that foreign currencies are basically fully liquid assets for the domestic economy, while in the case of crawling pegs or dirty floats, foreign exchange is warranted to be a very liquid, but not a fully liquid asset.

If a government refuses to assure the public on gold convertibility (i.e. the country is off the gold standard), then the government is no longer the ultimate gold market maker, and in so doing has at least partly deposed gold from its tyrannical position in matters of international payments adjustment and international efficiency earnings coordination. Moreover, if governments refuse to use gold to clear payments imbalances between national banking systems, then gold would be fully deposed as an instrument for attempting to forge the international coordination of policies.

The simplest case to analyse is one where a government is off the gold standard but still pursues a policy of fixed exchange rates by having its monetary authority 'peg' the exchange rate.[3] Assume nations A and B have agreed to fix the exchange rate between their currencies. The two nations have therefore agreed to operate as if they were in a UMS. When a payments deficit develops in A's trade relations with B, the initial impact will be a net increase in sales to B of liquid assets (formerly owned by those in A) or an increase in B's deposits in A's banking system as A's importers scramble to obtain B's currency to meet their contractual obligations. This growth in B's ownership of liquid assets either deposited in A's banks or formerly owned by A will be financed, *ceteris paribus*, by an expansion of B's money supply to meet the net needs of A to meet its international contractual settlements in terms of B's currency. Hence, the *initial* difference between government agreements to maintain a fixed exchange rate without gold convertibility and a gold standard system is that the immediate impact of a *ceteris paribus* trade imbalance will be entirely on the expansion of money in the surplus nation; and there will be no direct pressure necessary to reduce or limit A's money supply, finance availability, or the fully liquid assets denominated in terms of A's currency. The *initial* monetary accommodation (endogenous change) remains entirely with the expansion of B's financing facilities. Of course, the velocity of A's money may initially decline during the period of time when B's holdings of bank deposits in A increase, if B is not vigilant in keeping such wealth-holding active; but there will be no initial pressure on A's monetary authority to separately and endogenously reduce the total volume of deposits at domestic banks plus domestic currency outstanding.[4]

It is, however, highly unlikely that B's bankers and their clients will permit increased deposit holdings in A's banks to sit idle for any length of time. Consequently, it is at this stage that a fixed exchange rate system without gold convertibility can provide a decided advantage for the deficit nation *vis-à-vis* a gold (or any international commodity) convertibility system. Under the gold standard system, deficit nation A is under pressure to staunch the outflow of gold before it is bled white and its gold reserves completely depleted, even if this means creating havoc with domestic economic activity and imposing tremendous misery on domestic entrepreneurs and workers. The surplus nation, on the other hand, could continue to absorb international liquidity by passively accepting gold (the fully liquid international asset under the gold standard) as long as it so desired.

In a fixed exchange rate system without gold (commodity) convertibility, however, the boot can be on the other foot. Deficit nation A, while pursuing a policy of maintaining domestic aggregate demand, can continue to finance the external payments deficit by selling titles to deposits in A's banks which B's monetary authority is under agreement to accept to maintain the exchange rate. As long as B's monetary authority plays according to the rules of this game for fixing exchange rates, and in the absence of a coordinated deliberate incomes policy to cure the trade imbalance, B must either continue to accumulate bank deposits in A, or adopt a deliberate policy to encourage the spending of these accumulating liquidity claims on the products of A's industry, thereby eliminating the trade imbalance. Alternatively, B can 'recycle' this purchasing power to A via special loans or grants. In essence therefore, where there is no universal international reserve asset for a deficit nation to run out of – but only domestic liquid assets that national Central Banks can create and support – cooperative international agreements to maintain (or at least influence) exchange rates will force surplus nations such as B to behave in a globally and socially responsible manner (similar to a central government in a closed economy) by recycling surplus funds to deficit regions either via direct spending on the new goods and services produced in the deficit regions or by providing special grant or loans to such deficit areas. Economic civilization has surely progressed sufficiently to recognize these obvious advantages of this expansionist adjusting mechanism *for all parties*. What is urgently needed is the development of an internationally guaranteed system of sticky (if not absolutely fixed) exchange rates *without gold (commodity) convertibility*.[5]

Surplus nation B can recycle A's money by either (a) encouraging additional purchases of A's exports by B's residents, or (b) by lending B's holdings of A's money or other liquid assets to A's residents in exchange for promissory claims on A's future income and wealth, or (c) making grants to residents of A. If, on the other hand, B's increased ownership of liquid hoards of A's money increases and thereby slows down the velocity of money in A (assuming no offsetting increase in A's money stock), then a reduction in A's effective demand is encouraged, forcing a *ceteris paribus* decline in output and employment in A. (Depending on the institution of wage bargaining and price setting in A, increases in the money costs of production in A may (or may not) slow down significantly as spending on the products of A's industries is retarded.)

A loan recycling process can finance a continuing trade deficit for A, as long as B is willing to hold an increasing stock of A's promissory notes or other liquidity time machines. If, however, B is unwilling to increase its holdings of A's denominated liquid assets or promissory notes, then a fixed exchange rate cannot be maintained as B's Central Bank will ultimately stop exchange convertibility at the fixed rate of exchange when its reserves of A's currency are deemed 'too large'.

It is exactly at this point that the need for an ultimate international fully liquid asset becomes obvious. Trade is beneficial to both trading partners, yet in this case B is exporting (in value terms) more than it is receiving in imports. The case is analogous to an individual whose income – obtained by selling exports that he or she has produced to the rest of the world – is greater than consumption. The difference between the individual's exports and imports is his or her savings, an addition to net wealth which the individual is free to store in any liquid asset desired. (An individual is, of course, also free to reduce his or her productive activities to bring income into equality with a lower level of consumption, if leisure is preferred to increased liquidity or higher material consumption.) If, however, a saver desires to continue to work to earn an income in excess of his or her consumption level, then the saver must find accumulating liquid assets an enjoyable activity, while no-one else in the entrepreneurial economy suffers *as long as the aggregate demand is maintained*.

In the case of international trade, individuals in B are willing to produce goods to trade with A, but if B's exports exceed its imports, it means that residents of B prefer, *ceteris paribus*, an increment in liquid asset holding rather than spending the whole of their income earned by sales to A on the products of A.

As long as nation B is willing to hold bank deposits in A as liquid assets, no difficulty occurs. Nor would difficulties occur if A had gold (or other liquid assets) which B was willing to continually absorb as additional time machines.

A problem only develops, however, if holders of deposits in A's banks decide they wish to hold as liquid assets deposits in B's banks instead, but B's Central Bank will not accommodate this demand by creating new deposits in B's banks by buying deposits in A's banks. The public having expressed a preference for B's money over A's as a liquidity time machine has forced B's Central Bank to either expand B's money supply or let its exchange rate and/or interest rate rise. As long as B's Central Bank is willing to hold additional liabilities of A's banking system as a liquid reserve asset, there is no problem. If there is a universally accepted fully liquid asset such as gold, then B's Central Bankers will be willing to hold gold instead of excess stocks of A's bank liabilities, thereby forcing an outflow of gold from A as A's monetary authority redeems foreign held bank deposits. (There can never be an internationally fully liquid asset such as gold unless Central Bankers agree to such convertibility, at least between national banking systems.) Of course, if A runs out of this ultimate reserve asset, then it has no choice but to stop two-way convertibility and the game is over *unless it can be reconstituted by some new rules or a resharing of the fixed stock of the reserve asset, or additional reserve assets are made available to the Central Bank of the deficit nation.*

But why should Central Bankers be so perverse as to show a preference for one asset to hold as their bookkeeping entries over another as their reserve assets? One can understand the private sector's desire to switch liquid assets in their portfolio in a speculative search for capital gains or in avoiding possible capital losses. But are not Central Bankers supposed to be motivated by what is good for the nation or even multinational trade, rather than these more mundane money-grubbing activities? At this stage of human civilization, we surely should not need to encourage the waste of resources to dig gold out of the ground merely to bury them in Central Bank vaults and then 'ship' them from nation to nation via earmarking?

Why should Central Bankers of surplus nations not permit their bank balances in deficit nations to rise above normal 'reserve' levels, while leaving it to the two governments to cooperatively negotiate a coordinated incomes policy (as well as coordinated tariff and quota policies and even loans and unilateral transfers if necessary) to bring the trade balance to whatever level is deemed desirable and consistent with full employment in each nation? Such civilized behaviour is surely preferable to both trading partners instead of bleeding the deficit nation of its reserves, and in the course of time forcing recession on both parties, no matter what the cause of the initial deficit.

The eventual purchasing power of assets held by the surplus nation's Central Bank in order to finance the trade imbalance should not be an important or overriding economic issue. The citizens of B could, at the moment of the trade imbalance, purchase more goods from A at the current price level if they so desired. Instead, they prefer to 'save' i.e. to accumulate more liquid assets. The Central Bankers of B who are the ultimate recipients of B's excess holdings of bank deposits in A, are unlikely to ever purchase significant quantities of goods and services from A. Moreover, as long as a fixed exchange rate system (a UMS) is maintained, the purchasing power over producible goods of liquid assets denominated in terms of either domestic currency will vary with the rate of inflation (i.e. the rate of change of efficiency wages) of producible goods over time. Hence, a fixed exchange rate system with Central Banks required to hold either foreign deposits or an international reserve asset which can be only used for clearing purposes among national banking systems, gives nations not only the opportunity but the incentive to cooperate internationally to control inflation and payments imbalances via coordinated incomes, and tariff, quota and capital flow policies in each trading partner.

GOLD, INTERNATIONAL FULLY LIQUID ASSETS, AND CLEARING

Gold and other precious metals have, in the past, served as the ultimate liquidity time machine for Central Banks as well as for the general public of many economies. Today, there is a yearning on the part of some to return to such a system for international liquidity. Gold, which Central Bankers cannot produce via the exertion of labour (since it has a negligible elasticity of production), and which would be converted into legal tender money under a gold standard, would become a fully liquid international asset if enough governments agree to abide by such a system.

'Gold' need not be the 79th element in Mendelyéeff's periodic table of chemical elements. Anything

    (1) whose elasticity of production is negligible;

    (2) whose supply can expand endogenously with the needs of international trade;

    (3) whose carrying costs are negligible; and

    (4) which Central Bankers commit themselves to (a) freely convert into domestic money at a *fixed* exchange rate and (b) to always hold as a liquid asset (time machine) in whatever quantities are offered for conversion in excess of what is needed for international banking settlements;

will serve *better than gold* as a fully liquid international asset to settle clearing imbalances between national banking systems, *as long as Central Bankers abide by the simple rules of the game of international liquidity.*

As long as the world's Central Bankers agree to use the same thing as the international liquid asset for settling clearing imbalances, then bookkeeping holding of any quantity of such an asset is assured, for it will be the international time machine *par excellence*, as it will be able to be used to meet any monetary contractual obligation at any future date in any currency at a given exchange rate.

As Keynes pointed out in his famous chapter 'Auri Sacra Fames', the chemical element gold has no special or magical properties other than, like many other things, 'the increment in the total supply in any year is likely to be small',[6] i.e. its elasticity of production is negligible. If gold does not possess any mystical powers, why then has it so often, in the recent past, been chosen as the medium of ultimate settlement for payment imbalances between nations?

As long as multilateral trade for entrepreneurial economies is a process in historical time, an efficient organization for settling contractual payment obligations will involve a clearing mechanism where the transfers of assets and/or debts, such as bank deposits, are utilized for payments. The clearing instruments must be denominated either in the monetary unit which discharges the contractual obligation, or else in terms of a fully liquid international asset which each nation's monetary authority is legally bound to change into legal tender money. To promote confidence in the system, there should be institutional assurances that uncleared private debts can be converted at a *specified parity* into some asset of ultimate settlement (which by international agreement would make this asset an internationally fully liquid asset) at the option of the holder of the debt. Finally, it is essential that, in a world whose future is uncertain and non-predictable, there are well stated and agreed rules on the issuance of either private debts or any running or reserve assets used in the clearing system. Such rules are necessary to provide confidence that there will be no 'misuse' or misapplication of private debt facilities (in violation of the agreement) nor the spontaneous generation of additional clearing assets which might permit a trading partner to 'get something for nothing'. As long as the public has *confidence* in the operations of such a payments clearing system, market-oriented, productive entrepreneurial economies can engage in as much trade as their citizens desire without fear of financially caused disruptions, as long as none of the participants face the possibility of running out of the ultimate reserve asset. (As in the board game 'Monopoly' as long as all participants have sufficient funds to meet all expected – and unexpected – contractual obligations, the game can continue to be played with fun and zest!)

If the genius of human beings can devise instruments to physically transport their fellow creatures to the moon and to visually inspect via TV the outer planets of the solar system, it should not be beyond the intelligence of mankind to devise a practical clearing system for international liquidity as suggested. A system of managed exchange rates where international payments moved through a clearing house while 'paper gold' is used solely to settle payments between Central Banks is an obvious first step towards such a system. In recent years, developed nations have tried such human created paper substitutes for gold as *SDR*s (Special Drawing Rights) and *ECU*s (European Currency Units) – mock tests for the use of a fullfledged 'paper gold' international system. It must be admitted that these recently created systems have not been very successful. The failure to do better than these limited ventures must be attributed mainly to the political–psychological state of major trading nations, with their passions, economic dogmas, and lack of mutual trust and confidence. Progress is virtually impossible as long as each subgroup of economic agents in each nation wrestles for any potential advantage in any new proposed system, while those with vested interests in the existing – even if chaotic – international liquidity state encourage the almost universal lack of confidence in our political and economic leaders to develop a better way. It is no wonder that some want to turn back to the barbarous relic of an earlier day to restore some sense of order to the growing international financial chaos – and this despite the vast historical evidence that the order imposed by that tyrannical ruler, Gold, led to the economic collapse of the Great Depression.

Apparently, it will take another great collapse of the developed entrepreneurial economies before a serious reformation of the way in which these nations organize their payment clearings can occur. It is an unfortunate human trait that major reforms of economic institutions and processes are judged to be acceptable (and even desirable) only after the experiencing of a period of disaster and devastation. Economic retrogradation sets in during periods of *relative calm* and the warnings of economic Cassandras go unheeded![7] Nor is this backsliding economic behaviour surprising, for orthodox neoclassical theory teaches that 'free' markets (i.e. existing private sector institutions and power relations) are the best guides for improving the welfare of society. When the economic seas are calm, therefore, neoclassical theory encourages the dismantling of hard won institutional reforms considered unnecessary to cope with 'normal' economic conditions. (At best, the reforms are grudgingly admitted as a temporary expedient for alleviating an existing calamity, but in the long run, it is averred that such legislative reforms must promote misallocations and inefficiencies, and hence must be abandoned.)

As conditions change and storm clouds gather on the economic horizon, neoclassical theorists will declare that the earlier enacted legislative reforms 'caused' the impending storm; the only recourse is to reinstitute the pre-reform institutional relations which they claim will cause the storm clouds to disperse sooner, so that in the long run the economic seas will again be calm. Little is said (or known by these neoclassicists) about whether the dismantled economic ship can weather the storm and reach the 'long run' calmed seas.

On the other hand, those who warn that the threatening storm can be weathered by building a better ship via a further evolution of economic and social institutions and processes, and not by a regression to a nineteenth century economic Darwinian approach, go either unheard or unheeded, and are dismissed as mountebanks by the economic and political Establishment.

In the current context, it is the Post Keynesian monetary theorists who are in the Cassandra role regarding the existing international and national monetary systems, the same role filled by Keynes over a half century ago. History indicates that Keynes' warnings were ignored as orthodox economists, Central Bankers, and heads of government marched lock-step down the path of destruction by reinstituting nineteenth century institutions and practices. Only the storm of the Great Depression provided the climate for the rapid adoption of some of Keynes' revolutionary ideas to save the entrepreneurial system of production and distribution.

It may take a great monetary collapse in the 1980s to promote an environment for establishing needed new changes in the way that international monetary production and income distribution processes operate. Post Keynesian economists should be working on developing a set of detailed blueprints of how to construct a better system for international liquidity for entrepreneurial economies. Until the time when such blueprints are socially, economically, and politically acceptable, however, metallic gold may remain the only available fully liquid international asset. For everyone knows that gold's elasticity of production is so low that its stock supply cannot be expanded significantly, while paper and bookkeeping entries (whose production elasticities are also zero) can be expanded unless assurances are given *and* accepted that such 'abuse' of supply will not occur.

REPRISE FOR AN INTERNATIONAL FULLY LIQUID ASSET

As long as the governments of major trading nations announce that they will 'manage' the exchange rate (either in a fixed rate or managed float situation), then each government is making the domestic money supply endogenously responsive to imbalances in international payment flows over time. Surplus nations will *always* have to expand their domestic money supplies as, *ceteris paribus*, foreigners demand funds to meet international payment commitments. Deficit nations will initially find the velocity of circulation of their domestic bank deposits declining as titles to these deposits accrue to B's banking system and/or the latter's customers. To the extent that B recycles these deposits to finance A's spending, A's problems are not pressing – but if B refuses to accept liquid titles or promissory claims on future income, or to invest directly in A's stock of fixed capital or buy more of A's exports, then intergovernmental cooperation on the exchange rate and bank clearings between A and B can continue *only* if the Central Banks of A and B can agree on some medium which ultimately settles the international payment imbalance.

Gold, of course, has played the role of the ultimate reserve asset among Central Banks for part of the nineteenth and twentieth centuries. But what is really required is not any particular metal as an ultimate reserve asset; rather, what is needed is an asset which cannot be created by any single national Central Bank without the agreement of others, but with which each Central Bank is *legally bound* to maintain two-way convertibility with its legal tender money. In other words, what is essential is the development of an international fully liquid asset which possesses the assurance that no one nation can independently produce it without cost and then use it on the outside world 'to get something for nothing'. Just as with domestic money and liquid assets, international money and internationally liquid assets must have similar 'essential' elasticity properties, and customary assurances of acceptability and direct or indirect use as the medium of contractual settlement.

As long as there is no international law of contracts, as far as the general public is concerned, enforcement of private contractual obligations must always be in terms of a local currency, and there is no need to provide a universal currency for public use. Instead, the international 'gold' reserve, the *ultimate* fully liquid asset, can, by international agreement, be limited in use to settlements between national Central Banks. This permits and ensures established and customary institutional linkages for international transactions without requiring all contracts to be denominated in terms of the ultimate reserve asset.

SUMMARY

The classical specie-flow mechanism for restoring international trade balance without a permanent loss in global real income requires

(1) a fixed exchange rate between local currencies;

(2) relative changes in money costs of production resulting from induced changes in factor prices (in money terms) due to gold flows; and

(3) a high elasticity of substitution between exports and imports so that the induced change in the terms of trade redressed the trade imbalance.

Unfortunately, money prices of factors of production must be sticky during the production period in an entrepreneurial world, and therefore the adjustment process of the specie-flow mechanism has been diverted to one of creating global depressionary effects. Flexibility of nominal factor prices, which is a necessary condition for the proper operation of a neoclassical specie-flow adjusting mechanism, would destroy the institution of forward money contracts which are an *essential* characteristic of monetary, entrepreneurial, production economies which are market-oriented. Hence, neoclassical theory is in a logical dilemma – the price flexibility necessary for its assumed equilibrium mechanism to work (via the gross substitution axiom) is incompatible with entrepreneurial, market economies.

There are, of course, good sociological and game theoretical reasons,[8] as well as entrepreneurial and institutional arrangements, to explain why factor prices do not, and should not, respond in the freely flexible manner assumed by neoclassical theory, and therefore why relative money costs of production in trading nations do not automatically follow the adjustment process assumed in the specie-flow mechanism. In the unconscious recesses of their beings, nineteenth century entrepreneurial economies knew what it was all about. Production could be undertaken and the economic well being maintained or improved only if entrepreneurs' liabilities were limited by fixed money costs of production over the production period. The golden ages of economic growth, from 1832 to 1912, and 1950 to 1970, occurred during periods of sticky money wages (relative to productivity) in capitalist nations and stable exchange rates among major trading partners.

Of course, in a world of sticky money wage rates and structures, relative money costs of production between trading partners can still change (as hypothesized under a specie-flow mechanism) if nations institute a system of flexible exchange rates (i.e. a crawling peg, a managed float, or even a free float). It is often claimed that trade payments deficits can be 'cured' via exchange rate depreciation in such flexible rate systems. The goal of flexible exchange rate systems operating in tandem with a system of non-flexible money costs of production, is to alter the foreigner's cost of production in terms of domestic money in each trading partner, whenever a trade deficit occurs. The resulting relative change in the prices of exports and imports when denominated in any single currency means that the deficit nation's goods are less expensive and the surplus nation's goods more expensive to residents of both nations. Given the gross substitution axiom, there is then always some change in relative prices which ensures that the payments imbalance will be cured.

Unfortunately, exchange rate depreciation must normally be done at one fell swoop or at least relatively rapidly if it is to be effective. This means a large change in the terms of trade which (via equation 4.13 in Chapter 4) increases inflationary pressures in the deficit nation and lowers similar pressures in the surplus nations. Thus, *ceteris paribus*, workers in the deficit nation are likely to demand higher money wages, while their counterparts in the surplus country will be willing to accept less rapidly rising money wages – thereby vitiating the change in relative prices of exports and imports which would be necessary to restore a payments balance.

Instead of exchange depreciation.to cure a trade deficit, a practical alternative would be to maintain fixed exchange rates and develop a coordinated money incomes policy between trading partners to slowly eliminate the trade imbalance, while utilizing a temporary tariff or quota policy for short-term adjustments. A coordinated incomes policy is preferable to a deliberate exchange rate depreciation policy in a world of uncertainty, for it guarantees inelastic price expectations which are always stabilizing, while floating exchange rates always have the potential of unleashing elastic price expectations in international trade when unexpected events occur.

Deficit nations have found to their dismay that exchange rate depreciation is the most potent cause of uncontrolled domestic price inflation, for such a policy involves the redistribution of income from the deficit to surplus nation by raising the domestic money price of imports in the deficit nation. This increase in the domestic price of imports will, *ceteris paribus*, create inflationary tendencies, the size of which will depend on the degree of openness of the economy. Furthermore, when factor price contracts are indexed[9] directly (or indirectly with a lag via collective bargaining practices) in a vain attempt to maintain real living standards in the face of a lowering of real income due to the change in the terms of trade, the rise in the domestic price of imports induces rapid increases in the money costs of all domestic production. These factor price reactions quickly dissipate and frustrate the intended impact of the exchange depreciation. This, in turn, will require another exchange depreciation which will feedback into the cost of living index, etc. As Harrod noted many years ago

> The policy of relying on exchange depreciation to cure deficits really throws the objective of price stability to the winds. For this reason alone an incomes policy is to be preferred to exchange depreciation. Price stability is desirable, not only as helping to obtain equilibrium in the external balance of payments, but also for its own sake, on grounds of equity and efficiency . . . As regards efficiency, price inflation makes forward planning more difficult, but in modern industry, with its growing complexities and dependence on research and development, forward planning is becoming ever more important.
>
>   Thus, an incomes policy, if only it can be achieved, is much preferred to exchange flexibility.[10]

A persistent trade payments deficit due to an adverse trade balance may mean that, *ceteris paribus*, it is necessary for average real income in the deficit nation to increase more slowly than its average productivity, *unless* foreigners are willing *to finance* the deficit at the existing terms of trade indefinitely. Normally, with fixed exchange rates, the deficit nation should expect the money price level associated with aggregate domestic expenditures (E_D) to rise *relative to money wages and other domestic factor prices*. An incomes policy which involves, as Harrod reminds us, 'a campaign of education and, if you like, propaganda, to bring these facts home',[11] can encourage the sharing of this loss of real income among all inhabitants of the deficit nation in some politically and equitably acceptable manner, instead of unleashing a competitive game strategy in which each group in the deficit economy tries to push off their share of the nation's real income loss to other less powerful groups. In a modern democratic system, such competitive game behaviour is likely to exacerbate inflationary tendencies and lead to a 'solution' where *all* groups in society are worse off.[12]

But even with internationally coordinated incomes policies, it may be difficult to eliminate trade payment imbalances, especially if exports and imports in the two countries are not very good substitutes, i.e. if the demand for exports and imports is very price inelastic. This principle has often been recognized under the 'Marshall–Lerner Condition' where exchange depreciation, i.e. a change in the relative money costs of production between two nations in terms of either local currency, does *not necessarily, ceteris paribus*, improve the balance of payments. In other words the poorer the substitutes imports are for exports in each country (i.e. the weaker the applicability of the gross substitution axiom), the less likely that a mere change in the prices of domestically produced v. foreign produced goods (in terms of either local currency), whether due to (a) exchange rate changes or (b) coordinated incomes policies altering relative money costs of production in the two nations, will completely eliminate the trade imbalance. Hence, it may also be necessary to use tariff and quota policies *in conjunction with* an internationally coordinated incomes policy to maintain external equilibrium while simultaneously permitting each nation to freely pursue policies which encourage the full employment of domestic resources.

Any incomes policy, even if coordinated with those of other nations, cannot work instantaneously towards the elimination of payments imbalance. Hence, ample reserve assets will be required to finance the deficits during the transition period. Tariff and quota policies will also be required, especially if reserve assets are not sufficient to tide the nation over, even if the gross substitution axiom were to ensure payments equilibrium in the long run.

14 Freely Flexible Exchange Rates

In the normal course of events, even if fixed exchange rates are set so that over a period of years total outpayments from nation A to nation B equalled inpayments from B to A, there is little likelihood that in each subperiod an exact payments balance could be maintained. In an uncertain world, there will be oscillations in the trade balance merely because of seasonal factors, or variations in stockpiling, or different phases of the production and business cycle in each nation, etc. As long as exchange rates are fixed and are expected to move no more than a small percentage one way or the other (e.g. between gold export and import points), a large measure of the discrepancy between the value of exports and imports in any subperiod will be offset by movements in private funds. During a temporary trade deficit period, for example, importers and exporters will observe that the deficit nation's currency is relatively cheap. Since these individuals will always have a schedule of contractual payments coming due in the future, they will find it *in their best interests* to buy the deficit nation's currency spot as long as they expect to have an obligation due at a future date when they expect the exchange rate to return towards its 'normal' level. Similarly, bankers who hold funds in various nations for precautionary and speculative purposes, even if they have no expected contractual obligations coming due in the deficit nation's currency, will buy the cheap currency spot, while those who already hold nation's A currency will try to rearrange scheduled payments on international contracts denominated in B's currency to avoid selling A's money while it is 'temporarily' depressed. Harrod has termed the sum total of such financial movements 'the adjustment of balances and the leads and lags in trade payments'.[1]

EXPECTATIONS AND FLEXIBLE EXCHANGE RATES

As long as the public is *completely confident* in the government's willingness and ability to pursue a policy of fixed exchange rates (as, for example, is usual under an automatic gold standard), then the elasticity of expectations will be close to zero. A small price movement below the normal exchange rate will always be perceived as temporary; consequently such a movement would imply a substantial rate of return on moving forward in time any needed purchases of the weakened currency (or other liquid assets denominated in that currency) to meet future spending commitments.

If, however, a freely flexible (or even a crawling peg) exchange rate system is in operation, then the elasticity of expectations is not constrained to values close to zero by the prevailing institutional structure of the foreign exchange market. Thus a small decline in the spot exchange rate would *not* automatically induce an expectation that this was a temporary deviation from a normal rate. Uncertainty about future gains or losses will (by definition) necessarily be significantly greater than in a fixed exchange rate system. Movements in exchange rates can, if the future is sufficiently clouded and there are no institutional constraints limiting exchange rate changes, cut adrift the elasticity of expectations. Thus, price movements can induce expectations which can only further destabilize the exchange market. Thus, the more flexible per unit of time the exchange rate is thought to be, the less likely that 'leads and lags in trade payments' tend to offset random or transient trade imbalances. Instead, flexibility in an uncertain world can induce adverse, destabilizing and self-justifying expectations. If the elasticity of expectations equals unity, then flexible foreign exchange rate markets are on a knife edge where any initial movement in the exchange rate can induce further movements in the same direction and magnitude. Moreover, if the elasticity of expectations exceeds unity, then any change in the exchange rate, no matter how ephemeral, can create an accelerating movement away from the original rate. The magnitude of the elasticity of expectations can, of course, vary over time. Nevertheless, for any given set of *ceteris paribus* conditions, it is obvious that a fixed exchange rate system is likely to have economic agents who, on average, exhibit a smaller (or at least no larger) elasticity of expectations as compared to the expectational elasticity of agents in a freely flexible system. In other words, in a world of uncertainty and truly flexible exchange rates (where the government announces that it will never enter into the exchange market to stabilize prices, but will leave it to private banks to be exchange 'market makers'), economic agents are likely to exhibit more elastic expectations, *ceteris paribus*, except in conditions that are so static that no changes have occurred and hence no changes are expected. In the real world, unpredictable disturbances are part and parcel of international economic relations. Hence, as a practical matter, governments can never allow the public to believe that they will permit *truly* free floating exchange rates *without any official* intervention. The possibility of unstable foreign exchange markets, no matter how slight, is an anathema to all entrepreneurial trading economies.

Those who advocate truly freely flexible exchange rates are imprudent. In reality, the only relevant policy question is the degree of government intervention in the foreign exchange market which should be publicly announced in advance. The less the degree of intervention as stated government policy, the more reserve assets the nation must hold for emergency purposes, since under such an announced policy of free markets, if the government does intervene, the public in both countries will interpret such deliberate action as an attempt to head off an almost inevitable calamity. The empirical evidence is that since the breakdown of the Bretton Woods Agreement in the 1970s, governments have had to intervene more often than they did under the system of fixed exchange rates.[2]

Government action in such circumstances can prompt panic selling of the weakened currency, thereby exacerbating the situation unless the government has sufficient reserves to assure all that it can withstand any speculative run. If reserves are deemed insufficient for calamitous times, speculative runs will develop, thereby exacerbating inflationary tendencies in the depreciating local currency while reducing markets (and therefore employment) for the export industries of the nation whose currency exchange rate is rising. Furthermore, the more free market flexibility permitted by the announced government policy, the greater the potential *ceteris paribus* exchange uncertainties for those entrepreneurs contemplating long-term international arm's-length contractual commitments, thereby reducing, *ceteris paribus*, the level of international real investment and long-term trade.

Those who advocate freely flexible exchange rates to resolve trade balance deficits and the resulting payments imbalances are ultimately and solely relying on changes in exchange rates to alter the relative money costs of production (in terms of a single currency) in the trading nations so that, through the gross substitution axiom, relative demands for exports and imports will alter sufficiently to eliminate the deficit. In the real world, however, the mere announcement of a freely flexible exchange rate policy will require greater reserve holdings, and bring on the possibility of exaggerated movements and inflationary and depressionary tendencies in trading partners. If flexible rates do display actual significant movements in short periods of time, they will encourage competitive game strategies among economic agents,[3] which can only magnify inflationary tendencies in one trading partner and unemployment in the other. Thus, in the real world, a flexible exchange policy has little to recommend it, for in essence its claim to equilibrium ultimately rests on lowering the money efficiency wage or unit labour costs in the nation with the depreciating exchange rate relative to the cost of production in the surplus trading partner; but expectational phenomena can, in an uncertain world, push both countries to the brink of economic disaster. An intelligent, planned, and internationally coordinated incomes policy can surely achieve the same result without the potential for the disastrous expectational side effects.

MONETARISM AND FLEXIBLE EXCHANGE RATES

For many years before the breakdown of the Bretton Woods fixed exchange rate system, economists of the Monetarist school claimed that a freely flexible system would prevent the international transmission of inflation as each nation would be free to pursue its own domestic price level policy. Since 1971, however, the facts have proved just the opposite, as inflation has spread across the globe in epidemic proportions. Recent history might dishearten weaker spirits, but dedicated Monetarists will not be dissuaded by the 'short run' facts. Instead, they have proclaimed a new rationalization to explain why current events have not been a good test of the curative powers of a flexible exchange rate system. It is now accepted doctrine among Monetarist economists that one cannot pursue both a money supply target and an exchange rate target simultaneously; hence, the former must have the nation's priority. The lower the money supply growth target, however, the higher the interest rates, thereby encouraging net foreign lending inflows and, *ceteris paribus*, higher exchange rates. Avowed Monetarist governments such as that of Mrs Thatcher have claimed that these higher exchange rates will, in the long run, break the back of the accelerating inflation tendencies observed in the 1970s in countries such as the U.K. The rising exchange rate will force British manufacturers to compete against the world price so that, as Blackaby explains, British firms are 'forced to keep down the rise in their labour costs, and so they will concede smaller increases in money earnings. This wage moderation will spread from the manufacturing sector to the rest of the economy. In this way, "exchange-rate discipline" will bring down the British rate of inflation.'[4] Blackaby, however, notes that for Britain during the period 1977–80, 'this doctrine failed and in the light of experience', Blackaby concludes, 'it is not possible to maintain that we have in the exchange rate a powerful weapon for bringing down the rate of inflation'.[5]

If one strips away the plethora of new theoretical clothes (e.g. rational expectations, natural rates of unemployment and output growth, exchange rate discipline) in which Monetarism is currently garbed, one discovers an old policy skeleton – namely, a policy of deflating (or disinflating) an economy by reducing aggregate demand, output, and employment until the increase in domestic money efficiency earnings is reduced (at least relative to the growth of foreign efficiency earnings in terms of domestic money). The bitter pill of Monetarism always involves forcing, via market forces, a money incomes constraint (relative to productivity) policy down the throat of entrepreneurial economies. Massive doses of slack product markets, unemployment, business losses and bankruptcies, and human misery are the potent medicines hidden in the simple policies of rigid control of the money supply growth and freely flexible markets advocated by Monetarists. These economists belittle the development of prophylactic policies which establish, via legislative and cooperative actions, rules of the entrepreneurial game to limit money income increases. Such direct incomes policies are to be shunned, according to Monetarists, with as much fervour as the Amish community avoided the rise of modern conveniences such as electricity and the automobile as the work of Satan. Such quaint behaviour can be tolerated as long as its detrimental effects are limited to a small isolated group of practitioners and the majority of the population do not suffer deprivation due to the religious fervour of those advocates of suffering as a purifying concept. The quaint views of the small Amish minority can be accepted within a democratic entrepreneurial system for they do not attempt to foist their views on others. Unfortunately, Monetarists possess a more evangelistic fervour.

The side effects of the Monetarists' depressing medicine for limiting money income claims are very injurious to the body politics and economics of modern society. Lower profits or actual business losses not only reduce entrepreneurial expectations of future profits which are the bedrock basis for investment and innovation, but they simultaneously reduce internally generated financial flows which firms require for reinvestment. National productivity growth slows, stops or even declines when Monetarist policies are involved. This merely exacerbates the inflationary tendencies in the system as it increases, *ceteris paribus*, upward pressures on the money costs of production.

Moreover, in modern democratic entrepreneurial economies, wage bargains are relatively insensitive to restraints on aggregate demand. In periods of rising prices, money wage rate changes are much more closely related to current and recent past inflation rates and to previous disturbances in the relative wage structures. Consequently, any policy aimed at restraining aggregate demand to induce constraints on future money wage increases is bound to reduce productivity growth and hence be self-defeating.

If the rising prices faced by domestic residents are to be moderated, then current money wage settlements will have to, on average, be lower than the rise in prices since the previous settlement, *for each group of workers* in the economy and not only for those in the weak sectors. It is very difficult, if not impossible, to bring about this moderation in money income demand in all sectors of a *laissez-faire* economy, unless entrepreneurs and their workers in all sectors are so impoverished that none have the means or the stomach to continue the struggle over the distribution of income. Clearly, voluntary and/or legislative cooperation rather than coercion obtained by grave threats to economic life is the proper solution for enlightened societies. Governments should not permit the terrorism of slack markets to force 'voluntary' cooperation with any indirect incomes policy, any more than governments would legitimize the 'voluntary' transfer of income that would occur whenever a robber points a gun at a victim and states 'Your money or your life'.[6] If actions are forced under the threat of grave consequences to almost all groups of the economy simultaneously, then, the political system which fosters such intimidations is unlikely to survive! And democratic systems are even more in peril under these conditions than authoritarian ones – but neither are immune to political upheaval resulting from economic policies which coerce its residents into accepting economic hardships. If the economy has undergone a loss in real economic resources and hence the realities require belt-tightening, then civilized systems are surely more likely to minimize hardships via policies which coordinate sacrifices and encourage a spirit of cooperation and fair treatment, rather than those which encourage a Darwinian struggle among society's members.

15 Coordinating International Payments and Incomes

A fundamental argument developed in this volume is that any balance of payments problem due to current (or income) account transactions between open economies moving through calendar time towards an uncertain and unknowable future should be resolved primarily via an intergovernmentally coordinated incomes policy designed to achieve the maximum degree of stickiness in flow–supply prices (and incomes claims) while reducing the trade deficit. To enunciate this as a guiding principle is relatively easy. To transfer this principle into the arena of practical policies which are politically acceptable is more difficult, but not impossible. The goal of 'stickiness' does mean that one accepts the current distribution of domestic and global income – however arbitrary and unequal it might be – as a healthy position. Validation of the *status quo* does not mean that the distribution of income and wealth is sacrosanct and therefore cannot be changed over time as the economic process moves on. It does imply, however, that in a developed interdependent entrepreneurial system, significant changes in the distribution of income can be achieved without potentially severe damage to *all* participants only by a cooperative, negotiated agreement which is compatible with the potential flow and growth of full employment real income. Change in the relative distribution of income is a much more socially acceptable phenomenon in a non-zero positive sum economic system; in an era of economic growth, changes in the relative distribution can occur where most citizens suffer little or no reduction in absolute real income levels.

The alternatives to a peaceful coordinated incomes policy for affecting incomes distribution are either a Darwinian free market struggle in which the resulting stagflation is likely to impoverish all or most of the inhabitants, or a bloody political revolution. Darwinian struggles as well as political revolutions should be banished as uncivilized behaviour in real world democratic systems. In either case, the existence of large economic entities and/or groups with significant economic power sufficient to devastate the economic landscape if a struggle should break out, threatens the basis of any entrepreneurial system and the standard of living of all its inhabitants.

The rich and the powerful should adopt a view *of noblesse oblige* towards those lower down in the economic distribution, while the poor must not act on the basis of a 'misery loves company' view which delights in reducing all to the lowest common denominator. Instead those in the lower ranks of the distribution of income must recognize that greater net gains are most likely to be achieved within an entrepreneurial system of cooperation and growth which fosters equitable changes at a rate which is compatible with the social conscience of most. Education, not extermination, of the rich is necessary if the latter are unaware of the needs of the poor. The realities of the political economy of the world we live in must be faced if progress on these basic macroproblems of entrepreneurial economies is to be made. Only in the fantasy world of neoclassical 'large' economies populated solely with 'small' economic agents can the devastating short-term effects of a struggle over the distribution of income be ignored.

THE BASIC PRINCIPLES

This chapter outlines the basis for an ambitious and far-reaching scheme for economic cooperation among the trading nations of the world. Cooperation and goodwill are essential prerequisites for the success of any visionary proposal. There is, however, no alternative to co-operation, for our planet has become, through modern communications and transportation systems, so economically interdependent that, as Benjamin Franklin once said, 'We must all hang together, or we will all hang separately.'

Any proposal for reconciling trade payments problems should possess biased mechanisms of adjustment – biased towards the forcing of clearing conformability under a regime of economic expansion rather than contraction. The history of modern economies has clearly demonstrated that unionized monetary systems (UMS) have been more compatible with an environment of expansion than NUMS. It would therefore appear essential that the principles of money and banking associated with a UMS be established for financing the trading between open national economies. Keynes' original proposals for an International Clearing Union with an 'international money' to be utilized solely for clearing payments between national Central Banks was such a plan. It can be revised and updated to provide a payments clearing system that is designed to put more pressure for adjustment on creditor nations than on debtor nations.

In a well organized international clearing system operating on principles related to a banking system in a UMS, each national Central Bank would be obliged only to maintain two-way convertibility (at specified bid and asked prices) between its local currency and deposits at a supranational bank and clearing union. Consequently, access to foreign exchange by residents of any particular nation would be controllable by their own Central Bank working in cooperation with other Central Banks in an international clearing union. The ultimate reserve asset for purposes of international liquidity – which could not be held for precautionary or speculative purposes by the public – would be deposit liabilities of the supranational bank. These deposit liabilities would be denominated in whichever unit all Central Bank members agreed upon. The reserve unit, however, would not be used as a national or international money by the general public.

As in Keynes' original proposal, a rule should be adopted when the supranational bank is created, that any nation which accumulates excessive credit balances because of continuing trade surpluses will be required to take various steps to reduce these balances. If a nation either fails to take such actions and/or if the balances continue to accumulate, there should be a rule which triggers the confiscation of these excessive balances at the clearing house when they exceed a pre-determined level. This threat of confiscation of wealth, however, would never become operational, 'for obviously, it would always be in the interest of the country concerned to find some way of dealing with the surplus other than that . . . The main point is that the creditor should not be allowed to remain passive.'[1]

At this stage there would be no purpose in delineating in practical detail the steps that would be incumbent on the creditor nation, but they would primarily involve revaluing domestic money efficiency wages *vis-à-vis* foreign efficiency wages as denominated in terms of local currency. Instead of utilizing either devaluation of the deficit nation's currency and/or even appreciation of the surplus nation's money (which creates exchange uncertainties which will inhibit, *ceteris paribus*, international investment and long duration sales contracts), trading nations should develop internationally coordinated incomes policies to solve payments problems. A surplus nation would be required to *primarily* increase domestic money efficiency wages rather than to appreciate its currency.

Under pre-determined rules, surplus nations, at their option, could even split the required excess of money *income* growth, say, in half, and permit an equivalent appreciation of their exchange rate *vis-à-vis* the clearing bank's currency.[2] Such a provision would permit 'surplus' nations to make an adjustment to the balance of payments without forcing a significant inflation in the price level of goods purchased by the residents of the credit balance nation.

Deficit nations, on the other hand, would always be required to hold money incomes below productivity gains, and could, if they wished to, temporarily use tariffs, quotas and loans or grants from surplus nations as auxiliary mechanisms to buy time to bring their trade balance close to payments equilibrium. (Loans and overdraft facilities from the international clearing union would also be available.) Currency devaluation for deficit nations would be limited in advance to some small pre-determined annual rate. Surplus nations would be required to reduce and continue to phase out all existing tariffs and quotas at some pre-specified rate as long as the nation continued to accumulate credit balances at the supranational Central Bank and clearing union.

Each nation would be free to choose the form of incomes policy it believed most desirable for its inhabitants, given the sociology, politics and economics of its current mode of determining income distribution. Thus some nations might desire to control incomes via wage and price controls, others through some variant of a tax based incomes policy (TIP), etc. Nevertheless rules would be set where nations whose credit balances exceeded certain pre-determined levels would be required to increase domestic money incomes relative to domestic productive increments by pre-agreed rates.

These rules for coordinating international incomes and trade payments would force nations accumulating excessive international liquidity to adopt a somewhat inflationary domestic incomes policy to reduce their trade surplus. Of course, the surplus nation could avoid this inflationary incomes policy if instead it (a) devised import expansion programmes and/or (b) provided loans or grants to deficit nations. Either of these two policies would recycle finance and avoid the internationally stagnating effects from the excessive accumulation of international liquidity by trade surplus nations.

In sum then, surplus trading nations would be under pressure to eliminate payments imbalances by instituting a combination of deliberate policies to increase imports, inflate money efficiency earnings, and/or provide grants and loans to trading partners, or else face confiscation of excessive international liquidity hoards. Surplus nations will therefore bear the brunt of payments adjustment policies, but which, because of their credit surplus, they are more able to afford than deficit nations. In the current institutional environment on the other hand, adjustments are forced primarily on the deficit nations, many of whom (e.g. LDCs) are least able to afford it. Even if deficit nations are wealthy (e.g. oil consuming nations of Europe, U.S.A. and Japan), however, adjustments policies for deficit nations are inherently employment and output depressing. The result is stagnation and a slowing progress in the improvement of average standards of living throughout the globe. Currently (1980) the tremendous surplus being accumulated by the OPEC nations threatens the economic vitality of the entire world.

Once this Post Keynesian principle of fostering payments adjustments primarily on surplus nations is widely understood and recognized as a necessary condition for the mutual survival and growth of inter-dependent entrepreneurial economies, it should not be difficult for the technical 'experts' to engineer an international payments system which promotes such behaviour.

BALANCE OF PAYMENTS AND CAPITAL ACCOUNTS

Little has been said in this volume about exogenous capital movements and their effects on the balance of payments. It is obvious that large unfettered capital flows can create serious international payments problems for nations whose current accounts would otherwise be roughly in balance. Unfortunately, in free capital markets there are no ways of distinguishing between the movement of floating and speculative funds that take refuge in one nation after another in the continuous search for speculative gains (or for even precautionary purposes), and funds being used to promote genuine new investment for developing the world's resources. Capital movements of the latter kind are to be applauded. As long as net speculative and precautionary flows between nations are unimportant they can be tolerated. Such flows are likely to be insignificant, however, only when exchange rates are sticky *and* international liquidity is protected via internationally coordinated banking and incomes policies. Otherwise the international movement of speculative and precautionary funds (sometimes called 'hot money') can be so disruptive to entrepreneurial production processes as to impoverish most, if not all, nations who organize their production and exchange processes on an entrepreneurial basis. 'Loose funds may sweep round the world disorganizing all steady business . . . [and therefore] nothing is more certain than that the movement of capital funds must be regulated.'[3]

One of the more obvious dicta following from the Keynesian revolutionary view of liquidity in open economies is that

There is no country which can, in future, safely allow the flight of funds for political reasons or to evade domestic taxation or in anticipation of the owner turning refugee. Equally, there is no country that can safely receive fugitive funds which cannot safely be used for fixed investments and might turn it into a deficiency country against its will and contrary to the real facts.[4]

The techniques for controlling capital fund movements can be left to the practitioner as long as the principles are clear.[5]

With control of capital transactions – or at least, with each country to decide what degree of free capital funds enter and exit it permits while simultaneously cooperating with the desires of other nations as to what controls of capital movement they desire, each nation will be able to institute the degree of control over its domestic money supply that it desires. Cooperation between nations in detecting, reporting and stopping disruptive capital funds movements among nations whenever one of the payments partners requests such cooperation, guarantees that each nation can maintain control over that portion of the domestic money supply that is not used to finance the output of industry. Each nation should be free to judge its own needs for domestic interest rate and liquidity policy, while cooperating in an international payments scheme which is explicitly expansionist in design. Moreover, the successful implementation of an international liquidity and payments system based on the principle of coordinating incomes policies among nations will, in itself, ensure very inelastic expectational elasticities. This will mean that individuals will no longer be as greatly impelled to engage in disruptive international speculative and precautionary financial transactions when unexpected changes occur. Thus, within a short span of time, the problems of trade imbalances and 'hot money' flows which can now create economic havoc from which no nation is immune may fade away.

Notes and References

PREFACE

1. A UMS, on the other hand, has either a single nominal unit to denominate all contracts, or if there are various nominal units, there are absolutely fixed exchange rates amongst the units.

CHAPTER 1: SOLVING THE CRISIS IN ECONOMIC THEORY

1. J. M. Keynes, *The General Theory of Employment Interest and Money* (New York: Harcourt, Brace, 1936) pp. 260–2.
2. P. Davidson, 'The Dual Faceted Nature of the Keynesian Revolution: The Role of Money and Money Wages in Unemployment and Production Flow Prices', *Journal of Post Keynesian Economics 2*, 1980, pp. 291–307.
3. E. R. Weintraub, 'The Microfoundations of Macroeconomics: A Critical Survey', *Journal of Economic Literature*, 15, 1977, p. 2.
4. Ibid. p. 2.
5. J. R. Hicks, 'Mr. Keynes and the "Classics"', *Econometrica*, 5, April 1937. In private correspondence (letter to author dated 23 Nov. 1980) Sir John Hicks indicates his objection to being placed in the Neoclassical Synthesis–Keynesian column of Table 1.1. Hicks writes 'there are two [tenets] at least in the column where my name appears which are tenets I simply abhor. I do not assume full employment. I don't even say that there must be full employment in equilibrium; indeed, I regard that statement as nearly meaningless . . . nor do I have any serious belief in marginal productivity . . . I would accept more of the tenets in your middle column, though I don't really feel that that is where I belong . . . .

'Of course the trouble is that I have changed my mind – over fifty years! – and go on changing it. I think it is right to do so, partly because (one hopes) one's understanding improves, partly because, in a changing world, the things one wants to emphasize also change. I suppose there was a time when your classification of me would have fitted better; but surely, for your readers, it is my *Crisis* book of 1974 which it would be natural to take as representing my position. As I know, there is practically nothing in that book with which the Cambridge economists of your left-centre column disagree. But I don't want to go into that column either!'

272

6. Keynes, *The General Theory*, p. 177.

7. For example, see R. M. Solow, 'Discussion', *American Economic Review Papers and Proceedings*, 61, 1971, p. 63, where Solow states 'in short we neglect radical economics because it is negligible'.

8. There is no hyphen between the words Post and Keynesian. In the past there has been a lack of uniformity in labelling schools of thought; hence perceptive readers will note that others have used the term Post-Keynesian (with the hyphen) to designate the school that I have labelled Neo-Keynesian. In order to provide a non-ambiguous terminology I have eliminated the hyphenated term from this text and hope others will do likewise.

9. If by inflation we mean a non fully-anticipated rise in the *money* price level of newly produced goods over a period of time, then a logical analysis based on general equilibrium can *never* explain such phenomena. There is no logical niche for money, calendar time, a money price level, and non fully-anticipated future events (at least in an actuarial sense) in any GE system. If the inflation is 'fully anticipated' then all economic agents will have taken actions to insure themselves against the inflation and hence *the inflation can have no real effects on the economy*! Consequently, neoclassical theorists must always impose an outside (logically incompatible) non-Walrasian factor or relationship such as rigid money wages, or the equation of exchange, or the Phillips Curve to the total system of general equilibrium in order to attempt to handle the disruptive real world phenomena which continually plague our economic system.

10. The Monetarists have attempted to shore up their collapsing system by adding various expectational formation hypotheses to their system. Expectations permit any outcome in the short run, while expectations either 'adapt' or are 'rational' and therefore Monetarists assume that economic actors either know *at the initial instant* what are the true parameters of the economic system or learn (adapt to) these unchanging parameters. Consequently, 'in the long run', though we are all dead, the Monetarist expectational analysis will be verified! Elsewhere I have demonstrated that even with such expectational formation models added to general equilibrium systems, one cannot rescue the neoclassical system [See P. Davidson, *Money and the Real World*, 2nd ed. (London: Macmillan, 1978) pp. 370–2].

11. Of course, if one insists on analysing a problem which has no real world equivalent or solution, then it should not be a surprise that a model developed to respond to real world situations rather than imaginary queries will not suffice. Thus Post Keynesian models cannot determine how many angels can dance on the head of a pin, or how to specify *in advance* the optimal allocation of resources over calendar time into the uncertain, unpredictable future. On the other hand, models designed to provide answers of the angel-pin head variety, or on the optimal allocation path over time, will be unsuitable for resolving practical real world economic problems!

12. Intelligent advocates of general equilibrium systems have come to realize that the one and only useful function of general equilibrium analysis is to

demonstrate why optimal allocations can *never* be achieved in the real world. In this view, neoclassical systems are only

> very useful when for instance one comes to argue with someone who maintains that we need not worry about exhaustible resources because they will always have prices which ensure their 'proper' use. Of course there are many things wrong with this contention but a quick way of disposing of the claim is to note that an Arrow–Debreu equilibrium must be an assumption he is making for the economy and then to show why the economy cannot be in this state. The argument will here turn on the absence of futures markets and contingent futures markets and on the inadequate treatment of time and uncertainty by the construction. This negative role of Arrow–Debreu equilibrium I consider almost to be sufficient justification for it, since practical men and ill-trained theorists everywhere in the world do not understand what they are claiming to be the case when they claim a beneficent and coherent role for the invisible hand. But for descriptive purposes of course this negative role is hardly a recommendation. [Hahn, *On the Notion of Equilibrium in Economics* (Cambridge University Press, 1973) pp. 14–15].

13. J. R. Hicks, *Economic Prospectives* (Oxford University Press, 1977) p. vii. The Rational expectation hypothesis, on the other hand, assumes that the public has complete knowledge of the parameters of the real economic system and hence cannot be 'fooled' by government intervention.

14. J. R. Hicks, *Critical Essays in Monetary Theory* (Oxford University Press, 1967) p. vii.

15. J. R. Hicks, 'ISLM – An Explanation', *Journal of Post Keynesian Economics*, 3, Winter 1980–1, p. 139.

16. J. R. Hicks, 'Some Questions of Time in Economics', in A. M. Tang *et al.* (eds), *Evolution Welfare and Time in Economics* (Lexington Books, 1976) pp. 140–1.

17. A. Marshall, *Principles of Economics*, 8th ed. (New York: Macmillan, 1950) p. vii.

18. Keynes, *The General Theory*, pp. 293–4.

19. D. Laidler and M. Parkin, 'Inflation – A Survey', *Economic Journal*, 85, 1975, p. 795.

20. D. Laidler, 'Expectations and the Phillips Trade Off: A Commentary', *Scottish Journal of Political Economy*, 23, 1976, p. 59.

21. Ibid. pp. 62–3.

22. Ibid. p. 69.

23. Laidler and Parkin, 'Inflation', p. 743. Yet, to provide one obvious counter example, the efficient operation of spot security markets and hence the determination of the short-run rate of interest require the existence of two groups, the bulls and the bears, each possessing (by definition) opposing views about the spot price of securities at any given date in the future. Thus, when the future becomes the present, either the

bulls or the bears will be proved wrong if security prices change over time, or *both* will be wrong if the rate of interest remains unchanged. Thus, spot security markets exist only because the bulls have differing views about the future than the bears, and each group 'knows' the other group has an alternative erroneous view.

Thus, the very notion of a stable market rate of interest is incompatible with a market for securities in which that interest rate is determined. Moreover, there are many economic agents who gain their income from trying to forecast the short-run waves of bullishness and bearishness — not to stabilize the market, but to be one step ahead of the ebbs and flows of security price movements.

24. K. S. Arrow and F. H. Hahn, *General Competitive Analysis* (San Francisco: Holden-Day, 1971) pp. 356–7. Italics added.
25. Ibid. p. 361.
26. It would be foolish for entrepreneurs in a free enterprise, market-oriented system to enter into a production process whose gestation period greatly exceeded the duration of forward contracts with his workers (or even his material suppliers), for to do so would be to undertake a potentially unbounded liability with no controls over the costs of production and hence no assurance that the entrepreneur had sufficient finance to meet his future payrolls and complete the production process.
27. Keynes, *The General Theory*, Chapter 17.
28. 'The attribute of "liquidity" is by no means independent of these two characteristics. For it is unlikely that an asset, of which the supply can be easily increased or the desire for which can be easily diverted by a change in relative price, will possess the attribute of "liquidity" in the minds of owners of wealth' (Keynes, *The General Theory*, p. 241). For a complete discussion of the rationale for these salient properties, see P. Davidson, *Money and the Real World*. In my published dispute with Professor Friedman's he specifically remarks that his theoretical framework specifically assumes *easily reproducible commodities are good substitutes for money*. (See M. Friedman *et al.*, *Milton Friedman's Monetary Framework: A Debate With His Critics* (University of Chicago Press, 1974) pp. 27–9, 107–10.) Moreover, Friedman argued that 'actual' money can be a 'commodity capable of being produced by the execution of labor, often at roughly constant costs' (p. 153). Post Keynesian theory suggests, on the other hand that if a 'commodity money' is adopted by a modern production, money-contracting economy (as opposed to a system which organizes production on the basis of tradition or custom) the economy will utilize something which is not easily reproducible *within its boundaries* either because (a) the commodity is subject to rapid diminishing returns in production or (b) there are institutional arrangements to control its supply.

Since, as every student of general equilibrium knows, peanuts will do the job of money as well as anything else, if only peanuts were money, full employment would be an inevitable outcome as the involuntarily unemployed could always be put to work in the peanut fields!
29. F. H. Hahn, 'Keynesian Economics and General Equilibrium Theory',

in G. C. Harcourt, (ed.), *The Microfoundations of Macroeconomics* (London: Macmillan, 1977) p. 31. As long as spot markets exist for the purchase and sale of assets, however, they can be 'resting places for savings' only if the elasticity of substitution between nonreproducible assets and reproducible goods are zero, i.e. as long as the axiom of Gross Substitution does not apply.

30. Keynes, *The General Theory*, p. 16, italics added.
31. Solow, on the other hand, believes that 'thus far so-called Post Keynesianism seems to be more a state of mind than a theory' (Solow, 'Alternative Approaches to Macroeconomic Theory: A Partial View', *Canadian Journal of Economics*, 12, 1979, p. 344). Of course, Solow (as he readily admits) is far from an impartial judge of the merits of Post Keynesian analysis *vis-à-vis* Neoclassical Keynesianism. Although Solow concedes that he now finds 'bits of unorthodoxy incomparably more credible than the things that impeccably orthodox equilibrium theory asks me to believe about the world' (p. 348), he still concludes 'It is much too early to tear up the IS − LM chapters in the textbooks' (p. 354). Perhaps it is 'too early' for professors who have made fame and fortune out of such models to be ready to abandon them despite their common sense which suggests the incredible nature of neoclassical theory; but for others who have an earnest desire to resolve the economic problems which are threatening the 'Second Great Crisis of Capitalism in the Twentieth Century', and who have no vested interest in neoclassical theory, time is running out.
32. P. Davidson, *Money and the Real World*.
33. M. Friedman *et al.*, *Milton Friedman's Monetary Framework*, p. 154.
34. J. M. Keynes, *A Tract on Monetary Reform* first published in 1923, reprinted as Volume IV of *The Collected Writings of John Maynard Keynes* (London: Macmillan, 1971) p. 65.

CHAPTER 2: THE CONCEPTUAL FRAMEWORK

1. Hicks insists that if a theory is to be applicable to the real world, it must begin with some inductive axioms. See J. R. Hicks, *Causality in Economics* (New York: Basic Books, 1979) p. 28.
2. Some may be surprised that I assert that 'existence' is an assumption of neoclassical analysis rather than a conclusion. In fact, the neoclassical research programme has been to assume existence, stability, and uniqueness of full employment equilibrium, and then search out the *sufficient* conditions for achieving such an equilibrium.
3. Ferguson, a devout, but honest neoclassical scholar indicated that neoclassical theory could not be proved. It was to be accepted as 'a statement of faith'. C. E. Ferguson, *The New Neoclassical Theory of Production and Distribution* (Cambridge University Press, 1969) p. 269.
4. R. W. Solow, 'The Economics of Resources or the Resources of Economics', *American Economic Review Papers and Proceedings*, May 1974.

5. J. R. Hicks, *Causality in Economics*, p. 39.
6. Ibid. p. 38.
7. *The Collected Writings of John Maynard Keynes* [hereafter cited as *CWK*], xiv (London: Macmillan, 1973) p. 296.
8. Ibid. pp. 296–7.
9. R. F. Harrod, *The Life of John Maynard Keynes* (London: Macmillan, 1963) p. 463.
10. J. M. Keynes, *The General Theory of Employment, Interest and Money*, (New York: Harcourt, 1936) p. 37. [Reprinted as *CWK*, vii.] In earlier drafts of *The General Theory*, Keynes struggled to develop proper definitions with which to elucidate his various 'propensities'. See *CWK*, xiii, pp. 398–444.
11. Keynes' fundamental psychological law about the propensity to consume was based on both inductive knowledge ('the detailed facts of experience') and deductive views of human nature. See *CWK*, vii, p. 96.
12. Ibid. p. vi.
13. G. L. S. Shackle, *Epistemics and Economics* (Cambridge University Press, 1972) p. 73.
14. In P. Davidson, *Money and the Real World* (London: Macmillan, 1978), this is done in great detail. Chapter 3, however, provides a more limited and concise perspective.

CHAPTER 3: DEFINITIONS FOR A CLOSED ECONOMY

1. How many economists have carefully read and comprehended Keynes' definitional Chapter 6 and its Appendix in his *General Theory*? How many have similarly worked through Chapters 1 and 2 of Friedman's *Theory of Permanent Income* and realize that in Friedman, saving is defined (p. 11) to include the purchase of new durable goods including clothing, etc. while in Keynes, saving involves the decision *not* to purchase durables or nondurables by households? [Cf. J. M. Keynes, *The General Theory of Employment Interest and Money* reprinted as Volume vii of *The Collected Writings of John Maynard Keynes* [hereafter cited as *CWK*] (London: Macmillan, 1973) with M. Friedman, *Theory of Permanent Income* (Princeton University Press, 1957).]
2. Since the term 'income' is associated (in common usage) with contributions to the production of current output in the economy, therefore aggregate income should be limited to the money receipts arising from the *contractual* sale of current services of the factors of production. (Profits occupy a sort of halfway house – since they are not directly determined by contracts. Instead they are the residual due to the difference between the contractually determined receipts on the sale of products and the contractual costs of the hired factors of production.)

Income-in-kind payments should be conceived of as the combination of two separate contractual transactions, namely money income payments to factor owners from the employer, with a simultaneous purchase commitment of goods by the factor owner to the employer.

3. For simplicity we can assume each firm self-finances its investment projects in this case, although in reality there is likely to be equity and debt financing between firms.

4. For the moment we are ignoring saving by governments or foreigners. Government saving would be defined as equal to its money tax receipts less its money purchases of new goods and services, while foreigners' saving as far as the domestic economy is concerned is equal to foreigners' sales of new goods and services (imports) to domestic residents less foreigners' purchases of new goods and services (exports).

5. Milton Friedman on the other hand, in developing his analytical position, has used strange (to the layman) definitions of consumption and savings. Friedman designates consumption as 'the value of services' consumed (i.e. destroyed) during the period. Thus for Friedman consumption is equal to depreciation (or wearing out) of existing durables each year plus the purchase of non-durables (Friedman, *Theory of Permanent Income*, p. 11). Saving then, in Friedman's analysis, is any part of income not so consumed; thus, a layman might be shocked to discover that the purchase of a gas-guzzling sports car is, in Friedman's analytical system, a form of private saving in the year of its purchase (except for the portion of the car which depreciates in that year). Friedman prides himself on *not* defining the purchase of such durables as consumption. Instead he boasted that his definitions are superior to others (including the ones used in this chapter) because in Friedman's logical framework, 'much that one classified as consumption is reclassified as savings' (Ibid. p. 28). Thus, for example, when windfall (unplanned) income is received in Friedman's permanent income model, Friedman suggests 'Is not the windfall likely to be used for the purchase of durable goods?' (Ibid. p. 28). Hence, almost by definition, Friedman has demonstrated that current windfall (or transitory) income receipts will always be 'saved', since how many additional non-durables can a household purchase in the current period? The average layman would be surprised to learn that, if a household won the Irish Sweepstakes and spent the receipts on yachts, fast cars, mink coats, etc., such purchases are not, in Monetarist theory, conspicuous consumption but are instead private saving!

    Such uncommon use of language can be highly misleading for the unwary. For example, does anyone truly believe that a policy which stimulates private saving in the form of say mink coats, etc. improves productivity in the U.S.?

6. This section has benefited from considerable private correspondence with Sir John Hicks.

7. If the date of payment differs from the date of delivery, we can allow for this difference by reckoning that the actual contract includes an elemental loan contract.

8. Individual entrepreneurs in the non-integrated chain may also produce for spot market sales, i.e. for sales from shelf industry. In the housing industry in the United States, for example, builders producing for the spot market are said to produce 'on speculation' – a term suggesting such home builders differ considerably from those who only 'custom-

build' (on forward contract) houses. Nevertheless, a spot market for a producible good can continue to exist over time only if it is expected that the spot price will equal or exceed the costs of production plus the carrying costs.

9. Of course, some real world retail markets may sell forward as well as spot, e.g. subscriptions v. newstand sales of magazines. In a world where these markets are continuous, the spot price will normally exceed the subscription (forward) price while the latter will be closer to the costs of production.

Moreover, most retail spot markets are not efficiently organized and orderly, and it is very difficult if not impossible for households and entrepreneurs not in the normal distribution marketing chain (from producers to wholesaler to specialized retail stores) to resell consumer goods purchased at retail stores and at a price close to that prevailing in the retail market.

10. See *CWK*, xxix (London: Macmillan, 1979) p. 88. Keynes defined consumption goods as finished 'When they are ready for sale to a consumer or to a Capitalist for the purpose of holding them in stock as a speculation [for later sale on a spot market]', while capital goods are 'finished' when they are ready for use by consumers as consumption-capital (e.g. houses) or by producers as instrumental capital' (Ibid. p. 88).

11. Durables with high carrying costs are 'expensive' modes of time transportation, just as 'gas-guzzlers' are for space transport. All other things being equal, savers will attempt to find time machines with the lowest carrying cost among those available, just as car buyers might, *ceteris paribus*, choose the lowest 'gas guzzler' even if only guzzlers are available.

Milton Friedman, however, would permit (by definition) the household saver to store his liquidity in retail consumer durables such as clothing and household appliances (see M. Friedman *et al.*, *Milton Friedman's Monetary Framework: A Debate With His Critics* (University of Chicago Press, 1974) p. 28). Thus is Friedman's models, households' purchasing power is stored in durables which, in the real world, have very large carrying costs and are not readily resaleable, since, most consumer markets are not efficiently organized and orderly and hence, most consumer durables are, as far as households and entrepreneurs not in the normal distributive chain are concerned, illiquid.

In a Post Keynesian analysis, in order to be a liquidity time machine, not only must a durable be resaleable but also its carrying costs must be significantly less than the expected profit from future resale in order to make its holding as a store of value worthwhile. Since the marginal carrying costs of tangibles tend to rise rapidly with the size of stock held, those tangibles that are readily reproducible (at roughly constant costs in terms of the wage unit) will rapidly lose any time machine capabilities they might be thought to possess if the public attempts to buy (and hold as a store of value) any surplus over current consumption at the cost of reproduction of the tangible.

12. J. M. Keynes, *The General Theory of Employment Interest and Money*, p. 160.
13. This implies that the distinction of real rate of interest and the money rate of interest does not make any sense as an *ex ante* concept, if the future is 'fully anticipated' or everyone has homogeneous expectations. (See Keynes, Ibid. p. 142 and *CWK*, xiii, p. 518.)
14. A. Marshall, *Principles of Economics*, 1st ed. (London: Macmillan, 1890) p. viii.
15. To the extent that the public demand change is not offset by a change in reservation demand of the market makers of these spot markets. Even in spot (auction) markets the degree of price flexibility depends on this reservation demand of market makers, i.e. their reactions and interpretation of sudden changes in the public's market behaviour and the institutional rules governing how market makers are supposed to maintain 'orderliness'.
16. G. Debreu, *Theory of Value* (New Haven: Yale University Press, 1959) p. 32.
17. Ibid. p. 98. From a Knight–Keynes view, this is risk, not uncertainty!
18. Ibid. p. 98.
19. Ibid. p. 100. Italics added.
20. It should be noted that the neoclassical concept of commodity prices in a timeless dimension of a neoclassical world will not permit any logically consistent analysis of either inflation or the indexing of contracts, despite some airy policy suggestions by both Monetarists and mainstream Keynesians on the causes of inflation and the desirability or undesirability of indexing. Inflation (which is a rise in commodity prices over a period of calendar time) and indexing (which involves increasing contractual cash inflows over time in response to *unanticipated* inflation) are logically impossible in a neoclassical world where all commodity prices and their concomitant cash flows occur simultaneously at the initial instant of time. Inflation and indexing are phenomena which can be analysed only in a world where the passage of time is recognized by economic agents who utilize forward contracts to require delivery and payments in the future.
21. Cf. J. R. Hicks, *Critical Essays in Monetary Theory* (Oxford University Press, 1967) p. 36.
22. As *The Economist* (10–16 March 1979, p. 12) noted, the Japanese auto industry became an important world force when Toyota

> implemented its radical production control system, known as the 'just in time' method. This process was quickly copied by the rest of Japan's motor industry. It likens each manufacturing stage to a customer . . . The customer collects his goods in the precise quantity and at the exact time he needs them. The component producer, which may be part of the same company, thus has an orderly market and so can adjust its production (using the same approach) accordingly.

23. Since the fabrication of fixed capital goods is normally undertaken after the buyer-investor has entered into a forward contractual commitment

to accept delivery and make payment at a specified (near) future date, the fixed capital goods producer can use this purchase order as the basis for obtaining short-run construction fund finance from the banking system.

24. What is a sufficient rate of return for investment (in the aggregate) is primarily psychologically determined by what the entrepreneurial class deems to be sufficient. Nevertheless, it is not necessary for the stimulation of these productive activities that the game should be played for such high stakes as at present.

As Keynes noted

> Much lower stakes will serve the purpose equally well, as soon as the players are accustomed to them. The talk of transmitting human nature must not be confused with the talk of managing it. Though in the ideal commonwealth men may have been taught or inspired or bred to take no interest in stakes, it may still be wise and prudent statesmanship to allow the game to be played, subject to rules and limitations, so long as the average man, or even a significant section of the community, is in fact strongly addicted to the money-making passion (Keynes, *The General Theory*, p. 374).

25. Although it may appear that the floatation of new issues ties investment directly to private sector saving, it is demonstrated in Chapter 13 of my *Money and the Real World* that the existence of financial markets and a modern banking system rupture any direct and unchanging connection.

26. J. R. Hicks, *Critical Essays in Monetary Theory*, p. 47.

27. For a discussion of what increase of the money supply will be sufficient in this case, see P. Davidson, *Money and the Real World*, Chapter 13.

28. In general, fixed capital goods are produced 'to order' rather than 'to market'. In other words because of the specificity of the production process, its geographical location etc., producers of plant and equipment generally produce goods only when buyers have executed orders (forward contracts) for the purchase of these goods to be delivered at a specified future time and place. Purchasers of fixed capital goods (investors) are willing to enter into these forward commitments because they believe they possess the expertise to utilize this equipment to earn an expected series of monetary annuities (dated money income flows) over a period of years which will be sufficient to pay off ('realize') the illiquid position taken in fixed capital and yield a *monetary* return which will make it worthwhile to take on the risks of illiquidity and incorrect forecasts of the future.

29. J. M. Keynes, *The General Theory*, p. 212.

30. Thus the existence of an organized securities market where sale of title does not require delivery of fixed assets, ensures that the spot market for titles (corporate equities) is used for liquidity purposes, while the spot market for purchase (and delivery) of fixed capital goods is not (for a more complete discussion, see Davidson, *Money and the Real World*, Chapter 4).

31. As long as a legal title of ownership does *not* require delivery to, and

physical possession of, the good to the owner. See P. Davidson, *Money and the Real World*, pp. 59–69.

32. Cf. Keynes, *Treatise on Money, CWK*, v, p. 13.

33. Ibid. p. 13.

34. These debt clearing mechanisms could not be developed without the invention of a system of double-entry accounting. Consequently, it is not an exaggeration to claim that double-entry bookkeeping has done more to improve the lot of mankind than anything else including the wheel. It is probably reasonable to assume that if there is intelligent life in outer space, they will not be able to communicate with us until they develop a system of double-entry accounts.

35. J. R. Hicks, *Critical Essays in Monetary Theory*, p. 9.

36. Thus, any 'incomes policy' system should have a Supreme Court to adjudicate incomes disputes.

37. Of course if all that the SOS advocates wish to accomplish is the stimulation of investment spending, then they should come out explicitly for policies which directly accomplish this objective – e.g. making easy financing available. In an economy which is stagnating with excess capacity and unemployed labour it is unnecessary to cut consumption (or government spending) in order to free resources!

38. In the analytical model of Professor Friedman, on the other hand, if households initially demand additional money in order to hold some of their increased saving, and if the supply of money is limited, the price of money will rise and savers will substitute 'cheaper' producible durables as 'temporary abodes of purchasing power'. These 'cheaper' durables include easily producible durables such as appliances and clothing (M. Friedman *et al.*, *Milton Friedman's Monetary Framework: A Debate With His Critics*, pp. 27–9, 107–10). Hence in Friedman's system unemployment is avoided *and* real wealth is accumulated at a faster rate as the increased desire to save via purchasing 'temporary abodes of purchasing power' spills over into the purchase of all kinds of durables. But does even the non-professional economist believe that appliances and clothes are really efficient 'temporary abodes of purchasing power', i.e. do households buy such durables for resale?

39. P. Davidson, 'Rolph on the Aggregate Effects of a General Excise Tax', *Southern Economic Journal*, 27, 1960.

40. Unless exports are excluded from VAT. As a practical matter, however, a complete exclusion is not possible, e.g. invisible exports via purchase of tourist services cannot be readily excluded.

41. For example, see Davidson, *Money and the Real World*, pp. 325–9.

42. Ibid. Chapter 14.

43. This assumes that social or community capital accumulation is not a problem. In his book on *The Affluent Society* (Boston: Houghton Miflin, 1958), Galbraith spotlighted the problem of private affluence v. public squalor. Little has been done to ameliorate that problem. Nevertheless, a more rapidly growing economy could, if its policy makers desired, afford to produce *more* social investment goods as well as private affluence. Of course, this assumes that (a) we adopt a National Policy to Coordinate Income Claims – an incomes policy – to resolve the inflation problem,

and (b) a fiscal policy which specifically ensures the accumulation of social capital. Unfortunately at the time of writing, little has been done at the policy level to achieve either (a) or (b). If anything, because inflation problems have been improperly treated, the resulting stringency in monetary and fiscal policy has exacerbated the shortage of social as well as private capital.

44. Even if the initial position is full employment, the availability of finance will permit an expansion of NAO. If the market for goods is unfettered, a growth in demand for NAO which is financed will result in increased demand for AO (through the multiplier process) and consequently windfall profits in the AO industries, thereby causing an income redistribution towards groups with higher than average saving ratios. This redistribution raises aggregate private saving out of income into line (without a deliberate government policy) with a higher proportion of GNP produced in the form of capital (or NAO). If, for social and political reasons, this redistribution is considered undesirable, then a deliberate explicit incomes policy and fiscal policy must be put in its place to meet the objective of higher investment *at* full employment. In any case, a tight monetary policy cannot be utilized to prevent the resulting incomes inflation, for monetary policy, to the extent that it is successful in fighting inflation will do so by *reducing* actual investment activity.

45. Keynes, *Treatise on Money*, II, pp. 148–9.
46. *CWK*, XIV, p. 219.
47. A. Smith, *The Wealth of Nations*, Modern Library ed. (Random House, 1937) p. 325.

APPENDIX TO CHAPTER 3: MONEY AND GENERAL EQUILIBRIUM

1. This appendix appeared as an article in a symposium on General Equilibrium and Money published in *Economic Appliquée*, 30, no. 4, 1977, pp. 541–63. This journal is a publication of the *Institut des Sciences · Mathématiques et Economiques Appliquées*, a research institution founded in 1944 in Paris by François Perroux, Professeur Honoraire au Collège de France.

2. J. M. Keynes, *A Treatise on Money* (London: Macmillan, 1930) I, p. 31.

3. 'It is, however, interesting to consider how far those characteristics of money as we know it . . . are bound up with money being the standard in which debts and wages are usually fixed . . . The convenience of holding assets in the same standard as that which future liabilities may fall due . . . is obvious.' J. M. Keynes, *The General Theory of Employment, Interest and Money* (New York: Harcourt, 1936) pp. 236–7.

4. 'The attribute of "liquidity" is by no means independent of these two characteristics. For it is unlikely that an asset, of which the supply can be easily increased or the desire for which can be easily diverted by a change in relative price will possess the attribute of "liquidity" in the minds of owners of wealth.' Ibid. pp. 241, no. 1.

5. Davidson, *Money and The Real World*, 2nd ed. (London: Macmillan, 1978) Chapters 6 and 9.
6. K. Arrow and F. H. Hahn, *General Competitive Analysis* (San Francisco: Holden-Day, 1971) p. 356.
7. Ibid. p. 367.
8. E. R. Weintraub, 'The Microfoundations of Macroeconomics: A Critical Survey', *Journal of Economic Literature*, 15, 1977, p. 2.
9. D. Patinkin, *Money, Interest and Prices*, 2nd ed. (New York: Harper and Row, 1965) p. 50.
10. M. Friedman *et al.*, *Milton Friedman's Monetary Framework: A Debate With His Critics* (University of Chicago Press, 1974) p. 150.
11. B. Hansen, *General Equilibrium Systems* (New York: McGraw Hill, 1970) p. 3.
12. D. Patinkin, *Money, Interest and Prices*, p. 35. See also R. J. Barro and H. I. Grossman, 'A General Disequilibrium Model of Income and Employment', *American Economic Review*, 61, 1971, p. 88.
13. D. Patinkin, *Money, Interest and Prices*, pp. 337–8.
14. J. R. Hicks, *Value and Capital* (London, Oxford Univ. Press, 1939) pp. 1–4.
15. D. Patinkin, *Money, Interest and Prices*, p. 11.
16. Ibid. p. 35.
17. Ibid. pp. 209–11.
18. Ibid. p. 50. Friedman, however, claims this is a long run GE position and not an actual state of the economy. See Friedman *et al.*, *Milton Friedman's Monetary Framework*, pp. 44–8, 150–1.
19. Borrowing for via bonds, on the other hand, can only take place on Monday morning and *all* bond redemptions are 'fixed for the last hour of the week'. Debt obligations are, therefore, completely certain *and* are never carried over from one week to the next (Patinkin, *Money, Interest and Prices*, p. 81).
20. Ibid. p. 82.
21. J. R. Hicks, 'Some Questions of Time in Economics', in A. M. Tang *et al.* (eds), *Evolution Welfare and Time in Economics* (Lexington Books, 1976) p. 140.
22. Ibid. pp. 135–6.
23. Ibid. pp. 140–1.
24. D. Patinkin, *Money, Interest and Prices*, p. 643.
25. P. Davidson, 'A Keynesian View of Patinkin's Theory of Employment', *Economic Journal*, 77, 1967.
26. *CWK*, VII, pp. xxii–iii.
27. J. M. Keynes, *The General Theory*, p. 53.
28. As I have demonstrated elsewhere, Patinkin did not correctly introduce the aggregate supply function (and hence the demand for labour) into his model (see P. Davidson, 'A Keynesian View of Patinkin . . . ', *Economic Journal*, pp. 565–75), and hence did not correctly analyse a Keynes world in which equilibrium can occur without Walras' Law. In 1976, Patinkin admitted that his analysis of Keynes' aggregate supply function was wrong (see D. Patinkin, 'Keynes' Monetary Theory',

History of Political Economy, 8, 1976, no. 12, p. 91), and he attempted to provide a new formulation for the aggregate supply function. Unfortunately, Patinkin's 1976 supply analysis was still faulty and a further correction was forthcoming (see D. Patinkin, 'Keynes' Aggregate Supply Function: A Correction', *History of Political Economy*, 9, 1977). Nevertheless, I still believe that Patinkin's specific aggregate supply of goods and demand for labour, and the similar analysis in GE systems in general are inadequate and incorrect.

29. If for example current expectations are disappointed but the elasticity of expectations is zero (so that there is no substitutability between present and future goods) then nothing tends to change in the system.

30. R. W. Clower, 'The Keynesian Counterrevolution: A Theoretical Appraisal' in F. H. Hahn and F. P. R. Brechling (eds), *The Theory of Interest Rates* (London: Macmillan, 1965) p. 124.

31. Ibid. p. 103.

32. Ibid. p. 304.

33. Ibid. p. 111.

34. Ibid. p. 123.

35. Actually Clower's dual decision hypothesis is similar to Keynes' analysis of the classical doctrine of 'supply creates its own demand'. For Keynes this doctrine meant that the aggregate demand function $f(N)$, and the aggregate supply function $\phi(N)$, were 'equal for *all* values of N, i.e. for all levels of output and employment, and that when there is an increase in $Z(=\phi(N))$ corresponding to an increase in N, $D(=f(N))$ necessarily increases by the same amount as Z'. In other words, if $f(N) = \phi(N)$, then if firms hire less than the full employment level of workers, income will be constrained and aggregate demand will equal supply at less than full employment. Thus, any level of income can be an equilibrium one if $f(N)$ and $\phi(N)$ are equal for all levels of N, i.e. there 'is an infinite range of [equilibrium] values all equally admissible'. Thus, if firms hire initially the full employment level of output and if $f(N) = \phi(N)$, then there would be no shortage of effective demand, i.e. there is 'no obstacle to full employment'. J. M. Keynes, *The General Theory*, pp. 25–6.

36. Clower, 'The Keynesian Counterrevolution', p. 120.

37. Keynes, *The General Theory*, p. 230.

38. Clower, 'The Keynesian Counterrevolution', p. 305.

39. Ibid. p. 116.

40. *The Collected Writings of J. M. Keynes*, XIII, pp. 408–9.

41. Arrow and Hahn, *General Competitive Analysis*, pp. 15, 215, 305.

42. Clower, 'The Keynesian Counterrevolution', p. 121.

43. G. L. S. Shackle, *The Years of High Theory* (Cambridge University Press, 1967) pp. 91–3.

44. Cf. P. Davidson, *Money and the Real World*, pp. 270–80, Chapters 13 and 16.

45. R. F. Clower, 'The Keynesian Revolution: A Theoretical Appraisal', in R. W. Clower (ed), *Monetary Theory* (Middlesex Penguin, 1969) p. 289.

46. Ibid. p. 290. Italics added.

47. Ibid. p. 289.

48. Since the major borrowers in the modern economy are business firms and governments who (normally) have a perpetual life, they may never retire their outstanding debt. In fact, bankruptcies occur when borrowers are unable to refinance their obligations, and if such debtors are large organizations these can create monetary crises for the economy (e.g. in the U.S. Penn–Central Railroad in 1966, Lockheed in 1970, and New York City in 1975).
49. Keynes, *The General Theory*, p. 16.
50. Ibid. p. 16.
51. Grossman has demonstrated the *ad hoc* nature of Clower's system. See H. I. Grossman, 'Was Keynes a "Keynesian"? A Review Article', *Journal of Economic Literature*, 10, 1972, pp. 29–30.
52. Arrow and Hahn, *General Competitive Analysis*, p. 107.
53. E. R. Weintraub, 'The Microfoundations of Macroeconomics', p. 2.
54. Ibid. p. 11.
55. M. Shubik, 'The General Equilibrium Model is Incomplete and Not Adequate for the Reconciliation of Micro and Macroeconomics', *Kyklos*, 28, 1975.
56. J. M. Grandmont and G. Laroque, 'On Temporary Keynesian Equilibria', *Review of Economic Studies*, 43, 1976, p. 54.
57. Ibid. p. 53.
58. A zero elasticity of expectations is the basis of Keynes' static model. (See P. Davidson, *Money and the Real World*, pp. 379–81.)
59. Grandmont and Laroque, 'On Temporary Keynesian Equilibria', p. 53.
60. Keynes, *The General Theory*, pp. 260–2.
61. E. R. Weintraub, 'The Microfoundations of Macroeconomics', p.2.
62. Ibid. p. 2.
63. F. H. Hahn, *On the Notion of Equilibrium in Economics* (Cambridge University Press, 1973) p. 3.
64. F. H. Hahn, 'Equilibrium with Transactions Costs', *Econometrica*, 39, 1971, p. 417.
65. F. H. Hahn, *On the Notion of Equilibrium*, p. 14.
66. Ibid. p. 16.
67. Thus Friedman's claim that his monetary theory is based on a long run set of Walrasian equations is logically incorrect. The Arrow–Debreu (Walrasian) system is not a harmless 'as if' assumption since it is logically incompatible with other assumptions which are necessary in macromodels of monetary, production economies where money plays a unique and important role, i.e. where money really matters!
68. F. H. Hahn, *On the Notion of Equilibrium*, p. 6.
69. F. Perroux, 'The Economic Agent, Equilibrium, and the Choice of Formalisation', *Economie Appliquée*, 1973.
70. Ibid. p. 273.
71. Arrow and Hahn, *General Competitive Analysis*, p. 126.
72. F. H. Hahn, *On the Nature of Equilibrium*, p. 25.
73. Ibid. pp. 26–7.
74. Ibid. p. 28.
75. Ibid. p. 26.

CHAPTER 4: THE TAXONOMY OF INTERNATIONAL MONEY

1. G. L. S. Shackle, *Epistemics and Economics* (Cambridge University Press, 1972) pp. 72–3. One of the clearest examples of the successful use of the classificatory approach was Marshall's conception of inelastic, unitary elastic, and elastic cases of demand and supply factors.
2. For a complete discussion of the importance of theory before measurement, see P. Davidson and E. Smolensky, *Aggregate Supply and Demand Analysis* (New York: Harper and Row, 1964) Chapter 15.
3. It is not an exaggeration to suggest that the most important invention ever made by man was double-entry bookkeeping! This system provides a method of control over complex economic production and exchange activities. Without such controls, modern economies could not survive. Many societies have developed other important inventions such as the wheel, gunpowder, etc., but it was only after the development of double-entry bookkeeping in the Italian merchant states that Western European nations (and later their territorial possessions) led the world into the Commercial and Industrial Revolutions which truly revolutionized the production and exchange system and led to tremendous rates of increase in living standards after centuries of economic stagnation.
4. J. M. Keynes, *The General Theory*, p. 54: 'the income of the rest of the community [in a closed system] is the entrepreneurs' factor costs', while gross entrepreneurial income is defined as the excess of market value of final output over entrepreneurial factor costs. Hence, aggregate income is the sum of gross entrepreneurial income plus factor costs and therefore 'aggregate income . . . , thus defined, is a completely unambiguous quantity'.
5. In his *Treatise on Money* (see *The Collected Writings of John Maynard Keynes* [hereafter cited as *CWK*], v, 1971, Chapter 9) Keynes defined the concept of aggregate income differently from the familiar income definition of *The General Theory*. In the *Treatise*, even in a closed economy, the equality between the actual (as opposed to planned or *ex ante*) market value of final output and gross aggregate income was an equilibrium condition rather than a definitional (accounting) identity. In the *Treatise*, aggregate income was the sum of factor costs, monopoly rents, and the 'normal remuneration of entrepreneurs' (p. 111). Thus whenever the actual market value of final goods differs from the expected (or warranted) sales revenue of entrepreneurs, entrepreneurs receive windfall profits (or losses) which are not part of the defined aggregate income since actual entrepreneurial revenue exceeded (fell short) of their 'normal' remuneration. Thus, in any period when aggregate income as defined in the *Treatise* exceeds (is less than) actual aggregate expenditure on final goods and services, entrepreneurs receive windfall losses (or profits) and such windfalls are market signals inducing entrepreneurs to contract (expand) their level of economic activity.

   Unfortunately most economists failed to comprehend the implications of Keynes' *Treatise* analysis. In 1936, Keynes appeared to change the definition of aggregate income by slurring the difference between expected and actual market values. He simultaneously simplified the analytical model from an open NUMS to a closed UMS in order to focus economists' attention on his revolutionary concept of effective demand rather than Say's Law. As I have indicated in my *Money and the Real World* the logical structure of *The General Theory* is simpler but fundamentally the same as that of Keynes' *Treatise on Money*.

6. *CWK*, v, p. 118.

7. Especially when these include vertically integrated subsidiaries which are corporations chartered and therefore based (owned) in different nations.

8. Even more complicated is the accounting for such transactions as the production of crude oil in, for example, Saudi Arabia in the 1970s by Aramco (an American chartered corporation), with four American multinational companies and the Saudi Government as stockholders. The market value of Saudi crude oil landed in the U.S. is a complicated sum of before-tax profit margins, royalties, a small share of wages to foreign workers, and wages paid to Americans working abroad as Aramco employees. Since the Saudi Government currently (as of January 1980) obtains most of its revenue from an 'income tax' on the gross profits of Aramco, rather than as royalties, normal accounting procedures may be perceived to overstate $Y^g_{f \to d}$, the actual gross income generated externally but earned by a U.S. resident, namely Aramco and its U.S. corporate stockholders. This becomes even more complicated when the purchase of crude at Persian Gulf ports, and its transportation and landing in the United States, are done by other (foreign chartered) subsidiaries of each of the four major U.S. oil companies, for then the 'market value' of the import and the amount earned by U.S. v. foreign firms involves internal intra–MNC accounting practices of transfer pricing, where the prices are based on avoiding tax liabilities or government regulations rather than on rational economic valuation principles. This is especially significant when a foreign subsidiary makes unusual losses or profits (see Chapter 12) on the accounting transfer price used to purchase oil from Aramco and 'resells' it to a domestic refinery.

9. Keynes, *CWK*, v, p. 118.

10. S. Weintraub, 'The Price Level in an Open Economy', *Kyklos*, 30, p. 27.

11. ϕ is not quite the complement of Weintraub's n, for the latter would use V_{DP} rather than E_D in the denominator of any ratio of equation 4.11 (V_{DP} will equal E_D only when $B = 0$). Thus, strictly speaking, the complement of Weintraub's n would be $\phi' = (V_M/V_{DP})$, and $\phi = \phi'$ only if $V_X = V_M$.

12. We are measuring, as all price indices do, price level changes for a given market basket of goods. The composition of this initial market basket was determined in part by the ratio (P_D/P_M) and we are not accounting for any substitution effects that may occur after the initial instant due to a change in relative prices. (Any more than we would account for an exogenous change in relative demands and hence the composition of the original market basket.)

13. For further discussion of the effects of imported oil prices on the U.S. economy, see Chapter 9.

14. If cash flow problems become pervasive in the economy, then a cumulative debt deflation process can occur which will threaten the very

structure of capitalist financial institutions. See H. P. Minsky, *John Maynard Keynes* (Columbia University Press, 1975).

15. Keynes, *CWK*, v, p. 6.

16. Thus, in a modern, bank money economy, the ability to write sight drafts for the immediate transfer of ownership of particular fully liquid assets through the clearing mechanism of the national banking system in effect 'monetizes' the fully liquid assets known as bank liabilities.

17. Of course, the same degree of unionization need not exist between the domestic economy and *all* its trading partners, since the exchange rate could be unchanged between some trading partners (e.g. the U.S. and Mexico) while it varied with others (e.g. the U.S. and Canada).

18. Thus there is *ceteris paribus* potential for a 'free lunch' in international trade if nations would organize their laws of contract on a UMS basis.

19. Keynes argued that it was the spread between the gold points which permitted interest differential between financial centres in different nations. The greater the spread between the points, the greater the possible differential in interest rates are, hence the greater the leeway for some independence of interest rate policies in the two nations. Keynes recommended a spread of at least 2 per cent between bid and ask prices for gold.

20. R. F. Harrod, *Money* (London: Macmillan, 1969) p. 75.

CHAPTER 5: TRADE, MONEY AND INTERNATIONAL PAYMENTS

1. In so doing, the problems of international capital account transactions (other than those necessary for the immediate financing of the deficit) are excluded. This exclusion should not be interpreted as suggesting that long-term capital transactions are either unimportant or that they cannot create balance of payments difficulties in themselves.

2. When all money costs of production are expressed in terms of the same nominal unit.

3. A change in aggregate supply originating in one of the trading partners can be more properly analysed as a form of change in relative money costs of production.

4. For an analysis of the income-generating finance process (which is based on Keynes' post *General Theory* finance motive analysis) see P. Davidson, 'A Keynesian View of Friedman's Theoretical Framework for Monetary Analysis' in R. J. Gordon (ed.), *Milton Friedman's Monetary Framework: A Debate With His Critics* (University of Chicago Press, 1974) p. 103 and P. Davidson, *Money and the Real World*, Chapter 7.

5. Even the Chicago School's 'monetary approach to the balance of payments' is not a monetary-oriented analysis. Instead it stresses *real* balances and a Walrasian equational structure where money has *no* role to play. Harry Johnson has claimed that 'In fact the difficulty of monetary theory can be seen as [merely] an extra complication of a problem in "real" or "barter" theory that has always given economists trouble'. (H. J. Johnson, 'Money and the Balance of Payments', *Banca*

Nazionale Del Lavoro Quarterly Review, March 1976, p. 5). Keynes, on the other hand, always argued that 'the theory which I desiderate would deal . . . with an economy in which money plays a part of its own and affects motives and decisions and is, in short, one of the operative factors in the situation, so that the course of events cannot be predicted either in the long period or in the short, without a knowledge of the behaviour of money between the first state and the last' (Keynes, The Collected Writings of John Maynard Keynes [hereafter cited as CWK], XIII, pp. 408–9). In other words, for Keynes and Post Keynesians, money is not just an 'extra complication' added to a real or barter theory analysis.

6. T. Scitovsky, Money and the Balance of Payments (New York: Rand–McNally, 1969) pp. 88–9.

7. H. G. Johnson, 'Money and the Balance of Payments', p. 16.

8. The specie–flow mechanism involves the sale of a 'perfectly integrated' asset (gold) by residents of A to those in B, with a consequent change in relative production prices and costs (in terms of gold).

9. T. Balogh, Fact and Fancy in International Relations (New York: Pergamon Press, 1973). Of course, the global real income effects are ignored (by assumption) in all neoclassical analysis.

10. Scitovsky, Money and the Balance of Payments, pp. 106–8.

11. For example, see J. M. Keynes, 'The General Theory of Employment', Quarterly Journal of Economics, 51, (1973) reprinted in CWK, XIV (London: Macmillan, 1973) pp. 115–16.

12. J. M. Keynes, The General Theory, pp. 293–4.

13. For example, see P. Davidson, Money and the Real World, Chapters 6–13.

14. Cf. J. M. Keynes, A Treatise on Money, I, reprinted as CWK, V (London: Macmillan, 1971) p. 6. The institutional relationship between the Central Bank and the national banking system determines which sight drafts for the transfer of ownership of private (bank) liabilities the Central Bank will accept in exchange for legal tender and hence which private debts are the monies of contractual settlement in the domestic economy.

15. Alternatively one can directly sell a liquid asset in a market located in the foreign nation whose currency is needed to settle the contractual commitment. (This assumes that well organized spot markets exist for the sale of these assets.)

16. J. R. Hicks, Value and Capital, 2nd ed. (Oxford University Press, 1967) Chapter XVI.

17. Ibid. p. 204. Italics added. Thus economic models which attempted to make all expectations formation processes endogenous (and/or rational) deny a role for policy by ignoring this fundamental warning of Hicks! The existence of autonomous causes of changes in expectations at t_1 is, however, logically incompatible with a completely endogenous general equilibrium system.

18. J. R. Hicks, Causality in Economics (New York: Basic Books, 1979) p. 94.

19. J. R. Hicks, Critical Essays in Monetary Theory (Oxford University Press, 1967) pp. 38–45.

20. The better organized the market, ceteris paribus, the lower the transaction costs of buying and selling and hence the more liquid the asset.

21. R. F. Harrod, *Reforming the World's Money* (London: Macmillan, 1965) p. 1.
22. See P. Davidson, *Money and the Real World*, pp. 159–84, 402–5.
23. Of course, to the extent that payment inflows can be better coordinated with payment outflows, the fewer running assets are needed for any level of international activity. The rising demand for transaction balances as planned spending increases assumes that better coordination cannot be achieved.
24. This, of course, was exactly the problem that Harrod was concerned with.

CHAPTER 6: INTERNATIONAL MONEY AND LIQUIDITY

1. R. F. Harrod, *Money* (London: Macmillan, 1969) p. 151.
2. J. M. Keynes, *The General Theory*, p. 195.
3. R. F. Harrod, *The Life of John Maynard Keynes* (London: Macmillan, 1951) p. 403.
4. For expositional ease, money holdings of either domestic or foreign currency by a Central Bank will not be included in the outstanding money supply.
5. See Chapter 11.
6. P. Davidson, *Money and the Real World*, p. 409; Cf. J. R. Hicks, *Critical Essays in Monetary Theory* (Oxford University Press, 1967) p. 36.
7. Those holding currency A and having a forward contractual commitment in terms of B will at the same time be trying to revise their financial arrangements in order to avoid selling currency A spot for as long as the exchange rate is weak. Those holding currency B and having a forward contractual commitment in currency B will purchase money of A to resell for B at the commitment date if the transaction costs of the foreign exchange market are less than the difference between the current spot price of A and the normal price, as long as the normal price is expected to prevail at the commitment date.
8. Cf. J. R. Hicks, *Value and Capital*, 2nd ed. (Oxford University Press, 1946) p. 255. Also see pp. 205–6, 250–2, 264–6.
9. See S. Weintraub, 'Flexible Exchange Rates', *Journal of Post Keynesian Economics*, 3, Summer 1981.
10. The possibility of bankruptcy however creates discontinuities which endanger *all* existence proofs of general equilibrium. Thus if a bankruptcy occurs, no general equilibrium may exist. See K. Arrow and F. Hahn, *General Competitive Analysis* (San Francisco: Holden-Day, 1971) pp. 355–61.
11. J. M. Keynes, *The General Theory*, p. 157. Italics added.
12. See S. Weintraub, 'Flexible Exchange Rates'.
13. Ibid. pp. 157–8. Italics added. See also *The Collected Writings of John Maynard Keynes* [hereafter cited as *CWK*], VI, pp. 323–4.
14. Those who place their beach blankets at the edge of the surf during midtide in order to have easy access to the sea must surely know they will have to retreat in front of the advancing tide if they are not to be

inundated – even if they know that *more than half the time* they will remain high and dry!

15. Cf. P. Davidson, *Money and the Real World*, p. 320.
16. Keynes, *The General Theory*, pp. 236–7.
17. *CWK*, xxix, p. 89. Italics added.
18. This can be conceived as equivalent to the case where individuals can hold either dollar coins or dollar bills. As long as a dollar coin always trades for a dollar bill in a fixed exchange rate situation, coins and bills are (except for some convenience factor) perfect substitutes, and individuals will be indifferent as to whether they hold their money in the form of coins or bills.
19. M. Friedman, 'The Case for Flexible Exchange Rates', in M. Friedman, *Essays in Positive Economics* (University of Chicago Press, 1953) p. 200.
20. Just as convenience and chance dictate the ratio of coins to currency one carries in one's pockets to meet our daily retail expenditures.

CHAPTER 7: FINANCE AND TRADE IN NUMS v. UMS

1. See *The Collected Writings of John Maynard Keynes* [hereafter cited as *CWK*], xiv, pp. 201–23; also P. Davidson, *Money and the Real World*, Chapter 7.
2. *CWK*, xiv, p. 222.
3. Ibid. Italics added.
4. P. Davidson, 'Keynes's Finance Motive', *Oxford Economic Papers*, 17, 1965, pp. 47–66.
5. Cf. *CWK*, xiv, p. 208. Since planned (or *ex ante*) investment flows which are currently being financed exceed (by hypothesis) actual investment flows, then current financial commitments must exceed current actual savings flows. Of course, if the marginal propensity to buy securities out of current savings is less than unity, then this is a further complicating factor creating a shortage of finance and funding at the initial interest rate. (See P. Davidson, *Money and the Real World*, Chapter 13.)
6. P. Davidson, 'A Keynesian View of Friedman's Theoretical Framework for Monetary Analysis' in R. J. Gordon (ed.), *Milton Friedman's Monetary Framework: A Debate With His Critics* (University of Chicago Press, 1974) pp. 103–6.
7. If entrepreneurs produce 'to order', they will only hire inputs *after* they receive forward contractual orders from buyers which specify *a future date* for delivery *and* payment. In such a system entrepreneurs will normally be required to make most of the production cost payments *before* the date when sales revenue are received. To produce 'to market' means producing goods before orders are received, and therefore sales are made in spot markets from the shelf inventory *after* goods have been produced and factors paid for. Most economic theory textbooks on the theory of the firm assume that production is 'to market'.
8. Of course, in the timeless analysis of general equilibrium on the other hand, the matching of production cash outflows with sales cash inflows *at the initial* instant is an essential *aspect* of the equilibrium solution.

9. See P. Davidson, 'A Keynesian View of Friedman's Monetary Theoretical Framework' in R. J. Gordon (ed.), *Milton Friedman's Monetary Framework: A Debate With His Critics* (University of Chicago Press, 1974) p. 103. This process was labelled *construction funds finance* in Chapter 3 *supra*.

10. R. F. Kahn, *Selected Essays on Employment and Growth* (Cambridge University Press, 1972) p. 80.

11. Keynes, *Treatise on Money*, *CWK*, ed. v, p. 118.

12. Cf. J. R. Hicks, *Critical Essays in Monetary Theory* (Oxford University Press, 1967) p. 51.

13. Sooner or later some of the debts of the bank's customers must mature. These need not be paid off, as long as refinancing is available at the maturity date, i.e. as long as the Central Bank and/or other creditors are willing to hold debt instruments as liquidity time machines. Thus, the monetary authority can ensure that the banking system looks after that part of the public's wealth that the public does not wish to hold. The alternative is to reduce the wealth available to the public by recession and depression to that which the public will hold.

14. The astute reader should recognize that similar 'morals' could be applied to international trade imbalances if there were an international Central Bank.

15. For example, a common European Currency Union or ECU.

16. As the elasticity of expectations increases, the system becomes less stable and substitution possibilities diminish. No possible gains from substitution will be perceived by economic agents who have a unit elasticity of expectations. With elastic expectations the system will be unstable due to perverse (negative) substitution effects!

17. M. Friedman, 'Comments on the Critics', in R. J. Gordon (ed.), *Milton Friedman's Monetary Framework: A Debate With His Critics* (University of Chicago Press, 1974) p. 151. Italics added.

18. J. M. Keynes, *The General Theory*, p. 191.

19. To the extent that the regions were independent in their economic development.

CHAPTER 8: THE STABILITY OF THE PURCHASING POWER OF MONEY

1. Regularity of employment and fair treatment are conditions which Hicks has specified as *necessary* for the operation of an efficient labour market. See J. R. Hicks, *The Theory of Wages*, 2nd ed. (London: Macmillan, 1966) p. 317.

2. For example, see J. M. Keynes' definitions of income in his *Treatise on Money*, I (London: Macmillan, 1930) pp. 123–6 and *The General Theory* (New York: Harcourt, 1936) pp. 52–4.

3. Only a vile scoundrel would state that a Walrasian recontracting process is in the public interest.

4. See J. R. Hicks, *Value and Capital*, 2nd ed. (Oxford University Press, 1946) pp. 205, 264–5, 270. Also see P. Davidson, *Money and the Real*

World, Chapter 16. The elasticity of expectations is defined as the ratio of the proportionate change in the expected future values of X to the proportionate change in the realized values of X *vis-à-vis* the previous expected value of the current X.

5. Hicks, *Value and Capital*, pp. 297–8.

6. Ibid. p. 298.

7. As Keynes notes, 'To suppose that a flexible wage (or price) is a right and proper adjunct of a system which on the whole is one of *laissez-faire*, is the opposite of the truth.' Keynes, *The General Theory*, p. 269.

8. For a complete discussion of various standards, see J. M. Keynes, *A Treatise on Money*, ı (London: Macmillan, 1930) Chapters 6–9, reprinted in *The Collected Writings of John Maynard Keynes*, v (London: Macmillan, 1971).

9. For a detailed discussion of the greater volatility of spot prices in periods of unanticipated changes, see P. Davidson, *Money and the Real World*, Chapters 4 and 16.

10. Or the average degree of domestic monopoly (i.e. profit margins) is falling most rapidly.

11. Such nations are likely to find that servants are becoming prohibitively expensive.

12. For a further analysis of the implications of the OPEC Cartel, see Chapter 9.

13. This requires, under the *ceteris paribus* assumption, that exchange rates reflect production and trade patterns and are not disrupted by unusual and/or speculative international capital flows. In essence, this is the basis of the purchasing power parity theory of exchange rate determination.

14. Two-way convertibility means that the government stands ready to buy *or* sell a standard commodity market basket at a given price per unit of domestic currency.

15. Such policies can include changing the relative importance (the degree of openness) of foreign commodities in the standardized market basket.

16. Since forward exchange markets for periods in excess of 270 days are not well organized, even if they exist, international forward contracts whose duration exceeds nine months always impose another uncertainty upon one or the other contracting party (depending on which currency the contract is denominated in). Hence, if there is uncertainty as to the purchasing power of a money in terms of the international standard in an open NUMS, then, *ceteris paribus*, international contracts of durations in excess of nine months are less likely to be entered into than the same contract where only domestic transactors are involved.

17. In a closed system utilizing a single currency, domestic entrepreneurs attempt to achieve price stability not necessarily in terms of some composite commodity or earnings standard, but in terms of the particular commodities and inputs each hires, and the goods each sells. To achieve this price stickiness over time, domestic entrepreneurs enter into forward wage and material purchase contracts while simultaneously attempting to sell forward (in terms of the domestic money) the product of their enterprise. If both input hire and forward sales contracts are geared to the same date of delivery of the finished product, the domestic

entrepreneur has protected (hedged) himself against losses (or windfall gains) due to an unforeseen change in domestic money prices. Thus, forward domestic money contracts, *ceteris paribus*, reduce the inhibitions of entrepreneurs to undertake long duration production activities, especially in periods where there might otherwise be fears about rapidly changing price levels. Moreover, forward sales contracts can be pledged as security to help entrepreneurs finance their contractual costs of productions via working capital loans from the banking system.

18. See P. Davidson, *Money and the Real World*, pp. 147–8, 385–401.
19. A. Marshall, *Principles of Economics*, 8th ed. (New York: Macmillan, 1950) p. 142.
20. Keynes, *A Treatise on Money*, I, pp. 123–5. This would occur if the spot price of finished output *at the date of delivery* differed significantly from the forward (flow–supply) price entrepreneurs would quote on the date they begin the production process as the delivered price.
21. Ibid. p. 125.
22. Keynes, *The General Theory*, p. 53.
23. For example, Keynes wrote 'expected and realized results run into and overlap one another in their influence . . . in practice there is a large overlap between effects on employment of the realized sales-proceeds of recent output and those of the sales-proceeds expected from current input'. Ibid. pp. 50–1.
24. P. Davidson, *Money and the Real World*, p. 341.
25. 'The All Saints Manifesto for a European Monetary Union', *The Economist*, Nov. 1, 1975, p. 33. The nine economists are G. Basevi, M. Fratianni, H. Giersch, P. Kortuveg, D. O'Mahoney, M. Parkin, T. Pieters, P. Salin and N. Thygesen.
26. Ibid. p. 34. By eliminating the real costs of exchange uncertainties there is a 'free lunch' in international trade and finance.
27. Ibid. p. 36.
28. Cf. J. M. Blatt, 'Classical Economics of Involuntary Unemployment', *Journal of Post Keynesian Economics*, 3, Summer 1981. Blatt notes that when a robber states 'Your money or your life!', it would be a perverse use of language to define the resulting income transfer as voluntary!
29. 'The commodity basket can be defined as the weighted sum of the national commodity baskets used to calculate the national consumer price indices. The weights ought to reflect the relative share of each country in community GNP, intra-community trade, etc. The Europa itself is expressed in terms of a (weighted) basket of national monies.' *The Economist*, op. cit., Ibid. p. 37.
30. Ibid. p. 38. Although the money rule to be followed is never specified, it must be whatever is necessary to limit average European money wage increases denominated in Europas to the average increase in productivity (assuming no change in the terms of trade with the rest of the world?).
31. Ibid. p. 38.
32. After adjusting for changes in the Europa price of imports from nations outside the European Common Market.
33. Private parties can of course specify in advance the currency, or other

commodity they wish to get paid in. Such stipulations, however, are not legally enforceable unless legal tender currency has been specified or any other thing the State agrees to exchange for compulsory legal tender. Thus, if nations refused to permit the private sector to have Europas (or say gold), only Central Banks and their governments could use it as the mode of contractual settlement, and it would be unavailable to private sector transactors.

34. From 1974 to 1979, the OPEC current surplus totalled $224 billion. The ensuing payments and inflationary problems encouraged all consuming nations to be very cautious regarding demand management to avoid recession and unemployment. Cf. A. Maddeson, 'Western Economic Performance in the 1970's: A Perspective and Assessment', *Banca Nazionale Del Lavoro Quarterly Review*, September 1980, pp. 247–90.

35. For illustration of such a tax scheme, see P. Davidson, 'The United States Internal Revenue Service: The Fourteenth Member of OPEC', *Journal of Post Keynesian Economics*, 1, 1978–9.

CHAPTER 9: CAN WE HAVE AN INTERNATIONAL STANDARD WHEN THERE IS AN OPEC CARTEL?

1. Of course, energy producers within each nation, motivated by their own self-interest, will claim that they are entitled to the same real income (on a BTU equivalent basis) for their products as the members of the OPEC Cartel. Such claims will have to be rejected if inflation is to be avoided. Instead, income will have to be distributed in some manner which limits the domestic energy producers and landowners' claims to producers' surplus, and the economic rents due to either monopoly power or diminishing returns.

2. M. A. Adelman, 'Prepared Statement' in *Energy Independence or Interdependence: The Agenda with OPEC*, Subcommittee on Energy, Joint Economic Committee, 12 January 1977 (Washington: Government Printing Office, 1977) p. 8.

3. Not only should the Cartel be broken, but it must be broken if Western capitalist nations (as we know them) are to remain vigorous and healthy economies. Even if the U.S. can as a nation afford to turn over in the next few years a few per cent more of its GNP to Persian Gulf nations and also permit, because of wellhead price decontrol, smaller crumbs from the Cartel cake to fall into the laps of our own domestic producers *and* royalty owners, and even if the regional impact of this domestic redistribution of income and wealth is politically tolerable (and I believe it is not), the ultimate impact of continued Persian Gulf greed (and their continued ability to exercise it over subservient consumer nations) will be to exacerbate and make unmanageable the stagflation disease afflicting all capitalist consumer nations, and bring about the 'Second Great Collapse of Capitalism in the Twentieth Century'. This must be avoided at all costs, for the strength of these capitalist economies is not only necessary to improve the standard of living of their own citizens but it is also an essential factor in providing similar benefits for the LDCs of the Third World.

4. J. E. Hartshorn, *Politics and World Oil Economics* (New York: Praeger, 1962).

5. R. M. Solow, 'The Economics of Resources or the Resources of Economics', *American Economic Review Papers and Proceedings*, 64, 1974.

6. In Appendix A, the concept of 'workably competitive' is discussed.

7. M. A. Adelman, 'The World Oil Cartel', *Quarterly Review of Economics and Business*, 16, 1976, p. 11.

8. P. Davidson, L. H. Falk and H. Lee, 'The Relations of Economic Rents and Price Incentives to Oil and Gas Supplies' in G. Brannon (ed.), *Studies in Energy Tax Policy* (Lexington: Ballinger, 1974) and P. Davidson, L. H. Falk and H. Lee, 'Oil: Its Time Allocation and Project Independence', *Brookings Papers on Economic Activity*, 1974.

9. This does not mean that the day of the $3 barrel of oil will return. It only signifies that current world prices are more than sufficient to cover the real resource costs of oil.

10. Proved reserves are company estimates of the volume of oil underground which it is known (with considerable reliability because of drilling information) it is *profitable* to produce at the current market price.

11. See Davidson *et al.*, 'Oil: Its Time Allocation and Project Independence', pp. 413–20.

12. J. M. Keynes, *The General Theory*, p. 73.

13. Ibid. p. 159.

14. P. W. MacAvoy and R. S. Pindyck, 'Alternative Regulatory Policies for Dealing with the Natural Gas Shortage', *Bell Journal of Economics and Management Science*, 4, 1973.

15. Ibid. p. 467.

16. It also assumes a purely competitive market.

17. MacAvoy and Pindyck, 'Alternative Regulatory Policies', pp. 463–4.

18. Federal Power Commission Docket AR 61–1, transcript p. 7095.

19. If, for example, when wellhead prices were raised, this encouraged producers to believe this was only the beginning, and if supplies did not cascade forth, the market, susceptible to economic blackmail, would agree to even further raises. Since the demand for oil is inelastic, producers' income would rise even if they continued to hold back. Such expectational phenomena are especially realistic when a cartel is thought to control world energy prices and will keep them increasing more rapidly than inflations.

20. MER is defined as the highest rate of production that can be sustained over a long period of time without reservoir damage or significant loss of ultimate oil and gas recovery. Efficiency is measured in terms of an oil flow which maximizes the use of 'natural' drive forces to bring underground oil to the surface.

21. Keynes, *The General Theory*, pp. 149–50.

22. D. Harkin, 'The Oil Controversy', *Challenge*, Nov/Dec 1979, pp. 69–70. For a very different perspective see J. L. Simon, *The Ultimate Resource* (Princeton University Press, 1981).

23. U.S. Congress, Senate Subcommittee on Multinational Corporations,

Multinational Corporations and United States Foreign Policy, 93rd Congress, 2nd Session, 1974, Part 7, p. 539.

24. Ibid. p. 537.
25. Ibid. p. 310.
26. According to a U.S. government study, however, 'since 1979 there has been a massive and continuing illegal switching of crude oil by sellers from price controlled categories to the stripper [uncontrolled] category'. (*The Case of the Billion Dollar Stripper*, Subcommittee on Oversight and Investigations, Committee on Interstate and Foreign Relations, U.S. Congress (Washington: Government Printing Office, October 1980) p. 6). This fraudulent activity which has been labelled 'miscertification' by the Department of Energy, makes it potentially profitable to produce 'old oil' and sell it at uncontrolled prices before the phased deregulation period ends. Hence, this illegal activity may offset our *ceteris paribus* conclusion.
27. A minority of economists were less sanguine. In 1974, I first proposed a National Energy Policy requiring deliberate government action to the U.S. Senate Committee on the Budget. At that time I warned

> If, on the other hand, the government permits an unregulated market price for oil without altering existing market institutions and conditions, the 1980 domestic wellhead price for crude oil could easily be higher than the $11 per barrel that the government's Project Independence forecasts as domestic oil prices will in essence be set by the Sheiks on the Persian Gulf; I see no reason to believe that the OPEC cartel will *necessarily* unravel of its own accord. The OPEC nations are engaged in an economic war with the major consuming nations over the distribution of the world's wealth. Existing economic and political conditions in consuming nations such as the U.S. have made the OPEC cartel's job of preventing price cutting competition from alternative sources easier. Until the consuming nations recognize that the dispute underlying this economic warfare can only be negotiated from a position of internal strength, the consuming countries will remain at the mercy of the producing nations *and* domestic conglomerates and royalty owners who have a vested interest in redistributing wealth from consumers to producers and property owners.

   Also see Adelman, 'Prepared Statement'.
28. At various Congressional hearings over the years, some economists (e.g. see M. A. Adelman, 'Prepared Statement') have recommended policies to fight OPEC. In the 'National Economic Policy' section *infra*, is a proposal which I have presented in testimony to approximately a dozen Congressional Committees since 1973.
29. Saudi Arabia is used for illustrative purposes. Due to variations in government 'take' arrangements, the terms of trade will vary somewhat between the U.S. and each oil exporting nation. After 1980, Aramco will apparently only be a 'service' company as the Saudis 'buy' the productive facilities from the U.S. stockholders; nevertheless a portion

of the Saudi Arabian oil market price is equal to the value added of Aramco, and hence is not part of the oil terms of trade.

30. See Keynes, *A Treatise on Money*, I (London: Macmillan, 1930) Chapter 11, for an early discussion of this process and Davidson, *Money and the Real World*, 2nd ed. (London: Macmillan, 1978) Chapter 14.

31. Moreover, the loss in real income could have been reduced had the U.S. Government recognized in 1970 that OPEC was engaged in economic warfare with the consuming countries.

32. In essence each subgroup will attempt to emulate the Arab sheiks and obtain and protect as much wealth for themselves as possible. Many economists in the U.S. are willing to force groups in our own country to bite-the-bullet and to accept economic impoverishment to fight inflation, but are strangely silent about encouraging bullet-biting remedies on the Sheiks of the Persian Gulf.

33. A NPCIC is not as shocking as it seems. The government already deliberately affects the after-tax income distribution via fiscal policy. It is not a big step forward to coordinate pre-tax income distribution as it is determined in 'free' markets. Most people might find they like the results of such a policy, once they get over the shock of it.

34. The Nobel Prize winning economist, Sir John Hicks, has suggested that the reason the U.S. did not experience the same higher rates of inflation of Western Europe in 1974 and 1975 was due to the fact that the price rise of imported oil, 'while it has a large effect on the American import price index, has not been allowed to soak through to the domestic American economy. The American oil producers have not been allowed to raise their prices' (J. R. Hicks, 'What's Wrong With Monetarism', *Lloyds Bank Review*, October 1975, p. 12).

35. See footnote 20.

36. The government could tax oil that is *not* produced. For example, any oil property in the U.S. which is producing less than MER can be taxed on a per barrel per day basis on the difference between actual daily production and MER (or even say 10 per cent above MER). Similarly one can tax oil properties being withheld from development and production.

37. P. Davidson, 'The United States IRS: The Fourteenth Member of OPEC', *Journal of Post Keynesian Economics*, Winter 1978–9.

38. Simply stated, the concentration ratio measures the share of the market held by the four largest firms in an industry. There is nothing magic about using the top four rather than three, or five, or any other number. The top four are chosen simply because government agencies, in order to prevent identification of the activities of individual firms, publish data in that format.

39. Control of energy supply is concentrated in the hands of large conglomerate corporations and a few producing governments (OPEC, plus Canada, Norway, Mexico). Some oft-cited facts on concentration include: 7 firms produce 70 per cent of the world's supply of oil: in the U.S. 20 firms produce 76 per cent of the supply of oil; 23 firms control 85 per cent of refining capacity; 23 firms control 72 per cent of natural gas production; 4 firms in the petroleum industry produce approximately 25

per cent of coal; 20 major petroleum companies control 95 per cent of U.S. oil reserves, 70 per cent of natural gas reserves, 50 per cent of uranium reserves. Furthermore, of 18 major oil companies all are in natural gas. Sixteen of the 18 are in oil shale, 10 are in coal, 16 in uranium, and 10 in tar sands. Moreover such concentration statistics ignore the increased control of supply due to the pervasive nature of joint ventures by the oil companies and the interlocking directorates resulting from representatives of major banks being on the boards of many major oil companies.

CHAPTER 10: CAN WAGES BE FIXED IN TERMS OF AN INTERNATIONAL STANDARD?

1. In modern times, perhaps oil or gold are more relevant concepts.
2. Many Monetarists (e.g. Friedman) advocate the indexing of all contracts, i.e. wages, debt, rental and even tax liabilities. Consequently, they recommend a sticky 'money' earnings standard in terms of indexed units!
3. Even if it were possible to index security prices, bank notes, and bank liabilities (i.e. all financial assets including money) to the current money price of 'wheat', there would be of necessity some posterior time lag for the indexing to become effective as *it takes time* to collect, process, and interpret the information on the market price of 'wheat', therefore making 'wheat' preferable to money.
4. Only if money production costs and therefore spot market prices were expected to rise in the future at an annual rate which exceeded carrying costs would it pay to hold 'wheat' for liquidity purposes. Cf. Keynes, *The General Theory*, pp. 237–8.
5. *The Collected Writings of John Maynard Keynes* [hereafter cited as *CWK*], XIV, p. 501.
6. If domestic money wages were indexed to a foreign exchange rate, then the value of output in terms of foreign exchange would vary with the foreign exchange efficiency wage.
7. Except for filling teeth or serving as jewellery, gold has a very limited use in production or consumption activities.
8. Keynes, *The General Theory*, p. 374. Italics added.
9. For a discussion of the operation of such a clearing system, see Chapter 15.
10. *CWK*, xxv.
11. J. R. Hicks, *Causality in Economics* (New York: Basic Books, 1979) p. 94.
12. Of course, if there is a lack of confidence in the money contractual system, then long duration production processes will not be undertaken in a market-oriented entrepreneurial system!
13. This does not mean that Central Bankers have always acted properly as the 'lender of last resort' to prevent balance of payments (liquidity) crises between banks within their jurisdiction. All that is implied is that they could have done so!

14. As for example, in the board game of 'Monopoly', when every time a player passes 'Go', he collects $200.

15. For a further discussion of the importance of liquidity in a simple model, see Hicks, *Causality in Economics*, pp. 96–100.

CHAPTER 11: EUROMONEY

1. Cf. P. Davidson, *Money and the Real World*, pp. 145, 152–3.

2. Contracts for standardized commodities in international trade (e.g. oil, wheat) are often denominated in a single monetary unit (U.S. dollars) despite the nationalities of the buyers and sellers. Contracts for heterogeneous (branded) commodities, on the other hand, are often denominated in the currency of choice of the seller (e.g. Volvos in Swedish kroner).

3. Weintraub indicates that Central Bank intervention has been greater for developed nations since the abandonment of the Bretton Woods fix rate system in 1971. See S. Weintraub, 'Flexible Exchange Rates: New Wine in Old Bottles', *Journal of Post Keynesian Economics*, 3, 1981.

4. Orderlines involves trading rules which limit the permissible rate of change in market prices of the asset.

5. Permitting savings depositors to write drafts against their bank liabilities and using the banking clearing mechanism to clear such private bank debts monetizes these savings bank liabilities, as long as such 'savings' bankers can issue and refinance their liabilities when necessary via borrowing from the public, or via the resale of 'savings' bankers' assets directly or indirectly to the lender of last resort (as described *supra*).

6. This information was provided by Dr. Ed. Williams who is an active participant in Eurodollar markets. Dr. Williams notes that 'I should emphasize this is a negotiated phenomenon and good customers are able to obtain better rates than can others.' (Private correspondence, 3 April 1980.)

7. R. F. Harrod, *Money* (London: Macmillan, 1969) p. 324. For a further discussion, see *infra*.

8. For example, G. Dufey and I. H. Giddy, *The International Money Market* (New Jersey: Prentice Hall, 1978); also see *Some Questions and Brief Answers About the Eurodollar Market*, Joint Economic Committee, U.S. Congress 95th Congress, 1st Session (Washington: U.S. Government Printing Office, 1977).

9. In reality, Eurobanking is a separate function of many banks who also engage in normal domestic banking activities. Currently (Autumn 1980) Eurobanking is an illegal function for any bank office physically located in the United States, but it is a legal activity for overseas branches of U.S. banks.

10. V. Chick, *The Evolution of the International Monetary System: Some Lessons From National Experience* (University College, London, 1979, mimeo).

11. R. F. Harrod, *Money*, p. 319.

12. Ibid. p. 324. See S. Weintraub, *Price Theory* (New York: Pitman, 1949)

Chapter 14, for a complete discussion of different degrees of price discrimination.

13.   R. F. Harrod, *Money*, pp. 324–7.

14.   Thus, as Harrod notes, this arrangement can, *ceteris paribus*, leave the total U.S. dollar deposits committed to Eurobanks unchanged while increasing the domestic money supply. Ibid. pp. 326–7.

15.   Just as the Central Bank gives up control when it pegs the interest rate on government debt, thereby giving the holders of the said debt the option of monetizing it whenever they desire.

16.   If the trade deficit is equal to the last period's deficit, then, *ceteris paribus*, the sale of the Eurobankers' liability for domestic money need *not* induce an expansion of the domestic money supply, as long as the value of the export surplus financed by Class B borrowers equals the average propensity to buy Eurodollar assets out of domestic aggregate savings. If, however, the average propensity is less than the value of the export surplus, and/or the trade deficit is larger than last period's *and* the marginal propensity to buy Eurodollar deposits out of domestic savings is less than unity, then some portion of Class B borrowers' spot transactions will be met by the domestic banking system validating the increase in the money supply necessary to finance the initial working capital used in the production of the export surplus.

Whether the initial working capital loan by the domestic producer of exports or the financial arrangements of the Class B borrower of Eurodollar deposits should be viewed as the force leading to an endogenous increase in the money supply is partly a semantic question. Clearly, unless the producer of export goods expects the Class B borrower to finance his orders for exports, the producer for export will not (and often cannot) go to his local banker to finance his working capital. Thus, if the Eurodollar market, because of its lower interest costs, induces Class B borrowers to raise funds which they would be unable or unwilling to if only domestic credit markets at higher borrowing costs were available, then the Eurodollar Class B loans have induced an increase in the domestic money supply.

17.   Of course, if interest payments can also be borrowed, then we have a case of Rising Fund Finance or Ponzi Finance. See H. P. Minsky, *John Maynard Keynes* (Columbia University Press, 1975) and P. Davidson, *Money and the Real World*, Chapter 16.

18.   And if they do not, it is unlikely that stable international monetary relations could long endure.

19.   See footnote no. 13 for qualifications to this statement.

20.   R. F. Harrod, *Money*, p. 327.

21.   That is, when profits, royalties, taxes and other non-wage incomes are the major components of value added (e.g. crude oil).

22.   At the moment, we are therefore visualizing the possibility of different monies discharging the non-labour factor service contractual obligations and the payroll liabilities.

23.   Every year we see new statistical categories of money supply discovered in Monetarist econometric models and Central bank statistics, e.g. M_{1A} M_{1B}, etc.

CHAPTER 12: MULTINATIONAL CORPORATIONS AND
INTERNATIONAL TRANSACTIONS

1. F. H. Hahn, 'General Equilibrium Theory', *The Public Interest*, Special
Issue, 1980, p. 132.
2. United Nations, Department of Economic and Social Affairs, *Multinational Corporations in World Development* (New York, 1973) pp. 13–
14.
3. J. N. Behrman, J. J. Boddwyn and A. Kapoor, *International Business–
Government Communication* (Lexington Books, 1975) p. 160.
4. V. Chick, 'Transnational Corporations and the Evolution of the
International Monetary System' in G. J. Crough, *Transnational Banking
and the World Economy* (Transnational Corporations Research Project,
University of Sydney, 1979) p. 142.
5. Ibid.
6. 'Foreign Tax Credits Claimed by U.S. Petroleum Companies', *Hearings
Before a Subcommittee of the Committee on Government Operations*,
House of Representatives, 95th Congress (Washington: Government
Printing Office, 1977).
7. Ibid. pp. 516–18.
8. Ibid. p. 411. The producer affiliate of the MNC produces crude oil from
wells and ships it to an ocean terminal; the offtaker is an affiliate of the
MNC who 'buys' the oil at the terminal and ships it by tanker to the
refinery affiliate of the MNC, who in turn 'buys' the oil and refines it into
products.
9. Such practices probably continue even today as many of the major oil
companies have set up affiliates in Bermuda and elsewhere. Such
affiliates may have less than a half dozen employees but they provide
services for the affiliates of the same MNC involving the purchases and
sales of millions of dollars of oil each year – adding 'value' via such
trading activities, e.g. Mobil Oil Abu Dhabi, Inc. which, despite its
name, has its principal office in Bermuda!
10. Chick, 'Transnational Corporations', p. 143.
11. J. M. Keynes, *A Treatise on Money*, *The Collected Writings of John
Maynard Keynes*, v, p. 4. Chartelism, Keynes noted, 'is the doctrine that
money is peculiarly a creation of the state'.
12. Chick, 'Transnational Corporations', p. 145.

CHAPTER 13: GOLD: THE 'BARBAROUS RELIC'

1. For example, see T. Scitovsky, *Money and the Balance of Payments*
(Chicago: Rand McNally, 1969) pp. 106–9.
2. A crawling peg is where the maximum periodic exchange rate change is
agreed in advance, and governments agree to intervene in exchange
markets to ensure that these maximum rates of change are not
surpassed. A dirty float is where the government pays lip service to freely
floating (flexible) exchange rates, while warning that if the exchange rate
changes are 'too drastic' in the government's (unannounced) view, the

government will intervene in the foreign exchange market. The timing and the degree of intervention are less certain, therefore, in the case of a dirty float, than in the case of crawling pegs or fixed exchange rate systems.

3. This is, of course, equivalent to the case of the monetary authority in a closed system, pegging the rate of interest on government bonds by fixing their price (which would permit the public to monetize the entire national debt if it so desired).

4. In the unlikely case that A's currency, rather than its bank deposits, is used to buy B's money, then A's currency will pile up in B's vaults preventing it from circulating in A's domestic currency. If B were not vigilant in returning these notes to A, it might create a temporary shortage of hand-to-hand money in A.

5. In the next chapter the advantages and disadvantages of managed v. freely flexible exchange rate systems are analysed in greater detail.

6. *The Collected Writings of John Maynard Keynes*, VI, p. 262.

7. For example, Keynes was considered a Cassandra during the 1920s. In recent years see the writings on the financial fragility hypothesis (e.g. H. P. Minsky, *John Maynard Keynes* (Columbia University Press, 1974) and the possible collapse of the monetary system (see P. Davidson, 'Is Monetary Collapse in the 1980s Inevitable?', *Nebraska Journal of Economics*, 18, Spring 1979, and my written Congressional Testimony before the Subcommittee on Domestic Monetary Policy, House Banking Committee, U.S. Congress, 14 March 1979).

8. See S. Maital and Y. Benjamini, 'Inflation as a Prisoner's Dilemma', *Journal of Post Keynesian Economics*, 2, 1980.

9. See P. Davidson, *Money and the Real World*, 2nd ed., pp. 388–401.

10. R. F. Harrod, *Reforming the World's Money* (London: Macmillan, 1965) p. 38.

11. Ibid. p. 38.

12. Cf. S. Maital and Y. Benjamini, 'Inflation as a Prisoner's Dilemma'.

CHAPTER 14: FREELY FLEXIBLE EXCHANGE RATES

1. Harrod, *Reforming the World's Money*, p. 46.

2. Cf. S. Weintraub, 'Flexible Exchange Rates', *Journal of Post Keynesian Economics*, 3, Summer 1981.

3. Cf. S. Maital and Y. Benjamini, 'Inflation as a Prisoner's Dilemma', *Journal of Post Keynesian Economics*, 2, 1980.

4. F. Blackaby, 'Exchange-Rate Policy and Economic Strategy', *The Three Banks Review*, June 1980, p. 6.

5. Ibid. p. 7. The collapse of the pound in 1981 destroys the last vestige of belief in Thatcherism's exchange rate discipline.

6. Cf. J. Blatt, 'Classical Economics or Involuntary Unemployment?', *Journal of Post Keynesian Economics*, 3, 1981, and W. J. Samuels, 'Survival and Pareto Optimality in Public Utility Rate Making', *Journal of Post Keynesian Economics*, 2, 1980.

CHAPTER 15: COORDINATING INTERNATIONAL PAYMENTS AND INCOMES

1. *The Collected Writings of John Maynard Keynes*, xxv, p. 49.
2. Ibid. p. 80.
3. Ibid. p. 31.
4. Ibid. p. 53.
5. Cf. Ibid. pp. 53–4.

Index